Understanding Popular Music

Understanding Popular Music is an accessible and comprehensive introduction to the history and meaning of popular music. It begins with a critical assessment of the different ways in which popular music has been studied and examines the difficulties and debates which surround the analysis of popular culture and popular music.

Drawing on the recent work of music scholars and the popular music press, Roy Shuker explores key subjects which shape our experience of music, including music production, the music industry, music policy, fans, audiences and subcultures, the musician as 'star', music journalism, and the reception and consumption of popular music. This fully revised and updated second edition includes:

- case studies and lyrics of artists such as Shania Twain, S Club 7, The Spice Girls and Fat Boy Slim
- the impact of technologies including on-line delivery and the debates over MP3 and Napster
- the rise of DJ culture and the changing idea of the 'musician'
- a critique of gender and sexual politics and the discrimination which exists in the music industry
- moral panics over popular music, including the controversies surrounding artists such as Marilyn Manson and Eminem
- a comprehensive discography, guide to further reading and directory of websites.

Roy Shuker is Associate Professor in Media Studies at Massey University, New Zealand. He is the author of *Key Concepts in Popular Music* (Routledge 1998).

LONDON AND NEW YORK

Understanding Popular Music

Second edition

 **Roy Shuker**

First published 1994
by Routledge
11 New Fetter Lane, London EC4P 4EE

Simultaneously published in the USA and Canada
by Routledge
29 West 35th Street, New York, NY 10001

Reprinted 1995, 1997
Second edition published 2001

Routledge is an imprint of the Taylor & Francis Group

© 1994, 2001 Roy Shuker

Typeset in Goudy by Taylor & Francis Books Ltd
Printed and bound in Great Britain by Biddles Ltd,
Guildford and King's Lynn

ISBN 0–415–23509–X (hbk)

British Library Cataloguing in Publication Data
A catalogue record for this book is available from
the British Library

Library of Congress Cataloging in Publication Data
Shuker, Roy
Understanding popular music / Roy Shuker.
  p. cm.
Includes bibliographical references and index.
1. Popular music–History and criticism. 2. Popular
culture–History–20th century. I. Title.
ML3470 .S54 2001
781.64'0973–dc21
00-053356

ISBN 0–415–23510–3 (pbk)

Contents

Acknowledgements   vii
Introduction   ix

1 **'What's goin' on?'**   1
  Popular culture, popular music, and media literacy

2 **'Every 1's a winner'**   27
  The music industry

3 **'Pump up the volume'**   51
  Technology and popular music

4 **'We are the world'**   67
  State music policy, cultural imperialism, and globalisation

5 **'On the cover of the *Rolling Stone*'**   83
  The music press

6 **'I'm just a singer (in a rock 'n' roll band)'**   99
  Making music

7 **'So you want to be a rock 'n' roll star?'**   115
  Stars and auteurs

CONTENTS

8   'Message understood'   139
    Musicology and genre

9   'Sweet dreams (are made of this)'   155
    Musical texts

10 'U got the look'   175
    Film and television, music video and MTV

11 'My generation'   193
    Audiences and fans, scenes and subcultures

12 'Pushin' too hard'   217
    Popular music and cultural politics

    Conclusion: 'wrap it up'   241
    Popular music and cultural meaning

    Appendix 1: chapter/song titles   245
    Appendix 2: discography   247
    Further resources and bibliography   253
    Subject index   277
    Name index   279
    Song and album title index   284

Acknowledgements

'Black Eyes, Blue Tears' © 1997 Out of Pocket Productions Ltd (admin. by Zomba Music Publishers Ltd) and used by kind permission of Universal Music Publishing Ltd.

'Born in the USA' © Bruce Springsteen (ASCAP) Admin. by Zomba Music Publishers Ltd.

'Bring It All Back' © 1999. Words by Eliot Kennedy, Mike Percy, Tim Lever, Rachel Stevens, Hannah Spearritt, Bradley McIntosh, Jonathan Lee, Paul Cattermole, Joanne O'Meara and Tina Barrett. Taken from the song 'Bring It All Back'. By kind permission of Sony/ATV Music Publishing, Universal Music Publishers Ltd, and Music Ltd/BMG Music Publishing Ltd. All Rights Reserved.

'Cop Killer' © 1992 (Ice T/Cunningan). By kind permission of Rhyme Syndicate/Universal/MCA Music Ltd/Universal Music Publishers Ltd.

'Love in Vain Blues' Robert Johnson. Words and music by Robert Johnson. © (1978), 1990, 1991 King of Spades Music. All Rights Reserved. Used by Permission.

'My Generation' © 1965 Fabulous Music Limited, Suite 2.07, Plaza 535, King's Road, London, SW10 0SZ. International Copyright Secures. All Rights Reserved. Used by Permission.

'Spoonful' Written by Willie Dixon. © 1960 (renewed) 1988 Hoochie Coochie Music Inc (BMI) (administered by Bug). All Rights Reserved. International Copyright Secured. For more information on Willie Dixon and the blues please contact: The Blues Heaven Foundation, 2120 South Michigan Avenue, Chicago, IL, 60616, Tel: (312) 808 1286, Fax: (312) 8080273.

'Stand by Your Man'. Print rights controlled by Warner Bros Publications Inc/IMP Ltd. Used by permission of IMP Ltd.

ACKNOWLEDGEMENTS

'Wannabe' (Stannard/Rowe/Brown/Adams/Halliwell/Bunton/Chisholm) © 1994. By kind permission of Universal Music Publishers Ltd.

Every effort has been made to contact the owners of copyright material. In the event of a copyright query, please contact the publishers.

Introduction

As was its predecessor, this second edition of *Understanding Popular Music* is situated in the general field of cultural studies. While there in no sense exists a cultural studies 'orthodoxy', there is a general recognition that cultural studies embraces the analysis of institutions, texts, discourses, readings, and audiences, with these all best understood in their social, economic, and political context. The cultural studies 'project' is eloquently put by Grossberg: 'Popular culture is a significant and effective part of the material reality of history, effectively shaping the possibilities of our existence. It is this challenge – to understand what it means to "live in popular culture" – that confronts contemporary cultural analysis' (Grossberg 1992: 69).

This project is explored here through the detailed consideration of a central form of contemporary popular culture, popular music, a label which is obviously problematic. In the first edition of this book, for convenience, I used the term 'rock' as shorthand for the diverse range of popular music genres produced in commodity form for a mass, predominantly youth, market. This led to charges of my being 'rockist' (Negus 1996), since fans of genres such as rap, techno, and reggae would hardly equate their preferences with 'rock'. As indicated by genre divisions used in the music press, popular music has become a broad label encompassing a variety of musical styles and their accompanying record label and retail categorisations. At the same time, the very title of the book led some reviewers to make the obvious point that 'popular music' indicated a far greater range of music than 'rock' and its associated genres, and would also embrace national contexts other than the 'Western' countries I concentrated upon. Recognising these points, but also conscious of the difficulty of finding any acceptable 'shorthand' signifier, I have used the term 'popular music' in this second edition. My focus remains a narrow one within this, equating 'popular music' with commercially mass produced music for a mass market, and including the variety of genres variously subsumed by terms such as rock 'n' roll, rock, pop, dance, hip-hop, and R&B.

Historically , my discussion of such music is largely restricted to the period since the early 1950s and the emergence of rock 'n' roll, and geographically limited to the Anglo-American nexus of production and consumption (see the discussion in Chapter 1). I emphasise the historical and contemporary production of popular music, within an international industry, predominantly as recorded music in various formats, or texts; the nature of these texts; and their cultural significance, reception and consumption. These topics are examined principally in relation to their expression in the United States and Canada, the United Kingdom, and New Zealand. The United States and the UK are the key historical sites in the development of popular music, and represent the continuing, albeit declining, Anglo-American dominance of the international market. Canada and New Zealand are examples of countries largely incorporated into this hegemony; essentially on the periphery of the global market, they illustrate questions of the status of the local within the internationalisation of popular music.

The core question addressed is how meaning is produced in popular music. Cultural interpretations and understandings are embedded in musical texts and performances – records, tapes, music videos, concerts, radio airplay, film soundtracks, and so on. Such meanings are, in one sense, the creations of those engaged in making the music in these diverse forms, but they are also the result of how the consumers of these forms interact with the music. Further, music texts and performances are cultural commodities, produced largely by an international music industry ultimately concerned with maximising profits. Meanings, or, rather, particular sets of cultural understandings, are the result of a complex set of interactions between these different parties. Accordingly, the question of meaning in popular music cannot be read off purely at one level, be it that of the producers, the texts, or the audience. It can only be satisfactorily answered by considering the nature of the production context, including State cultural policy, the texts and their creators, and the consumers of the music and their spatial location. Most importantly, it is necessary to consider the interrelationship of these factors.

Such a position is, of course, hardly new. Writing in 1980, Stuart Hall distinguished three key 'moments' in the sociological analysis of any cultural form: production, text, and appropriation. As Hall argued, it is not simply a question of examining each of these independently, but rather the way in which they fit together. This interlinking is central to the consideration of the relationship between forms of popular culture and the ideologies associated with these (Hall 1981).

The impetus for the first edition of this study arose from what I then saw as a contradiction between the prominence of 'rock' as a cultural form and its marginalisation and relative neglect in media and cultural studies. Even then (1993), however, this imbalance was changing, with new work reflecting a recognition of the economic and cultural prominence of popular music, and signalling a maturing of academic analysis of the form. Since then, further writing has seen the consolidation of established areas of inquiry and the forging of new insights. This includes studies of the political economy of the music industry (Negus 1999); textual analysis of the meanings embedded in popular music forms, both aural and audio visual (Brackett 1995); and ethnographic studies of subcultures, club cultures, and music scenes (e.g. Bennett 2000; Thornton 1995). In addition, there are fresh attempts to introduce and theorise the field (e.g. Frith 1996; Longhurst 1995; Negus 1996; Swiss *et al.* 1998). Further, there is considerable work in languages other than English (see the summaries in *RPM, The Review of Popular Music*, the journal of the IASPM – the International Association for the Study of Popular Music). Such work indicates the present vitality of popular music studies and the maturation of the field. In mapping this new terrain, *Understanding Popular Music* offers a contribution towards this process.

In the first edition of this book, I accepted Weinstein's view that popular music studies do not constitute a discipline, and that 'academic discourse on popular music since the 1980s has been a bricolage' lacking 'any paradigmatic theory, focus of study, method or voice' (Weinstein 1991b: 97–8). She attributed this to the diversity of 'rock' as a cultural form; the lack of clear ideological distinctions, such as that historically made between authentic and commercial music; and the claim that the music's meaning is, in part at least, attributable to the positioning of its various audiences. This claim remains valid, although various attempts to 'map' the field suggest there is an emergent sense of its constituent elements and concerns (see Shuker 1998; Horner and Swiss 1999). Even the continued lack of a disciplinary focus should not be regarded as necessarily a drawback, since the study of popular music is necessarily an interdisciplinary one. As I have argued throughout this text, it embraces the economic base and associated social relations within which the music is produced and consumed, textual analysis, auteur study, and the nature of the audience. Indeed, popular music studies reflects the state of media studies in general, as a field of inquiry, drawing on relevant disciplines and methodologies, rather than being a clearly defined discipline.

The discussion here draws together material from several national contexts and places this within a historical dimension, both aspects frequently absent from contemporary-oriented and nation-bound studies of popular media. A more historical and international sweep enables us to make firmer conclusions about the nature and impact of popular music, particularly given the continued growth of global multimedia conglomerates and the increasing evidence of the globalisation of culture.

It is, of course, not possible to deal with every aspect of popular music. Themes, topics and examples have been selected partly for their importance in exemplifying the diverse activities of the field of popular music, but primarily for their relevance to the general argument: the need to consider context, texts and their producers, and the consumers of popular music, and their interrelationship. After the initial exercise in theoretical sign posting, the organisational logic of the text is to begin with issues of the economic and technological context, the music industry, music and technology, and State cultural policy. I move from these to the nature of texts and the cultural practices of their production. This leads on to a consideration of consumption, particularly the sites (scenes), social groups and practices involved; and finally to the manner in which popular music is a form of cultural politics, involving processes of regulation, restriction, and empowerment. This is to see meaning in popular music as the product of a somewhat circular process, operating at a number of cultural levels in the personal and social and institutional domains.

The original book has been heavily revised. Reflecting current emphases in popular music studies, I have paid greater attention to the role of technology; gender politics and music; the process of making music, and the associated continuum of success involved; the current popularity of dance/electronic music; and the crossover success of country music. The volume has been reorganised; two new chapters have been added, and most of the other chapters recast. I have added more contemporary examples to the discussions of performers and recordings (necessitating the curtailment of those included earlier). A discography has also been included. More fully, the scope of the book is as follows.

Chapter 1 examines the difficulties and debates surrounding the definitions and key terms used throughout the study, and some of the central questions and topics embraced in any serious analysis of popular culture. It then outlines, in necessarily abbreviated fashion, the major approaches evident in cultural studies, and the popular music variants of these.

Chapter 2 deals with the music industry as an example of the cultural industries. The historical development and contemporary nature of the record industry shows how a number of factors have influenced the manufacture, distribution, promotion, and reception of popular music at particular historical conjunctures. Central here is the debate over determinations, with audience consumer sovereignty in tension with the attempts of the music industries to shape music as a commodity form, to determine tastes and maximise profits.

Chapter 3 considers the impact of technology on popular music. Technological changes in recording equipment pose both constraints and opportunities in terms of the organisation of production, and innovation in musical instrumentation has allowed the emergence of 'new' sounds. New recording formats and modes of transmission and dissemination alter the nature of musical production and consumption, and raise questions about authorship and the legal status of music as property. I sign-post some of the cultural implications of these, with brief examples of the interaction of technological, musical and cultural change.

Chapter 4 considers the musical cultural policies of local and central government (the State). The validity of the 'cultural imperialism' thesis, and the concept of globalisation are discussed in relation to popular music in Canada and New Zealand. In both countries, the State's response to the dominance of Anglo-American music provide possible models for wider emulation, and useful insights into the question of what constitutes the 'national' in cultural forms.

Chapter 5 takes up the neglected role of the music press, a term used here for the whole corpus of writing on popular music, ranging from the popular press to cultural journalism. Within this, the focus is on music magazines and music critics as cultural gatekeepers, promotional adjuncts to the music industry, and general purveyors of lifestyles.

Chapter 6 deals with those who make the music. I examine the process of music-making and sites of production; conceptions of the term 'musician'; and the status hierarchy accorded various categories of performer.

Chapter 7 examines the nature and relevance of 'auteur' theory and 'stardom' in popular music, with case studies of producer Phil Spector, and performers Frank Zappa, Bruce Springsteen, Madonna, the Spice Girls, Shania Twain, and Norman Cook, better known as Fat Boy Slim. The interrelationship of ritual, pleasure, and economics involved operates to create audiences, to fuel individual fantasy and pleasure, and to create musical icons and cultural myths.

Chapter 8 discusses the application of musicology, the question of lyric analysis, and the nature and significance of genre, using heavy metal and dance music as case studies.

Chapter 9 provides examples of textual analysis, to illustrate a modified musicology, which places pieces in their social and historical contexts and takes account of listeners' affective responses to the music. The analysis of music videos is included here.

Chapter 10 deals with the visual (re-)presentation of popular music, examining the relationship between popular music and film, television, and, in particular, music video and MTV. While the bulk of this literature has been preoccupied with textual analysis, and this remains part of the discussion here, my emphasis is rather on the industrial aspects of these audio-visual texts.

Chapter 11 examines the place of music in the lives of 'youth' as a general social category, as a central component of the 'style' of youth subcultures, and as integral to fan culture. I then move to particular consumption practices: dance; concert going, and record collecting. Two factors are seen to underpin consumption: music as a form of cultural capital, and as a source of pleasure and empowerment. Lastly, musical scenes and sounds, the musical geography of place, are introduced as significant new concepts in popular music studies.

Chapter 12 discusses two aspects of music as cultural politics. First, historical and contemporary case studies are used to show how attempts to regulate popular music, its fans and performers have constituted a form of 'moral panic', related to broader attempts to maintain and reconstitute cultural hegemony. Second, I consider popular music as a vehicle for political views, through an examination of Live Aid, and as gender and sexual politics. Music as cultural politics returns us to the significance of the socio-economic context in shaping cultural meaning in the music.

Each of these topics is substantial, and clearly there will not be scope to explore each one in detail; at times particular aspects can merely be introduced and further lines of inquiry suggested. Generic texts inevitably suffer from the sins of omission and over-simplification, and I am sure that both are evident here. That said, I will be content if the discussion encourages readers to pursue further their investigations into popular music.

Acknowledgements

As in the original edition of this book, this heavily revised version has relied extensively on the work of many critics and 'colleagues at a distance', who have written extensively on cultural studies and popular music. Many of the 'best' ideas here are theirs; the errors of fact and argument – the bum notes – remain mine. To list them risks leaving out someone, and a check of my text and references provides a roll call of sorts; my thanks to you all. I have also benefited enormously from my membership of IASPM (the International Association for the Study of Popular Music), through its conferences, publications, e-mail discussions, and, above all, from the friendships and insights its members have provided me with. Further acknowledgement is due to my students in various media studies and popular culture courses over recent years, who provided a critical initial sounding board for much of the material and many of the ideas here. A particular debt of gratitude is due to Emma, my daughter and keen research assistant, whose input added greatly to my discussions of The Spice Girls, Shania Twain, and contemporary dance pop. Thanks also to Mary Jane, for undertaking the bibliography, and being there.

Finally, for their input and patience, my thanks to my Routledge editors, Christopher Cudmore and Ruth Graham.

Roy Shuker, Palmerston North, New Zealand, August 2000.

Chapter 1

'What's goin' on?'

Popular culture, popular music, and media literacy

To study popular music is to study popular culture. While this would appear to be a self-evident claim, much writing on popular music tends to treat it in isolation from the literature in the general field within which it is situated. The initial concern here is with the general nature and role of popular culture as a social phenomenon, primarily in contemporary society, but also in terms of its historical development. Within this broader ambit, my interest is with questions about the nature and production of popular culture, its social reception, and consumption; the value of studying popular culture, and the ways in which such studies can best be pursued. These questions embrace the dynamics of popular culture, cultural hierarchies and the politics of taste. In examining these questions, I have drawn on a range of theoretical and case-study material from media studies, cultural studies, history, sociology, and women's studies. This overview indicates what seem to me to be the starting points and preoccupations that should inform the study of popular culture.

I move from this general discussion to focus on the study of popular music. Academic analysis of popular music and its associated manifestations was initially slow to develop. During the 1970s and 1980s, even the increasingly popular field of media studies tended to concentrate its attention on the visual media, particularly television, and neglected popular music. There were notable exceptions, with the work of scholars such as Simon Frith, George Lipsitz, Iain Chambers, Angela McRobbie, Richard Middleton, John Shepherd, Dave Laing, Lawrence Grossberg, and Nelson George. During the 1990s, there was a veritable flood of material, as well as a marked increase in the number of courses either directly on popular music, or on it as an aspect of popular culture and media studies. While 'established' popular music scholars continued to produce important new work (e.g. Frith 1996; Grossberg 1992;

1

Lipsitz 1994), they were joined by writers such as Andy Bennett, Marcus Breen, Mavis Bayton, Sara Cohen, Reebee Garofalo, Phil Hayward, Steve Jones, Tony Mitchell, Keith Negus, Will Straw, and Deena Weinstein.

The new prominence of popular music studies reflects recognition of rock/pop music's centrality as a global cultural phenomenon, associated with a multi-billion dollar industry, and a many faceted pop-youth culture reaching out into every aspect of style. This emerging literary explosion takes a number of forms and approaches the topic from a range of perspectives, including political economy, cultural studies, feminist studies, and media studies, this last with its own rich theoretical mix of film theory, semiotics, psychoanalysis, feminism, and social theory (see the useful Bibliographies in Gratten 1995; Haggerty 1995; and, especially, Shepherd *et al.* 1997; also Shuker 1998).

The discussion here is necessarily selective and highly condensed, concentrating on those questions, theoretical positions and approaches which loom in the background throughout the text. I have attempted to make theoretical material accessible to those not familiar with the more extensive original discussions, while the interested reader can follow these up via the references provided.

As Horner and Swiss (1999: 7) observe, the different meanings given terms common to the vocabulary of popular music studies, including the very terms 'popular' and 'music', help shape the music and our experience of it. Accordingly, we begin by clarifying some key terms, especially 'culture', 'popular', and 'popular music', then move on to a brief examination of several central issues in any attempt to analyse the popular: the relationship between lived culture and cultural preferences; the question of ideology and preferred readings; the pleasures of the text; and recurring anxiety and debate over the effects of popular culture. A number of 'ways in' to the examination of popular culture are then outlined: the high culture tradition, identified with Leavisite English criticism; the mass society thesis associated with Frankfurt School Marxism; three variants of critical media theory – political economy, structuralism, and culturalism; and, finally, attempts to articulate postmodern analyses of the popular. In each case, examples of the application of the theoretical perspective to popular music are presented.

SETTING AGENDAS

The meaning and utility of terms such as 'popular' and 'mass', especially in relation to 'culture' and 'media', have been the subject of considerable discussion and debate (see, for example, Williams 1981; Edgar and Sedgwick 1999). Similarly, 'popular music' and associated terms such as 'rock', 'rock 'n' roll', and 'pop', are used by musicians, fans, and academic analysts in a confusing variety of ways. Then there is 'media literacy', a term which refers to attempts to reconceptualise print-oriented literacy towards the critical 'reading' of all forms of media, including popular music. In all these cases, it needs to be remembered that it is difficult to define phenomena which are social practices as well as economic products or pedagogic concepts, and which are not static but constantly evolving. Indeed, precise definitions can be constraining; they should be regarded as frameworks for exploration and elaboration, rather than factual declarations to be defended. That said, let us try at least to pin down the general nature of some of the concepts which are central to cultural studies.

Popular culture and the mass media

'Popular' is a contested term. For some it simply means appealing to the people, whereas for others it means something much more grounded in or 'of' the people. The former usage generally refers to commercially produced forms of popular culture, while the latter is reserved for forms of 'folk' popular culture, associated with local community-based production and individual craftspeople. In relation to popular music, for example, this is the distinction often made between folk music, especially when acoustically based, and the chart-oriented products of the record companies. As we shall see, however, such a clear-cut distinction has become increasingly untenable.

While not all popular culture is associated with the mass media, there is a reciprocal relationship between the two. The mass media involve large-scale production, by large economic units, for a mass, albeit segmented, market. The term 'mass media' refers to print, aural, and visual communication on a large scale – the press, publishing, radio and television, film and video, the recording industry, and telecommunications, to mention only the more obvious mediums of production and dissemination. Used as an adjective, 'popular' indicates that something – a person, a product, a practice, or a belief – is commonly liked or approved of by a large audience or the general public. Applied to the media, this means that particular television programmes, films, records, and books and magazines are widely consumed. Their popularity is indicated by ratings surveys, box-office returns, and sales figures. To a degree, this definition of 'popularity' reifies popular cultural texts, reducing them to the status of objects to be bought and sold in the marketplace, and the social nature of their consumption must always be kept in mind. This study equates the 'popular' with commercial, cultural forms of entertainment, and regards markets as an inescapable feature of popular culture.

Popularity is central to popular culture, as its various products and figures (stars, auteurs) attain general social acceptance and approval. In a sense, a circular argument holds here: the popular are mass, the mass are popular. As Turner puts it: 'popular culture and mass media have a symbiotic relationship: each depends on the other in an intimate collaboration' (K. Turner 1984: 4). Contemporary popular culture in the United States and Canada, the United Kingdom, and New Zealand – to mention only the national settings we are primarily concerned with in this study –

3

forms the majority of mass media content, while the majority of popular culture is transmitted through the mass media.

Commercial forms of popular culture increasingly depend on mass marketing and publicising on a multi-media basis. Mass marketing campaigns promoting a range of products accompany the release of major feature films such as *Star Wars: The Phantom Menace* and *Toy Story*. What we have here is the creation and marketing of a cultural phenomenon, with the cinema film, its video and music soundtrack, the posters, T-shirts, souvenir books, games, and children's toys, not to forget revivals of the original comics, films, or television series which established the popularity of these programmes and their characters. Increasingly, popular films also have 'the making of' programmes accompanying their release. These promotions and their various associated texts are carefully orchestrated, using large-scale advertising, and practices such as nationwide saturation release, achieved by the block booking of cinemas. Tie-ins of related products and the marketing of logos create lucrative secondary incomes; the best-known recent examples being the ubiquitous Pokémon and Teletubbies.

A similar process is evident in the mass marketing of popular music. The music can be reproduced in various formats (or 'texts') – vinyl, audio tape, compact disc, DAT (Digital Audio Tape), and video – and on variations within these: the dance mix, the cassette single, the limited collector's edition, the remastered CD, and so on. The music can then be disseminated in a variety of ways – through radio airplay, discos and nightclubs, television music video shows and MTV-style channels, live concert performances, and the Internet and MP3. Accompanying these can be advertising, reviews of the text or performance, and interviews with the performer(s) in the various publications of the music press. In addition there is the assorted paraphernalia available to the fan, especially the posters and the T-shirts. The range of these products enables a multi-media approach to the marketing of the music, and a maximisation of sales potential, as exposure in each of the various forms strengthens the appeal of the others.

Culture and the popular

It is already obvious that my use of the term 'culture' rejects the argument that anything popular cannot, by definition, be cultural. Although a high–low culture distinction is still very strongly evident in general public perceptions of 'culture', the traditionally claimed distinction between 'high culture' and 'low culture' has become blurred. High art has been increasingly commodified and commercialised, as with classical music's star system of conductors and soloists, while some forms of popular culture have become more 'respectable', receiving State funding and broader critical acceptance. Yet clear distinctions and cultural hierarchies remain widely held, not least within particular cultural forms, by those involved in their production and consumption.

My use of the word culture, one of the most difficult words in the English language (see Williams 1983), is in a sociological rather than an aesthetic sense. Williams argues that contemporary usage of 'culture' falls into three possibilities, or some amalgam of these: 'a general process of intellectual, spiritual, and aesthetic development'; 'a particular way of life, whether of a people, period, or a group'; and 'the works and practices of intellectual and especially artistic activity' (Williams 1983: 90). This can be seen as a useful, if overly expansive, definition. Our interest here will be primarily between the second and third of these definitions; and in the relationship between them – the way particular social groups have used popular music within their lives. This is to shift the focus from the preoccupation, evident in much media/cultural studies, with the text in and of itself, to the audience. This is also to stress 'popular culture', rather than accept the reservation of the term culture for artistic pursuits associated with particular values and standards, sometimes referred to as elite or high culture – Williams' third definition. In addition to this emphasis on the audiences and consumption aspects of popular culture, we are concerned with the relationship between the creation of cultural products and the economic context of that creation, a process which involves creating or targeting audiences, and an active engagement between texts and their consumers. This is to recognise that neither texts nor their consumers exist in isolation.

In short then, the main concern of this study is with the interrelationship of context, texts, and consumption, as demonstrated by the manufacture, distribution, and consumption of popular music, primarily in its various recorded forms. But what is popular music?

Popular music

Popular music defies precise, straightforward definition. Accordingly, some writers on popular music slide over the question of definition, and take a 'common-sense' understanding of the term for granted. Historically, the term popular has meant 'of the ordinary people'. It was first linked in a published title to a certain kind of music that conformed to that criterion in William Chapple's *Popular Music of the Olden Times*, published in instalments from 1855. Not until the 1930s and 1940s did the term start to gain wider currency (Gammond 1991; see also Williams 1983). Middleton (1990) observes that the question of 'what is popular music' is 'so riddled with complexities … that one is tempted to follow the example of the legendary definition of folk song – all songs are folk songs, I never heard horses sing 'em – and suggest that all music is popular music: popular with someone'. However, the criteria for what counts as popular, and their application to specific musical styles and genres, are open to considerable debate. Classical music clearly has sufficient following to be considered popular, while, conversely, some forms of popular music are quite exclusive (e.g. thrash metal).

Most definitions are based on identifying the constituent genres making up 'popular music', though views vary on which genres should be included. For instance, *The Penguin Encyclopedia of Popular Music* (Clarke 1990) never attempts to define 'popular music' in any generic sense, instead noting that popular music 'has always been a great mainstream with many tributaries' (Introduction), it deals with an impressive range of these, including jazz, ragtime, blues, rhythm and blues, country, rock (and rock 'n' roll and rockabilly), pub rock, punk rock, acid rock, heavy metal, bubblegum, and reggae. The point that this is a shifting topography is shown by the lack of reference to rap, only just emerging into the mainstream market when Clarke wrote. A similar approach is evident in other attempts to survey the field, most notably the *Rolling Stone* histories of rock 'n' roll (Miller 1980; Ward *et al.* 1986; DeCurtis and Henke 1992), and various consumer record guides to 'rock', a term which became roughly contiguous with 'popular music' post the emergence of rock 'n' roll in the 1950s (AMG 1995; Shapiro 1991; Sinclair 1992). For example, Sinclair (1992: Introduction) observes: 'I have kept my definition of "rock" fairly loose, assuming the scope to cover the more obvious of the country, soul, rap and blues artists whose work has had a significant impact on the rock mainstream'.

Linked to this broad genre approach, are those definitions based on the commercial nature of popular music, and embracing genres perceived as commercially oriented. Many commentators argue that it is commercialisation that is the key to understanding popular music: e.g. 'When we speak of popular music we speak of music that is commercially oriented' (Burnett 1996: 35). This approach places the emphasis on the 'popular', arguing that such appeal can be quantified through charts, radio airplay, and so forth. In such definitions, certain genres are identified as 'popular music', while others are excluded (e.g. Clarke 1990; Garofalo 1997). However, this approach can suffer from the same problems as those stressing popularity, since many genres, especially meta-genres such as world music, have only limited appeal and/or have had limited commercial exposure. Moreover, popularity varies from country to country, and even from region to region within national markets.

It also needs to be noted that this commercially oriented approach is largely concerned with *recorded* popular music, that is usually listened to in a fairly conscious and focused manner. Kassabian makes the useful point that what she terms 'ubiquitous musics' are frequently left out of such discussions: music in films, in stores, on the phone, in the office, on television, and so on. 'These are the kinds of music that no one chooses for herself or himself but that nevertheless wash our everyday lives with sound' (1999: 113). This acoustic wallpaper is also the subject of Joseph Lanza's book *Elevator Music* (1995), while 'Muzak' is a corporate trademark.

A further facet of attempts to define popular music is its relationship to technology, with some writers seeking to maintain a distinction between a 'folk mode' predicated on live performance, and a mass culture form associated with recording. The latter is criticised as 'only commercial ... leaving the profound and innate potential of the medium for cultural and aesthetic expression still undeveloped' (Cutler, cited in Jones 1992: 4). But as Jones points out,

> the widespread use of inexpensive multitrack recorders and the spread of home-made cassette networks are giving rise to another form of folk music that fits neither category. Likewise the use of turntables and microphones in rap music contradicts the easy combination of recording and mass culture.
>
> (Jones 1992: 5)

The nature of popular music cannot be simply reduced to whether or not it uses technology. The obvious point here is that those who wish their music to reach a wider audience must record, a process which is increasingly technological in character (see Chapter 3). Further, technology's relationship to popular music can be related to the varying levels of affluence of different social groups. Those without access to instruments are more likely to make music which either doesn't need them, or can be achieved with relatively cheap equipment. Doo-wop, close harmony singing on street corners in the 1950s, needed no instruments. In the 1980s, hip-hop was developed by underprivileged urban blacks, using the voice, the turntable, and cheap drum machines. In comparison, jazz-funk ('fusion') is preferred by many wealthier black musicians, who can afford to purchase and learn instruments (Blake 1992: 42).

Tagg (1982), in an influential and much cited discussion, characterises popular music according to the nature of its distribution (usually mass); how it is stored and distributed (primarily recorded sound rather than oral transmission or musical notation); the existence of its own musical theory and aesthetics; and the relative anonymity of its composers. The last of these is debatable, and I would want to extend the notion of composers and its associated view of the nature of musical creativity (see Chapter 6). However, musicologists have usefully extended the third aspect of this definition, while sociologists have concentrated on the first two dimensions.

It seems that a satisfactory definition of popular music must encompass both musical and socio-economic characteristics. Essentially, all popular music consists of a hybrid of musical traditions, styles, and influences, and is also an economic product which is invested with ideological significance by many of its consumers. At the heart of the majority of various forms of popular music is a fundamental tension between the essential creativity of the act of 'making music' and the commercial nature of the bulk of its production and dissemination (see Frith 1983: chap. 1).

Rock, pop, and authenticity

This ongoing tension between art and commerce in popular music is evident in the widely used terms 'pop' and 'rock 'n' roll' (with 'rock' often used as shorthand for the latter, if not both). I have used them somewhat interchangeably here, regarding both as commercially produced music for simultaneous consumption by a mass market. But beyond similarities of production and consumption, aesthetic distinctions and ideological weight are generally attached to these labels: 'in rock, there is the ethos of self-expression which draws an intimate tie between the personal and the performance. ... Rock and pop stars play to different rules' (Street 1986: 5). Hill offers a fuller version of the same sentiments:

> Pop implies a very different set of values to rock. Pop makes no bones about being mainstream. It accepts and embraces the requirement to be instantly pleasing and to make a pretty picture of itself. Rock on the other hand, has liked to think it was somehow more profound, non-conformist, self-directed and intelligent.
>
> (Hill 1986: 8)

To identify particular artists with either pop or rock 'n' roll attempts to keep commerce and artistic integrity apart on a central yardstick. It was part of a tendency in the 1980s (and still evident) to view popular music in terms of a series of dichotomies: mass versus community/local; commerce versus creativity; manufactured versus authentic; major record companies versus independents. This approach was a legacy of the mythology of 'rock' which was a product of the 1960s, when leading American critics – Landau, Marsh, and Christgau – elaborated a view of rock as correlated with authenticity, creativity and a particular political moment: the 1960s protest movement and the counterculture (for example, Marsh 1987). Closely associated with this leftist political ideology of rock was *Rolling Stone* magazine, founded in 1967 (see Chapter 5). The key term in these perspectives was 'authenticity'.

I would argue, however, that the pop/rock distinction was never really valid to any significant extent. As much as anything else, 'rock' has been a marketing device. Even rock's frequent refusal to admit to commodity status, and its attempt to position itself as somehow above the manufacturing process, all too easily become marketing ploys – 'the Revolution is on CBS' slogan of the late 1960s being perhaps the best example. Nevertheless, using authenticity to distinguish between pop and rock continues to serve an important ideological function, helping differentiate particular forms of musical cultural capital.

The 'classic' distinction between rock and pop also runs into difficulties when we consider the various forms of 'alternative' music, illustrating the difficulties of forcing genres into too rigid a typology. Similarly, 'world beat', the rephrasing of traditional folk music in a dance-pop mode, initially exemplified by Ofra Haza's 'Im Nin Alu' (on *Shaday*, Sire, 1988), has frequently ignored geographical and musical boundaries. These examples illustrate how, in the 1990s, the old 'rock constituency' has splintered even further, continuing a process already evident since the late 1970s and the punk–new wave explosion.

In sum, only the most general definition can be offered under the general umbrella category of 'pop/rock': essentially, it consists of a hybrid of musical traditions, styles, and influences, with the only common element being that it is characterised by a strong rhythmical component, and generally, but not exclusively, relies on electronic amplification. Indeed, a purely musical definition is insufficient, since pop/rock's dominant characteristic is a socio-economic one: its mass production for a mass, predominantly youth, market. At the same time, of course, it is an economic product which is invested with ideological significance by many of its consumers.

As this discussion suggests, as with a term like 'popular culture', it is misguided to attempt to attach too precise a meaning to what is a shifting cultural phenomenon. For convenience, and despite its own associated difficulties (see my Introduction), I use the term 'popular music' throughout this study as shorthand for the diverse range of popular music genres produced in commodity form for a mass, predominantly youth, market, primarily Anglo-American in origin (or imitative of its forms), since the early 1950s.

Critical media literacy

The study of popular music is part of the more general project of critical cultural studies: to 'read' the commercial media in a critical manner, in order to acquire media literacy. Literacy is still generally understood as a shorthand for the social practices and conceptions of reading and writing (with reading still equated with print media). Media literacy essentially involves a process of 'reading' the popular media, be it print, visual or aural, in a critical manner. Media literacy emphasises the development of critical autonomy, enabling students 'to establish and maintain the kind of critical distance on their culture that makes possible critical autonomy: the ability to decode, encode, and evaluate the symbol systems that dominate their world' (Ontario Ministry of Education 1989: 10). This is a view which has much in common with other media educators who see the dominant purpose of media studies as ideological demystification (Masterman 1989).

The arguments in support of media literacy are various, but centrally involve two facts of contemporary life, already touched on in our discussion of 'popular culture'. First, the mass/popular media's saturation of society, and the high levels of its consumption among young people; and, second, the pervasive influence of these media, which act as 'consciousness industries'.

The obvious argument for a media literacy which encompasses the development in the learner of a critical perspective on all popular media, be they print, visual, or aural, is the sheer pervasiveness of such media and its enormous appeal among the young. The experience of most of us is saturated by the popular mass media: I wake up, shower and dress to the clock radio and the (New Zealand) National Programme's 'Morning Report', and during breakfast catch up on the weather forecast and the local radio news. If driving to work, depending on traffic delays, I listen to music tapes or the radio. My working day begins with checking my e-mail, and, classes and student consultations aside, frequently encompasses sessions of previewing audio or video recordings, checking web sites, and breaks to catch up on recent journals and newspapers. In the early evenings I may watch television or a video, play music, sometimes on the headphones, or go to a movie, while the late evening usually sees me in bed with 'a good read'. All of this means a considerable level of media consumption, and, as Masterman observes, 'the real significance of these different uses of the media is that they are frequently integrated not simply with other activities but with one another', via different levels of engagement – flicking through a magazine or the paper, while watching television (Masterman 1989: 3). It is also important to note that they vary from activities which isolate the individual (headphones, reading), to home-based entertainments usually shared with others (television, video), and social forms outside the home – going to the 'movies' with one's partner/family/friends.

Some idea of people's level of engagement with the popular media is provided by the US Census Bureau, which found that in 1999 the average American above the age of eighteen spent 3,405 hours on consuming media and entertainment products; or roughly some eight hours per day! (Greco 2000: v; of course, such statistics beg the question of the nature of such 'consumption'). The consumption of popular media is particularly high among young people. In the United Kingdom, a survey of homes found children and teenagers had almost universal access to audio equipment of some kind (Livingston and Bovill 1999).

The second core argument for media literacy is the sheer influence of the media, reflecting its pervasiveness and high levels of consumption. As is frequently pointed out by commentators, the media operate as consciousness industries, shaping our perceptions, values and norms, and confirming or denying these. This process involves delivering audiences to advertisers, and, in the case of television, presenting an apparently transparent window on the world. While official and public attention tends to focus on the 'effects' of various media in terms of its perceived links to violence and sexuality, the general ideological effects of the media are less obvious and less addressed. It can be readily seen that the majority of codes and practices operating within popular media texts are frequently reinforcing and reproducing dominant interests in society; for example, the representation in television news and press coverage of disputes between capital and labour (see the work of the Glasgow

Media Studies Group). At the same time, however, within this dominant discourse there exist spaces and possibilities for opposition, resistance and alternative messages.

Despite the pervasiveness of the popular mass media, schooling continues to be preoccupied with teaching 'high culture'. We often find embedded in school curricula and teaching practices the assumption that the only 'culture' worth transmitting is that of a national and classless 'high' culture, of equal relevance to all pupils. The school curriculum has often been a selection from the cultural experiences and artifacts available, a selection which generally embodies two attitudes: Arnold's 'the best that has been thought and said'; and a critique of the mass communications industry which uses education to 'inoculate' pupils against the fatal charms of mass/'pop' culture: the seduction of advertising, the sexism of rock videos and so on.

Accordingly, children's preferred media are frequently at odds with the school curriculum. This situation is changing, with media studies now a firmly established part of the curriculum in a number of countries – including New Zealand, several Australian states, Canada (notably Ontario), and the United Kingdom. Media studies programmes usually reflect, implicitly rather than explicitly, the dominant theoretical perspective(s) by which they are underpinned. Generally, there is a tendency to privilege one aspect of the media: context, text, or audiences. What is needed, I have argued throughout this study, is an approach which links these three central aspects, an approach best achieved through a consideration of the question: 'who/what is determining meaning in popular culture?' In a sense, then, *Understanding Popular Music* is an attempt to provide a basis for the study of 'popular' music as part of a critical media literacy.

Media literacy, with its concentration on popular culture, or mass media produced for a mass audience, challenges the traditional emphasis on high culture and the preoccupation with print media. In its place, it emphasises the critical consideration of the various forms and genres of popular media, in terms of their nature as commercial and ideological texts, their constructions of reality, the nature of their consumption, and attempts to regulate them. It is to these we now turn.

ANALYSING THE POPULAR

The study of popular music is situated in the general field of cultural studies, which addresses the interaction between three dimensions of popular culture: lived cultures, the social being of those who consume popular cultures; the symbolic forms, or texts, that are consumed within the lived culture; and the economic institutions and technological processes which create the texts.

Analysis of the interrelationship of these dimensions raises a series of complex issues, including:

1   The tension between the economic, market determinants of popular culture and the consumer sovereignty exercised by those who actually buy, view, read, and listen to mass-marketed television, films, magazines, bestsellers, and popular music.

2   The nature of lived cultures and the interrelationships between particular cultural preferences and factors such as class, gender, ethnicity and age.

3   The ideological role of popular culture in perpetuating dominant values, and the possibilities for subverting and opposing such preferred readings.

4   The nature of the appeal of popular culture (the pleasures of the text), and its role as a form of cultural capital.

5   The frequent 'moral panic' reaction to popular culture, and the associated notions of 'effects' and causality at work in such episodes.

Obviously, while these questions have been framed separately here, they are far from discrete. Further, we can only indicate here in shorthand fashion, issues which have been the subject of extended debates in cultural theory (see the useful overviews in Edgar and Sedgwick 1999; O'Sullivan *et al.* 1994).

Market determination and consumer sovereignty

As already observed, popular culture products are generally mass produced for a mass market, with that production process dominated in most spheres by a few large companies. Consider the highly lucrative international market for pop/rock music. This is currently dominated by a small group of 'majors' or multinational companies: British based EMI; BMG (Bertelsmann Group, Germany); Sony Music Entertainment (Japan); Warner Music Group (USA); and Universal/Polygram (USA, Holland).

The move into Hollywood by Japanese corporate capital since the late 1980s is a clear indication of the ongoing battle for global dominance of media markets. This battle reflects companies' attempts to control both hardware and software markets, and distribute their efforts across a range of media products – a process traditionally termed 'vertical integration', but now labelled 'synergy' – which enables maximisation of product tie-ins and marketing campaigns and, consequently, profits. As commentator Nigel Cope observed after Sony purchased both CBS Records (for $2 billion) in 1988 and Columbia Pictures (for $3.4 billion) in 1989:

Now Sony can control the whole chain. Its broadcast equipment division manufactures the studio cameras and the film on which movies are produced; in Columbia it owns a studio that makes them and, crucially, determines the formats on which they are distributed. That means it can have movies made on high definition televisions, and videoed with Sony VCRs. It can re-shoot Columbia's 2700-film library on 8mm film, for playing on its video Walkmans.

(Cope 1990: 56)

Such moves reflected the economies of scale and global integration required to compete on the world media market in the 1990s (Herman and McChesney 1997). Some commentators see the natural corollary of such concentrations of ownership as an ability to essentially determine, or at the very least strongly influence, the nature of the market's desire or demand for particular forms of popular culture. On the other hand, more optimistic media analysts, with a preference for human agency, empha-sise the individual consumers' freedom to choose, their ability to decide how and where cultural texts are to be used, and the meanings and messages to be associated with them (see Chapter 2).

The debate in this area is one of emphasis, since clearly both sets of influences or determinations are in operation, and it is a question of integrating rather than opposing them. For example, if I want to purchase a record, and have the necessary money to do so, I can make a 'free choice' from the records held at the local shops; however, this freedom is seriously constrained by the availability of particular formats and genres in the stores (unless, of course, I have access to the Internet and a credit card – see Chapter 3). I will certainly be able to purchase the latest charting performers on album, audio tape, or CD, and even in some cases as a video; but the retailer may well not have a relatively obscure blues musician on a small independent label, particularly if it is only putting the artist out on vinyl.

Cultural capital: lived cultures and cultural preferences

The comprehensive investigations of Pierre Bourdieu have showed how different cultural texts, practices, and values may be accorded differing worth among various social groups, thereby constituting forms of cultural capital (see especially Bourdieu 1984). Such work also illustrates that while the contemporary mass media are 'popular' in the sense of being a widely shared experience, they are arguably less class-specific than traditional cultural forms, and their appeal is more complexly based. As already suggested, mass media are frequently associated with popular or 'mass culture', commercially provided forms of leisure and entertainment. While such products are directed at all sections of the community, they are not, as some critics maintain, undifferentiated. Various forms of mass/popular culture in fact address different target audiences; further, they are actively mediated by these audiences in terms of their cultural experiences, age, and class, ethnic, and gender locations. For example, a piece of 'gangsta' rap music by Ice-T will be received very differently by an inner-city ghetto young black male (arguably the genre's primary target audience), and a middle-class suburban white woman. The woman would probably find the idiom itself 'boring', its sexism offensive and its 'blackness' threatening. For the black youth, however, the music would speak to his general economic experience of power-lessness, while asserting his black masculinity and perceived gender superiority within his ethnic group. This is to see the audiences social position as a mitigating factor in determining 'taste'.

As Bourdieu has observed, 'nothing more clearly affirms one's class, nothing more infallibly classifies, than tastes in music' (1984: 18). Academic sociology was initially slow to explore the relationship between popular music and its largely adolescent consumers, but there is now a history of studies exploring youth's tastes in music and factors such as class background, ethnicity, gender, location, and attitudes towards school (see Chapter 11). Bourdieu's notion of cultural capital has been usefully reworked and applied to various patterns and styles of music preferences (e.g. Thornton's discussion of club cultures in the UK).

Culture, ideology, and preferred readings

Another point of debate around popular culture is its ideological role in reinforcing or reproducing dominant values. Writers who concentrate on the text itself, often using concepts from semiotic and psychoanalytic analysis, argue that there frequently exists in the text a 'preferred reading', that is, a dominant message set within the cultural code of established conventions and practices of the producers and transmitters of the text.

This assumes that there is a dominant culture, a view strongly debated in cultural theory. Even if we accept the notion of ideologically dominant values, and while some consumers may, at least implicitly or subconsciously, 'buy into' the preferred readings containing these values, it must be kept in mind that it is not necessarily true that the audience as a whole do so. In particular, subordinate groups may reinterpret such textual messages, making 'sense' of them in a different way. This opens up the idea of popular resistance to, and subversion of, dominant cultures.

The 'meaning' of any engagement between a text and its consumers cannot be assumed, or 'read off', from textual characteristics alone. The text's historical conditions of production and consumption are important, as is the nature of its audience, and the various ways in which they mediate their encounter with the text. Conversely, nor can meaning be simply read off from the structural location of the consumer. Text and audiences interact. Herman and Hoare (1979) point to a number of examples of this occurring with popular music texts: the Strawbs' 'Part of the Union', intended as a direct attack on trade unionism, achieved the opposite effect when sung by Coventry car workers, while a traditional ballad, 'You'll Never Walk Alone', taken up by Liverpool Football Club supporters became an anthem of solidarity. As they conclude: 'Because records are interpreted, because they stimulate song, their consumption is not merely passive. A song's meaning is not immutable, independent of context' (Herman and Hoare 1979: 53). The study of 'pop' music fans also reminds us that cultural meanings are ultimately made by consumers, even if this process is under conditions and opportunities not of their own choosing (see Chapter 11).

The pleasures of the text

Some audience commentators will admit to being 'addicted' to popular culture, the use of addicted conveying here a hint of guilty pleasures, an abdication of aesthetic judgement through the implied suggestion that 'I couldn't help myself'. Yet to enjoy Batman and Darth Vader, ER and the Simpsons, Madonna and Springsteen, Raymond Chandler's Marlow and Robert Parker's Spenser, is to simply acknowledge that we are all immersed in popular culture, and that it plays a significant role in our lives. This is the case even with those who largely reject it, in part because the production of popular culture frequently subsidises the economic ability to meet minority market tastes. For example, some 90 per cent of recorded music sold is pop/rock music and its associated genres, the income from this core market arguably in effect subsidising the smaller market for musical forms such as classical and jazz.

The above list of popular culture heroes and texts indicates the word-games played by adherents. To be able to participate in the morning coffee-break ritual of discussing last evening's television programmes ('Wasn't George Clooney great in that emergency room scene in ER?'), presupposes a knowledge of the particular programme, its main characters and narrative dynamics. The process is a similar one with music fans' arguments over the relative merits of artists, or the various works of a particular performer: 'Surely you'd agree that Dylan's 1960s albums are superior to his subsequent work?' The insider is able to join in the game, provided he or she has the necessary background knowledge – cultural capital – to do so. All this is part of what has been termed the pleasures of the text, the ability to identify with particular forms of popular culture and a familiarity with its codes and conventions, thereby contributing to an aesthetic and emotional enjoyment of the form.

The pleasures of the text can also be physical: the solitary pleasures of being absorbed in 'a good read', creating an oasis of privacy and self isolation among family routines and distractions; the sheer tactile pleasure of handling record albums, with the accompanying rituals of setting the scene for listening, cleaning the record, and studying anew the sleeve notes; and the physical pleasures of those forms of popular culture which involve active participation, most notably dance. Then there are the emotional pleasures to be derived from both the anticipation and consumption of familiar pleasures: a well-loved record or film, a favourite author or television programme, or another concert by a favourite performer. Frequently, such pleasure includes an element of catharsis, the release from everyday tensions and concerns as we are 'lost' in the moment of consumption. There is the social dimension to all this, where consumption takes place with friends, family and lovers, and provides a context for the pursuit of other agendas, from catching up on gossip, to the time-honoured 'back row of the pictures' – now probably replaced by the lounge sofa and the rented video, or the Internet chat room! Consumption as a social activity brings into play the individual's knowledge of the text, which provides a focal point for much of the in-group or personal discussion.

Popular culture, 'effects' and moral panic

The audience reaction to popular culture/mass media has frequently provoked anxiety among those concerned for social stability and social order. In England in the nineteenth century, popular culture (sometimes referred to as 'folk culture') was associated with the customs, rituals, values and beliefs of working-class and lower middle-class groups. The middle classes largely conceived of these lower-class beliefs and behaviours as annoying, wasteful, immoral, and, at times, threatening and dangerous. Accordingly there emerged a desire to regulate and control popular culture, particularly those expressions of it associated with crowds, public spaces, noise, excessive drinking and violence.

The degree of success the Victorian ruling class enjoyed in this project, and working-class resistance to it, is beyond our scope here, but since the turn of the century, concern over the impact of popular culture has periodically surfaced with the advent of each new mass medium – silent cinema and the talkies, dime novels and comics, television, rock 'n' roll music, and video. The controversy surrounding the introduction of each popular medium frequently represented a form of moral panic; that is, the social concern generated by them was greatly exaggerated, and the perceived threat to social harmony was by no means as ominous as many regarded it. Such moral panics were episodes in cultural politics, in part representing struggles to maintain dominant norms and values. Popular culture was seen by its critics as diametrically opposed to 'high' culture and something to be regulated, particularly in the interests of the susceptible young.

Such debates have been preoccupied with the perceived negative effects of popular culture, and are generally based on simple notions of causality. Television provides the clearest recent example of this, but popular music has provided its own series of moral panics, from the teds and bodgies of the 1950s, to the mods and rockers of the 1960s, punk in the 1970s, goths in the 1980s, and gangsta rappers and rave culture in the 1990s (see Chapter 12).

READING POPULAR MUSIC

At this point, to place the discussion which follows in context, I address the various approaches and attitudes towards popular music displayed in the critical literature.

Six dominant points of entry can be identified: a high cultural, conservative critique and dismissal of popular music; the closely allied mass culture critique of the Frankfurt School; political economy; the structuralist-oriented approach of musicology; culturalist perspectives including populist positions and subcultural analysis; and contemporary discussions of popular music as a leading example of postmodernist cultural theory. These perspectives in turn reflect major approaches to cultural analysis. Of course, these broad labels are no more than cursory signposts in what is a complex field, with considerable intermixing of intellectual traditions. (For fuller discussions of approaches to culture, and cultural studies, see Johnson 1979; Swingewood 1977; Turner 1994; Grossberg *et al.* 1992.)

High culture and popular music

The high-culture tradition is essentially a conservative one. It encompasses a defence of a narrowly defined high or elite 'culture', in the classic sense of Arnold's 'the best that has been thought and said' (Arnold, *Culture and Anarchy*, 1869). This is an artistic conception of culture: the only real and authentic culture is art, against which everything else is set. It offers a mass society thesis, in which the valued civilised culture of an elite minority is constantly under attack from a majority or mass culture which is unauthentic and a denial of (the good?) life. Its main task in analysis is evaluation and discrimination – a search for the true values of civilisation, commonly to be found in Renaissance art, the great nineteenth-century novels, and so on.

A version of this view is ably expressed by Peter Abbs, most fully in his book *Reclamations* (1975). The very title of this study indicates its author's concern to return to an educational emphasis on the practice of discrimination, selection, and evaluation. Abbs uses the term 'mass-culture', which he regards as more satisfactory than 'popular culture', since 'unlike traditional folk-culture (which it often seeks to simulate) mass-culture is not made by the populace, nor does it generally express the authentic experience of a particular people' (53). Mass culture refers to the manufacture of culture as a commodity on a massive scale to mass markets for massive profits (78), and, as such, clearly includes much popular music. Mass/popular culture, for Abbs, represents a form of cultural debasement, epitomised by its trivialising of the emotions:

> In true culture we invariably find a high degree of specificity, a strong sense of context, of time and of location, a sense of unique relationships, of binding existential meanings; in false culture we tend to find the reverse, we find a high degree of generality in which all things prickly, problematic and diverse have been conveniently dissolved.
>
> (Abbs 1975: 53)

This passage epitomises the conservative critique of popular culture: its perceived lack of authenticity and its triviality, attributable to its mass commodification for the lowest common denominator, and its debasement of the emotions and human relationships.

Such high cultural critiques of popular culture have frequently reserved their most vehement efforts for popular music. Writing in 1839, Sir John Herschel claimed:

> Music and dancing (the more's the pity) have become so closely associated with ideas of riot and debauchery among the less cultivated classes, that a taste for them, for their own sakes, can hardly be said to exist, and before they can be recommended as innocent or safe amusements, a very great change of ideas must take place.
>
> (cited Frith 1983: 39)

Through the 1950s and 1960s, there were a succession of commentators who regarded much popular music as mindless fodder, cynically manufactured for mindless youthful consumers. In his best-selling book *The Closing of the American Mind*, Allan Bloom argued that rock music presents life as 'a nonstop commercial prepackaged masturbational fantasy', which he charges as responsible for the atrophy of the minds and bodies of youth (Bloom 1987).

Underpinning such views are assumptions about the potentially disruptive nature of 'the popular', and the need for social control and the regulation of popular pleasures. The high culture view of popular culture has been criticised for failing to recognise the active nature of popular culture consumption; failing to treat the cultural forms seriously on their own terms; biased by aesthetic prejudices, which are rarely explicated; and resting on outmoded class-based notions of a high–low culture split. The traditionally claimed distinctions between high and low culture have become blurred. High art has being increasingly commodified and commercialised, while some forms of popular culture have become more 'respectable', receiving State funding and broader critical acceptance.

The high culture perspective remains evident in the application of aesthetics to popular music, and the tendency of musicology to ignore or dismiss popular music genres. It also underpins some State attitudes towards the funding and regulation of cultural forms. At an everyday level, it is implicit in the manner in which musicians, fans and critics make distinctions of value both between and within particular genres.

Popular music and the mass society

Though politically on the left, the influential 'Frankfurt School' of social theory has a good deal in common with the high culture conservative commentators. The

Frankfurt theorists criticised mass culture in general, arguing that under a capitalist system of production, culture had become simply another object, the 'culture industry', devoid of critical thought and any oppositional possibilities. This general view was applied more specifically to popular music by Adorno, especially in his attacks on Tin Pan Alley and jazz. When Adorno published his initial critique 'On Popular Music' in 1941, the music of the big bands filled the airwaves and charts, operating within the Tin Pan Alley system of songwriting that had been dominant since the early 1900s, characterised by simple rhyming formulas and harmonies.

At the heart of Adorno's critique was the standardisation associated with the capitalist system of commodity production:

> A clear judgement concerning the relation of serious to popular music can be arrived at only by strict attention to the fundamental characteristic of popular music: standardization. The whole structure of popular music is standardized even where the attempt is made to circumvent standardization.
>
> (Adorno 1941: 17)

In this essay and his subsequent writings on popular music, Adorno continued to equate the form with Tin Pan Alley and jazz-oriented variations of it, ignoring the rise of rock 'n' roll in the early 1950s (Adorno 1976). This undermined his critique and resulted in his views generally being strongly rejected by more contemporary analysts of popular music (see, for example, Frith 1983: 43–8; and the section below on populist perspectives).

Gendron forcefully recapitulates 'the failings' of Adorno's theory, particularly his exaggeration of the presence of industrial standardisation in popular music, but also suggests that 'Adorno's analysis of popular music is not altogether implausible', and merits reconsideration (Gendron 1986). To support this argument, Gendron examines the standardisation of the vocal group style doo-wop, rooted in the black gospel quartet tradition, which had a major chart impact between 1955 and 1959. So far, so good, but he then asserts: 'What is true for doo-wop also holds true for other rock 'n' roll genres: rockabilly, heavy metal, funk etc.' This claim is not teased out, and runs counter to the clear differentiation that is evident within genres such as heavy metal and techno/dance music (see Chapter 8).

What happens when you read, hear or view something is that you mediate the experience; further, this process of mediation is not purely at an individual, psychological level, but is influenced by the context within which the activity occurs. It is that context, especially its economic dimension, that is the focus of political economy.

Music as political economy

The political economy approach to the popular/mass media has as its starting point the fact that the producers of mass media are industrial institutions essentially driven by the logic of capitalism: the pursuit of maximum profit. The fact that these institutions are owned and controlled by a relatively small number of people, and that many of the largest-scale firms are based in the United States, is a situation involving considerable ideological power. Schiller (1999) has traced the pervasive and increasing inequality in access to information and cultural products due to the commercialisation and privatisation of broadcasting, libraries, higher education, and other areas of public discourse. Commenting on the United States, Bagdikian (1997) observes how 'a small number of the country's largest industrial corporations have acquired more public communications power than any private business has ever before possessed in world history', together creating 'a new communications cartel'. The music industry has been part of this process of consolidation of 'imperial corporations' (Barnett and Cavanagh 1994). At issue is the consequent question of control of the media and whose interests it operates in, and the relationship between diversity and innovation in the market.

Classical political economy analysis (the Frankfurt School is, arguably, an example), tended to devalue the significance of culture, seeing it primarily as the reflection of the economic base of society. The influence of political economy is evident in the argument of those contemporary Marxists who emphasise the power of corporate capitalism to manipulate and even construct markets and audiences:

> More than any of the other performing arts, the world of song is dominated by the money men on the one hand and the moral censors of the media on the other. The possibility of alternative voices making themselves heard is always small and at times, such as now, non-existent. The illusion is that song is a freely available commodity. ... The reality is that song is the private property of business organisations.
>
> (Rosselson 1979: 40)

The picture of a powerful corporate capitalist music industry, able to manipulate and even construct markets and audiences, stresses how the music business is now an integral part of a global network of leisure and entertainment corporations, typified by a quest for media synergy and profit maximisation (Barnett and Cavanagh 1994). An extension of this is the classic form of the cultural imperialism thesis, popularised in the 1970s, which implied that mass manufactured popular culture, primarily from the US, is swamping the integrity and vitality of local cultural forms.

Such positions can all too easily slip into a form of economic determinism, married to (capitalist) conspiracy theory; seeing culture as produced by economic relations,

20

and omitting any sense of the relative autonomy of the superstructure. They ignore the crucial point, already made but worth reiterating, that the consumption of music is not (necessarily) a passive activity. Classical political economy also tends to overlook or negate the many instances of oppositional politics in rock music, including the symbolic revolt of subcultural lifestyles, 'conscience rock', and the didactic use of song lyrics (see the reply to Rosselson from Herman and Hoare 1979; and Chapter 12).

Contemporary political economy theorists have become more sophisticated in their appreciation of the reciprocal relationships between base and superstructure. Media institutions have been examined by asking of media texts: who produces the text? For what audience? In whose interests? What is excluded? Such an interrogation necessitates examining particular media in terms of their production practices, financial bases, technology, legislative frameworks, and their construction of audiences. As regards global cultural consumption, the classic cultural imperialism view has undergone major revision, with the status of the 'local' and its relationship to globalisation being seen in more complex and dynamic terms (see Wallis and Malm 1984; Robinson *et al.* 1991; and the discussion in Chapter 4). This new work has reasserted the importance of political economy, which has come into its own in the last decade in reframing popular music studies.

Structuralism and musicology

Structuralist views of popular culture/media concentrate on how meaning is generated in media texts, examining how the 'structure' of the text (visual, verbal, or auditory) produces particular ideological meanings. Such study is primarily through semiotics, the study of signs, a method which attempts to establish how the various elements of a text combine to present a 'preferred reading' (or a most likely, or dominant, message or meaning) for the consumer (viewer, listener, or reader). Such an approach involves systematically uncovering the various layers of meaning in a text. At its most sophisticated (or esoteric, depending on your point of view), this involves the application of psychoanalysis, in conjunction with semiotics, to examine how media texts shape the individual unconscious of the consumer. Structuralist media theory, for example, will refer to how films and television programmes 'position the viewer' and 'construct subjectivity' in accordance with certain ideological positions.

The musicological approach can be regarded as a structuralist form of cultural analysis, since it privileges the text by placing the emphasis firmly on its formal properties. Musicologists tackle genres such as pop and rock as music, using conventional tools derived from the study of more traditional/classical forms of music: harmony, melody, beat, rhythm, and the lyric. Academic musicology, however, remains sparse (see Mellers 1986; Shepherd 1991; Middleton 1990), and has had limited impact on popular music criticism. This state of affairs reflects most 'non-classical' musicians' and rock critics' general lack of formal musical training, and the latter's preoccupation with the 'sociology of rock'. The obvious difficulty with the musicological approach is that the preoccupation with the text in and of itself omits any consideration of music as a social phenomenon. The music itself becomes a disembodied presence, lacking any social referents.

Indeed, it can be argued that much popular music is largely a music of the body and emotions, and its influence cannot easily be reduced to a simple consideration of its formal musical qualities. Attempts to do so can all too easily become pretentious, as shown by Frith's comparison of two explanations of the Animals' 1964 hit 'I'm Crying'. Richard Middleton, a musicologist, emphasises in his explanation the formal musical qualities of the composition, including the point that:

> The cross relations in the ostinato (which is melodic and harmonic) are the equivalents of blue notes, arising from a similar conflict between melodic and tonal implications. The modal melodic movement of the ostinato, with its minor thirds, clashes with the tonal need for major triads imposed by the 12-bar blues structure.
>
> (cited Frith 1983: 13)

Compare this with Alan Price's description: 'I wrote the music and Eric (Burdon) did the words and we just threw it together in rehearsal in Blackpool. We just stuck it together and recorded it and by chance it was successful' (ibid.).

Such examples aside, musicology deserves a better press than it has received, and we can point to a number of recent examples of its helpful application to popular music (e.g. Moore 1993; Brackett 1995; Covach and Boone 1997); its value, and its application to particular texts, are examined in Chapter 8.

Culturalism and popular music

Culturalist perspectives on popular culture have examined the question of how the media actually undertake the production of 'consent' for social, economic and political structures which favour the maintenance of dominant interests (see, for example, the early work of Stuart Hall). Those working in this area have been markedly influenced by the ideas of the Italian Marxist theoretician, Antonio Gramsci, particularly the concept of ideological hegemony, advanced by Gramsci to explain how a ruling class maintains its dominance through achieving a popular consensus mediated through the various institutions of society, including the schools, mass media, the law, religion and popular culture. Ideological hegemony thus represents the organisation of consent, a process underpinned by the threat of actual physical coercion by the State. An important aspect of hegemony is that it mystifies and conceals existing power relations and social arrangements. Particular ideas and rules are constructed as natural and universal 'common sense' and the popular media

22

play a leading role in this process. However, hegemony is never absolute, but is instead constantly being challenged and redefined.

Those who stress the consumption of popular music as an active, rather than a passive process, who identify the many instances of oppositional politics in popular music, and who emphasise the tensions and contradictions at work within the music industry can be broadly described as 'culturalist'. In the writing on popular music, culturalism is best represented by the work on music and youth subcultures associated with the Birmingham Centre for Contemporary Cultural Studies (BCCCS) during the 1970s (Willis 1978; Hebdige 1979; Hall and Jefferson 1976). This broad body of work emphasised the place of the individual in the determination of cultural meaning. For example, Chamber's theme is the constant interplay between commercial factors and lived experience:

> For after the commercial power of the record companies has been recognised, after the persuasive sirens of the radio acknowledged, after the recommendations of the music press noted, it is finally those who buy the records, dance to the rhythm and live to the beat who demonstrate, despite the determined conditions of its production, the wider potential of pop.
>
> (Chambers 1985: Introduction)

In similar fashion, Middleton (1990) places popular music in the space of contradiction and contestation lying between the 'imposed' and the 'authentic', and also emphasises the relative autonomy of cultural practices.

Postmodern rock

Finally, the impact of postmodernism needs to be acknowledged, with its challenge to the established notions of representation in the verbal and visual spheres. Postmodernism seeks to blur, if not totally dissolve the traditional oppositions and boundaries between the aesthetic and the commercial, between art and the market, and between high and low culture. The precise nature of postmodernism, however, proves hard to pin down, and there is a marked lack of clarity and consistency in all the varying usages of the term.

In a key early contribution, 'Postmodernism, or the Cultural Logic of Late Capitalism', Jameson overviews postmodernism as the cultural expression of a new phase of capitalism, characterised by communications technologies facilitating the virtually instantaneous shifting of international capital, the emergence of new centres of capital (e.g. Japan) in a global economy, new class formations breaking with the traditional labour versus capital division, and a consumer capitalism which markets style, images and tastes as much as actual products. The commodification of culture has resulted in a new populism of the mass media, a culture centred around

23

the marketing and consumption of surfaces and appearances, epitomised by the ubiquity of commercial television (Jameson 1984; see also the writing of French postmodern theorists Baudrillard and Lyotard).

Despite its obvious plausibility as a general explanation of developments in popular culture, postmodernism suffers from a number of difficulties. To heavily generalise (since, as already stated, postmodernism is hardly a unitary theoretical position), these are: its frequent lack of specificity; its over-preoccupation with texts and audiences at the expense of locating these within the economic and productive context within which cultural products reside; its reduction of history and politics and its ignoral of 'traditional' sociological notions of production, class and ideology (see Milner 1991).

A form of postmodern thesis was popular in the 1980s with academic commentators on popular music, who saw the music, once associated with youthful rebellion and political activism, as now thoroughly commercialised and incorporated into the postmodernist capitalist order. What was once revolt had become style. In his collected essays, *Music for Pleasure* (1988b), and in his contribution to his edited volume *Facing The Music* (1988a), Simon Frith suggested the arrival of a curious entity, postmodernist pop, a value-free zone where aesthetic judgements are outweighed by whether a band can get its video on MTV and its picture in *Smash Hits*. In an analysis of a number of major contemporary pop stars, Hill echoed Adorno's critique of popular music as manufactured mass culture. Appropriately subtitled 'Manufacturing the '80s Pop Dream', Hill's study of performers such as Michael Jackson, Duran Duran, and Madonna, argued that 'this fresh species of genuinely talented practitioners are *ready and willing* to manufacture themselves' (his emphasis), and that 'never before have commerce and creativity so happily held hands' (Hill 1986: 9). While both Frith and Hill concede that 'rock' has always been about more than just music, they argued that it had never been more so, and was now increasingly subverted to the services of commercialism. This is to misrepresent the history of popular music, which has always been at least partly about style, and, once again, downplays the continued political force of many of its constituent genres.

More recently, the application of postmodernism to popular music is primarily based on two perceived trends: first, the increasing evidence of pastiche, intertextuality, and eclecticism; and, second, increased cultural fusion and the collapsing of high–low culture type distinctions in rock. Postmodernist views of music videos, for example, frequently regard it as exemplifying the collapse of traditional distinctions between art and the commercial, the aesthetic and the unaesthetic, and the authentic and unauthentic (e.g. Kaplan 1987). However, this conflation of postmodernism and music video is open to serious question, with music television, if anything, actually becoming more traditional in form during the later 1990s.

In addition to music television such as MTV, Goodwin (1991; also 1993) identi-

24

fies a number of points where the debate around postmodernism intersects with popular music: the music itself, where claims are made for textual exemplars of post-modernism; the use of sampling and pastiche; the emergence of particular social formations of consumers 'which celebrate pastiche and ahistorical modes of consumption' (175); and 'postmodern rock' as a sales category. In his insightful analysis of these, Goodwin concludes that 'while it is possible to discover categories of post-modern music and perhaps practices of postmodern consumption, the grand claims of postmodern theory remain insubstantial as an account of the current state of popular music' (Goodwin 1991: 174). Almost a decade later, there is little evidence to contest this view (see Longhurst 1995; Gracyk 1996: 220–6).

The general approach adopted in *Understanding Popular Music* draws primarily from critical media theory, particularly its contemporary political economy and culturalist strands. Popular cultural texts are regarded as dynamic not static, medi-ated both by patterns of economic and social organisation and the relationship of individuals and social groups to these patterns. This puts politics in a position of central importance, as culture is viewed as a site of conflict and struggle, of negotia-tions which constantly confirm and redefine the existing conditions of domination and subordination in society. Against the backdrop of these cultural studies' sign-posts, the construction of meaning in popular music can be seen as embracing a number of factors: the music industry and its associated technologies, those who create the music, the nature of musical texts, the constitution of audiences and their modes of consumption, and attempts to influence and regulate all of these. The role of the music industry, in its drive to commodify its performers and texts, and to maximise profits, is the starting point for analysing popular music.

Chapter 2

'Every I's a winner'

The music industry

The music industry embraces a range of institutions and associated markets: the recording companies (my main focus in this chapter) and the retail sector, producing and selling recordings in their various formats; the music press; music hardware, including musical instruments and sound recording and reproduction technology; merchandising (posters, t-shirts, etc.); and royalties and rights and their collection or licensing agencies. These facets are increasingly under the ownership/control of the same parent company, enabling the maximum exploitation of a particular product/performer.

While reliable data is difficult to obtain, various sources indicate the economic significance of the products of the music industry. In 1984, the annual revenues from the sale of records, tapes and CDs in the US was estimated by Billboard at $4.37 billion, while internationally such revenues brought in $US 12 billion annually (Garofalo 1987: 79). In 2000, the Recording Industry Association of America observed that, as the world's universal form of communication, music touches every person of the globe to the tune of $40 billion annually, and the US recording industry accounts for one-third of that world market (www.riaa.com).

Aside from the sales of recorded music in its various formats, there is also the considerable revenue to be gained from associated activities and products, as a few examples suggest:

- The summer 1996 'Can't Not' world tour by Alanis Morissette, to promote her album *Jagged Little Pill*, grossed over $23million (Cantin 1997).
- A full page, colour advertising spread in UK music magazine *Q* costs almost £8,000.

27

- The original MTV channel now reaches 287 million households in Europe, Latin America, and Australia.
- The Rolling Stones are believed to have earned US$10 million when Microsoft launched its software campaign with the group's song 'Start Me Up'.
- The financial outlay on music hardware – the performers' amplifiers, guitars, drum kits, synthesisers, etc.; and the consumers' sound systems – is unestimated, but the adverts in the proliferation of musicians' magazines (see Chapter 4) testify that it is clearly enormous, as is the expenditure on sound systems.
- The size of 'megastar's' deals has reached unprecedented levels. In August 1996, REM signed a five album contract with Warner Bros records worth an estimated US$80 million, the largest recording contract ever rewarded. The band was paid a $10 million signing bonus plus, as a further 'sweetener', a $20 million royalty advance on future sales of its existing six album Warner catalogue (*LA Times* press report, August 1996).

All of the above emphasise the economic aspect of popular music; but cultural meanings are not created by economics alone.

This chapter begins by considering the theoretical debate around the relative value of economic and cultural determinations in popular music. The recording industry is seen as a cultural industry, in which cultural meanings are constrained by economics, but not entirely so. Drawing on the work of Peterson, I then give an overview of the various explanations, cultural and economic, that have been offered for the emergence of rock 'n' roll in the mid-1950s. These illustrate the importance of the production 'context' in enabling the emergence of artistic 'creativity'. The discussion of subsequent trends in the music industry emphasises vertical and horizontal integration at work, with a general tendency towards consolidation. These are related to explanations for the perceived alternation of periods of creativity and conservatism in musical genres. I then briefly consider the roles of A&R (Artist and Repertoire) and marketing in the production process. A case study of Bob Marley and the Wailers, and the commodification of reggae, demonstrates the operation of the industry at the level of particular artists and genres.

POPULAR MUSIC AS A CULTURAL INDUSTRY

First coined by Adorno, as a descriptive term, 'cultural industries' refer to those institutions in our society 'which employ the characteristic modes of production and organization of industrial corporations to produce and disseminate symbols in the form of cultural goods and services, generally, though not exclusively, as commodities' (Garnham 1987: 25). Such industries are characterised by a constant drive to expand their market share and to create new products, so that the cultural commodity resists homogenisation. The cultural industries are engaged in competition for limited pools of disposable income, which will fluctuate according to the economic times (see Vogel 1994). The cultural industries are also engaged in competition for advertising revenue, consumption time, and skilled labour. Radio especially is heavily dependent on advertising revenue. Not only are consumers allocating their expenditure, they are also dividing their time among the varying cultural consumption opportunities available to them. With the expanded range of leisure opportunities in recent years, at least to those able to afford them, the competition among the cultural, recreational, and entertainment industries for consumer attention has increased.

The sound recording industry demonstrates most of the features identified by Vogel (1994) as characteristic of the entertainment industries:

1 Profits from a very few highly popular products are generally required to offset losses from many mediocrities; overproduction is a feature of recorded music, with only a small proportion of releases achieving chart listings and commercial success, and a few mega sellers propping up the music industry in otherwise lean periods (e.g. Michael Jackson's, *Thriller*, 1982, with sales of some twenty million copies through the 1980s).

2 Marketing expenditures per unit are proportionally large; this applies in the music industry to those artists and their releases with a proven track record.

3 Ancillary or secondary markets provide disproportionately large returns; in popular music through licensing and revenue from copyright (e.g. for film soundtracks).

4 Capital costs are relatively high, and oligopolistic tendencies are prevalent; in the music industry this is evident in the dominance of the majors, in part due to the greater development and promotional capital they have available.

5 Ongoing technological development makes it ever easier and less expensive to manufacture, distribute, and receive entertainment products and services. This is evident in the development of recording technology.

6 Entertainment products and services have universal appeal; this is evident in the international appeal of many popular music genres and performers, enhanced by the general accessibility of music as a medium, no matter what language a song may be sung in.

In addition to these characteristics, it is noteworthy that the music majors and their associated media conglomerates, reveal different patterns of ownership in relation to the levels of production, distribution, and retail (see the case studies in Barnett and Cavanagh 1994).

The music industry is big business, an international multi-billion dollar enterprise. Historically, the music industry has been centred in the United States, with the United Kingdom making a significant artistic contribution to an Anglo-American popular music hegemony. This Anglo-American dominance has waned in recent years, with the reassertion of the European market and the emergence of Japanese media conglomerates as major players in the music industry. Nonetheless, the Anglo-American market remains of major importance, not least for its commercial legitimation of emergent trends.

Recording companies are the most important part of the music industry. They fall into two main groups: the 'major' international companies and lower tiers of 'independents', although in terms of structure and operating practices, the distinction between these is frequently blurred (see Negus 1996). The 'indies' in many cases are dependent on the majors for distribution and also act as 'farm teams', finding and developing new talent for them. Record companies are hierarchically organised business structures, with clearly demarcated roles. In a larger enterprise these roles would include management, producers, marketing and public relations, publicity, promotion, business affairs, finance and legal, manufacture and distribution, administrative and secretarial (see Negus 1992: 38f.; Hull 2000). In the case of the record industry, while creating and promoting a new product is usually expensive, actually reproducing it is not. Once the master copy is pressed, further copies are relatively cheap and economies of scale come into operation. A video may well cost many thousands of dollars to make, but its capacity to be reproduced and played is then virtually limitless. It also needs to be noted that the advent of cheap reproductive technologies has made piracy difficult, if not impossible, to control.

As indicated in Chapter 1, the international recording industry is now dominated by five 'majors'. Each company is part of a larger communications or electronics conglomerate, each has branches internationally, and each embraces a number of labels. For example, Sony Music is part of Sony Corporation, the Japanese electronics manufacturing company. In addition to its extensive consumer electronics division, Sony also owns or has significant interests in film production and distribution (through Columbia Pictures and Tri-Star Pictures), home video production and distribution, and television production. Sony Music includes Sony Music Publishing, and the labels Columbia, Epic, and Epic Associated Labels; Sony also owns half the Columbia House record club, Sony Distribution, and CD and tape production facilities in the United States. Sony expanded its music interests substantially through its acquisition of CBS Records for US$2 billion in 1988 from CBS. Sony's music group revenues amounted to around $4.6 billion in 1997, some 56 per cent of Sony's entertainment business revenues of $8.2 billion, and about 10 per cent of Sony's total revenues for that year (Hull 2000: 81; Hull provides useful sketches of each of the 'big five'; see also Burnett 1996).

The continued concentration of the culture industries as a whole is increasingly obvious. In 1981, forty-six corporations controlled most of the business in daily newspapers, magazines, television, books, motion pictures, and music in the United States. By 1986 that number had shrunk to twenty-nine. In 2000, ownership of the United States media industry is in the hands of only six conglomerates, and global communication is dominated by twelve major corporations.

The music industry has been part of this process of consolidation, heading towards a system of oligopoly (where a few sellers occupy the market). In 1998 two of the majors, Universal Music Group and Polygram, merged, with the resultant record company, Universal Music Group, becoming the largest record company in the world, with an estimated market share of 23 per cent (Hull 2000: 79). This was surpassed with the January 2000 merger of Time Warner and EMI creating the world's biggest music company, worth around US$20 billion, and with a powerful foothold in the Internet through a planned merger between Time Warner and America Online. This will enable the new Warner EMI Music group to have access to millions of web, cable and magazine subscribers at a time when the Internet is transforming the music industry (see Chapter 3).

The crucial issue here is what this means in cultural terms. How does such concentration affect the range of opportunities available to musicians and others involved in the production of popular music, and the nature and range of products available to the consumers of popular music? In other words, what is the cultural significance of this situation, and what role does it play in the creation of meaning in popular music?

DETERMINATIONS AND MEANINGS

Studying the cultural industries involves utilising the general insights of political economy theory, and engaging in the debates that have surrounded this classic approach. These involve the relative importance of the economic base and the associated social institutions of the superstructure: the family, the church, the school and the media. This is not purely a question of economics, since what is at stake is the nature of cultural products and their associated ideological messages.

Studies of the music industry often fall into one of two broad perspectives: those which emphasise corporate power, and those which, critiquing this, emphasise the active role of the consumers of the music. More recently, a 'middle ground' has emerged, informed by critical political economy, which views the industry as in tension between these two polarities (see Sanjek 1997, for a useful overview of 'divergent approaches to the music industry'). A number of studies have emphasised the power of the corporate music industry, a view encapsulated in their titles: *Rock 'n' Roll is Here to Pay* (Chapple and Garofalo 1977); *Rockonomics* (Eliot 1989); *One for the Money* (Harker 1980); *The Mansion on the Hill: Dylan, Young, Geffen, Springsteen, and the Head-On Collision of Rock and Commerce* (Goodman 1997). Those who see the economic base as calling the tune, at the risk of making a bad pun, argue for the commodification of rock under the conditions of capitalist production and the constant quest for profit. Chapple and Garofalo, for example, argued that the concentration of ownership (among the major recording companies), enabled capitalist corporations to 'colonise leisure', and that the music business was by then 'firmly part of the American corporate structure' (1977: 300). Marc Eliot, in his damning study of the American music industry, concludes:

> In light of the music industry's profitable involvement in all facets of the commercial mainstream, the story of rock and roll should be used by the Harvard School of Business as one of its case studies. Far from the threat that social and political critics would have it seem, rock and roll has become the corporate spine of American entertainment.
>
> (Eliot 1989: 201)

This association of art and economics was seen as particularly evident with the British 'New Pop' performers of the early 1980s, and with the rise of music video and MTV.

> The New Pop isn't rebellious. It embraces the star system. It conflates art, business and entertainment. It cares more about sales and royalties and the strength of the dollar than anything else and to make matters worse, it isn't in the least bit guilty about it.
>
> (Rimmer 1985: 13; see also Hill 1986)

A linked body of more journalistic work exposed the graft and corruption in the music industry, features seen as a by-product of its preoccupation with profit-making (Goodman 1997; Dannen 1991). While these studies focused on mass-produced popular music in largely Western contexts, studies of the production of music in non-Western societies showed a similar pattern (Wallis and Malm 1984; Robinson *et al.* 1991).

In *Music for Pleasure*, Frith takes a hard line on the side of the commodification and co-option of rock thesis. In his introduction he states:

> My starting point is what is possible for us as consumers – what is available to us, what we can do with it is a result of decisions made in production, made by musicians, entrepreneurs and corporate bureaucrats, made according to governments' and lawyers' rulings, in response to technological opportunities. The key to

'creative consumption' remains an understanding of these decisions, the constraints under which they are made, and the ideologies that account for them.

(Frith 1988b: 6–7)

The ideological side of this view is that rock as the language of rebellion has meta-morphosised into the language of the cash register. The first line of Frith's book is: 'I am now quite sure that the rock era is over' (ibid.: i).

This is to see the process of consumption, whereby social meaning is created in the music, as constrained by the processes of production: production determines consumption. While Frith clearly has an argument, this emphasis is too simply deter-ministic. Both production and consumption are not to be regarded as fixed immutable processes, but must be regarded as engaged in a dialectic. Indeed, Frith's own case studies in the same volume suggest the operation of human agency in both spheres remains highly important. While the elements of romance and imagination that have informed particular moments in both our personal histories and the history of genres such as rock are marginalised in the commodification process, they remain essential to the narratives we construct for ourselves through popular music.

At the heart of the associated debates is the issue of the influence and nature of concentration: how does the music industry concentration affect the range of oppor-tunities available to musicians and others involved in the production of popular music, and the nature and range of products available to the consumers of popular music? Initial analyses of the relationship between concentration, innovation, and diversity in popular music suggested a negative relationship between concentration and diversity in the (Western-dominated) international recording industry, relating this to a cyclical pattern of market cycles (Peterson and Berger 1975; Rothenbuhler and Dimmick 1982). This view was challenged by Lopes (1992), who argued that a very high level of concentration was accompanied by a high level of diversity. Lopes concluded that innovation and diversity in popular music in a period of high market concentration depends on the system of development and production used by major record companies (see also Burnett 1996).

It needs to be acknowledged that those writers emphasising 'the incorporation of rock' did allow some limited cultural space for consumer autonomy, the autonomy of the 'local', and the radical potential of popular music. More recent music industry studies have revisited, reworked, and revitalised the political economy tradition, to develop a 'middle way' between the polarities of corporate power and consumer autonomy. Greater attention is being paid to the filtering processes at work before a particular piece of music reaches the charts (Blake 1992; Cusic 1996; Sanjek 1988). For example, Christianen (1995: 91) points to the importance of the number of deci-sion makers within a firm as a variable in explaining the diversity and innovation generated by a major record company.

Negus has been a key contributor to this perspective. In a detailed account of the music industry in the United Kingdom, his central concern is the process of discovery and development of recording artists, which he uses 'as an organising principle to provide a more general account of the recording industry and the production of pop music' (1992: vi; see also Negus 1999). Negus draws on Bourdieu's notion of 'cultural intermediaries', which he sees as more flexible than the traditional concept of 'gate-keepers', to examine the role of personnel in the music industry in terms of their active role in the production of particular artists and styles of music, and the promotion of these.

While Negus stresses the anarchic aspect of many of these industry practices, which he sees as the result of the essential uncertainty endemic to the music business, he also demonstrates how the industry 'has come to favour certain types of music, particular working practices and quite specific ways of acquiring, marketing and promoting artists' (1992: vii). Such established modes of operating work against new artists, styles outside of the historically legitimated white rock mainstream, and the employment of women. This process is confirmed in studies of the operation of particular recording companies, including the 'independents' (Lee 1995; Hesmondhalgh 1997); the marketing of specific genres, notably 'world music' (Garofalo 1993; Mitchell 1996: chap. 2) and America's black popular music tradition (Garofalo 1994; George 1989; Neal 1999); and studies of artists' engagement with the recording process.

While Negus is at pains to emphasise 'the cultural worlds being lived and constantly remade, highlighting the webs of relationships and multiple dialogues along and around which the musical and visual identities of pop artists are composed and communicated' (1992: vii; see also Negus 1996: chaps 2 and 3), his work has been subject to strong critique, notably from Harker. Harker argues that Negus 'quietly absorbs the terminology (of the industry and the Harvard Business School) and its ideological premises and implications into his discourse' (1997: 47). Harker reasserts the value of the classic Marxist critique, with an emphasis on disposable wealth or the lack of it, and class location (1997: 73), in interpreting 'official' data on trends in the music industry.

Also central to left analyses emphasising the economic, is the conception of 'authenticity', which is imbued with considerable symbolic value. Authenticity is underpinned by a series of oppositions: mainstream versus independent; pop versus rock; and commercialism versus creativity. Inherent in this polarisation is a cyclical theory of musical innovation as a form of street creativity versus business and market domination and the co-option of rock. Such views of mass art forms – like rock – as compromised by its association with capitalist commodity production, are flawed:

> Art has always in some sense been propaganda for the ruling classes and at the same time a form of struggle against them. Mass art is no exception. It is never

simply imposed from above, but reflects a complicated interplay of corporate interests, the conscious or intuitive intentions of the artists and technicians who create the product, and the demands of the audience.

(Willis 1981: intro.)

The uneasy alliance between art and commerce is frequently placed at the heart of the history of popular music, but it must be seen as a false dichotomy. Rare is the performer who has not been concerned to ensure the fullest possible return for their talents, and a concern with marketability is not necessarily at odds with notions of authenticity and credibility; indeed, the latter are themselves marketable commodities, as the recent commercial success of the band Rage Against the Machine testifies.

I wish to argue here, as elsewhere in this account, for a Gramscian modified, political economy thesis. While the commodity form which popular music takes, and the capitalist relations of mass industrial production in which the bulk of popular music is created, do significantly determine the availability of these texts and the meanings which they produce, such determination is never absolute. Meanings are mediated, the dominant meanings of texts subverted, and 'alternatives' to 'mainstream' commercial music are always present. Music is a site of the ongoing political struggle in the cultural sphere.

The discussion so far has been at a general theoretical level. The relative merits of base versus superstructure, or the economic versus cultural explanations of rock, are now examined through two case studies: (1) the historical development of the music industry, particularly why rock 'n' roll established itself in the mid-1950s United States; and (2) with reference to the role of A&R and marketing, how the music industry attempts to maximise profit and mould 'product', genres, and artists, using the example of Bob Marley and the Wailers.

WHY 1955?

At the most general explanatory level, it is accepted that 'the rock formation emerged out of and was articulated into the particular social, economic, and political context of post-war America' (Grossberg 1992: 138). However, the various attempts to sketch more precisely the nature of this context, and its relationship to the emergence of the new music, privilege different contributing factors: demographics, cultural politics, musical innovation, and shifts in the nature of the music industry.

Demographics

The emergence of rock 'n' roll in the mid-1950s is usually explained in terms of a combination of age group demographics and individual musical creativity. The post-

35

war baby boom was 'a crucial condition of the rearticulation of the formations of popular culture after the Second World War and the Korean War'; there were 77 million babies born between 1946 and 1964, and by 1964, 40 per cent of the population of the United States was under twenty (Grossberg 1992: 172). The baby boom and the emergence of a youth market made the young a desirable target audience for the cultural industries: 'post-1945 American teenagers enjoyed an unprecedented level of affluence. Their taste in film, music, literature and entertainment was backed up by enormous purchasing power which record producers and film-makers were quick to satisfy' (Welsh 1990: 3). Certainly, there were indications that 'American teenagers were rejecting, consciously or not, the quasi-official popular culture which had flourished during the Depression and war years, a highly idealised, romanticised picture of family and national life' (ibid.). The popularity of books like *Catcher in the Rye*, films about alienated youthful loners – *The Wild One*, and *Rebel Without a Cause* – and an increasing interest in black subcultures, were all indicative of some young peoples' search for alternative explanations about American life from beyond the mainstream. One aspect of this search was the development of a white audience for rhythm and blues, which was to give rock 'n' roll its twelve bar structure (see Miller 1999; Ennis 1992).

American suburbia, where the baby boomers were concentrated, neither represented nor catered for the desires of American youth. As Grossberg (1992: 179) puts it: 'Rock emerged as a way of mapping the specific structures of youth's affective alienation on the geographies of everyday life'. This is to usefully emphasise the point that the social category of youth 'is an affective identity stitched onto a generational history' (ibid.: 183); the particular configuration of circumstances in the 1950s forged an alliance of 'youth' and rock music as synonymous with that particular age cohort of young people. For Grossberg, 'Rock's special place (with and for youth) was enabled by its articulation to an ideology of authenticity', an ideology which involved providing youth with cultural spaces 'where they could find some sense of identification and belonging, where they could invest and empower themselves in specific ways' (Grossberg 1992: 204–5). Authenticity, in Grossberg's sense of the term, is here equated with the ability of rock to resonate with youth's common desires, feelings and experiences in a shared public language.

Music innovations

There is no denying the significance of the baby boom in elevating youth to a new social, political and economic visibility, and clearly the emergence and vitality of any cultural form is dependent on the existence of an audience for it. Music is a form of communication, and popular music, as its very name suggests, always has an audience. However, we must not over privilege the 'audience explanation' for the emergence of rock in the 1950s. Audiences select their cultural or leisure texts from what is available to them, and the nature of the market is determined by more than the constitutive qualities of its potential audience. Recognising this, some analysts add musical innovation to an emphasis on the new youth audience. At the same time as the baby boom gathered momentum, this view runs, several key performers – Elvis Presley, Little Richard, Bill Haley, Buddy Holly, and Chuck Berry – revitalised popular music. Presley is the most lauded of these:

> Presley took the song ('That's All Right Mama'), and the strong rhythmic element in it, but kicked it out of the heavy almost ponderous groove Crudup (the original artist) used. What Presley succeeded in doing was injecting the blues with an abandoned hillbilly attitude. ... The result was a musical hybrid, destined to prove more exciting than either its blues or country parents, while retaining elements of both.
>
> (Welsh 1990: 36)

At one level, the impact of these performers is undisputed. Even though they were adapting existing styles and forms, they were innovative (see Gillet 1983; Miller 1999). But as Curtis observes, '*all* popular performers come along at the right time' and 'to explain the success of a given act, you need to make the social and cultural context of that success as specific as possible' (Curtis 1987: 5). To that context, we must add the economic dimension.

Both the demographic and innovative artists' arguments used to explain the emergence of rock 'n' roll are ultimately limited. A significant segment of youth in the early 1950s can be regarded as rejecting the established forms of popular culture, and searching for something fresh and more their own, but the post-war baby boom did not affect the market until the late 1950s and 1960s. In 1955 this age group were yet to hit their teenage years and did not yet represent a major segment of the rock audience. Furthermore, the 'radical' or oppositional nature of youth in this period must not be exaggerated, and nor must rock's only limited rejection of the dominant liberal consensus in everyday American life (Grossberg 1992: chap. 6). The creativity argument at first sight looks more attractive, yet a more thorough consideration of the antecedents of rock 'n' roll reveals that the musical form was present prior to the early 1950s. It merely awaited the right combination of technical, market, and musical factors to emerge in a more realised and commercially dominant form.

The production of culture

Following Peterson (1990), we can utilise a 'production of culture' perspective to explain the emergence of 'the rock aesthetic in American popular music ... in the

brief span between 1954 and 1956'. This approach examines the historical development and nature of the record industry by a number of interrelated factors: law and
regulation; technology; industry structure; organisational structure; occupational
career; and market. I have adopted Peterson's account here, supplementing his
discussion with reference to more detailed examinations of this historical process
(Eliot 1989; Sanjek 1988). I then extend his analysis to the international scene and
subsequent developments in the music industry, and conclude with an overview of
the state of the industry as it enters the twenty-first century. Against this 'empirical'
background, we can then reconsider the validity of the base versus superstructure
debate.

One important point demonstrated by such a historical analysis, is the significance of what could be considered contextual factors in the shaping of popular music:
for example, the relative importance of particular genres, the dominance of certain
forms of radio format, the role of technology, the shifting status of record company
majors and independents. Furthermore, the precise nature and relative importance of
these can be shown to have changed over time: the configuration of the political
economy of popular music is constantly shifting.

Copyright

First, copyright law, patent law and the Federal Government regulation of radio
station broadcasting licences were an important influence on the advent of rock and
roll, 'though in ways completely unintended and unanticipated as well' (Peterson
1990: 99). Copyright is central to the music industry. 'The basic principle of copyright law is the exclusive right to copy and publish one's own work' (Fink 1989: 36).
That is, the copyright owner has the right to duplicate or authorise the duplication of
their property, and to distribute it. The full legal nature of copyright is beyond our
scope here (see Fink 1989: 36–47); its significance lies in its cultural importance.

The first US copyright statute was enacted in 1909, and protected the owners of
musical compositions from unauthorised copying (pirating), while making a song
into a commodity product that could be bought and sold in the marketplace.

> With copyright protection, the aggressive New York sheet-music writer-
> publishers could afford to spend a great deal of money promoting a new song
> because other printers could not pirate the valuable properties thus created.
> Their activity fostered a quick succession of innovations in music and popular
> dancing, most notably ragtime and jazz.
>
> (Peterson 1990: 99)

Similar legislation was enacted in Britain in 1911. The development of recording raised the question of whether the publishers of recorded and sheet music could claim the same rights as literary publishers. British and American legislation differed on this, with the former being more restrictive in its approach: 'In Britain records cannot be copied, heard in public, or broadcast without permission; in America, the purchaser of a record (whether a private citizen or radio station) is its owner and can do what he or she likes with it' (Frith 1983: 133).

Royalties and genres

Copyright laws provided no mechanism for collecting the royalties from the public performance of music. In 1914, the American Society of Composers, Authors and Publishers – ASCAP – was formed, to issue licences and to collect all due royalties from three sources: the performance of songs, with recording artists receiving income based on the revenue made from the sale of their records; the sale of original music to publishers, and subsequent performance royalties; and money paid to the publishers for their share of the sales and performances, usually split 50–50 between composers and publishers (Eliot 1989: 21–2). ASCAP's initial efforts to build its membership and implement the collection of royalties met with only limited success, but its role was confirmed by a Supreme Court decision in 1917 validating the organisation's right to issue membership licences and collect performance royalties.

Though, in effect, 'mandating that only ASCAP licenced music could be played in Broadway musicals, performed on the radio and incorporated into movies … by the 1930s it effectively controlled access to exposing new music to the public' (Peterson 1990: 99). However, broadcasters resisted all ASCAP's attempts to collect royalties for music played on the radio, and went so far as to create their own organisation to break what they claimed were ASCAP's monopolistic tactics, establishing Broadcast Music Inc. – BMI – in 1939. In successfully challenging the ASCAP monopoly, BMI also undermined the dominance of a particular form of popular music, 'an aesthetic which accented well-crafted, abstract love themes, strong melodies and muted jazz rhythms and harmonies' (ibid.). Other genres, predominantly the work of black musicians, were systematically excluded from access to a wider audience. BMI, contesting ASCAP's stranglehold, was unable to lure many songwriters and publishers from their rival, so it turned to those who were not members of ASCAP. This included many working within jazz, rhythm and blues and the country music traditions. In 1940, when the long-running dispute between ASCAP and the radio stations over user fees still remained unresolved, all ASCAP-licensed songs were excluded from radio airplay. This left the way open for BMI's artists to create a space for themselves in the public consciousness. While ASCAP soon came to terms with the radio stations, the genres represented by BMI continued to receive airplay. The dominant aesthetic of swing and crooner music remained secure, but 'for the first time it became possible to make a living as a songwriter or publisher in these alternative genera that in fusing formed the foundations of the rock aesthetic' (Peterson 1990: 100).

Formats

Developments in patent law were another factor in shifting the nature of the music industry towards a position conducive to the emergence of rock 'n' roll in the 1950s. The two major American phonograph companies, Columbia (established in 1889) and RCA (established in 1929, incorporating Victor, formed in 1901), joined by Decca (established in 1934 in the United States), had been engaged since the inception of the industry in a battle over alternative recording and reproducing technologies. At stake was the all important market share. The ten-inch 78 rpm shellac disc had emerged as the standard by the 1930s, but experimentation and research continued. Not only was sound quality a consideration, arguably even more important was the amount of music that could be placed on a record, offering the consumer 'more value for money'. In the early post-war years, Columbia developed a long-playing hi-fidelity record using the newly developed vinyl. In 1948 Columbia released its twelve inch 33-and-a-third rpm LP. Refusing to establish a common industry standard, RCA responded by developing a seven inch vinyl record, with a large hole in the middle, that played at 45 rpm. After several years of competition between the two speeds, the companies pooled their talents and agreed to produce in both formats. By 1952, the LP had become the major format for classical music and 'the 45' the format for single records for popular radio airplay, jukeboxes and retail sales (Sanjek 1988). The 45 was a significant change in format because it was virtually unbreakable, compared with the delicate 78s, making it easier for smaller distribution companies to enter the national market, and compete with the established national distribution systems of the majors. This enabled the emerging independent labels to distribute across the country and have national hits, and to mail promotional copies of new songs to radio stations.

Radio

The part played by the Federal Communications Commission (FCC), which licensed broadcasting stations throughout the United States, was also significant in influencing the timing of the advent of rock 'n' roll. During the peak of radio in the 1930s, when virtually every American home had a set, the FCC restricted the number of stations licensed to each market to between three and five. The major networks (NBC, CBS, and Mutual) accounted for the majority of these licenses, and lobbied successfully for maintenance of the *status quo*. While many applications for new stations were submitted, these were denied or deferred. This situation changed dramatically in 1947 when the networks, concerned at the threat posed by the emergent medium of television, withdrew their former objections. The FCC was now able to gradually approve the backlog of applications, with the result that in the next four years the number of radio stations authorised in most markets doubled.

A growing symbiotic relationship between phonograph record makers and commercial radio station owners also contributed to the flowering of rock 'n' roll in the 1950s. Radio broadcasting in 1948 was dominated by four competing national networks, each trying to increase their share of the total American radio audience. This meant they had essentially similar programmes and schedules. In contrast, the newly emergent independent radio stations varied widely in their programming, in several cases playing records aimed at black buyers. The record industry in 1948 was similarly highly concentrated. Four firms – RCA, Columbia (CBS), Capitol, and American Decca (MCA) – released 81 per cent of all the records making the Top 10 during that year. These few firms were able to effectively dominate the recorded music market through controlling three key aspects of the hit-making process: (1) getting creative people on long-term contracts and establishing them as 'names' in the eyes of the public; (2) monopolising record distribution; and (3) maintaining close ties with network radio programmers.

Both radio and the record industry were transformed in the years 1954–58. In radio, what had effectively been one single national market with four competing networks, fractured into upwards of a hundred autonomous local markets, each with eight to a dozen or more radio stations competing with each other. The old radio networks, financed by national advertisers, could afford expensive dramatic programmes, comedy shows, and live music. This format was beyond the resources of the proliferating independent radio stations, which turned to playing records as their staple form of programming. From a situation of direct competition, radio and the record industries shifted to one of symbiosis. Radio depended on the industry for programming material, while the record industry rapidly came to appreciate the value of radio exposure for commercial success. Competition between the numerous radio stations, focused at the local rather than a national level, encouraged greater programming differentiation through the playing of different kinds of records. The aim became the capture of a local market segment rather than a slice of a homogeneous national audience.

The rise of the independents

The cultural upshot of all this was a marked expansion of the aesthetic range of records played on air by the mid-1950s. The majors were slow to shift their focus from the established crooner and swing aesthetic, leaving the way open for a number of recently started record companies. Sun Records, Atlantic Records, Stax, Chess, Vee Jay, Dot, Coral, and Imperial were able to successfully compete in the national market, promoting the genres neglected by the majors: 'The 1950s decade was the golden era for small independents, which embraced blues, gospel, modern jazz, country, R&B, and rock 'n' roll'. From 1948 to 1954, about one thousand new record labels were formed, and for many of these 'it came down to what music could be recorded most cheaply' (Kennedy and McNutt 1999: xvii; this study provides an excellent history of the 'little labels', from 1920 to 1970). Radio stations sought new, attention-getting material regardless of its source. The independents developed new talent – Presley on Sun is the best known example – and the majors no longer dominated distribution. In 1951, industry magazine *Billboard* recognised the broadened appeal of black music by changing its 'race' chart to the R&B chart.

The structure of the music industry and radio stations also changed. Between 1948 and 1958 radio shifted from large-scale in-house production by the major networks, involving a high level of job differentiation, to localised, small-scale operations with fewer specialised departments and jobs. The bureaucratically organised oligopolistic record companies of 1948 were well suited to efficiently producing a large number of standard products, but were slow to adjust to the demand for a more varied product. In the new situation of successful challenge by the independents, the majors lost three-quarters of the market share. Yet they gradually recaptured their preeminent position by becoming financing and distribution companies for a series of divisions, that were allowed to operate, in effect, as independent small firms.

New careers

The nature and relative balance of general career patterns in radio and the music industry changed dramatically in the mid-1950s. In radio, the most conspicuous change was the transformation of the functionary position of radio announcer into the showman-entrepreneur DJ. Exemplified by Alan Freed, this new approach became termed in the industry 'personality radio'. This promotional role, including the controversial use of 'payola' (paying DJs to play records, sometimes through giving co-credit for the songwriting), enabled many artists on small labels to receive airplay. In the record industry, the emergence of new style producers, first in the new record companies, was important for the marketing of new artists and styles. These new-style producers sought out promising singers and groups, helped them to find appropriate material, and facilitated the recording process by selecting the suitable studio musicians, and saw that the record, once marketed, got appropriate promotion (Peterson 1990: 111). Examples included the Chess brothers in Chicago, and Jerry Wexler at Atlantic in New York.

There was also a shift in the market, from a relatively homogeneous one in 1948 to a heterogeneous one by 1958, perceived by industry executives as youth oriented and segmented into specialist audience niches. In sum, these various shifts saw an industry geared to maintaining a 'steady state' situation and to managing the slow evolution of new styles, changing to become an industry able to respond to the emergence of rock 'n' roll in 1955–56. The constraints on the operation of the industry had changed at the contextual level, enabling change at the cultural level.

MARKET CYCLES?

An influential attempt to explain both this initial historical development and subsequent genre shifts in popular music, is the market cycles explanation offered by Peterson and Berger (1975). Briefly, this suggests that original musical ideas and styles, generated more or less spontaneously, are taken up by the record industry, which then popularises them and adheres to them as the standard form. Meanwhile new creative trends emerge which have to break though the new orthodoxy. Thus develops a cycle of innovation and consolidation, a cycle reflected in the pattern of economic concentration and market control. Monopolistic conglomerates are formed during periods of market stability, and inhibit the growth of independents – who are usually the source of new ideas. Yet under conditions of oligopoly there is also a growing unsatiated demand, from those who are not satisfied with the prevailing product available. Bursts of musical innovation – rock 'n' roll, the West Coast sound, punk – are often associated with youth subcultures, who help draw attention to them (see Chapter 11). Small record labels emerge to pioneer the new sound and style, followed by reconcentration and market stagnation once more as the majors regain control. The main evidence used by Peterson and Berger is the relative chart shares (in the Top 20) of the competing labels and the relative chart performance of established artists, and new and emerging artists.

This is a seductive thesis, not least because it offers an economic rationale for the bewildering historical shifts in rock tastes, which do seem to see swings between blandness and innovation. To test its validity, we must first sketch it out more fully. As already discussed, the period 1948–55 certainly saw an initial period of oligopoly, with four firms accounting for 70 per cent of the market, and along with the next four largest taking almost all the total market. This dominance, achieved by vertical integration, was starting to break down with the emergence of rock 'n' roll, abetted by structural shifts in radio. The years 1956–59 were characterised by competition, according to Peterson and Berger, as independent labels carved out a prominent market share and the majors attempted to reassert their dominance. Innovation was also prominent, as evidenced by the decline in the number of charting cover versions, new artists grabbing a bigger share of the hits, and a greater diversity in lyric content. There followed a period of 'secondary consolidation' (1959–63); the number of firms in the market stabilised at about forty, though with eight firms getting about half the market share. Several important new players emerged: film companies (Warner, MGM) diversifying in the face of competition from television, and strong independents such as Dot, Imperial, and Liberty. The majors acknowledged rock was not a passing fad after all; they moved to expand their rosters of performers, buying up contracts and developing new talent (the Beach Boys at Capitol, Dylan at Columbia). Renewed growth occurred between 1964 and 1969, with innovation and transition fuelled by Beatlemania and the California sound of the late 1960s. Many artists tackled previously largely unmentioned themes: sexual freedom, black pride, drugs, oppositional politics, and war. 'Black' labels – Motown and Atlantic – moved into the majors. At the same time, reconcentration began: Warner bought Reprise, United Artists bought Liberty, and Paramount bought Dot.

In the early 1970s, reconcentration fully emerged once again. The majors increased their market share, with four firms dominant: Columbia, Warner Brothers, Capitol, and Motown. Of firms in the top ten, only two – Motown and A&M – were independents, that is, not part of a media conglomerate. The majors were able to capitalise on each new fad: 'Since they have a wide range of artists under contract with one or another of their various subsidiary labels, they can take advantage of every changing nuance of consumer taste' (Peterson and Berger 1975: 155). Revolt, as George Melly (1970) put it, had become style, with bands like Alice Cooper and the New York Dolls appearing self-conscious and posed in their apparent anti-social stances. The independents were increasingly squeezed out of the game by the high costs of promotion associated with breaking new bands. The structure of the industry appeared to have returned, full circle, to the early 1950s.

The market cycles notion can be applied to developments post-1975 (Rothenbuhler and Dimmick 1982). The advent of punk (1978–82) in part represented a reaction to the majors' market domination and the associated musical blandness of the 1970s. But its moment was short-lived as the majors soon incorporated it, and consolidation returned stronger than ever. Motown first signed a distribution deal with MCA in 1983, then in 1988 the company was sold by founder Berry Gordy to MCA (and the investment firm Boston Ventures) for US$61 million. In 1989, the major independent label Island Records, which had popularised reggae in the West, went to Polygram for £200 million. At the end of the decade rap offered a burst of creativity, but it too was soon commercialised: MC Hammer's dance-pop, watered-down rap, *Please Hammer Don't Hurt 'Em*, was the best-selling album of 1990 (Light 1991).

In the 1990s, media conglomeration firmly became the name of the game, one that was enacted increasingly on a global scale. The industry as a whole became progressively more integrated, both vertically and horizontally (see Hull 2000).

Record companies continued to be at the power centre, because of their control of distribution, and, as we have seen, the international market is now dominated by a handful of companies. The 1980s marked the saturation of the US domestic market, and the efforts of media conglomerates to secure their market share globally.

While the theory of market cycles provides a useful perspective on the economic development of the music industry, particularly the vexed relationship between its economic organisation and the nature of its cultural product, there are some significant caveats that need to be applied to it. First, there is a major methodological difficulty posed by its reliance on commercially successful singles, with the underlying assumption that the diversity of rock music is to be found in the hit parade. This overlooks the predominance of LP sales over singles since the early 1970s (see Chapter 3: Formats), and the generally accepted tendency to accord greater aesthetic weight to the longer format. Further, it sees market diversity as a direct function of the number of individual hit records in any one year. But, as Laing (1986: 335) points out, to confirm this argument it would be necessary to undertake a critical stylistic analysis of the actual recordings that were hits, on the basis of their musical features rather than the companies that released them. On this point, it could also be argued that the products of the independents are by no means always characterised by innovation. Indeed, frequently they themselves copied styles already popularised by their major competitors. Finally, as Peterson and Berger themselves acknowledge, the distinction between majors and independents has not been clear-cut since about 1970, while the two tiers of the industry have historically been linked through the majors' control of distribution.

MARKETING CONSUMPTION

Marketing has come to play a crucial role in the circulation of cultural commodities. It is a complex practice, involving several related activities: research, product planning and design, packaging, publicity and promotion, pricing policy, and sales and distribution, and is closely tied to merchandising and retailing. Central to the process is product positioning and imbuing cultural products with social significance to make them attractive to consumers (for insightful discussions, see Ewen 1988; Ryan 1992). In popular music this has centred on the marketing of genre styles and stars, which have come to function in a similar manner to brand names, 'serving to order demand and stabilize sales patterns' (Ryan 1992: 185). Above all, it involves utilising star images, linking stars and their music with the demands/emotions/desires of audiences.

It is noteworthy that by the 1990s the cant term for music within the industry was 'product'. This relates to popular music being an increasingly commodified product: merchandise to be packaged and sold. The major problem faced by record companies is the uncertainty of the music market: only one in eight of the artists A&R sign and record will achieve sufficient sales to recoup the original investment and start to earn money for the artists and generate a profit for the company. This situation has led to major record companies looking for acts already partially developed and indicating commercial potential.

The artists and repertoire (A&R) department of a recording label are responsible for working with acts who are already under contract, and finding new talent. They are constantly seeking out new material and acts to sign, attempting to develop a roster of artists for the company. A&R staff are frequently involved in all aspects of an artist's relationship with the record company, including the initial negotiations and the signing of the contract, the rehearsal, arrangement and recording of songs, and liaising with the marketing, video production and promotion divisions of the recording company (see Barrow and Newby 1996: chap. 7; Cusic 1996). It is a male-dominated sphere, a hierarchy divided according to seniority and experience, with successful A&R people among the highest paid employees in the music industry. The criteria A&R personnel generally use for judging potential artists are identified by Negus: 'the live, stage performance; the originality and quality of the songs or material; the recorded performance and voice; their appearance and image; their level of personal commitment, enthusiasm and motivation; and the achievements of the act so far' (1992: 53). A&R staff base their acquisition and development of artists on a mix of information about rapidly shifting styles and who are 'hot' new performers, acquired through extensive networks of contacts, and assessed largely through intuition and subjective response ('gut feeling').

To consider more precisely the relationship between industry marketing practices and consumer sovereignty, it is necessary to examine how record companies attempt to shape the marketplace. The case of Island and the Wailers is particularly instructive.

Packaging reggae

Island Records was begun by Chris Blackwell, the Jamaican-born son of an English plantation owner, in 1962, to supply Jamaican music to West Indian customers in Britain. The company diversified to black music in general, setting up Sue Records in 1963 as a subsidiary to market (under licence) American soul, blues, ska, and rhythm and blues tracks. In 1962, the company had its first major success when Millie Small's ska tune 'My Boy Lollipop' reached Number 2 in the English pop charts. In the later 1970s, Island hooked into the commercial end of the British counterculture, releasing records by Traffic, Fairport Convention, and Free. In 1972 Blackwell signed the Wailers, with Bob Marley.

Conventional histories see this move as inevitably successful, riding the burgeoning Western interest in reggae. But in fact the marketing of reggae and the Wailers is illustrative of record company attempts to maximise their investment at their most successful moment. Island shaped and marketed Marley and the Wailers as ethnic rebellion for album buyers, both black and white (Jones 1988; White 1989; Barrow and Dalton 1997). The strategies used included recording *Catch a Fire* (Island, 1972), the Wailers' first album, in stereo; doubling the pay rates for the session musicians involved, enabling them to record for longer; employing the latest technical facilities of the recording process to 'clean up' the music; and remixing and editing the backing tracks in London, after they had been recorded in Jamaica. Blackwell also accelerated the speed of the Wailers' basic rhythm tracks by one beat, thinking that a quicker tempo might enhance the appeal of reggae to rock fans (Jones 1988: 64). The result was a more 'produced sound', with keyboards and guitars, moving away from reggae's traditional emphasis on drums and bass.

Catch a Fire had an elaborate pop-art record cover, designed as a large cigarette lighter, while the Wailers' second album, *Burnin'* (Island, 1973), pictured Rastas in various 'dread' poses, and printed the song lyrics. 'These ploys seemed to confirm Island's intention to sell the Wailers as "rebels" by stressing the uncompromising and overtly political aspects of their music' (Jones 1988: 65). At the same time, however, this stance was watered down for white consumption. The group's third album had its title changed from *Knotty Dread*, with its connotations of rasta militancy and race consciousness symbolised by dreadlocks, to *Natty Dread*, with its white connotations of fashionable style.

Island carefully promoted the Wailers concert tour of Britain in 1973 to include appearances on national radio and television. This level of exposure was new for reggae, previously constrained by the genre's limited financial support. Later marketing of the band, following only fair success for their first two albums, included pushing Bob Marley to the fore as the group's frontman and 'star'. This strategy proved particularly successful during the 1975 tour of Britain, as the band – now 'Bob Marley and the Wailers' – commercially broke through to a mass white audience. Original founding members Peter Tosh and Bunny Wailer left towards the end of 1974, both feeling that too much attention was now being given to Bob. In another strategic marketing move, instead of simply replacing them with similar characteristically Jamaican male harmonies, the more gospel-inflected backup vocals of the I-Threes were brought in to supply a sound more familiar to rock audiences at that time (Barrow and Dalton 1997: 131). A string of record hits and successful tours followed in the late 1970s, due at least in part to the music becoming more accessible and pop oriented. In 1981, Bob Marley's worldwide album sales were estimated to be in excess of US$190 million.

The success of Island with the Wailers helped usher in a period of the international commercialisation of reggae. For the multinational record companies, 'reggae was a rich grazing-ground requiring low levels of investment but yielding substantial profits' (Jones 1988: 72). Jamaican artists could be bought cheaply compared to the advances demanded by their Western rock counterparts. Yet while reggae spurred the success of dub and the ska revival of the early 1980s, and was a crucial influence on commercially successful bands like the Police, Bob Marley remained the only major star to emerge from reggae. His international success arguably owed as much to Blackwell and Island as to his personal charisma and the power of the music.

Marley's death in 1981 did little to diminish his commercial worth, as Island successfully marketed a greatest hits package, *Legend* (1984), which was number 1 in the UK for several months. Indeed, the continued appeal of Marley was indicated by the album's remarkable longevity: it has remained the top-selling 'catalogue' album in *Billboard* since that chart's creation in 1991 (it is still there as I write this), and by 1997 had sold twelve million copies worldwide (Barrow and Dalton 1997: 135). By 1984, Dave Robinson was running Island, and his market research indicated that:

> you should keep the word 'reggae' out of it. A lot of what people didn't like about Bob Marley was the threatening aspect of him, the revolutionary side. So the (album cover) picture chosen was one of the softest pictures of Bob. It was a very well conceived and thought-out package. And a very well put-together record.
> (Chris Blackwell, owner of Island records; cited Stephens 1998 :145)

This approach set the trend for the subsequent marketing of the reggae star, as his image was subtly remoulded, moving from the Rastafarian outlaw of the 1970s to the natural family man of the 1980s to the 'natural mystic' in the 1990s. This process reflected the incorporation of his music along with his image and message. A new CD compilation, *The Natural Mystic* (1995) and a four CD boxed set *Songs of Freedom* (1992), both reflected how 'The Marley of the 1970s, rude boy, revolutionary, Rastafarian, needed to be exorcised for the singer to appeal to a more mainstream white audience' (Stephens 1998: 142). The cover of *Natural Mystic*, a profile head shot of a gently smiling Marley with his hand at his chin, was similar to that used on the *Legend* cover, and indeed came from the same photo session in 1977. The booklet accompanying the 1992 boxed set tells the story of Marley's origins as a rude boy in Trenchtown, Jamaica, the turn to Rastafari in the late 1960s, and his rise to international stardom in the 1970s, and the accompanying CDs parallel this history. Both the booklet and its images, and in the choice of songs for inclusion in the package, emphasise Marley's growing commitment to spiritual and social issues, playing down his increased political consciousness and desire to connect with a black audience as illness looked likely to end his career.

We are left with a picture of the music industry as a classic example of a culture industry. On the one hand, there is the concern to maximise profit, a quest involving the creation of market stability and predictability; on the other hand, the majors, in that same quest for profit, have to offer their customers innovation and change – or at least the appearance of it. 'Perhaps more than any other mass-produced commodity, popular music is a contested form' (Bennett 2000: 41). There is a constant tension between the homogenisation of the product and the presentation of something new and fresh. This process operates at two levels: the software – the production of the music, in its various formats – and the hardware, the technology to reproduce the recorded sound. Despite industry attempts, which at times have proven highly successful, to control or determine this situation, the meanings of their cultural texts essentially remain open to (re-)interpretation by their consumers.

Chapter 3

'Pump up the volume'
Technology and popular music

The history of music is in part one of a shift from oral performance to notation, then to music being recorded and stored, and disseminated utilising various mediums of sound (and visual) transmission. These are hardly discrete stages, but they do offer an organising logic for the overview here. Any new medium of communication or technological form changes the way in which we experience music, and this has implications for how we relate to and consume music. Technological changes in recording equipment pose both constraints and opportunities in terms of the organisation of production, while developments in musical instrumentation allow the emergence of 'new' sounds. New recording formats and modes of transmission and dissemination alter the process of musical production and consumption, and raise questions about authorship and the legal status of music as property.

It is not possible here to cover all aspects of these topics, which have been the subject of intensive study (major books include Jones 1992; Cunningham 1996; Millard 1995; Chanan 1995; Théberge 1997). Rather, I have attempted to signpost some of their cultural implications, with brief examples to illustrate the interaction of technological, musical and cultural change. As Théberge observes, 'technology' is not to be thought of simply in terms of 'machines', but rather in terms of practice, the uses to which sound recording and playback devices, recording formats, and radio, computers and the Internet are put: 'in a more general sense, the organization of production and consumption' (Théberge 1999: 216–17). The discussion covers:

1   Sound production, the influence of new instrumentation on music making; examples: nineteenth-century brass bands; the microphone; the electric guitar.
2   Sound recording: the recording studio; amplification; formats.

3 Sound reproduction: the phonograph and its descendants.
4 Sound dissemination: the historical impact and contemporary importance of radio, and the Internet and MP3.

As the focus here is on music as sound, mediums which combine sound and visuals – film, television, and music video and MTV – are treated separately (Chapter 10). A further example of the deployment of new technologies is the area of music retail. Electronic Data Processing, combined with greater concentration of music retailing (the megastores), permitted retail, distribution, and production 'to be arranged as an interconnected logistic package', allowing 'music retailers to delineate, construct and monitor the "consumer" of recorded music more intricately than ever before' (Gay and Negus 1994: 396). It is also important to acknowledge that prior to recorded sound, print was central to the transmission of music. Even before the invention of the printing press, hand-written songs were circulated. The printing press facilitated the circulation of Broadside ballads from the early sixteenth century, and sheet music, which peaked at the end of the nineteenth century (see Negus 1996).

SOUND PRODUCTION

New technologies of sound production are democratising, opening up performance opportunities to players and creating new social spaces for listening to music. However, these opportunities and spaces are selectively available, and exploited by particular social groups. Three brief examples of this process are the impact of nineteenth-century brass band instruments; the microphone in the 1930s; and the electric guitar in the early 1950s.

Victorian England saw an unprecedented expansion in participative music, with brass bands a major part of this. Herbert (1998) examines how and why brass bands developed, their distribution and extent, and the nature and significance of their impact. In doing so, he illustrates the complex intersection of technology, urbanisation, and musical forms at work in shaping the brass band movement. The first half of the nineteenth century was the most important period in the history of brass bands. They emerged as a new form of leisure activity, with the development of new brass instruments made possible by the invention of the piston valve: 'Suddenly brass instruments possessed a new musical facility, and potentially a new social identity' (Herbert 1998: 110). The advent of new instruments made possible new musical techniques, and an expanded band repertoire.

The introduction of the microphone in the 1920s revolutionised the practice of popular singing, as vocalists could now address listeners with unprecedented intimacy. This led to new musical creativities and sites of authorship. Johnson traces the emergence of the microphone as a 'performance accessory' in Australia, showing how it was inscribed by gender politics. Masculinist resistance to this 'artificial' aid left it primarily to women singers to exploit its possibilities in the 1930s. 'In particular, they experimented with projection, timbre and sensibility in a way that placed the intimate "grain of the voice" in the public arena, laying the foundations for the distinctive vocalisation of rock/pop' (Johnson 2000: chap. 4; see also Chanan 1995: chap. 7).

In a similar manner, the amplification of the guitar transformed popular musician-ship: 'amplification allowed guitarists to play fluid and hornlike solos, while the country and jump blues genres popular in the late Forties encouraged them to elaborate a more percussive and riffing style' (Miller 1999: 41). The Fender Esquire in 1950, the first mass-produced solid body electric guitar, changed the range and variety of people who could play, reducing the importance of controlling each string's resonance precisely, covering fingering mistakes.

SOUND RECORDING

Sound recording is the process of transferring 'live' musical performance on to a phys-ical product (the recording). The history of sound recording is one of technical advances leading to changes in the nature of the process, and the tasks and status of the associated labour forms. Such changes are not narrowly technical, as different recording technologies and their associated working practices (e.g. multitracking, overdubbing, tape delay) enable and sustain different aesthetics (for a detailed history, see Cunningham 1996; for a concise overview, Millard 1995: chap. 14). In the recording studio, the work of the sound mixer, or sound engineer, 'represents the point where music and modern technology meet' (Kealy 1979). Initially designated as 'technicians', sound mixers have converted a craft into an art, with consequent higher status and rewards.

Particular recordings illustrate advances in sound recording, at times accompa-nied by greatly increased use of studio time. Approaching the history of popular music from this perspective creates quite a different picture of artistic high points and auteur figures, in comparison with the conventional chronologies. Compare, for example, the following recordings (see Cunningham 1996, for a fascinating account of each):

1   Les Paul and Mary Ford, 'How High the Moon', which occupied the number one position on the American chart for nine weeks in Spring 1951, launched the concept of sound-on-sound recording, coupled with Paul's discovery of tape delay. The technique for recording Ford's voice was also innovative, as Paul recalls: 'The unwritten rules stated that a vocalist should be placed no closer than two feet from the microphone, but I wanted to capture every little breath

and nuance in Mary's voice. So I had her stand right on the mike, just a couple of inches away. Then, what happened? Everybody started to record vocals that way!' (Cunningham 1996: 25).

2   Elvis Presley, 'That's All Right Mama' (Sun, 1956), was recorded at the session in which producer Sam Phillips introduced the slapback delay sound, used on Presley's other Sun singles and the label's recordings by other rockabilly artists (see Escott 1991).

3   The Beach Boys, 'Good Vibrations' (Capitol, 1966), Brian Wilson's 'pocket symphony', utilised a huge range of instruments, including a Theremin (a pre-synthesiser electronic gadget), made possible partly by his extensive use of overdubs.

4   Pink Floyd, *Dark Side of the Moon* (Capitol, 1973) set a new precedent in sound recording techniques; for example, in its use of Noise Gates, devices which allow audio signals to be heard once they rise above a predetermined volume threshold, and an extensive use of synthesisers.

Through the 1980s and 1990s new recording technologies opened up creative possibilities and underpinned the emergence of new genres, notably techno, dance , and rap and hip-hop. Beadle (1993) addresses the profound changes being wrought by samplers, MIDI, and other new technological phenomena, which he credits with giving new life to a moribund music industry in the 1980s. Sampling can be viewed as part of rock's historic tendency to constantly 'eat itself', while also exemplifying its postmodern tendencies:

> The wilfull acts of disintegration necessary in sampling are, like cubism, designed to find a way ahead by taking the whole business to pieces, reducing it to its constituent components. It's also an attempt to look to a past tradition and to try and move forward by placing that tradition in a new context.
>
> (Beadle 1993: 24)

Digital sampling allows sounds to be recorded, manipulated, and subsequently played back from a keyboard or other musical device (see Théberge 1999). Introduced in the late 1970s and subsequently widely used, digital sampling illustrates the debates surrounding musical technologies. Its use is seen variously as restricting the employment of session musicians, and as enabling the production of new sounds, e.g. the use of previously recorded music in the creation of rhythm tracks for use in rap and dance remixes. The increasing emphasis on such new technologies is significantly changing the emphases within the process of producing popular music: 'As pop becomes more and more a producer's and programmer's medium, so it increasingly is a sphere of composition, as opposed to performance' (Goodwin 1998: 130).

Formats

With the advent of recorded sound 'music became a thing' (Eisenberg 1988), with recording technology in the late nineteenth century enabling its development in commodity form, independent of its 'live' performance aspects. Subsequent shifts in the popularity of various recording formats are important in explaining the historical evolution of popular music. Each new recording format offered fresh recording and marketing opportunities, and affected the nature of consumption. Historically, these constitute a procession of formats, though each is never totally superseded: the shellac 78, the vinyl 45, the EP and the LP, cassette audio tape, the compact disc, and digital audio tape and the erasable compact disc. The discourse here revolves around the search for realism, fidelity, and portability.

The question is the cultural significance of such developments. For example, the domestic relocation of music consumption, facilitated by the phonograph, raised questions of the listening process:

> Anyone, living no matter where, has only to turn a knob or put on a record to hear what he likes. Indeed it is just in this incredible facility, this lack of necessity for any effort, that the evil of this so-called process lies. For one can listen without hearing, just as one can look without seeing. The absence of active effort and the liking acquired for this facility make for laziness. … Listeners fall into a kind of torpor.
>
> (composer Stravinsky, in his autobiography, 1935, cited Eisenberg 1988)

The search for fidelity in sound recording reprised the concerns expressed during the development of formats, especially in debates over whether the authenticity, or sound 'aura', of the recording was comparable to hearing the piece in live performance (see Eisenberg 1988; Frith 1996: chap. 11).

Changing technologies and formats usually appeal to consumers wanting better sound (though what constitutes 'better' is debated) or greater convenience, and to those who possess a 'must have' consumerist orientation to such new technologies. New markets are created as older consumers upgrade both their hardware and their record collections. The balance sheet with regard to the declining status of the vinyl single and album, versus the ascendancy of the CD, is a mixed one. Yet there were opportunities in this even for those still emotionally tied to vinyl, as the early 1990s saw a boom in the used record store business as CD converts sold off their record collection on their way to buying their first disc player (Plasketes, 1992).

A short history of the single

The history of the single (historically often referred to as 45s – the rpm) is an example of the relationship between music making, marketing, and consumption. As observed in Chapter 2, the introduction of the virtually unbreakable vinyl 45 in the early 1950s was an important factor in the emergence of a proliferation of smaller independent record labels, who were significant in popularising rock 'n' roll. The single was originally a seven inch vinyl format, with an 'A' side, the recording considered most likely to receive radio airplay and chart 'action', and a 'B' side, usually seen as a recording of less appeal. Also important was the EP, an 'extended play' single, a vinyl seven inch, usually with four songs. In the UK the EP represented an early form of 'greatest hits' package, with attractive record covers, and outsold albums until the early 1960s.

In the early 1950s, the vinyl single overtook its shellac 78 counterpart as the dominant music industry marketing vehicle. Singles became the major selling format, the basis for radio and television programming, and the most important chart listing, with the last two in an apparently symbiotic relationship. Singles appealed to young people with limited disposable income. For the record companies, singles were cheaper to produce than an album, and acted as market 'testers'. While singles' success was important for performers and the record companies, it was also important as a means of drawing attention to the accompanying, or subsequent album, with the release of both being closely related. With a few significant exceptions (e.g. Led Zeppelin), performers generally relied on the single to promote their album release. This approach became the 'traditional' construction of record marketing through the 1960s and 1970s. Album compilations of singles, either by one performer or from a genre or style of music became an important market. While some performers with high charting singles were 'one hit wonders', singles' success frequently launched careers, leading to an album deal and moves from independent to major labels.

In the 1980s new single formats gained an increasingly significant market share. There was a massive increase in sales of cassette singles in America, and Swedish band Roxette's 'Listen to Your Heart' (1990) became the first single to hit number 1 in the United States without being released as a vinyl 45. Twelve-inch singles, including remixes, became an important part of the dance music scene, and, accompanying the general rise of the CD format, the CD single also began to emerge as a popular marketing form and consumer preference. Negus (1992: 65) documents the consequent decline of the vinyl single through the 1980s. In the US 1979–90, sales of singles declined by 86 per cent (from 195.5 million to 27.6 million units), and despite the growth of new formats, total sales of singles declined by 41 per cent. In Britain the single's decline was less dramatic, with total sales falling by 21 per cent, from 77.8 million in 1980 to 61.1 million in 1989. This reflected the continued industry practice in the UK of releasing one or two singles prior to the issue of an album. The relative decline of the single reflected the higher costs of the new formats, and the pressure to produce a video to accompany a single, a practice which was regarded as necessary for supporting radio airplay and chart success (see Chapter 7).

Performers were effected by the shift to the CD format. Whatever the aesthetic status of the rock/pop single, its material significance lay in its availability to artists with limited resources. The seven-inch 45 and the 12-inch dance single, with their specialist market tied to the club scene, offer such performers only a partial substitute. Linked to this, is the point that many of the independent record companies can't afford to produce CDs, restricting the market options available to their artists.

In the 1990s, the overall life of the single in the charts, due to radio airplay, remained important for drawing attention to the album. The single is now less important, with sales in all formats having continued to decline in the past decade. Nevertheless, the single remains crucial to commodifying pop music for the teen market. The appeal of particular singles is assessed primarily by the placing achieved on the charts, as well as longevity there. (It should be noted that these are not quite the same; sustainability indicates a broader market appeal, following initial sales to a performer's niche market or cult support). Making subsequent assessments of the commercial, and thereby presumed cultural, impact of a single on the basis of total sales and the length of time spent in the charts is a common practice (see Whitburn 1988).

SOUND REPRODUCTION

The historical development of the phonograph and various subsequent sound systems (hi fi; home stereo; the transistor radio; audio tape players; the walkman; the CD player) is more than simply a succession of 'technical' triumphs. Reflecting changes in the technologies of sound recording and production, each new form of sound reproduction has been accompanied by significant changes in how, when, and where we listen to music.

A talking machine

Edison invented the phonograph, a 'talking machine', in November 1877. This followed his work, along with researchers such as Bell and Watson, on the transfer of speech electrically, which led to the development of the telephone. The phonograph represented the true beginning of the reproduction of recorded sound, replacing 'the shared Victorian pleasures of bandstand and music hall with the solitary delight of a private world of sound' (Millard 1995: 1). Edison's phonograph used cylinders and was able to record and reproduce sound. Other researchers developed the new technology further: Berliner developed the gramophone (1888), using a disk instead of a cylinder, while Edison considerably improved on his original in 1887.

Various commentators have identified a succession of phases in the technological history of the phonograph: an acoustic one from 1877 to the 1920s; the use of electrical/magnetic tape, from the 1920s; and the digital age, with the CD, from 1982:

'the industry built on the phonograph was driven forward by the constant disruption of innovation: new systems of recording, new kinds of machine, and newer types of recorded music' (Millard 1995: 5–6; see also Jones 1992; Read and Welch 1977). By the 1970s, most homes in 'developed' countries had a home stereo system, the modern phonograph, consisting of an amplifier, a record player, tape recorder, and radio.

The phonograph was originally intended primarily as a business tool, but moved into entertainment initially through coin-operated phonographs (from 1889). With the development of pre-recorded cylinders in the early 1900s, the phonographic industry took off. While in 1897 only about 500,000 records had been sold in the United States, by 1899 this number had reached 2.8 million, and continued to rise. The impact of the talking machine was international. Farrell's (1998) discussion of the early days of the gramophone in India presents a fascinating story of the intersections between commerce and technological innovation and their impact on traditional Indian modes of music patronage and music making. Economics underpinned the move of GLT (Gramophone and Typewriter Ltd) into the Indian subcontinent. As John Watson Hawf, their agent in Calcutta, put it: 'The native music is to me worse than Turkish but as long as it suits them and sells well what do we care?' (cited in Farrell 1998: 59). For the first time 'Indian musicians entered the world of Western media' (ibid.: 58), as photography and recorded sound turned 'native' musics into saleable commodities.

The gramophone arrived in India only a few years after its invention in the West, and recorded sound brought many forms of classical Indian music out of the obscurity of performance settings, such as the courtesan's quarter, and on to the mass market. Recording these was a formidable exercise: the visits to various parts of India in the early 1900s were quite correctly termed 'expeditions', involving complex logistical problems. For the emergent Indian middle class, the gramophone was both a technological novelty and a status symbol. The images in the company catalogues, reproduced by Farrell, illustrate this, along with the use of traditional images of Hindu deities to add to the appeal of the new medium. The constraints and possibilities of the new technology affected the style and structure of the music recorded. While Farrell is cautious not to generalise too far from the one detailed example he presents, he suggests that one possible limitation of the limited duration of the early recordings 'was to lead artists to give greater weight to the composed or fixed parts of the performance than they would normally have done in live recitals' (1998: 78).

Stereo and the sound system

Stereophonic sound was first developed for use in film theatres in the 1930s, with home stereo systems as scaled down versions. In 1931 the first three-way speaker systems were introduced. The sound was divided into high, middle and low frequencies, with each band sent to three different transducers in the loud speaker, each designed to best facilitate that part of the sound spectrum: the large 'woofer' for the bass, a mid-range driver, and the smaller 'tweeter' for the treble. Due to the depression, and the difficulty of reaching agreement on a common stereo standard (compared with the battle over recording formats), this system was not turned into a commercial product until the late 1950s.

In the 1950s, tape was the format to first introduce stereo sound into the home. Read and Welch (1977: 427) observe that the 'introduction of the stereo tape recorder for the home in 1955 heralded the most dramatic increase ever seen for a single product in home entertainment'. The increased sales of magnetic tape recorders and prerecorded tape forced the record companies to develop a competing stereo product, particularly for the classical music audiophile. By the 1960s, stereo sound was incorporated into the loudspeakers used in home stereos. December 1957 saw the first stereo records introduced to the market. These were not intended for the mass market, and sales were initially not high, but home stereos became popularised during the 1960s.

In addition to home stereo systems, there are more mobile forms of sound reproduction, important for decentring the listening process, and sometimes identified with particular lifestyles and social groups. 'Sound system' is the term given to large, heavily amplified mobile discos and their surrounding reggae culture. These initially emerged in Jamaica, from the 1950s onwards, and were subsequently transplanted to Britain with the influx of Caribbean immigrants.

> The basic description of a sound system as a large mobile hi-fi or disco does little justice to the specificities of the form. The sound that they generate has its own characteristics, particularly an emphasis on the reproduction of bass frequencies, its own aesthetics and a unique mode of consumption.
>
> (Gilroy 1997: 342)

Compact cassette audio tape and cassette tape players, developed in the mid-1960s, appealed because of their small size and associated portability. Initially a low fidelity medium, steady improvement of the sound, through modifications to magnetic tape and the introduction of the Dolby noise reduction system, enhanced the appeal of cassettes. The transistor radio (made possible by the invention of the transistor in 1948) and the audio cassette had become associated technologies by the 1970s, with widely popular cheap radio cassette players, and the cassette player incorporated into high-fidelity home stereos. The development of powerful portable stereo players (boom boxes), associated with inner-city African-American youth, created a new form of social identification and a new level of noise nuisance. Another mobile form of sound system is the walkman, which had a major impact when it was introduced during the 1980s, enabling the listener to maintain an individual private experience in public settings (see Negus 1992).

An efficient format for the expansion into remote markets, tape cassettes became the main sound carriers in 'developing' countries, and by the end of the 1980s cassettes were outselling other formats three to one. As a portable recording technology, the tape cassette has been used in the production, duplication and dissemination of local musics and the creation of new musical styles, most notably punk and rap, thus tending to decentralise control over production and consumption. Home taping is individual copying (to audio or video tape) from existing recordings, or off-air, and was made possible by the development of cassette audio tape and the cassette tape player. The term cassette culture has been applied to the 'do it yourself' ethic that underlies such practices, and the network of musicians and listeners it embraces. Such practices pose a considerable threat to the music industry, with their violation of copyright.

CD-ROM

CD-ROMs are 4.5 inch plastic, aluminium-looking disks, the same size as the musical CD, which can each hold up to seven hundred megabytes of data, in multimedia form. This is equivalent to approximately one thousand 300 page books. Although they have gone largely untreated in the critical literature on popular music, the music CD-ROM represents a new marketing niche and a new advertising avenue for the popular music industry.

CD-ROMs are part of the explosion of multimedia in the 1990s. While this term is often loosely used, it generally refers to the communication of messages or information through the combined use of text, graphics, animation, audio, and motion video. In the modern sense, it goes with another basic concept of new technology – interactivity. Multimedia has come to imply more than just the convergence of voice, music, alpha-numeric text and so on, it also implies that the user has some degree of interactive control over these, instead of being a passive viewer, as with broadcast TV. In a broader perspective, multimedia is a synonym for convergence: major media companies working together, often under corporate umbrellas.

Music CD-ROMs are one aspect of the ongoing convergence of the electronics and music industries which began in the 1980s (see Chapter 2). By the early 1990s, record companies, including EMI and the Warner Music Group, began forming multimedia distribution divisions, which started exploring the possibilities of new technologies, including music CD-ROMs. For example, in 1994 EMI spokesperson Don Harder (senior VP of information technology) announced a CD-ROM featuring heavy metal band Queensryche, to be released with the band's new album:

'We are looking at creating as much synergy as possible between the CD and the CD-ROM. With both of those titles being carried in many of the same locations, we want to do a lot of cross marketing' (*Billboard*, 30 April 1994: 1, 98).

CD-ROM became an important and influential part of the music industry, extending the possibilities for listeners/viewers to interact with the musical perform-ance (see Hayward 1995; Shuker 1998). An increasing number of popular music CD-ROM titles have become available. These are usually artist-specific (a pioneering example is *XPLORA 1 Peter Gabriel's Secret World* (Interplay, 1993, and updates), but there are also music CD-ROMs which let users compose, play guitar, and edit music videos, along with music encylopedias (e.g. *Music Central 96*, and updates). Increasingly, regular CD releases now include multimedia material which can be accessed when the recording is played through the appropriate computer; e.g. The Rolling Stones, *Stripped*, 1996). In addition to CD-ROMs, there are now music/artist specific computer screen savers and video and computer games, complete with sound bites. A logical extension of this, has been the current links between the major record and on-line companies.

SOUND DISSEMINATION

I now turn to the role of communications media in bringing music to consumers, examining the historical impact and contemporary importance of radio, and the Internet and MP3.

Radio

Until the advent of MTV in the late 1980s, radio was indisputably the most impor-tant broadcast medium for determining the form and content of popular music. The organisation of radio broadcasting and its music formatting practices have been crucial in shaping the nature of what constitutes the main 'public face' of much popular music, particularly rock and pop and their associated sub-genres. Radio has also played a central role at particular historical moments in popularising or margin-alising music genres (for detailed discussions, see Barnard 1989; Crisell 1994; Pease and Dennis 1995).

Radio developed in the 1920s and 1930s as a domestic medium, aimed primarily at women in the home, but also playing an important role as general family entertain-ment, particularly in the evening. Radio in North America was significant for disseminating music in concert form, and helped bring regionally based forms such as western swing and jazz to a wider audience. Historically the enemy of the record industry, during the disputes of the 1930s and 1940s around payment for record airplay, radio subsequently became its most vital promoter. The reshaping of radio in the 1950s was a key influence in the advent of rock 'n' roll, while radio airplay became central to commercial success, especially through the popular new chart shows. 'Hit radio was "one of America's great cultural inventions", revitalising a medium threatened by television' (Barnes 1988: 9). The DJ (disc jockey) emerged as a star figure, led by figures such as Bob 'Wolfman Jack' Smith and Alan Freed (see Miller 1999: 57–61).

FM radio was developed in the early 1930s, using a frequency modulation (hence FM) system of broadcasting. It did not have the range of AM, and was primarily used by non-commercial and college radio until the late 1960s, when demand for its clearer sound quality and stereo capabilities saw the FM stations become preeminent in the commercial market. They contributed to what became a dominant style of music radio in the 1970s and 1980s (radio friendly; high production values; relatively 'easy listening'; for example, the Eagles, Fleetwood Mac). With the appeal of FM, the 1970s witnessed a consolidation of the historically established role of radio in chart success: 'Independent program directors became the newest power brokers within the industry, replacing the independent record distributors of the early sixties' (Eliot 1989: 169). Eliot is referring here to the way in which most radio stations followed formats shaped by consultants, with a decline in the role of programme directors at individual stations, a situation that persisted into the 1990s. Though video became a major marketing tool in the 1980s, radio airplay continues to play a crucial role in determining/reflecting chart success.

'No rap, no crap' (1990s 'Classic Rock' station slogan)

Radio stations are distinguishable by format: primarily the type of music they play, but also the style of their DJ's, and their mix of news, contests, commercials and other programme features. Radio broadcasts can be seen as a flow, with these elements merging. Historically, radio formats were fairly straightforward, and included 'top 40', 'soul', and 'easy listening'. Later formats became more varied, and included 'adult oriented rock', classic hits (or 'golden oldies'), contemporary hit radio, and urban contemporary (Barnes 1988). The main types of radio station include college, student, pirate, and youth radio (e.g. the US College stations; New Zealand's campus radio, and Australia's Triple J network); State national broadcasters, such as the BBC; community radio; and, the dominant group in terms of market share, the commercial radio stations. There is a longstanding contradiction between the interests of record companies, who are targeting radio listeners who buy records, still largely those in their teens and early twenties, and private radio's concern to reach the older, more affluent audience desired by advertisers. To some extent, this contradiction has been resolved by niche marketing of contemporary music radio.

As channel switching is common in radio, the aim of programmers is to keep the audience from switching stations. Common strategies include playing fewer commercials and running contests which require listeners to be alert for a song or phrase to be broadcast later, but the most effective approach is to ensure that the station does not play a record the listener does not like. While this is obviously strictly impossible, there are ways to maximise the retention of the listening audience. Since established artists have a bigger following than new artists, it makes commercial sense to emphasise their records and avoid playing new artists on high rotation (i.e. many times per day) until they have become hits, an obvious catch-22 situation. The most extreme example of this approach is the format classic rock, or classic hits, which only plays well-established hits from the past. This format remains very popular, capitalising on the nostalgia of the demographic bulge who grew up during the 1960s, and who now represent a formidable purchasing group in the marketplace.

The concern to retain a loyal audience assumes fairly focused radio listening. Paradoxically, while the radio is frequently 'on', it is rarely 'listened' to, instead largely functioning as aural wallpaper, a background to other activities. Yet high rotation radio airplay remains vital in exposing artists and building a following for their work, while radio exposure is also necessary to underpin activities like touring, helping to promote concerts and the accompanying sales of records. The very ubiquity of radio is a factor here; it can be listened to in a variety of situations, and with widely varying levels of engagement, from the walkman to background accompaniment to activities such as study, domestic chores, and reading (see Crisell 1994).

Station and programme directors act as gatekeepers, being responsible for ensuring a prescribed and identifiable sound or format, based on what the management of the station believes will generate the largest audience – and ratings – and consequent advertising revenue. The station's music director/the programme director – at smaller stations the same person fills both roles – will regularly sift through new releases, selecting three or four to add to the playlist. The criteria underpinning this process will normally be a combination of the reputation of the artist; a record's previous performance, if already released overseas; whether the song fits the station's format; and, at times, the gut intuition of those making the decision. In the case of the first of these factors, reputation and previous track record, publicity material from the label/artist/distributor plays an important role, jogging memories or sparking interest in a previously unknown artist. Chart performance in either the US or UK is especially significant where the record is being released in a 'foreign' market.

In choosing whether or not to play particular genres of popular music, radio functions as a gatekeeper, significantly influencing the nature of the music itself. This is illustrated in the shifting attitude of radio to heavy metal, moving from its ignoral in the 1970s to marginal status in the early 1980s, followed by acceptability and the hold it gained on the airwaves in the late 1980s with the rise of lite metal (see Weinstein 1991a: 149–61).

The importance of radio for disseminating popular music is also indicated by State regulation of the medium. The State has, at times, attempted to encourage 'minority' cultures, and local music (with the two frequently connected), through quota and other regulatory legislation (see Chapter 4, for a discussion of the application of a radio airplay quota in Canada). The State also shapes the commercial environment for radio, primarily through licensing systems, but also by establishing codes of practice – a form of censorship. This State practice has at times been challenged, most notably by pirate radio: broadcasts made by unlicensed broadcasters as alternatives to licensed, commercial radio programming (see Chapman 1992; Shuker 1998).

Music in cyberspace

The Internet is a computer linked global communications technology, with dramatically increasing numbers of people accessing it through the 1990s. The World Wide Web (WWW), a major part of the Internet, is the graphical network that contains web sites dedicated to one topic, person, or company. These locations are known as homepages and allow seamless jumping to other locations on the Internet. The Internet has added a major new dimension to the marketing and reception of popular music, while creating new problems for the enforcement of copyright. It includes on-line music shops; web sites for record companies and performers; on-line music journals; on-line concerts and interviews; web radio, and bulletin boards (see the Bibliography herein). In sum, web sites represent new ways of inter-linking the audience/consumers of popular music, the performers, and the music industry. Most discussions of the significance of such electronic commerce emphasise the business/economic aspects: the benefits to firms and consumers; the barriers and difficulties associated with doing business via the Net; the demographics of Net users; and the opportunities for companies on the Net.

There are also significant cultural issues associated with popular music on the Net, which link up with ongoing debates in the study of popular music, such as the relative importance of the music industry and the consumers of popular music. The Net may create greater consumer sovereignty and choice by bypassing the traditional intermediaries operating in the music industry (primarily the record companies), but the majors, initially slow to recognise its potential, are now developing major sites (see Sony's Michael Jackson site). Any new medium or technological form changes the way in which we experience music, and this has implications for how we relate to and consume music. In the case of the Net, the question is what happens to traditional notions of the 'distance' between consumer and product, and its technological mediation? Finally, the nature of intellectual property rights, and the regulation of these, has been brought into even sharper focus with the electronic retrieval possibilities implicit in the Net, and the ongoing debates over sampling in popular music texts

(Gurley and Pfefferle 1996; Hayward 1995). The debates here have recently been brought sharply into focus by MP3.

I Want My MP3

MP3 is a technology encoding recorded sound so that it takes up much less storage space than it would otherwise. MP3 files are small enough to make it practical to transfer high-quality music files over the Internet and store them on a computer hard drive: CD quality tracks downloadable in minutes (for a detailed 'how to', see Mann 2000). MP3 has become very popular as a way to distribute and access music. According to Media Metrix, the number of people listening to digital music (primarily but not exclusively MP3) in the United States in June 1999 was 4 million, having grown from only a few thousand in June 1998 (Mann 2000: xxi). It is widely claimed that MP3 has become the most searched for word on web search engines.

There has been enormous debate over the economic and cultural implications of this new technology. For consumers, MP3 enables access to a great variety of music, most of it free, and they can selectively compile their own collections of songs by combining various tracks without having to purchase entire albums. For artists, MP3 means they can distribute their music to a worldwide audience without the mediation of the established music industry. Yet MP3 also raises concerns about potential loss of income. For Internet music publishers, MP3 opens up opportunities for smaller, more innovative companies.

For the major record companies, MP3 challenges their control over distribution and, since the format has no built-in way to prevent users from obtaining and distributing music illegally, can represent considerable lost royalties. The majors have joined to create the Secure Digital Music Initiative (SDMI; see www.sdmi.org), in an attempt to reassert control over music distribution. And the problem is international. A spokesperson for the Recording Industry Association of New Zealand, Terrence O'Neill-Joyce, argues that the problem is not with the actual technology of MP3, which he believes is being effectively used by many music producers, but rather the ineffective means of securing remuneration for artists: 'It's a case of technology outstripping legislation and a lack of a proper commercial framework being established as of yet' (cited Scovell 2000).

Alongside these misgivings, the music industry is making considerable use of MP3. Many on-line music retailers offer tracks for download by MP3, hoping these will act as a 'taster' for listeners' purchases. Recording companies have recognised the need to utilise the new technology to maintain their market dominance in the new world of on-line audio music, looking for new concepts in packaging and marketing to digitally retail songs via the Internet.

The discourse surrounding music and technology embrace divergent views about creativity and musicianship, artistic freedom, and property rights (copyright). New technologies are variously seen as democratising or consolidating established music industry hierarchies; rationalising or disruptive of distribution processes; confirming or challenging legal definitions of music as property; and inhibiting or enabling of new creativities and sites of authorship (Thornton 1995: 31). These transcend national boundaries, separating music from the time, place, and social context of their production. This process leads us to the nature of popular music as a global commodity and cultural form, and national attempts to ensure that 'local' music is not overwhelmed by international repertoire.

Chapter 4

'We are the world'

State music policy, cultural imperialism, and globalisation

State attitudes and policies towards popular culture are a significant factor in determining the construction of meaning in popular music. At the level of attitudes, State cultural policies are indicative of the various views held about the very concept of culture itself, debates over government economic intervention in the marketplace versus the operation of the 'free market', the operation of cultural imperialism, and the role of the State in fostering national cultural identity. As the Task Force Report on *The Future of the Canadian Music Industry* (1996) put it:

> Most industrialized states believe that cultural products must not be treated as commodities. The cultural exemption contained in international trade agreements reflects a recognition that it is in their diversity that the richness of human cultures is to be found and that the distinctive characteristics of each culture should be preserved.

The internationalisation of the music industry has historically been equated with 'cultural imperialism', with local cultures dominated and to varying degrees invaded, displaced and challenged by imported 'foreign' cultures. The solution to this situation is usually seen as some combination of restrictions upon media imports and the deliberate fostering of the local cultural industries, including sound recording. These are illustrated here by Canada's MAPLE test and Federal policies supporting local music; and New Zealand's quota debate and subsequent operation of NZ On Air. (For a further instructive example, see Breen 1999 on Australia. Fuller considerations of popular music and cultural policy, and a broad range of international examples, can be found in Wallis and Malm 1992; Robinson *et al.* 1991; Bennett *et al.* 1993; Ewbank and Papageorgiou 1997).

There are also examples of both the central and local State attempting to use popular music as one way to regenerate local communities, and stimulate community support for local music (see, for example, Cohen 1991, on Liverpool; Elderen 1989, on the Netherlands Pop Music Foundation; and Street 1993, on Norwich). For reasons of space, however, I have chosen to concentrate here on cultural policy at the national level.

CULTURE AND THE STATE

State cultural policies have been largely based on the idealist tradition of culture as a realm separate from, and often in opposition to, the realm of material production and economic activity. This means that government intervention in its various forms – subsidy, licensing arrangements, protectionism through quotas, etc. – is justified by the argument which has been clearly elaborated by Garnham:

> 1. that culture possesses inherent values, of life enhancement or whatever, which are fundamentally opposed to and in danger of damage by commercial forces; 2. that the need for these values is universal, uncontaminated by questions of class, gender and ethnic origin; and 3. that the market cannot satisfy this need.
>
> (Garnham 1987: 24)

Drawing on the Romantic cultural tradition, a key part of this view is the concept of the individual creative artist:

> The result of placing artists at the centre of the cultural universe has not been to shower them with gold, for artistic poverty is itself an ideologically potent element in this view of culture, but to define the policy problem as one of finding audiences for their work rather than vice versa.
>
> (ibid.)

This ideology has been used by elites in government, administration, intellectual circles, and broadcasting to justify and represent sectional interests as general interests, thereby functioning as a form of cultural hegemony.

Seeing classical music, ballet, and the theatre as 'high culture' or 'the arts', legitimates both their largely middle-class consumption and their receipt of State subsidy. 'Popular culture' is then constructed in opposition to this, as commercial, inauthentic, and so unworthy of significant government support. A comic example of this view was provided by civil servant Sir Humphrey Appleby, giving advice to his ministerial 'boss' in the television comedy series *Yes Minister*:

> Subsidy is for Art. It is for Culture. It is not to be given to what the people want, it is for what the people don't want but ought to have. If they really want something they will pay for it themselves. The Government's duty is to subsidize education, enlightenment and spiritual uplift, not the vulgar pastimes of ordinary people.
>
> (Episode: 'The Middle-Class Rip Off', BBC Television)

As already argued (Chapter 1), such a dichotomised high–low culture view is unsustainable, yet it nonetheless remains a widely held and still powerful ideology.

The assumptions and issues underpinning such a high–low culture distinction were also neatly illustrated by the contrasting attitudes of two former New Zealand Prime Ministers. In 1983, the then Prime Minister Robert Muldoon, heading a National (Conservative) administration, justified his continued rejection of arguments for a cut in the sales tax on records (such a tax did not apply to 'cultural' items like books), by claiming that pop music could not be considered cultural: 'If you use the word "culture" in its normal sense', he said, 'I don't think (leading local groups) Split Enz and Mi-Sex are cultural'. This view, of course, was a defensible consequence of the high culture position outlined above. In contrast to this, in 1986 Labour Prime Minister David Lange's objections to the Government being 'the inevitable funder' of the New Zealand Symphony Orchestra aroused considerable controversy. Mr Lange said he had nothing against what he was sure was an 'extraordinarily competent' group of musicians, but the example of the orchestra as a socially worthy purpose did not inspire him to reach for his cheque book! Asked if the Government would help foot the orchestra's costs, he noted that the local pop group Peking Man played to a wider audience while receiving no State assistance. When reporters observed that the orchestra was regarded as a national cultural treasure, Lange quipped that was because it lost money: 'Things are regarded as raving socialist or national cultural treasures if they lose a packet. I just happen to like Dire Straits more than I like Debussy', said Mr Lange, who took the British rock group to lunch during its 1986 New Zealand tour (Press Report, 4 November 1986).

CULTURAL IMPERIALISM, GLOBALISATION, AND MUSIC

The common preference of listeners and record buyers for foreign-originated sounds, rather than the product of their local artists and labels, is associated with the cultural imperialism thesis. Cultural imperialism developed as a concept analogous to the historical, political and economic subjugation of the Third World by the colonising powers in the nineteenth century, with consequent deleterious effects for the societies of the colonised. This gave rise to global relations of dominance, subordination and dependency between the affluence and power of the advanced capitalist nations, most notably the United States and Western Europe, and the relatively powerless underdeveloped countries. This economic and political imperialism was seen to have a cultural aspect:

> the ways in which the transmission of certain products, fashions and styles from the dominant nations to the dependent markets leads to the creation of particular patterns of demand and consumption which are underpinned by and endorse the cultural values, ideals and practices of their dominant origin. In this manner the local cultures of developing nations become dominated and in varying degrees invaded, displaced and challenged by foreign, often western, cultures.
>
> (O'Sullivan et al. 1994: 62; see also Robinson et al. 1991)

In terms of mass media and popular culture, evidence for the cultural imperialism thesis, as it became known, was provided by the predominantly one-way international media flow, from a few international dominant sources of media production, notably the USA, to media systems in other national cultural contexts. Not only did this involve the market penetration and dominance of Anglo-American popular culture, more importantly, it established certain forms as the accepted ones, scarcely recognising that there were alternatives:

> One major influence of American imported media lies in the styles and patterns which most other countries in the world have adopted and copied. This influence includes the very definition of what a newspaper, or a feature film, or a television set is.
>
> (Tunstall 1977: intro.)

The cultural imperialism thesis gained general currency in debates through the 1970s and 1980s about the significance of imported popular culture. Such debates were evident not only in the Third World, but in 'developed' countries such as France, Canada, Australia, and New Zealand, all subject to high market penetration by American popular culture. Adherents of the thesis tended to dichotomise local culture and its imported counterpart, regarding local culture as somehow more authentic, traditional, and supportive of a conception (however vaguely expressed it may be) of a distinctive national cultural identity. Set against this identity, and threatening its continued existence and vitality, was the influx of large quantities of slick, highly commercialised media products, mainly from the United States. Upholders of the cultural imperialism view generally saw the solution to this situation as some combination of restrictions upon media imports and the deliberate fostering of the local cultural industries, including music.

The cultural imperialism thesis has generally been applied to film, television and publishing; with a few exceptions (Wallis and Malm 1984; Lealand 1988; Laing 1986; Robinson *et al.* 1991), it has not been examined in relation to popular music. At first sight, its application here appears warranted, given that the major record companies are the dominant institutions of the music industry, and local pressings of imported repertoire take the major share of national music markets. But to what extent can this situation be seen in terms of cultural invasion and the subjugation of local cultural identity? Such figures present only the bare bones of the structure of the music industry, and tell us little about the complex relationship of the majors to local record companies in marginalised national contexts such as Canada and New Zealand.

Although the existence of cultural imperialism became widely accepted at both a 'common-sense' level and in leftist academia, its validity at both a descriptive level and as an explanatory analytical concept came under increasing critical scrutiny in the 1980s. The validity of the local/authentic versus imported/commercial dichotomy is difficult to sustain with reference to specific examples, while media effects are assumed in a too one-dimensional fashion, underestimating the mediated nature of audience reception and use of media products. More importantly, the cultural imperialism thesis is predicated on accepting the 'national' as a given, with distinctive national musical identities its logical corollary. However, the globalisation of Western capitalism, particularly evident in its media conglomerates, and the increasing international nature of Western popular music bring these notions into question.

There are three significant points to be made here: first, Anglo-American popular culture has become established as the international preferred culture of the young since the 1950s. This is not to subscribe to any reductionist view of an international youth culture (cf., Reich 1967), but to make the point that American rock 'n' roll was 'an instance of the use of foreign music by a generation as a means to distance themselves from a parental "national' culture' (Laing 1986: 338). Second, local products cannot be straightforwardly equated with local national cultural identity, and conversely (arising from the first point) imported product is not to be necessarily equated with the alien. Indeed local product is often qualitatively indistinct from its overseas counterpart, though this in itself is frequently a target for criticism. Third, while specific national case studies demonstrate the immense influence of the transnational music industry on musical production and distribution everywhere, they 'just as clearly indicate that world musical homogenization is not occurring'

(Robinson *et al.* 1991: 4). The process is rather one in which local musicians are immersed in overlapping and frequently reciprocal contexts of production, with a cross-fertilisation of local and international sounds. Mitchell (1996) provides an instructive analysis of this process, with reference to a range of national examples and musical genres. The global and the local cannot be considered binary categories, but exist in a complex interrelationship.

More recently, reflecting the internationalisation of capital – a trend particularly evident in its media conglomerates – the term 'globalisation' has replaced cultural imperialism. As an explanatory concept, however, globalisation is often used too loosely, and is open to similar criticisms to cultural imperialism. Currently, 'glocalisation' has emerged as a more useful concept, emphasising the complex and dynamic interrelationship of local music scenes and industries and the international marketplace (see Leyshon *et al.* 1998).

The major problem faced by record companies is the uncertainty of the music market. It is widely agreed that, at best, only one in eight (to ten) of the artists A&R sign and record will achieve sufficient sales to recoup the original investment and start to earn money for the artists and generate a profit for the company. This situation has led major record companies to look for acts that are already partially developed and which indicate commercial potential, especially in the international market (Hesmondhalgh 1996b; Negus 1999). This is an approach with considerable implications for local artists operating primarily at a regional or national level.

Local branches of the majors (e.g. Sony Canada) find that it is more economic to concentrate on local pressings of imported repertoire, usually from the United States, given the costs of developing master recordings. There is an economic advantage in releasing recordings based on foreign master tapes: no production costs are involved when importing a foreign master, while producing a Canadian content master involves costs from $10,000 to $200,000, plus the cost of one or more promotional videos. Risks are high in originating master tapes since only one in ten is financially successful.

Attempts at the national level to foster local popular music production are primarily interventions at the level of the distribution and reception of the music. They attempt to secure greater access to the market, particularly for local products in the face of overseas music, notably from the United Kingdom and the United States. Such attempts, along with the issues surrounding cultural imperialism and globalisation and the status of the local, can be more fully addressed through two national examples: Canada and New Zealand.

GLOBAL MUSIC, NATIONAL CULTURE: CANADA

Canadians value music: 70 per cent identify it as an important part of their lives, and 46 per cent buy music on a regular basis (DFSP 1999: 3). Reflecting this, the

Canadian music industry is economically significant; in 1996, Canadians spent C$107 per person on recordings, compared with C$76 on books (ibid.). In addition, popular Canadian artists such as Celine Dion, Bryan Adams, Alanis Morissette, Shania Twain, and Robert Charlebois are the country's best-known cultural ambassadors abroad.

The history of the Canadian music industry has been shaped largely by its relationship to the international marketplace, especially its proximity to the dominant United States market for popular music. During the 1980s and into the 1990s, the Canadian music industry was dominated by the local branches of the majors.

> The eight largest record companies in Canada are foreign-owned; 89 per cent of the revenues from the Canadian domestic market goes to multinationals. Their interest in Canadian music is restricted to those recordings which are marketed across the continent. This preference also shapes current government programs for subsidising domestic recording. All other recording remains economically, spatially, and discursively marginal.
>
> (Berland 1988; see also Robinson *et al.* 1991: chap. 5)

Economies of scale applied to production meant that indigenous product was far more costly to produce and frequently had inferior production values compared with imports (largely) from the United States. With record distribution also dominated by the majors, and commercial radio frequently tied to US programme formats and broadcast sound quality, the Canadian industry and musicians had only a small market share: in 1988 the independents received approximately 11 per cent of national revenues from record sales. One consequence of this situation was that only a small percentage of music bought in Canada originated there, even when it was made by Canadian artists (e.g. Bryan Adams). This economic situation sat uneasily with the historical Canadian concern to encourage nationhood and a cultural identity via communications technology, while at the same time resisting the intrusion of American media and messages. These concerns have pushed the State to the forefront in media and cultural policy (see Dorland 1996).

The Canadian music industry as a whole was considerably stronger by the mid-1990s. Recordings generated substantial economic activity: retail sales in Canada totalled C$1.3 billion in 1997, while the royalties paid to Canadian songwriters, composers and publishers (as public performance rights) totalled C$49 million in 1997, up from C$34 million in 1993 (DFSP 1999). While this overall picture is impressive, the historical dichotomy remained: Canadian firms earn about 90 per cent of their revenue from selling Canadian-content recordings, while 88 per cent of the revenues of foreign-controlled firms comes from selling recordings made from imported masters. Foreign firms have five times the revenue, eighteen times the profit, ten times the long-term assets, and sixteen times the contributed surplus and retained earnings of Canadian-controlled firms (Task Force 1996).

It should also be acknowledged, however, that the major's are not simply parasitic here. Brian Robertson, President of CRIA (Canadian Recording Industry Association), stresses the important investment in Canadian talent by the multi-nationals (majors), now around C$40 million a year in Canadian Content production. 'This has escalated tremendously in the last decade, and represents a huge investment per year in Canadian music and artists and their recordings' (author interview, July 1999). Canadian brewing giant Seagram's takeover of MCA in 1995 (and Polygram in 1998) meant that a major recording company was now based in Canada, but as yet this appears to have had little impact on the development of local repertoire.

Yet as Straw (1993, 1996) has observed, while the general picture of a margin-alised local sound-recording industry remains valid, contradictions are now evident. On the one hand, there is the increased international visibility and success of Canadian artists/music within the global sound-recording industry, although these artists frequently record in the United States, for US-based companies; e.g. Bryan Adams, Alanis Morissette, Shania Twain. On the other hand, there is also an increased share of the local market for music of Canadian content, with commer-cially significant sales for several locally based performers, including Bare Naked Ladies, Our Lady Peace, Red Rodeo, and Sarah McLachlan. In 1998, Our Lady Peace's CD *Clumsy* sold over 800,000 copies in Canada, along with well over half a million copies in the USA; Bare Naked Ladies had a top ten *Billboard* single ('One Week'), and their album *Stunt* reached sales of three million (Chauncey 1999: 57). Artists working in non-pop or rock genres are also having a national impact: singer and jazz pianist Diana Krall attained platinum sales (100,000 in Canada) with her CD *Love Scenes*, and her latest CD, *When I Look in Your Eyes*, went gold (50,000) on the day of its release in June 1999; both releases also gained significant exposure and sales outside of Canada.

At the same time, the popular music market has changed dramatically, with the splintering of 'mainstream rock', once the dominant genre, into a wide range of genre styles and performers, along with the willingness of the major record companies to market/exploit these. These trends have created uncertainty as to the future role and status of Canada's small, locally based firms, which have traditionally nurtured and been economically dependent on new musical styles. In other words, reflecting glocalisation, the relative market positions and relationship of 'majors' and 'inde-pendents' in the Canadian market has changed (Straw 1996). The growth of foreign markets has made artist development in Canada more globally oriented. The Canadian branches of the Majors, and Canadian owned independent labels such as Nettwerk Productions, Attic Music Group, True North, and Marquis Classics are increasingly looking to develop artists with international appeal. Randy Lennox, president of Universal Music Group (Canada) states: 'We're watching specific market trends worldwide when signing an artist today' (LeBlanc 1999).

In the midst of these shifts, positive Government policy toward the local music industry appeared to be more necessary than ever, a view shared by the comprehensive and influential Task Force Report, on *The Future of the Canadian Music Industry* (Task Force 1996). The Task Force was asked to develop proposals that would ensure that the industry could maintain its central role in promoting Canada's cultural identity by providing an increasing choice of Canadian music. Objectives set for the industry were to maintain its ability to compete in Canada and abroad; to be adequately compensated for use of its copyrighted material; and to benefit from new technologies. The Task Force concluded: 'While cultural objectives should provide the basis for music industry policy, measures that strengthen the creation, performance, production, distribution and marketing of Canadian music will also generate important economic benefits' (Task Force 1996). The Task Force report was a comprehensive document and here I concentrate on only two aspects of it: the operation and future of the 'Can Con' regulations, administered by the Canadian Radio and Telecommunications Commission (CRTC), and the Sound Recording Development Program (SRDP).

The CRTC and Can Con

The CRTC was established by Parliament in 1968. The Broadcasting Act requires the CRTC to ensure that each 'broadcasting undertaking ... shall make maximum use, and in no case less than predominant use, of Canadian creative and other resources in the creation and presentation of programming' (unless the specialised nature of the service makes it impracticable). The CRTC has responsibility for establishing classes of broadcasting licences, the allocation of broadcast licences, making broadcasting regulations, and the holding of public hearings in respect of such matters.

In pursuit of this goal, a Canadian Content quota on AM radio was introduced in 1971, and extended to FM radio in 1976. These quotas took into account particular station airplay formats, and expected a reasonably even distribution of Canadian selections throughout the day and through the broadcast week. What constitutes 'Canadian' was established by the MAPLE test, in which at least two of the audio components of a recording must be:

'M' – music is composed by a Canadian
'A' – artist (principal performer) is a Canadian
'P' – performance/production is in Canada
'L' – lyrics are written by a Canadian

Can Con, as the local content requirements came to be known, proved controversial, but had an undeniably positive impact on the Canadian recording industry:

> That simple regulation was a watershed. It was the expression of a protectionist policy designed to allow Canadian musicians to be heard in their own country, The overall effect of the regulations has been the creation of an active, vigorous, self-supporting, and surprisingly creative industry – one that hardly existed prior to the regulations.
>
> (Flohel 1990: 497)

It seems to be generally agreed that, while the current group of Canadian international stars would have 'made it' anyway, their early careers received a significant impetus from the airplay guaranteed by Can Con. Further, and perhaps more importantly, the quota allowed a 'middle' group of performers to make an impact – and a living – within the Canadian industry: 'there's a whole lot of middle ground Canadian artists who are fabulous acts and Can Con has helped to ensure that they get the airplay that allows them to become the stars that they have become in Canada and, in many cases, nowhere else in the world' (Doug Pringle, director of programming at Rawlco Communications, responsible for a number of newer radio stations, cited in Melhuish 1999: 73).

In early 1999, after a series of public hearings and a review of radio policy by the CRTC, the Canadian content requirement was increased to 35 per cent. This change did not indicate a 'failure' of the previous requirement, but was a recognition that the local industry was now in a strong enough position to provide sufficient acceptable recordings to meet such an increase.

The Sound Recording Development Program (SRDP)

The SRDP was created in 1986 to provide support to Canadian-owned companies for the production of Canadian audio and video music and radio programmes and to support marketing, international touring, and business development. This recognised that it was necessary to assist the industry to enable it to provide the local content required under the CRTC regulations. With the exception of the support provided to Specialized Music Production, which is administered by the Canada Council, SRDP support is the responsibility of two organisations, FACTOR and MusicAction, based on an agreement with the Department of Canadian Heritage.

The 1991 evaluation of the SRDP found that it had had a very positive effect on the sound recording industry, but that its resources (funding was initially C$5 million) were inadequate to significantly strengthen the independent sector of the industry and, in particular, that it provided too little support to marketing and distribution. This view was confirmed by the Task Force report, which regarded the scheme as now substantially under-funded: 'A major concern for both English and French language industries is the inadequacy of the resources available to support the marketing of recordings by Canadian artists' (Task Force 1996).

The Task Force (1996) recommended that the resources of the Sound Recording Development Program should be increased immediately to C$10 million annually and sustained at that level for a period of five years, but it was not until late 1999 that Government policy began to address this, and a comprehensive review of the programme was begun. Speaking in 1999, Brian Chater, President of CIRPA (the Canadian Independent Record Producers Association) emphasised there remained a pressing need to get 'serious structural funding' in the local industry:

> The music business has become very much like the film business; you have to have a lot of bucks to play the game, and a lot of the time it won't work anyway. Now if you don't invest three or four hundred grand on each project, nobody thinks you're serious. Do five of those and you've spent a couple of million dollars. The reality with project funding is that you're always scrambling from A to B trying to pay the bills with the project money. What we want to see indies have access to is structural funding, so that you can operate a company rather than do projects.
>
> (Melhuish 1999: 79; also discussed in author interview, July 1999)

The Canadian case raises crucial questions about the role of music as a form of discourse actively engaged in the uniting or fragmenting of a community. It presupposes that listeners consciously identify – and identify with – specifically locally produced music. The frequent negative reaction local product provokes is an important reminder of how what counts as popular music has been identified with a particular imported form, the result of the dominance of American radio formats, music videos, and production values.

Further, it is misleading to automatically assume that local musicians embody and support a Canadian cultural nationalism in their work. Indeed, Canada itself is characterised by considerable cultural diversity, with strongly developed regional music scenes and idioms. Attempts to include more French language music on Canadian radio illustrate the difficulties of conflating 'the national' in multicultural/bilingual settings. A 1989 hearing of the CRTC led to a 1990 regulation stipulating that at least 65 per cent of the vocal music played weekly by all Francophone AM and FM radio stations, irrespective of format or market, must be French-language. The tensions this created for an industry and artists wanting to remain 'culturally politically correct' but also needing to appeal to the larger, international market, illustrated the double-bind in which Quebec is caught. 'Like other small nations, it feels the need to protect its local products from multinational conglomerates but aims none the less at generating its own international hits ... the debate under study goes to the very heart of this double bind' (Grenier 1993: 124).

NEW ZEALAND ON AIR

These questions of the relationship between popular music, local cultural identity, and the internationalisation of the music industry are also evident in New Zealand. The 1989–90 debate over a compulsory quota for NZ music on the radio traversed the arguments over the importance of supporting the local music industry, the constitution of the 'local', and the relationship between airplay and commercial success (see Shuker 1994). When a quota was not introduced, New Zealand On Air (NZOA) was established, to administer the funds collected by the broadcasting fee. Its brief included provision for subsidising local music – a kind of quota default option.

As in Canada, New Zealand's local recording companies and their products are largely marginalised by the dominant position of the international record companies (the 'majors'), and the sheer quantity of 'imported' material (mainly New Zealand pressings of international repertoire). Given the economic and cultural significance of recorded music, this situation has been the focus of considerable public debate and Government cultural policy. New Zealand can best be regarded as an example of a country with a small market for recorded music, with a small share for local music within the major-dominated turnover of the local phonogram market, and with a relatively unimportant role for local sounds within the international music market. This places New Zealand on a similar footing to Canada and the Netherlands. As Rutten observes, the fact that there is a very limited domestic market for local music in such countries 'poses important problems, given the skyrocketing costs of recording and marketing. It is necessary to look to larger markets in order to recoup investments in a band or an artist' (Rutten 1991: 300).

There are a number of established NZ independent labels, along with branches of the majors who dominate the global music industry. According to industry sources, the subsidiaries of the multinational record companies continue to supply approximately 90 per cent of the domestic market. While any strict division between the majors and the 'indies' is no longer really tenable, with distribution deals tying the two sectors of the industry together, there remain interesting questions about the dynamics of their relationship. This is particularly the case with the operation of the majors with respect to local product.

The New Zealand popular music scene has experienced periodic highs and lows through the last decade. After a low period in the late 1980s (in terms of overall chart success), local artists made strong chart showings both at home and internationally during 1991–92, greatly assisted by the introduction of NZ On Air's music schemes. Flying Nun, the country's main independent label, saw continued sales growth, particularly in the United States. During the next few years, despite the continuation of NZ On Air's funding of videos and CD compilations of local artists, retail sales fluctuated and chart success failed to match the peak level achieved in 1992. This was followed in the mid-1990s by the international success of OMC ('How Bizzare'), Crowded House, and Neil Finn, and strong local showings by artists such as Bic Runca, Shihad, Che Fu, and The Feelers.

Despite occasional successes, the vital signs of the local recording industry remain mixed. The local scene remains insufficient to support full-time professional performers, there is still only limited radio and television exposure for local artists, and initiatives to support the industry remain limited. Several explanations have been offered for this: a general lack of effort on the part of the majors to sign and develop New Zealand artists; the general lack of an industry infrastructure, especially in terms of management and the opportunities for radio and television air play; and the inadequacies of the local industry, which is seen to have failed to grasp the opportunities open to it.

Logically, given the economies of scale involved, the majors concentrate more on promoting their overseas artists, with their local performers treated as a lower priority. The majors also in a sense feed off local labels, treating them in the same fashion as North American professional sports franchises use their 'farm teams' to foster talent and provide local back-up as necessary. But this is as much a symbiotic relationship as it is a parasitic one. The independents need the distribution and marketing support the majors can provide, particularly in overseas markets, while NZ performers who outstrip the strictly local need the majors to move up a league. This was evident with the two main New Zealand independent record labels operating in the late 1980s: Flying Nun, and Pagan (Mitchell 1996), and continues to be the case.

New Zealand artists who remain 'at home' will always remain marginal to the international music industry, since the country lacks the population base to support a music industry on the scale of neighbouring Australia. The result is a tension between the support for the purely local, and the need to go offshore to follow up national success. Shihad, arguably New Zealand's premier band, in late 1998 relocated to Los Angeles:

> We're not turning our back on New Zealand. A lot of people are coming to the realisation that as a climate for making music New Zealand is tremendously wealthy in terms of what we have available to us and what people can produce here. But the actual platform for getting music out into the market place is absolutely shit. We're crippled in comparison to places like Australia where they have local content quotas.
>
> (Tom Larkin, drummer, Shihad, *Rip It Up*, October 1998: 14.
> Shihad is now based in Melbourne, Australia)

Given the marginal status of New Zealand's recording industry in the international arena, and the difficulties facing local artists, the initiatives taken by New Zealand On Air (NZOA) to foster New Zealand music, in operation since July 1991, are of crucial importance. NZOA's brief is not restricted to 'popular music', but in practice this is the case, with classical music having its own sources of funding and support. NZOA is charged with ensuring that 'New Zealanders have a diverse range of broadcasting services that would not otherwise be available on a commercial basis'. A key strategy in pursuit of this goal is 'To encourage broadcasters to maintain a sustained commitment to programmes reflecting New Zealand identity and culture'. Working towards achieving this includes 'funding programming on television and radio about New Zealand and New Zealand interests, including the broadcasting of New Zealand music' (NZOA Annual Report 1995/96: Statement of purpose and goals).

NZOA's popular music programme has four main schemes related to radio and television. In addition, it has put out two major CD compilations: *Kiwi Gold Disc* (1996) and *Kiwi Gold Disc II* (1998), collections of 'classic' New Zealand hits from the past, which are sent to every radio station in the country to boost the amount of material they have available for airplay. The ongoing schemes are (from NZOA 1999: Annual Report).

1   Radio Hits, which provides incentives to record companies to produce records suitable for the commercial radio play list; and lessens the financial risk inherent in recording and releasing singles, by enabling partial recovery of recording costs.
2   The Hit Disc, which assists record companies to get airplay for new releases, and makes sure that 'every Programme Director in every NZ radio station has access to a broadcast quality copy of new singles which have commercial radio airplay potential'. The first of these, and still the most important, is the *Kiwi Hit Disc*, made up of 'new New Zealand music on release or about to be released by record companies'. The *Indie Hit Disc* and, most recently, the *Iwi Hit Disc*, are similar schemes with more of a niche market.
3   Music Video, 'funding NZ music videos as part of a campaign to get more NZ music on air', through subsidising production costs of selected videos.
4   New Zealand Music on Radio, which involves funding specialist radio programmes promoting NZ music, for commercial radio and student radio, aimed at the youth audience.

In each of the first three schemes the criteria for support is similar, or identical. First, 'It must be New Zealand music. The priority is original New Zealand music but we accept covers as well' (Music Video; Radio Hits; Kiwi Hit Disc). Second, there must be a confirmed record release: 'the video must back up the release of a single or EP in

80

NZ either by an independent or a major label' (Music Video); and 'A record company – either a major or one of the independents – must be involved in releasing the record' (Radio Hits). Priority goes to projects distributed nationally usually via one of the major record companies. Third, a key consideration is broadcast potential: 'our priority is videos which are likely to generate repeat screenings on national network television' (Music Video); 'To qualify for funding, the record must attract significant airplay on commercial radio' (Radio Hits); and 'the record must be a realistic contender for significant airplay on commercial radio' (Kiwi Hit Disc) Seven radio stations are used as barometers, and the schemes use programmers from TV shows and radio as consultants to identify broadcast potential.

A mix of cultural and commercial criteria are being applied here, with an emphasis on the latter. It is important to recognise that the schemes in themselves do not guarantee exposure through local television and radio. What they do is facilitate the production of local product, including an acceptable technical quality of these videos and recordings; and make it more available to local programmers. Recognising this, in early 1998 NZOA began employing a 'song plugger', whose role was to push (promote) the forthcoming Hit Disc to key radio station programmers. This represented a dramatic departure for NZOA, but was a necessary move given that, despite six years of effort, there appeared to have been only limited improvement in the levels of New Zealand music getting airplay on commercial radio.

The NZOA music schemes are in a very real sense the alternative to a local content quota. A recent improvement in the proportion of local content on radio suggests that NZOA may be close to its breakthrough goal of 'double digits'. Yet even with the more forceful presentation of the products of its various schemes, it remains to be seen if this goal can be achieved, thus making a quota unnecessary. In July 2000 the funding for the NZOA music schemes was virtually doubled, from NZ$2 million to NZ$3.78 million a year, to enable the implementation of strategies to get increased airplay for local recordings.

The transformation of the global circulation of cultural forms is creating new lines of influence and solidarity which are not bounded by geographically defined cultures, and popular music is not exempt from such processes. Accordingly, we need to be conscious of the danger of too easily dichotomising the local and the global, recognise the dynamism and intertextuality of at least the best of contemporary popular music, and avoid adopting a narrowly defined cultural nationalist position. Nevertheless, there remain important economic arguments for the support of the local. The continued development of the infrastructure of the Canadian and New Zealand music industries is central to generating opportunities for local musicians, and for providing a launching platform for access to the international market.

Debates over cultural policy and popular music embrace a volatile mix of the ideological and the economic. At the ideological level, there is the maintenance of an outmoded high–low culture dichotomy, which partly serves to legitimate the general neglect of the popular, including popular music. At the same time, however, the State is also concerned to respond to the significant level of community support for local culture, and the perceived necessity of defending the local against the continued and increasing dominance of international popular media. This concern is mediated by the difficulty of establishing the uniqueness of national 'sounds', be they New Zealand or Canadian.

Chapter 5

'On the cover of the Rolling Stone'

The music press

In order to be consumed in its various forms, popular music must be brought to the attention of those who listen to the radio, go to the clubs and concerts, and purchase its recorded products. Radio has served a crucial publicising role here, and continues to do so; 'live' exposure has been historically important, though it arguably became less so as MTV and television video programmes became key players during the 1980s. The role of each of these in creating musical constituencies and meanings is examined elsewhere here (see Chapters 3 and 10). Then there is the music press, which plays a major part in the process of selling music as an economic commodity, while at the same time investing it with cultural significance. In one of the few extended critical discussions of the music press, Frith correctly argues for its central role in 'Making Meaning': 'the importance of the professional rock fans – the rock writers', and the music papers, whose readers 'act as the opinion leaders, the rock interpreters, the ideological gatekeepers for everyone else' (Frith 1983: 165).

This chapter begins with a general consideration of the music press, which is viewed as a diverse range of publications, with music journalism a literary genre in which any distinction between 'rock journalism' and academic writing on popular music is frequently blurred. A typology of music magazines is then presented, encompassing industry reference tools, record collector magazines, fanzines, 'teen glossies', 'the inkies', style bibles and the new tabloids. Although these have many features in common, each serves a particular place in a segmented market, in which journalism becomes collapsed into, and often indistinguishable from, music industry publicity. Despite this symbiosis, popular music critics continue to function as significant gatekeepers and as arbiters of taste, a role examined in the concluding section of the discussion here.

'ROCK JOURNALISM'

While this chapter will focus on popular music magazines and the work of music critics within these, the term 'music press' obviously covers a wider range of publications. Most newspapers and general magazines include some coverage, with reviews of contemporary recordings, artist profiles/interviews, and, most commonly, lifestyles and associated gossip. There is a variety of more focused music journalism, present in a body of literature which increased dramatically during the early 1980s (Taylor 1985), and which has continued to do so through the 1990s (Doggett 1997). Although categories frequently overlap, with 'rock journalism' and academic work increasingly intertwined, we can distinguish between popular (auto)biographies, histories, and genre studies; similar 'academic' analyses; and various forms of consumer guides, including encyclopedias and dictionaries, discographies, and chart listings. There are also more esoteric publications, such as rock quiz books, genealogical tables plotting the origin and shifting membership of rock groups, and 'almanacs' dealing with the trivia and microscopic detail of stars' private lives. Taylor's summary of all this remains apposite: 'The variety of these publications is matched by the variation in the quality of their writing, accuracy and scholarship, which means one must approach them with a degree of discrimination and care' (Taylor 1985: 1). This work has been drawn on extensively throughout this study. At this point I want to make a few observations about the orientation and cultural significance of music journalism in determining how meaning is constituted in popular music.

Popular music journalism includes the proliferation of 'quickie' publications aiming to cash in on the latest pop sensation. Reading like press releases, these concentrate on the pictorial aspects of their subjects rather than provide any extended critical commentary, and are often little more than pseudo-publicity. This was particularly evident in the pop annuals accompanying the emergence of chart pop in the 1950s, which were largely rewritten PR (public relations) handouts, 'publicity hype disguised as journalism' (Doggett 1997: 37). These publications reinforce the star aspect of pop consumption, feeding fans' desire for consumable images and information about their preferred performers, as did pop and rock magazines aimed at the teenage market (*Record Mirror*, UK, which began publication in 1953; and *Disc*, UK, 1958).

In the 1960s this changed with the impact of the 'New Journalism', associated with the writing of figures such as Hunter S. Thompson and Tom Wolfe. The New Journalism set out to move journalism beyond simple factual reporting, by using conventions derived from fiction.

> Stylistic traits pioneered by the new journalists such as scene by scene construction, third person point of view, recording of everyday detail and the inclusion of

the figure of the journalist within the text were appropriated by US and UK music critics from the end of the 1960s.

(Leonard and Strachan 2002)

There was also a commitment to treating popular culture as worthy of serious analysis, an approach that has continued to be influential. *Rolling Stone* (US) magazine and a revamped *NME* in the UK, exemplified this, and elevated several rock critics to star status (Greil Marcus, Dave Marsh).

There is now a substantial, historically situated, body of critical journalistic work on popular music, particularly rock, directed at a popular readership. I have in mind here the work of critics like Greil Marcus, Lester Bangs, Robert Christgau, Anthony DeCurtis, James Miller, Ellen Willis, Mikhal Gilmore, and Dave Marsh in the United States, and Jon Savage, Dave Rimmer, Julie Burchill, Nik Cohn, and Charles Shaar Murray in the United Kingdom. (The male-dominated nature of this group reflects notions of 'rock' as a masculine genre; see Chapter 12.) One indication of the commercial and ideological significance of this writing since the late 1960s, has been its increasing (re-)appearance in books, as collected pieces by individual critics (e.g. Murray 1991); as anthologies (Heylin 1992); or in encyclopedias of popular music (e.g. Larkin 1995).

Most significant of all are a number of more thematic studies. For example, Greil Marcus uses a handful of rock artists, including Elvis Presley, Sly Stone, the Band, and Randy Newman, to illuminate the 'question of the relationship between rock 'n' roll and American culture as a whole'. His concern is with 'a recognition of unities in the American imagination' (Marcus 1991a: introduction). In a similar fashion, Miller's *Flowers in the Dustbin* (1999) documents the development of rock 'n' roll through a succession of key artists, recordings, technologies, and moments, relating all these to broader cultural currents in American life.

I will further consider the nature and influence of music journalism later in the chapter, but turn now to the main site of most of this writing: the music magazines.

MUSIC MAGAZINES

The print media can more easily cater for niche interests and audiences than its electronic counterparts. Magazines are generally cheaper to produce than radio and television programmes, and they are consumed more independently. Readers look at them at their own pace, selecting out which items they want to attend to, in what order, and with what degree of concentration. Music magazines don't simply deal with music, they are also purveyors of style. Through both their features and advertising, they provide dress models and hairstyles to emulate, and offer lifestyles and attitudes, an ideology, to their readers. As Weinstein aptly puts it, 'magazines freeze the signifiers of a subculture, allowing them to be learned and absorbed' (1991a: 175). At the same time, they continue to fulfil their more traditional function of contributing to the construction of audiences as consumers. More specifically, in relation to the music, critics perform an influential role as gatekeepers of taste and arbiters of cultural history, and are an adjunct to the record companies' marketing of their products. Reviews provide the record companies (and artists) with critical feedback on their releases. In the process, they also become promotional devices, providing supportive quotes for record adverts, and forming part of press kits sent to radio stations and other press outlets.

The various consumer or fan-oriented music magazines play a major part in the process of selling music as an economic commodity, while at the same time investing it with cultural significance. In the UK, a 1995 survey of the readers of twenty-seven music magazines showed *Smash Hits* to be the most-read title (3.3 million readers across an entire year, reaching 7.1 per cent of the group surveyed), followed by *NME* with 2.4 million readers (5.3 per cent) and *Q* with 2.3m (5.1 per cent). The survey showed that 57 per cent of those who read music magazines brought an album every month and a further 30 per cent did so every two to three months (*Music Week*, March 1996). This is a volatile and highly competitive market: *RAW*, the 'Britpop fortnightly' launched in 1995 to fill the gap between *Smash Hits* and the monthly *Select*, ceased publication after five months, despite selling around 40,000 copies per issue.

Given this role, the music press has received surprisingly little attention in the academic popular music studies (see Stratton 1982; Shuker 1998; and Leonard and Strachan 2002). General accounts of the development of pop/rock make considerable use of the music press as a source, while largely ignoring its role in the process of marketing and cultural legitimation. The music press is absent from otherwise far-ranging anthologies, studies of the music business, and even encyclopedias of popular music. It is ironic that *The Penguin Encyclopedia of Popular Music* (Clarke 1990) promotes itself with a cover quote from *Q* magazine, describing the Encyclopedia as 'an indispensable companion', when it contains no reference to *Q* or any other such publications! The only book-length study of the music press, on its most influential publication, *Rolling Stone* magazine (Draper 1990), deals in biographical exposé rather than extended cultural analysis.

We can usefully distinguish between industry-oriented, performer-oriented, and consumer-oriented music magazines. The music trade papers keep industry personnel informed about mergers, takeovers, and staff changes in the record and media industries, and changes in copyright, and regulatory legislation. They advise retailers about marketing campaigns, complementing and reinforcing their sales promotions; and provide regular chart lists based on extensive sales and radio airplay. The main publications are *Music Business International*, and *Music Week*, and, most important of all, *Billboard* (US).

There is a strong tradition of musicians' magazines: *Down Beat* (US) has been continuously published since 1934. These concentrate on the technical aspects of recording and performance, reviewing new musical hardware, and often including transcriptions. As Leonard and Strachan (2002) observe: 'Interviews in these publications are distinct as they are conducted with a focus on aspects of music making such as musical technique and discussions on musical equipment'. These magazines serve a general pedagogic function, informing their readers of new hardware and instrumental techniques, and, argues Théberge (1991), contributing to a sense of community among musicians. Leading titles include *Guitar* (US), *Making Music* (UK), and *Canadian Musician*.

I concentrate here, however, on the variety of magazines which focus on the performers of popular music (the artists), their products (predominantly in recorded form, but also as live performance), and the relationship of consumers (fans) to these. These publications fall into a number of fairly clearly identifiable categories, based on their differing musical aesthetics or emphases, their socio-cultural functions, and their target audiences. While the best-known ones are those published in English, there are also important 'foreign' variants (for a comprehensive bibliography of music magazines, see the RoJaRo index).

First, there are the fanzines, private publications normally available only on mail order subscription, or on sale from specialist and 'alternative' bookshops. Aimed at younger readers (12 to 18) are the teen glossies, emphasising vicarious identification with pop stars whose music and image is centred on this youth. Each country has its own versions of the form. Then there are the older, established 'serious' rock magazines: in the UK *Melody Maker*, *New Musical Express* and in the US *Creem*, *Rolling Stone*. These are often referred to as the 'inkies', because of their original use of cheap newsprint which would sometimes come off on readers' hands (though *Rolling Stone* had moved to a glossy tabloid format by the early 1980s, as did *Creem* in the early 1990s). Linked to the New Journalism of the 1960s, the inkies have reflected a tradition of critical 'rock journalism', with their reviewers acting as the gatekeepers for that tradition.

Frequently drawing on the same critical tradition, are a number of niche magazines which concentrate on specific genres, such as those for heavy metal (e.g. *Metal Hammer*, UK; *Aardschok*, Netherlands); hip-hop (*Black Music Review*, Japan; *Vibe*, US); 'alternative' (*Spin*, US); avant-garde (*Wire*, UK); dance music (*Muzik*, UK); and folk (*Folk Roots*, UK). Record collector magazines are a key part of the infrastructure of record collecting (see Chapter 11). They include extensively researched artist, label, or genre retrospectives with accompanying discographies, and extensive space devoted to advertising. Leading titles are *Goldmine* (US), *Discoveries* (US), and *Record Collector* (UK).

In the mid- to late 1980s there was an upsurge of style bibles – *The Face*, *Blitz*, and *ID* – which successfully challenged the market dominance of the older 'inkies'. These were very different: 'The enormous space in magazines like *The Face*, *Elle*, and *Blitz* given over to images and illustrations means that the printed word is pushed to the sidelines. There are few sustained reviews or critiques' (McRobbie 1988: xiv). Finally, there are several new magazines which offer a combination of the 'inkies' focus on an extensive and critical coverage of the music scene (and related popular culture), packaged as a glossier product with obvious debts to the style bibles. These magazines include *VOX*, *Q*, and *Mojo* in the UK, and *Vibe* and *The Source* in the US.

A further category is the 'free' music and general entertainment guides, such as New Zealand's *Rip It Up* (until 1998), and magazines associated with music retail chains, most prominently Tower Music's *Pulse*. These are combinations of local 'inkies' and trade papers, as their 'free' status is dependent on industry support.

These magazines can be studied and compared in relation to a series of generally common features:

1   Their covers: the cost, the title, and the featured artists are all indicative of the magazine's scope and target audience. Further 'clues' are in the visual design (layout, graphics, typeface), the level of language, and the use of promotional give aways (e.g. *Smash Hits* key rings compared with the compilation CDs used with *Q*).

2   The general layout and design: e.g. the use or non-use of colour, boxed material, sidebars, visuals, and even the actual size and length of the magazine.

3   Scope: the genres of music included; other media covered (the increasing references to Net sites and video-game culture); the relative importance accorded particular artists; language used; gender representation (including in the advertising).

4   Reviews: length, depth, tone and language used; e.g. *Rolling Stone*'s stars system; *Hot Metal*'s skull rating system. (For a helpful analysis of the evaluative criteria and rating systems underpinning reviews in Australia's *Rolling Stone* and *Juice*, see Evans 1998.)

5   Adverts: which products feature? (the links to a target readership; e.g. teen mags' feminine hygiene ads); the proportion of the content which is adverts (often the distinction between adverts and 'real' content is blurred, with much content rewritten press copy); the values and associated lifestyles projected by the advertising.

6   The readership involvement: letters to the editor; competitions; reader questions answered (*Q*'s 'where are they now?'); the use of their readers to survey taste and the popularity of artists and genres.

In sum, the answers to such questions provide a profile of particular music magazines, and an indication of their relationship to the wider music industry – a combination of gatekeeper and symbiotic marketing tool. While there is obvious overlap – and market competition – among these various types of music magazine, they each have distinctive qualities. At this point, I want to make a few comments on the various types of magazine, and some of the major titles currently available, beginning with one which is often not regarded as part of the music press, but whose importance is considerable; the fanzines.

Fanzines

Produced by one person, or a group of friends, working from their homes, fanzines are usually concentrated totally on a particular artist or group, and are characterised by a fervour bordering on the religious. This stance can be a reactionary one, preserving the memory of particular artists and styles, but is more usually progressive. Fanzines like *Crawdaddy* in the 1960s and *Sniffin' Glue* in the 1970s had tremendous energy, reflecting the vitality of live performances and emergent scenes.

The initial impact of punk rock in the UK in the 1970s was aided by a network of fanzines and their enthusiastic supporters (see Savage 1991). With photocopying cheap and accessible for the first time, the fanzines were a new medium tailor made for the values of punk, with its do-it-yourself ethic and associations of street credibility. There was an explosion of the new form as dozens of fanzines 'charted punk's diaspora in scrawled, montaged, xeroxed pages' (Savage 1991: 402). Several fanzines provided a training ground for a number of music journalists, and in some cases useful media expertise for those who, taking to heart their own rhetoric of 'here's three chords, now form a band', subsequently did just that.

The growth of the audience for heavy metal in the 1980s was accompanied by a proliferation of metal fanzines. As with fanzines based in similar youth cultures and genres, 'metal fanzines are characterized by a passionate, almost proselytizing, tone. Fanzine editors adhere fanatically to the metal conventions, standards, and practices' (Weinstein 1991a: 178). With radio giving metal little airplay and the mainstream music press hostile to it, the metal fanzines became an important part of the record companies' promotion activities, creating an information network connecting fans and bands globally, centred around particular bands (e.g. *Killing Yourself to Die*, an international Black Sabbath fanzine), sub-genres and regions.

During the 1990s, various local music scenes have owed much to the role played by fanzines in promoting musicians and styles (see Chapter 11). They have also created national and international networks, as with the proliferation of UK dance club zines, linking a network stretching from Manchester to London, and beyond. Despite their essentially non-commercial and often ephemeral nature, fanzines remain a significant part of the music scene, with many now available through the Internet.

The teen glossies

These music magazines are aimed at a teenage market, particularly young girls. All are similar in format, with the majority of coverage devoted to exposing the private personas of current pop stars whose careers are tied to the teenage market. The magazines thereby make these stars accessible to adolescent fantasies, forming part of what McRobbie and Garber (1976) termed the culture of the bedroom, complete with pinups. Teenage girls purchase *Smash Hits* and its competitors in part for the posters which are a feature of the magazine.

Some teen glossies are linked to television music shows. New Zealand's *RTR Countdown* was created by the *NZ Listener* (a guide to television and radio programmes) as a print media counterpart and compliment to the long-established *Ready to Roll (RTR)*, a popular television music programme. This obviously useful marketing tie-in was consolidated in 1988 when RTR added the word 'Countdown' to its name. As Television New Zealand's marketing magazine observed in 1990, this link 'provides a unique opportunity for cross promotion between the two very different but complementary mediums', and a link up for many successful competitions (*Networks*, September 1990: 3). Currently, similar links are evident with the *Top of the Pops* TV show and magazine, and *Smash Hits* televised awards shows.

The teen glossies are teen music/film/TV/lifestyle publications. There are adverts for films, cable TV channels, video games, and TV programmes appealing to younger readers. The goods and services advertised are generally relatively cheap, recognising the limited (but significant as a market segment) spending power of teenagers. They project a lifestyle that is healthy, youthful, glamorous, and fun, most notably through the frequent advertisements for cosmetics. A number of advertisements for feminine hygiene products are obviously projected at girls on the verge of puberty, and show active lifestyles involving attractive, clean-cut 'in group' girls. Such advertising is hardly surprising given adolescent experimentation with make-up, clothes and hairstyles, in their concern for appearance, and the establishment of a personal identity. The teen glossies have a major share of the music press market: *Smash Hits* 1999 circulation of 213,000 made it the UK's leading music magazine.

Packaging rebellion: metal mags

There are a range of Heavy Metal magazines, catering to various sub-genres of metal, and their fans. Most are primarily aimed at an adolescent male readership, and are similar to the teen glossies, with an emphasis upon the performer(s) and their pictorial representation. (More extreme forms of metal are catered for primarily by fanzines.) This is attractively packaged 'rebellion', allowing its consumers to vicariously identify with the genre. When it emerged in the 1970s, heavy metal was either ignored or heavily criticised by the mainstream music press, leaving the way open for specialised heavy metal magazines more sympathetic to the genre. The oldest of these is *Kerrang!*, which began in 1981, followed by *Metal Hammer* (UK, 1989; circulation in 1999 was 29,000) and *RAW* (standing for Rock Action Worldwide). With metal's increasing commercial success in the late 1980s, the established rock magazines awarded the genre fuller and more sympathetic coverage, but the specialist metal magazines continued to proliferate, with a large number of national variants. Heavy metal fans are linked internationally by these magazines, which promote the images and values of metal.

Supporting the indie scene: *NME*

Typical of the more serious 'inkie' rock press is the *New Musical Express* (NME), which began publication in 1952, marketed to the new generation of teenage record buyers in the UK. As with its main competitor, *Melody Maker*, the NME was closely tied into the record industry. In 1952, NME published 'the first regular and reasonably accurate list of British record sales'; the *Melody Maker* soon followed with a similar 'hit parade' based on retailers' returns, and both charts became closely tied to the industry's stocking and promotional policies (Frith 1983: 166). Through the 1950s, the NME focused on the stars of popular music, with little critical perspective on the music covered. This clearly met a market demand, and by 1964 the magazine was selling nearly 300,000 copies per week.

The orientation of the UK music press, including NME, changed with the emerging and critically self-conscious progressive rock market of the mid-1960s, and the development in the US of new, specialist music magazines such as *Creem* and *Rolling Stone*, characterised by their serious treatment of rock as a cultural form. In 1972 the NME was reorganised, with a new team of writers recruited from Britain's underground press. After a slump in the face of a late 1960s market assault by the now 'progressive' *Melody Maker*, by 1974 NME was back to 200,000 sales (Frith 1983). Biting 'new journalist' prose for many readers became part of NME's appeal – whether you agreed or not with the evaluations on offer was almost incidental.

Increasingly, the NME became associated with the British 'alternative' or indie music scene. It remains indispensable for those wanting to keep up with this scene, and invaluable for those performers and labels working within it. The magazine sticks closely to its traditional format: a tabloid-style layout, limited use of colour, on cheap newsprint; with a mix of features: reviews of records and concerts, as well as film, book, and video reviews; competitions and classifieds; a gig guide and tour news; and extensive chart listings, including retrospectives of these.

To a degree, *NME's* very hipness and cynicism in the 1980s proved its undoing, as two new groups of readers emerged in the music marketplace: ageing fans, no longer into clubbing and concerts, with an eye to nostalgia, Dire Straits, their CD collections, and FM 'solid rock'/'golden oldies' radio; and younger yuppies and style-oriented professionals. Both groups of consumers were largely uninterested in the indie scene, and turned instead to the lifestyle bibles and the new glossies like *Q*, and (later) *MOJO*. This competition saw a decline in *NME's* circulation, which stood at 85,000 in 1999.

Rolling Stone: from counter culture icon to industry staple

The American inspiration for the outburst of the rock press in the late 1960s, and its reorientation, *Rolling Stone* was launched in San Francisco on 9 November 1967. Jann Wenner, its founder, wanted the publication to focus on rock music, but it was also to cover the youth culture generally. The first issue of the new fortnightly established that it was aiming at a niche between the 'inaccurate and irrelevant' trade papers and the fan magazines, which were viewed as 'an anachronism, fashioned in the mould of myth and nonsense'. *Rolling Stone* was for the artists, the industry, and every person who 'believes in the magic that can set you free'; it was 'not just about music, but also about the things and attitudes that the music embraces' (cited Frith 1983: 169).

This rather earnest ideological mission resulted in considerable tension in the early years of *Rolling Stone* (see Draper 1990), as it attempted to fuse in-depth and sympathetic reporting of youth culture and the demands of rock promotion. *Rolling Stone* in its struggling early years was supported by the record companies, and the concern with radical and alternative politics was soon suborned by the dependence on the concerns of the music industry. In August 1973, *Rolling Stone* changed its format, becoming 'a general interest magazine, covering modern American culture, politics and art, with a special interest in music' (Frith 1983: 171). However, it retained its now preeminent place as an opinion leader in the music business, mainly because its ageing, affluent, largely white male readership continued to represent a primary consumer group for the record industry.

The development of 'regional editions' of *Rolling Stone*, beginning with Britain in 1969 and followed by an Australian monthly edition, along with subsequent Japanese and German language editions reflects the increasing internationalisation of popular music, and the global predominance of Anglo-American artists. In format, *Rolling Stone* retains its distinctive character through its famous cover picture feature (immortalised in the Doctor Hook single of 1972, which gained the band a cover story), but contents and presentation-wise it is similar to its newer competitors such as Q. This is hardly surprising, given that both magazines are oriented to older consumers with sufficient disposable income to allow them to purchase the music, clothes, spirits, and travel opportunities which *Rolling Stone* advertises. The US edition of *Rolling Stone* currently sells over a million copies per issue (1,221,000 in 1999), maintaining its place as the leading publication of this type (compared with *Vibe*'s 1999 circulation of 700,000 and *Spin*'s 535,000).

Style bibles: *The Face*

In the 1980s, a new strain of music journalism emerged, most markedly in the UK, with 'interest shifting from the music itself to a more general concern with the cultural phenomena which accompany it' (McRobbie 1988: xv). This new focus was strongly evident in the styles of the new 'style bibles', especially *The Face*. *The Face* was launched in May 1980 by Nick Logan, who had edited *NME* in its peak years and had also been responsible for the successful new teen pop glossy *Smash Hits* (launched in 1979). While its early covers announced *The Face* as 'Rock's final frontier', it rapidly became much more than a music monthly, with its preoccupation with style inspiring a host of imitators across Europe. Not everyone was quite so enthusiastic. Dick Hebdige (1988) wrote a sharply critical essay on *The Face*, seeing it as totally subordinated to postmodernity, flattening everything to the glossy world of the image, and presenting its style as its content. *The Face* reached its peak in 1987, with a circulation of 350,000 (in 1999, circulation is 38,000). In July 1988 it celebrated its 100th issue by wrapping up 'the style decade' and shifting towards a simpler, more natural look and a renewed focus on the music. It has, however, continued to combine high and popular culture in an innovative and engaging fashion, continuing to subvert the boundaries between them.

The new tabloids: *Q*

Q first appeared in October 1986, subtitled 'The modern guide to music and more'. Q is a high-quality 'glossy' magazine, aimed squarely at affluent consumers, usually in their twenties, with a strong interest in both contemporary popular music and its historical antecedents. Q's interviews and articles cover a range of performers, who are frequently allowed to 'speak' extensively for themselves, with most articles being hung around a loose interview format. Q has an extensive reviews section, with comprehensive coverage of new releases and re-releases. The reviews are frequently literary in orientation, and show a strong sense of popular music history and the interplay of its musical genres. This is also evident in standard features such as 'Where Are They Now?' responding to readers queries about (often rather obscure) bands of yesteryear, and retrospective pieces on key releases within particular genres. In addition to records, Q also reviews concerts, and provides a listing of upcoming UK concerts, a traditional function of its 'inkie' predecessors; critically surveys new stereo and VCR technology and hardware; and reviews music-related books and music videos. The advertising in Q is indicative of its affluent middle-class readership.

Following its 1986 debut, Q's sales tripled to stand at over 170,000 in August 1990, making it the success story of the UK music press. This success, suggests Reynolds, is based on the 'objectivity' of Q: 'its non-partisan approach and avoidance of vehemence', its non-confrontational style of interviewing, and an avoidance of the critic-as-star form of self-indulgence – all characteristics of the older 'inkies' in the 1990s, most notably NME (Reynolds 1990). Q has maintained its market share, in the face of stiff competition from new magazines like MOJO; with its (1999) circulation at 166,000.

Muzik: monitoring dance music

The increasing prominence of various styles of dance music since the late 1980s has seen a number of magazines catering to this broad genre and its participants (e.g. i-d; DJ). Muzik, subtitled 'The ultimate dance music magazine', is one of the most enduring of these. Launched in the UK in May 1995, as an addition to the IPC Magazine group, it adopted a critical stance reminiscent of the old 'rock' press: 'We will offer praise to those who deserve it, but not shirk from sticking the boot in where necessary' ('Muzik – The Story So Far', Issue no. 50, July 1999). In format and contents, Muzik is very similar to the new tabloids, but with its features, free cd's, regular columns, and advertising oriented to dance music, its creators, and the dance scene generally. The magazine is primarily oriented to the UK, but with some international coverage, especially the off shore dance scenes of Europe (Ibiza, etc.). Muzik has played a very active part in constructing the dance genre and scene, by sponsoring dance parties, holding annual awards (since 1996), issuing its own compilation albums, and spearheading a campaign in 1995–96 for free tap water in all clubs (to avoid the dangerous dehydration associated with ecstasy use). This illustrates the proactive role now played by music magazines.

Journalism or industry publicity?

Writing in 1983, Frith saw the music papers and their writers as operating in a symbiotic relationship with the record industry, with the blurring of the boundary between rock journalism and rock publicity reflected in the continuous job mobility between them: 'record company press departments recruit from the music papers, music papers employ ex-publicists; it is not even unusual for writers to do both jobs simultaneously' (Frith 1983:173). Nearly twenty years on, the situation Frith describes has become even more firmly consolidated. Popular music magazines have developed in tandem with consumer culture, and, as I have already shown, the variations evident among them reflect the diversity of readers' tastes and interests. They have also become part of a general magazine culture; while they are to be found in a separate section in the magazine racks, they are competing for advertising with a proliferating range of magazines. Accordingly, the market profile (especially the socio-economic status) of their readership must guarantee advertisers access to their target consumers. The advertising each carries firmly indicates their particular market orientation. They are providing not just an adjunct to popular music – though that dimension remains central – but a guide to lifestyle, especially leisure consumption.

The ideological role of the music press in constructing a sense of community and in maintaining a critical distance from the music companies had already become muted by the late 1980s: 'The music press has abandoned its pretensions of leading its readership or setting agendas, and contracted around the concept of "service": hard news, information, gossip, consumer guidance' (Reynolds 1990: 27). During the 1990s the music press has largely abandoned any residual post-punk sense of antago-nism towards the industry, realising that they share a common interest in maintaining consumption. This is achieved by sustaining a constant turnover of new trends, scenes, and performers, while also mining music's past using the links between older consumer's nostalgia, younger listeners' interest in antecedents, and the back catalogue.

CRITICS AS GATEKEEPERS

I turn now to the role played by popular music critics as gatekeepers of taste, arbiters of cultural history, and publicists for the record industry. This influence can some-times be spectacular, as with *Billboard* editor Timothy White's decision upon first hearing *Jagged Little Pill*, to make Alanis Morissette the focus of his 'Music to My Ears' column before the album's release; and then influencing the editors of *Spin* and *Rolling Stone* to follow suit. White's column (in the 18 May 1995 issue) was distrib-uted with some review copies of *Jagged Little Pill*, helping set the tone for the generally positive press and magazine reviews the record received. The album was exceptional, but this coverage provided a helpful initial boost (Cantin 1997: 142, 151).

Such episodes aside, there is general agreement that music critics don't exercise as much influence on consumers as, say, literary or drama critics. The more crucial intermediaries are those who control airtime (DJs and radio programmers) and access to recording technology and reproduction and marketing facilities (record compa-nies and record producers). Nonetheless, I would argue that the critics do influence record buyers, particularly those who are looking to make the best use of limited purchasing power. Many buyers purchase the latest boy band or Celine Dion release as a matter of course, acting as confirmed followers of that artist, style, or scene. But others are actively exploring the byways of fresh talent, new musical hybrids, or the back catalogue.

Such searches are aided by the way in which 'rock critics' don't so much operate on the basis of some general aesthetic criteria, but rather through situating new products via constant appeal to referents, attempting to contextualise the particular text under consideration. For example:

> The distinctive feature of the Specials' music is its rhythm: drawing on West Indian music of the 1960s – ska and rock steady – the group invested rock's usual 4:4 beat with the looseness, verve and cheerfulness that were missing from both punk's banged out messages and disco's expensive precision. The Specials' off beats, their rambling guitar and organ, have the warmth and ease of the 1960s soul and mod clubs from which this pop sound emerged the first time around.
>
> (Frith 1988a: 77)

While the various allusions here may well make some demands on the readers' cultural capital – their knowledge of rock's past and some basic musicology – this in itself is part of the appeal of such reviews. 'Yes, I know what this reviewer means', the informed reader can think, and therefore make a judgement about the appeal of the Specials.

Popular music critics construct their own version of the traditional high–low culture split, usually around notions of artistic integrity, authenticity, and the nature of commercialism. The best of such critics – and their associated magazines – have published collections of their reviews; most prominently *The Rolling Stone Record Guides* (Marsh and Swenson 1984; DeCurtis and Henke 1992). Along with recent series such as the *All Music Guides* and the *Rough Guides* (to Rock, Reggae, and, forthcoming volumes on hip-hop and drum 'n' bass), these reference tools have become bibles in their fields, establishing orthodoxies as to the relative value of various styles or genres and pantheons of artists. Record collectors and enthusiasts, and specialist and second-hand record shops, inevitably have well-thumbed copies of these and similar volumes close at hand.

Yet, this body of criticism is a field in which highly idiosyncratic and disparate standards are the norm. Particular performers and their efforts will be heaped with praise by one reviewer and denigrated by another. Evaluations reflect personal preferences and matters of taste. Rarely are evaluative criteria laid bare for critical scrutiny, and even where this occurs it creates as well as resolves difficulties (see Shuker 1994: chap. 3, for a discussion of the early editions of *The Rolling Stone Record Guide*; and Christgau's rating system).

A major contribution to this group of studies is the American critic Dave Marsh's *The Heart of Rock and Soul, The 1001 Greatest Singles Ever Made* (1989). There is a dominant tendency in 'rock' to accord value to albums as opposed to singles (the reverse is true of much dance music), although as Marsh observes, singles are the essence of rock 'n' roll: 'record production, promotion and marketing is entirely determined by the search for and exploitation of potential hit singles' (Marsh 1989: xii). Utilising singles as the frame of reference for rock history also alters the relative value of particular styles of music. Suddenly album-oriented 'progressive' music (non-rhythm and blues), which has produced few hit singles yet dominates critical discussion, is pushed to one side. Yet Marsh's approach has its own heroes and villains. For him, the 1960s are indisputably the most creative period of rock 'n' roll; just under half of the singles included are from that decade. Among his top choices, it is not until Number 24 (Springsteen's 'Born to Run') that we see a post-1970 single. The antipathy to punk is clear, though several post-punk 'New Wave' performers are prominent (Elvis Costello has five entries). There is also a predilection for American performers; English bands with considerable commercial success, such as the Troggs and the Small Faces, do not rate a mention. Indeed, it is a fascinating exercise in trivia to compare the American chart rankings of Marsh's selections with their English equivalents (see Gambaccini *et al.* 1987), an exercise which shows the commercial failure of many of Marsh's selections on the other side of the Atlantic (the exercise works equally well in reverse).

A similar gatekeeping role is played by the leading histories of popular music, which reveal a mix of distinctly national prejudices and aesthetic discrimination at work. In the *Rolling Stone* history *Rock of Ages* (Ward *et al.* 1986), only British bands and performers who had an impact on the United States charts are mentioned, though occasionally there is a gesture towards those who, despite their lack of sales success, influenced American styles (e.g. the Searchers). This is a history of rock 'n' roll as it happened in America. Furthermore, there is a high–low culture distinction at work within the idiom itself, with a great deal on bands seen as avant-garde, such as the Fugs and the Quicksilver Messenger Service, but commercially successful groups (e.g. Paul Revere and the Raiders) barely rating a mention. They are dismissed as 'teeny bopper', juvenile fodder, unfit to join the pantheon of 'authentic' performers. Yet which of these groups still get airplay, and sell respectable amounts of 'greatest hits' packages? Are all their admirers duped consumers, or does their music have a timeless quality which the *Rolling Stone* writers, in their reach for a high art, 'ideologically correct' approach to 'rock', have somehow overlooked?

All this is to simply make the point that popular music critics, and their histories, encyclopedias and consumer guides are playing a key role in defining the reference points, the highs and lows in the development of 'rock' and other styles of popular music. They imbue particular performers, genres, and recordings with meaning and value, and even their internecine arguments strengthen an artist or record's claim to being part of a selective tradition. The consumers of the music themselves frequently reflect (even if only to reject) such distinctions.

Music magazines play their part in the economics of popular music, encouraging readers to buy records (and posters, T-shirts, etc.), and generally immerse themselves in consumer 'pop' culture. Similarly, music critics act as a service industry to the record industry, lubricating the desire to acquire both new product and selections from the back catalogue. Both the press and critics, however, also play an important ideological function. They distance popular music consumers from the fact that they are essentially purchasing an economic commodity, by stressing the product's cultural significance. Furthermore, this function is maintained by the important point that the music press is not, at least directly, vertically integrated into the music industry (i.e. owned by the record companies). A sense of distance is thereby maintained, while at the same time the need of the industry to constantly sell new images, styles and product is met.

Up to this point, I have been concerned with the broad context within which popular music is produced: the music industry, the technology available, State cultural policy, and the role of the music press. Each plays a role in mediating between the music and consumers, and shaping the cultural meanings attached to the music. The discussion turns now to those who actually make music, primarily musicians, the creative process involved and the nature of their creations.

Chapter 6

'I'm just a singer
(in a rock 'n' roll band)'
Making music

In addressing the question of how meaning is produced in popular music, a central role must be accorded to those who actually make the music. This is not, however, to simply accept the 'creative artist' view of the production of cultural products, which sees 'art' as the product of the creative individual, largely unencumbered by politics and economics. Those involved in making music clearly exercise varying degrees of personal autonomy, but this is always circumscribed by the available technologies and expertise, by economics, and by the expectations of their audience. Once again, it is a question of the dynamic interrelationship of the production context, the texts and their creators, and the audience for the music.

This chapter is concerned with the nature of music making and the relative status of those who make music, primarily, but not exclusively, musicians. Indeed, the term 'musician' is not as straightforward as it seems, and it is worth acknowledging that people make music as an integral part of their everyday lives (see Crafts *et al.* 1993). Finnegan, in her study of music-making in Milton Keynes, found it difficult to distinguish 'amateur' from 'professional' musicians:

> local bands sometimes contained many players in full-time (non-musical) jobs and others whose only regular occupation was their music; yet in giving performances, practising, sharing out the fees and identification with the group, the members were treated exactly alike (except for the inconvenience of those in jobs that had to plead illness or take time off work if they travelled to distant bookings).
>
> (Finnegan 1989: 13)

99

Furthermore, the local musicians tended to use the term professional in an evaluative rather than an economic sense, to refer to a player's standard of performance, musical knowledge and qualifications, and regular appearances with musicians regarded as professional. While the term 'musician' has been associated with singing or playing an instrument, the development of sampling technology, computer-based composition, and DJ/mixer culture have undermined such easy equations.

My discussion begins with the initial creation of musical texts, through songwriting and the 'working up' of a composition, either original or a 'cover', for performance/recording. I then turn to the reproduction of the musical text as a material product – the sound recording, and the role of the producer, and the various styles of reproduction as performance. The second part of the chapter considers the differing roles and status of those who create music. I examine the distinctions frequently used by musicians themselves, as well as critics and fans, to label various performers. There is an obvious hierarchy of values at work here, both between and within various categories, and in the discourse around the application of terms such as creativity and authenticity. The bulk of my discussion is concerned with 'mainstream' commercial forms of music making, notably rock and pop, and the demarcations present within their musical production as sounds. Other genres, notably disco and dance music, and 'musicians' such as the contemporary dance DJ, subvert many of the traditional assumptions of the 'rock formation' about the nature of musicianship (see Straw 1999; Haslam 2000).

MAKING MUSIC

Our detailed knowledge of how performers actually create their music, and how they attempt to create an audience for their efforts remains sparse. A decade ago, Cohen's summary of the available literature observed that there had been a lack of ethnographic or participant observer study of the process of making music:

> What is particularly lacking in the literature (on rock) is ethnographic data and microsociological detail. Two other important features have been omitted: the grassroots of the industry – the countless, as yet unknown bands struggling for success at a local level – and the actual process of music making by rock bands.
> (Cohen 1991: 6)

Cohen's informative account of the music scene in Liverpool in the mid-1980s focused on two punk influenced bands to examine:

> the process of music making and the complexity of social relationships involved, analysing the way in which music not only reflects but affects the social environ-

ment, and highlighting the underlining conceptions of music which determine the musical terminology and categories used and the evaluation of music, musicians, musical knowledge and skills.

(Cohen 1991: 7)

In addition to Cohen's *Rock Culture in Liverpool*, one could then point to a handful of 'classic' accounts (Becker 1997; Bennett 1990; Finnegan 1989; Weinstein 1991a: chap. 3), along with a large body of biographical profiles of varying usefulness. To these we can now add several compendiums of reflections from musicians; indepth studies of the making of particular recordings; further accounts of musicians involved in local musical scenes, along with music making in 'native' or non-Anglo-American settings; and several insightful discussions of musical creativity (e.g. Berkenstadt and Cross 1998; Neuenfeldt 1997; Frith 1996). Here I can only gesture towards the complexity and associated insights of this body of literature.

Popular music is for the majority of its participants an essentially 'amateur' or 'quasi-professional' activity, which may become a career option. Indeed, the great majority of people who make their living playing rock music live near the poverty line: there are said to be 10,000 functional bands in the greater Los Angeles area alone, 'all slugging it out night after night in a never-ending cacophony of competition, strategic repositioning, and reconfiguration' (Kirschner 1998: 250). In either case, making music is a distinct form of labour process, with identifiable characteristics and various specialist roles within it. As shown in the discussion of record company cultural intermediaries in Chapter 2, there are a wide range of roles within the music industry, including record producers, music video directors, sound engineers and mixers, publicists and journalists, agents and managers. I concentrate here on the musicians, but it should not be overlooked that their ability to 'make music' is, to varying extents, dependent on the input of these other industry personnel. To begin with, there is composition and the role of the songwriter.

'Wrote a song' (Bob Seger)

With its romantic connotations of creativity and authenticity, composition is at the heart of discourses surrounding authorship in popular music. Examples of artistic and commercial success frequently accord songwriting a key place: 'Kurt Cobain's ability to write songs with such strong hooks was the crucial ingredient in Nirvana's eventual world-wide appeal. The melodies he wrote were so memorable, people found themselves singing along without even knowing or understanding the lyrics' (Berkenstadt and Cross 1998: 63).

While composition can encompass several modes, most recently the bricolage of

101

electronic practices underpinning dance music, I concentrate here on songwriting in relation to mainstream, chart-oriented rock and pop music. In comparison with the writing on other roles in the music industry, and the nature of the creative process in popular music, the role of the songwriter has received only limited attention. Published work has concentrated on song composition and the process of song-writing, and the contributions of leading songwriters, especially those associated with the Brill Building in New York.

There are numerous personal accounts of the process of songwriting; for example, Paul McCartney's recollections of his collaboration with John Lennon (Miles 1997), and Cantin's discussion of the collaboration between Alanis Morissette and Greg Ballard:

> she would sit on the floor. Ballard would perch on a chair. They'd both take acoustic guitars and fool around with melodies and lyrical ideas and see what happened. When they really got rolling, Alanis would fall into a kind of trance-like state.
>
> (Cantin 1997: 126)

Songwriters have historically exercised considerable influence over artists/styles. In the 1950s Leiber and Stoller got an unprecedented deal with Atlantic to write and produce their own songs; the resulting collaborations with performers such as the Drifters and Ben E. King produced sweet soul, a very self-conscious marriage of R&B and classical instruments, notably the violin. In the 1960s Holland, Dozier, Holland contributed to the development of the distinctive Motown sound. In the 1970s Chinn and Chapman composed over fifty British top ten hits in association with producers Mickie Most and Phil Wainman, 'using competent bar bands (Mud, Sweet) on to whom they could graft a style and image' (Hatch and Millward 1987: 141), to produce highly commercial power pop, glitter rock, and dance music. In the 1980s, Stock, Aitken, Waterman wrote and produced successful dance pop for performers such as Kylie Minogue.

In the late 1950s and early 1960s a factory model of songwriting, combined with a strong aesthetic sense, was evident in the work of a group of songwriters (and music publishers) in New York's Brill Building: 'the best of Tin Pan Alley's melodic and lyrical hall marks were incorporated into R&B to raise the music to new levels of sophistication' (AMG 1995: 883). The group included a number of successful song-writing teams: the more pop oriented Goffin and King; Mann and Weil; and Barry and Greenwich; the R&B oriented Pomus and Sherman, and Leiber and Stoller. Several also produced, most notably Phil Spector, Bert Berns, and Leiber and Stoller, who wrote and produced most of the Coasters hits. One factor which distinguished the group was their youth: mainly in their late teens or early twenties, with several married couples working together, the Brill Building songwriters were well able to relate to and interpret teenage dreams and concerns, especially the search for identity and romance. These provided the themes for many of the songs they wrote, especially those performed by the teen idols and girl groups of the period. Pomus and Sherman, and Leiber and Stoller, wrote some of Elvis Presley's best material. Collectively, the Brill Building songwriters were responsible for a large number of chart successes, and had an enduring influence (see Shaw 1992). The role of such songwriters, however, was weakened with the British invasion and the emergence of a tradition of self-contained groups or performers writing their own songs (most notably the Beatles), which weakened the traditional songwriting market.

Some songwriters have been accorded auteur status, especially when they have later successfully recorded their own material (e.g. Carol King: *Tapestry*, Ode, 1971; Neil Diamond), or are performing as singer songwriters. The term 'singer songwriters' has been given to artists who both write and perform their material, and who are able to perform solo, usually on acoustic guitar or piano. An emphasis on lyrics has resulted in the work of such performers often being referred to as song poets, accorded auteur status, and made the subject of intensive lyric analysis (see Chapter 9: texts). The folk music revival in the 1960s saw several singer songwriters come to prominence: Joan Baez, Phil Ochs, and, especially, Bob Dylan. Singer songwriters were a particularly strong 'movement' in the 1970s, including Neil Young, James Taylor, Joni Mitchell, Jackson Browne, and Joan Armatrading; all still performing/recording. In the 1980s, the appellation singer songwriter was applied to, among others, Bruce Springsteen, Prince, and Elvis Costello; and in the 1990s to Tori Amos, Suzanne Vega, Tanita Tikaram, Tracy Chapman, and Toni Childs. This recent female predominance led some observers to equate the 'form' with women performers, due to its emphasis on lyrics and performance rather than the indulgences associated with male-dominated styles of rock music. The application of the term to solo performers is problematic, in that most of those mentioned usually perform with 'backing' bands, and at times regard themselves as an integral part of these. Nonetheless, the concept of singer songwriter continues to have strong connotations of greater authenticity and 'true' auteurship.

The realities of practice

Once a song is composed, even if only in a limited form (partial lyrics only, or a riff to build on), it becomes 'worked up' for live performance and recording. A similar process occurs with 'covers' of recordings by other performers. There are very few formal study or apprenticeship programmes for aspiring popular musicians, in sharp contrast to the opportunities for classical and jazz instrumentalists. Learning the required musical skills takes time and perseverance as well as inclination and talent.

There is also the need for considerable financial investment, particularly with genres like heavy metal, which emphasise amplification and visual high-tech. In 1988 the leader of a still struggling and unsigned band mentioned to Weinstein that the band was financed by the $30,000 that his parents had saved for his college education! In 2000, New Zealand electronic duo Pitch Black can point to $25,000 worth of expensive technology.

Bennett's detailed account, 'The Realities of Practice', shows that song getting for most rock musicians is a process of 'copying a recording by playing along with it and using the technical ability to play parts of it over and over again' (Bennett 1990: 224). Interestingly, and reflecting the limitations of conventional notation when applied to rock music, little use is made of sheet music: 'It's so simple just to get things off the record, sheet music is just for people who can't hear' (piano player; cited Bennett 1990: 227). Copying initially takes place in private, with the next step the expansion of the song-getting experience to the group situation – transforming the song into a performable entity – and its extension to the creation of 'sets' of songs. These blocks of material, usually consisting of ten to fifteen songs to be played over a 45-minute period, are constructed to 'align the group's performance potential with particular markets for the group's services' (Bennett 1990: 233). That is, they are tailored for specific audiences and contexts (gigs), and, as such, usually represent a compromise between what bands want to play and what is marketable.

The two Liverpool bands that Cohen studied demonstrated a complex process of musical composition, rehearsal, and performance. Their musical world was based around a series of polarities: creativity versus commerce; musical content and quality versus image and superficiality; honest and natural versus false and deceitful; artistic integrity versus selling out; independent record companies versus major record companies; live music for community, experimentation and indulgence versus recorded music for profit and for a mass market (Cohen 1991: 134). The bands situated themselves into a combination of these various factors, with tension, constant debate and shifting allegiances evident among their members. Their creative process was typically incremental and participatory, as with the Jactars in rehearsal:

> Dave has come up with an idea for a new song and plays it to the others on his bass. It comprises a short sequence of notes (a 'riff') which he plays over and over to enable the others to get the feel of it. Trav tries out a few chords on his guitar before playing along with Dave. Gary begins to beat out the rhythm on the rim of his snare drum and then joins in on the whole drum kit followed by Tog on keyboards. Dave repeats the riff while the others experiment with different chords and beats. They stop for Trav to check over some chords with Dave and identify which notes he has been playing. Dave suggests that Tog play some

'deep' notes on keyboards to complement Trav's chords. Again they begin this process of repetition and experimentation using the same short riff as their base.

(Cohen 1991: 136)

Beyond creating a distinctive musical sound and original material, successful performers must also develop the different skills required of the live and studio recording settings (see Weinstein 1991a; Negus 1992). It is during the latter process that the role of the producer comes to the fore.

'Lookin' for that million-dollar sound' (Bruce Springsteen, 'The Promise')

The occupation of producer emerged as a distinct job category and career path in the popular music industry during the 1950s, initially as someone who directed and supervised recording sessions, and who also frequently doubled as sound engineer (e.g. Sam Phillips at Sun Records). Successful producers, such as songwriters Leiber and Stoller at Atlantic and George Martin at EMI, began exerting pressure on their recording companies to receive credits (on recordings) and royalties. By the mid-1960s, the studio producer had become an auteur figure, an artist employing multi-track technology and stereo sound to make recording 'a form of composition in itself, rather than simply as a means of documenting a performance' (Negus 1992: 87). The main example of this new status was Phil Spector (see Chapter 7). In the 1970s and 1980s, the producer's important role as a cultural intermediary was consolidated with the development of new technology: synthesisers, samplers, and computer-based sequencing systems. Producers became central figures in genres such as dub and techno, and, above, all with disco.

Currently, the way producers operate, their contribution to the session, and the level of reward they are accorded vary widely, depending on the stature of the musicians they are working with and the type of music being recorded (see, for example, Butch Vig's account of his work as producer on Nirvana's *Nevermind* in Berkenstadt and Cross 1998). Producers' approaches to recording vary from the naturalistic, 'try it and see what happens', to a more calculated, entrepreneurial attitude. Production practices represent an amalgam of established techniques and the possibilities offered by the new technologies.

Live performance

Once a band or performer has 'learned' some music, assuming ambition and confidence, they will usually seek to perform live in public. I use the term 'live' performance for those situations where the audience is in close physical proximity to the performance, and the experience of the music is contiguous with its actual performance. Historically of course, prior to the advent of recorded sound, all music was live, and was experienced as such. Live music is made in a variety of settings: by buskers in the streets or subways, in clubs and concert halls, and in the 'open air', most notably at outdoor concert venues and festivals. 'Pseudo-live' performances take place at one remove, as it were, from the original or actual performance, and are usually experienced through intermediary technology – film and TV (see Chapter 10), or in one of the various recorded formats via radio and sound reproduction systems, or web broadcasts (see Chapter 3). The pseudo-live experience of music is not usually in the same time frame as the original performance, although this can be the case with radio and satellite TV linkups with 'live' events. For both fans and musicians there is a perceived hierarchy of such performances, with a marked tendency to equate an audiences' physical proximity to the actual 'performance' and intimacy with the performer(s), with a more authentic and satisfying musical experience.

Various forms of performance, and associated venues, mediate the music, creating a diegetic link between performer, text, and consumer. Their significance in determining meaning in popular music lies in the interrelationship of ritual, pleasure, and economics in the music. Performance in its various guises operates to create audiences, to fuel individual fantasy and pleasure, and to create popular music icons and cultural myths. At times, performance events have had the capacity to encapsulate and represent key periods and turning points in popular music. The Woodstock festival represented the peak of the 1960s counterculture, at least at an ideological level, while the Rolling Stones' Altamont concert signalled its passing. The significance of such events is indicated by their use in a cultural shorthand fashion among fans, musicians, and writers – 'Woodstock' – with an assumed set of connotations (Shuker 1994).

'Downtown' (Petula Clark): clubs and pubs

Public performance venues are significant indicators of the nature of genre styles, the economic and critical status of performers, and the nature of their audience/fans. They range along a continuum, from performances on street corners etc., clubs and pubs, to smaller concert halls, to outdoor stadiums. Clubs and pubs remain the main venues for live music on a regular and continuing basis. Both serve as training grounds for aspiring performers operating at the local level, and provide a 'bread and butter' living for more established artists, often through being part of an organised 'circuit' of venues. Club appearances include 'showcase' evenings, similar to variety-style concerts, with a number of performers featured; 'one-nighters'; and extended engagements. All are important for gaining experience in live work, building an audience, and making contacts in the music industry. Clubs also remain the main site for most music fans' engagement with live music, particularly in smaller towns not on the national concert itinerary of touring performers.

The equation of live performance with musical authenticity and 'paying your dues' as a performer remains a widely held ideology among fans, musicians, and record company executives. Reflecting this, clubs have historically assumed mythic importance for breaking new acts, as with the Who at the Marquee in London, and the Doors at the Whisky in LA. They can also establish and popularise trends and musical genres, as in the 1970s with American punk at New York's Max's and CBGBs, and Cleveland's Clockwork Orange and the Viking Saloon, and English punk at London's 100 Club and the Roxy, and Manchester's Electric Circus (see Heylin 1993; Savage 1991), and disco in the 1980s, and DJ culture and techno and its various genres in the 1990s (Garratt 1999; Thornton 1995). A local network of clubs or pub venues can foster a local scene and arguably create a 'local' sound (see Chapter 11).

Where there is not a strong club scene, pubs will sometimes take on the same role. In the process they legitimate a particular sound and performance ethos around rock. In Australia, the strongly masculinist 'Oz Rock' which historically dominated the local music scene, was defined by its association with the pub circuit in the 1980s. Such venues do not function in a neutral fashion, merely supplying a physical locale:

> Bands starting out lack the power to deal effectively with pub owners, while the pub owners' dominance of the industry allows them plenty of options. The top bands may receive decent fees and conditions, but most bands are simply afraid to negotiate with their employers for fear of losing the gig. Coupled to this economic powerlessness, and insidiously connected to it in effect, is the influence pub venues can exert on the nature of the band's material, on the gender composition of the band, what members wear and so on. Of particular concern is the fact that pub owners like bands who are not well known to play songs that are.
>
> (Turner 1992: 19)

'On the road again' (Canned Heat): tours and concerts

As with club and pub gigs, concerts, usually part of a tour, expose performers and their music to potential fans and purchasers, building an image and a following. Tours were important historically for helping 'break' English bands in the United States during the 1960s, and for the commercial breakthrough of Bob Marley and the Wailers in the UK in the 1970s (see Chapter 2), and remain a crucial part of the present national and international music scenes. For example, the importation of name DJs from the UK has been a major factor in consolidating the present dance music scenes in Australia and New Zealand. During the 1990s, purely promotional 'tours' have become significant in building a fan base, for example Shania Twain's shopping mall stops in 1993–94 (see Hager 1998).

The nature of tour concerts is an oddly ambivalent one. On the one hand, for the fan it is a rare opportunity to see a favoured performer, especially if you live in locations where the opportunity may be literally a once in a lifetime one. On the other hand, for the performer each concert blurs into a series of 'one night stands' and the challenge is to maintain freshness at each performance. Tour books, band biographies, and many classic rock songs document 'life on the road', with its often attendant excesses, and exhilaration at audience enthusiasm coupled with fatigue. The monotony of touring is well captured in *The Big Wheel*, a 'novel' about a band's tour of America, written by Bruce Thomas, the bass player with Elvis Costello and the Attractions:

> I slept through some of the most spectacular scenery in the world, not because I wasn't interested but because I was bloody knackered. This was the band's third time round the world in three years. Round and round and round the world we had gone until it all blurred together.
>
> (Thomas 1991: 20)

Concerts are complex cultural phenomena, involving a mix of music and economics, ritual and pleasure, for both performers and their audience (for a detailed discussion, see Weinstein 1991a: chap. 6; Eliot 1989; Fink 1989). Different genres and performance styles create different forms of concert experience. Clearly a slickly lit and choreographed S Club 7 or Steps stadium pop concert is a different visual and aural experience from a drum and bass DJ's presentation in a club. At the heart of concerts is the sense of community which they engender, albeit a transient one. At their head, on the other hand, lie economics and promotion.

'Rock this town' (Stray Cats): rock concerts

The traditional 'rock' concert illustrates the nature of the concert experience, from the performers' point of view (for audience response see Chapter 11). To begin with, a clear backstage–frontstage divide exists in rock concerts:

> Backstage is the world of the media, governed by functional specialization, calculations of financial interest, and instrumental rationality. Frontstage is the realm of the audience, ruled by a sense of community, adherence to the codes of a valued subculture, and expressive-emotional experience. The stage itself is the

site of the mediation of these two worlds by the performing artist who binds them together with the music.

(Weinstein 1991a: 199–200)

The backstage area is a highly complex work site, with a range of specialised workers. The number of personnel reflects the size of the tour and the economic importance of the performers, but can include technicians in charge of the instruments and equipment (amplifiers, etc.); stage hands, who often double as roadies; people to work the sound and lighting boards; security guards; and the concert tour manager. The successful operation of the backstage area at concerts involves the integration of these workers into a stable and impersonal time schedule, where each person does their job as and when required.

Performers conform to ritual forms of behaviour in rock concerts (behaviour which has interesting parallels with classical music concerts; see Small 1987). The model of the rock band, at least at the level of image, is anti-hierarchical:

an anarchist commune or a group of friends. On stage the players come close to one another, even lean on one another, and circulate to interact with different members of the band. Off stage they live with one another when they are on tour. Poses for the ubiquitous photographs of the group require that the members be physically close to one another.

(Weinstein 1991a: 99)

This public image often conceals the personal animosities present within the group, which are frequently concealed or played down in the common interest of maintaining the group's career (for example, between Townshend and Daltrey in the Who in the 1960s; between Jagger and Richards in the Stones through the 1980s; between the Gallagher brothers in the 1990s). At times such clashes prove too much, especially when exacerbated during the stresses of touring, and members leave and are replaced, or the group breaks up.

There exists a clear hierarchy of rock and pop tours and concerts. For a relatively unknown act, seeking to publicise a new or first release and create an audience, opportunities for live work will be few and venues will be small. The pub and university campus circuit remains essential for such performers. The scale of most 'national' tours is very localised, 'hitting' only a dozen or so centres. For established visiting bands and local acts, which have 'broken' into the charts and the marketplace, there are larger-scale 'national' tours. These still largely play selected main centres, where venues and audiences are large enough to (hopefully) make the exercise economic. At the top end of the scale, are the global tours of the top international acts, which are massive exercises in logistics and marketing – and also hugely profitable.

109

Examples include tours by a reformed Eagles (the 'Hell Freezes Over' tour), and The Rolling Stones' 'Bridges to Babylon Tour'.

During the record industry's affluent years of the early 1970s, tours by major acts were associated with legendary excesses and expenses. Eliot cites one publicity manager: 'I was working with Zeppelin, Bad Company, the Rolling Stones. It was the heyday of rock excess, when everybody was rolling in money and there were limousines to take you to the bathroom' (Eliot 1989: 173). This was unsustainable when the record industry retrenched in the mid-1970s, and companies began to cut back on tour support and set such expenditure off against band's future earnings. Nevertheless, through the 1980s and into the 1990s, live concerts remained the best way to maintain audience interest in a successful act and a key factor in breaking a new one. 'Virtually every rock group eagerly toured behind the release of a new album, with record companies assuming all expenses, paying the acts nothing more than per diems' (Eliot 1989: 169). Tours work to strictly controlled budgets, with the act usually paying for everything out of record sales before the allocation of royalties. If record sales are good, the performer(s) make money. On the other hand, the Grateful Dead, who toured extensively in the 1970s without 'hits', became heavily indebted to their record label, Warner Brothers, and were on the road for five years before generating any income from royalties. Tours are about promotion as much as performance. Artists take part in radio and TV shows and make personal appearances at record stores, to create consumer interest and sales.

I turn now to the discourse surrounding various perceived categories of musician, and the hierarchy of value frequently attached to these.

'It's a long way to the top (if you want to rock and roll)', AC/DC

As most biographies demonstrate, the career trajectory of popular musicians still involves skill and hard work, not to mention a certain amount of luck. The few detailed ethnographic accounts we have, suggest that most bands are 'precariously balanced between fame and obscurity, security and insecurity, commerce and creativity' (Cohen 1991: 4). It is a Darwinian struggle, and there are thousands of unsigned bands:

> Most bands never make it beyond the start-up and early momentum phases of the drive to success. The obstacles prove to be too great to surmount. Disharmonies within the group, lack of financial resources, personal problems, fatigue, waning enthusiasm in the face of frustration, inability to make hard decisions to sacrifice weaker members, and lack of the requisite talents and skills all contribute to failure.
>
> (Weinstein 1991a: 75; see also Bennett 1990)

Even if a band gets signed to a major label, it has only a small chance of breaking even (see Eliot 1989: 193ff., for a fascinating case study of the economics involved in attempting to 'break' a band at the national level; for a more recent example, see Karlen 1994, on Babes in Toyland).

Writing in 1988, Frith identified a traditional model of the rock music career, which he termed 'The Rock', involving a rock career process that was established in the 1960s. Musicians started at the base of this pyramid model, working the local scene through clubs and pubs, building up a following. They then might move up through several tiers, first to regional live work, recording for small, indie labels, and gaining success and recognition at the regional level. Beyond this were a major recording contract, with national exposure and hits, and major touring. At the highest level, there beckoned international hits, tours, and media exposure, and 'superstar' status. Frith regarded this model as underpinned by a dynamic and ideology emphasising 'a Horatio Alger-type account of success being *earned* by hard work, determination, and skills *honed* in practice' (Frith 1988b: 112). Frith was concerned that while there were still careers (e.g. U2) which followed this model, the 1980s corporatisation of the music business and the key role of video in selling new pop groups had seen the rise of an alternative success story,

> The Talent Pool: The dynamic here comes from the centre. There are no longer gatekeepers regulating the flow of stardom, but multi nationals 'fishing' for material, pulling ideas, sounds, styles, performers from the talent pool and dressing them up for world wide consumption.
>
> (ibid.: 113; and see Chapter 9: music video)

As Frith acknowledged, the two models are ideal types. During the 1990s, there was both a reassertion of the significance of the traditional model and a merging of the two career paths. While video exposure remained important, it no longer had the status it enjoyed in the mid-1980s. Genre is a factor here, with clear differences between the success routes for recent dance pop bands such as The Spice Girls and S Club 7, and alternative and grunge performers in the early 1990s. For the latter, as the Seattle scene indicated, success at the local and regional level, or nationally on a smaller scale, with a niche or cult audience, on 'independent' labels and via college radio and the club scene, was necessary to attract the attention of the major record companies.

Creating and working-up new musical material for performance, studio recording and touring, and once again back to creating and recording to keep the momentum going, is the musicians' work cycle. As Weinstein observes: 'Such work may be gratifying because of the opportunities for creativity, sense of mastery, and experiences of social bonding it bestows, but it is still work' (Weinstein 1991a: 61). Furthermore, all of these activities involve not just musical skills. While the original basis of most groups is in peer friendships, this will change once things get 'more serious', with problems created by the differing levels of ability and commitment of group members (commitment to a practice schedule), and the need for group cohesion and leadership. Then there are the well-documented physical and emotional strains of 'the rock lifestyle'.

One reason, and probably the dominant one, behind the willingness of so many rock musicians to enter the Darwinian struggle for commercial success, is the ultimate possibility of stardom, with its allure of a lifestyle of glamour and affluence. This is not to ignore the appeal of gaining the approval of fans and critics, but it is clear that the majority of performers aspire to that *and* 'the money'. As Kirschner (1998: 252) observes, 'Success should be seen as a central trope in popular music, informing and motivating the entire domain of rock culture' and creating what he terms the 'continuum of success'. Talent aside, success is governed by access to the differing resources and opportunities in the process of making music. Accordingly, our interest now moves to the 'pecking order' of popular music.

THE SUCCESS CONTINUUM

There exists a status hierarchy among performers, a hierarchy endorsed by critics and fans, as well as by musicians themselves. This hierarchy ranges from those starting out, largely reliant on 'covers', to session musicians, to performers who attempt, with varying levels of critical and commercial success, to make a living from music. This last group has its own differentiations, with notions of 'journeymen' players, and hierarchies of 'artists' and stars, often likened to some sort of sports league table: a minor or major league band; first and second division performers; stars and 'megastars'. The bases for such evaluations remain tantalisingly vague, and the status of particular performers frequently varies among critics and over time. Taste and subjectivity necessarily feature, as much as any fully elaborated artistic and musical criteria.

At the base of this hierarchy are cover bands, which are generally accorded little critical artistic weight. The common view is that reliance on someone else's material concedes that you have nothing of your own to say. However, bands starting out rely on cover versions for a large part of their repertoire out of necessity, while even 'original' performers will play a few covers. The distinction remains important, since upward career mobility is directly tied to notions of originality (Kirshner 1998: 265). Learning such songs is part of the apprenticeship process in acquiring rock musicianship:

> song copying allows the novice to become a competent member of a musical tradition. This applies to both musicians and audiences. An example is the birth

of rock in Britain through copies of American rhythm and blues hits such as the Stones' version of Arthur Alexander's 'You Better Move On' (1964).

(Hatch and Millward 1987: 3–4)

Cover songs are literally music to the ears of the managers of smaller venues like clubs and pubs, as they are tapping into a proven product that the audience can identify with. Covers have featured strongly in the charts throughout the late 1980s and into the 1990s. There is a fresh generation of listeners and a new market for the recycled song, as reissues demonstrate – for example, boosted by the film *Ghost*, the 1990 success of the Righteous Brothers' 'You've Lost that Lovin' Feelin' ', which had originally topped the charts in 1965 (indeed, it had made the UK top ten again when first reissued in 1969). Even relatively straightforward carbon copies of songs can be successful, as with Wet Wet Wet's 1990s cover of the Troggs 1967 top ten hit, 'Love Is All Around'. For a new generation of record-buyers, a 'good' song is a good song, regardless of any historical memory. Some covers, such as the Chimes' 1990 version of the U2 song 'I Still Haven't Found What I'm Looking For', reinterpret the original song in a fresh and distinctive way.

The extreme example of cover bands are those performers who not only directly model themselves on established bands, but actually copy them, presenting themselves as simulacra of the originals. Such tribute bands, as the industry prefers to call them, rate few plaudits artistically, but they have become big business, with several enjoying lengthy and successful careers. Australian band Bjorn Again, primarily performing the music of Swedish band Abba, have played over 1500 shows in some forty countries worldwide, and undertook a highly successful tenth anniversary world tour in 1999. Regionally based tribute bands may become a focus for their local community, as with the Pink Floyd tribute band the Benwell Floyd, who regularly perform in the North East England pub and club circuit. Bennett shows how the appeal of the Benwell Floyd rests on a combination of their musical expertise, and the overlapping kinship and friendship networks shared by the band and its audience, which contribute to the construction of local identities (Bennett 2000: chap. 7).

During the 1990s, there were more than 150 tribute bands on the nostalgia circuit in Australia and New Zealand alone, imitating almost everyone from defunct groups, such as CCR, to bands which are still performing, like Midnight Oil. On the positive side, the imitators are bringing the music to a new audience of under twenty-fives, a generation who never saw the original performers, encouraging them to seek out the earlier material. Other views are less complimentary, pointing to the difficulties in policing copyright and the fact that the original artists are frequently having to share audiences with their imitators. In 1992, while ex-Cold Chisel guitarist Ian Moss was performing to a handful of people in a Sydney suburban hotel, Swing Shift, a Cold

Chisel clone featuring Moss' music, played to a crowd of a thousand at a nearby venue. The main objection made to the nostalgia and cover bands, however, is that they do not create new music. Ironically, the same charge has not been levelled at the industry's tendency through the 1990s to produce a steady stream of 'tribute' albums, in which various artists pay homage by covering the work of artists as varied as The Clash, Gram Parsons, and Jimi Hendrix.

Next up the pecking order are the session musicians. Generally anonymous, they function as the pieceworkers of the music industry. Some attain critical recognition for their contributions: reggae performers Sly Dunbar and Robbie Shakespeare established themselves as 'the' rhythm section, and 'house' or label bands such as Booker T and the MGs received considerable credit for their creative input. The efforts of a few session musicians attain near legendary status, as with Jeff Beck and Jimmy Page's guitar solos on a variety of records in the 1960s, but usually only when they later become successful in their own right, creating interest in this aspect of their back catalogue.

Beyond the bands at the base of Frith's performance pyramid of 'The Rock', are those who are working at the middling levels of the industry. These performers are sometimes regarded as 'journeymen': they may enjoy a fair measure of commercial success, but they are not seen as particularly innovative, even though they may have a distinctive style and themes. But this label is unnecessarily pejorative, resting as it does on contestable (in part because they are rarely fully articulated) aesthetic distinctions. It makes more sense to talk of 'mid-level' status performers, who enjoy a mix of commercial and critical recognition. These are performers whose names are recognisable to the majority of popular music fans, even when they may not necessarily buy their records or attend their performances. Mid-level rock success is illustrated by the career of performers such as Tom Petty and the Heartbreakers, and the critical response to their work (see Shuker 1994).

Beyond this are performers who are considered stars and auteurs. In Chapter 7 I turn to examples of these, to further consider the process of making music, and the associated concepts of 'musician' and musical creativity.

'So you want to be a rock 'n' roll star?'

Stars and auteurs

The concept of the auteur (broadly, author or creator) stands at the pinnacle of a pantheon of performers and their work, a hierarchical approach used by fans, critics, and musicians to organise their view of the historical development of popular music and the contemporary status of its performers. Auteurs enjoy respect for their professional performance, especially their ability to transcend the traditional aesthetic forms of the genres they work within. Stars go beyond this and indeed may not be stars primarily on the strength of their music, also enjoying wider public interest and public fascination with their personas and personal lives.

This chapter examines the nature and application of the concepts of auteur and star in popular music. I then provide capsule biographies of a number of popular music figures who provide a range of examples of the auteur/star: record producer Phil Spector; the iconoclastic composer and musician, Frank Zappa; Bruce Springsteen, the biggest white rock star since Elvis; Madonna, whose ability to reinvent herself has kept her life and music hugely popular for twenty years; Shania Twain, who has taken her country music into the mainstream; British dance pop phenomenon of the late 1990s, the Spice Girls; and the multiple identities of Norman Cook (Fat Boy Slim).

My intention is twofold: first, to provide an overview of their careers, and some indication of the nature and extent of their contribution to popular music; and, second, to offer a critical appraisal of this contribution and their status as auteurs. In this context, these examples can only be capsule summaries, and the interested reader is referred to the extensive literature available on figures such as Madonna and Springsteen.

AUTEURS, STARS, AND MUSIC HISTORY

There are popular music performers who can be considered both stars and auteurs, combining a high level of creativity and innovation in their work with broader media interest and public visibility (e.g. Madonna, the Beatles). Both auteurs and stars sell records, though it is possible to attain auteur status without necessarily enjoying high levels of commercial success (e.g. Frank Zappa, Elvis Costello, Richard Thompson). Longevity can also lead to greater artistic recognition, as with Madonna.

Stars are probably the most fascinating aspect of popular culture, yet also the most problematic. The enormous fascination with stars' personal lives suggests a phenomenon that cannot simply be explained in terms of political economy, although audience identification with particular stars is a significant marketing device. Film director Geoff Murphy, talking of his experience in working with Mick Jagger on the movie *Freejack* (1992), and the attention Jagger drew wherever they went in public, termed the singer 'a walking icon'. British singer Robbie Williams' brief promotional visit to New Zealand in August 2000 provoked a media frenzy, with a succession of front page stories, encapsulated by one journalist: 'He arrived, dropped his trousers on telly, had sex with someone from Hamilton, sang half a dozen songs, got a new tattoo and left' (Russell Baillie, *Weekend Herald*, 2–3 September 2000: D4).

The important question is not so much 'what is a star?' but 'how do stars function – within the music industry, within textual narratives, and, in particular, at the level of individual fantasy and desire?' What needs to be explained is the nature of emotional investment in pleasurable images. While there is a large body of theoretically oriented work on film stars, the study of stardom in popular music is largely limited to personal biographies of widely varying analytical value (notable exceptions are Straw's discussion of authorship, Straw 1999; and Marshall 1997: chap. 6, on celebrity in popular music. There are also some useful examinations of desire and identification in music fandom, in relation to stars; see Chapter 11).

The various histories of popular music are in large part situated around profiles of key performers, as too are more analytical works. This fairly standard approach serves an ideological function: by placing the emphasis on the individual artist – and their creative genius – it raises the status of particular genres (e.g. 'rock') and styles (e.g. the singer-songwriter) as cultural forms to that of the other 'arts'. Yet also widely recognised are the constraints placed on performers by the industry – the old art versus commerce mythology, which obscures the happy amalgam of the two. Individual biographies tell us a great deal about the dynamics of the relationship between performers, their record companies and other aspects of the music industry (technology), and their fans; and they can also be extremely informative about the nature of the creative process. This is particularly so of stars, and of musicians who are considered auteurs.

John Cawelti raised the possibility of applying auteur criticism, initially developed in the 1950s as a radical approach to film, to other forms of popular culture:

> In popular music, for example, one can see the differences between pop groups which simply perform without creating that personal statement which marks the auteur, and highly creative groups like the Beatles who make of their performance a complex work of art.
>
> (Cawelti 1971: 267)

Similarly, American critic Jon Landau argued that 'the criterion of art in rock is the capacity of the musician to create a personal, almost private, universe and to express it fully' (cited in Frith 1983: 53). This application of auteur theory to popular music elevated genres such as 1960s rock to the status of art. This involves distinguishing it from popular culture, with its traditional connotations of manipulated consumer taste and escapist entertainment, and instead relating rock music to notions of individual sensibility and enrichment. Such an approach is central to the work of musicologists (for example, Mellers 1974, on the Beatles). In this view, musical auteurs are producers of art, extending the cultural form and, in the process, challenging their listeners.

This 'some popular music can be considered art' view must be treated with caution, as it places aesthetic distinctions at the heart of the determination of cultural meaning. These are not to be rejected entirely, but such an emphasis on 'discrimination' needs to be balanced against considerations of the social production of meaning and the political economy of the cultural industries.

Frith suggests that by the early 1970s:

> self-consciousness became the measure of a record's artistic status; frankness, musical wit, the use of irony and paradox were musicians' artistic insignia – it was such self-commentary that revealed the auteur within the machine. The skilled listener was the one who could recognise the artist despite the commercial trappings.
>
> (Frith 1983: 53)

But as Frith himself points out, this once again too sharply distinguishes between art and commerce in popular music. Since all music texts are social products, musicians are under constant pressure to provide their audience with more of the music which attracted that same audience in the first place. This explains why shifts in musical direction often lose established audiences while, hopefully for the performer, creating new adherents. This, for Frith, is to emphasise the contradiction between being an 'artist' and being responsible to one's market (Frith 1983: 53–4). The other facet of this argument is to claim particular artists as auteurs despite their location within a profit-driven commercial industry. This is also to reprise the art versus commerce debate, leading us to pantheons of musical and cultural value which are problematic, since all musical texts 'arrive on the turntable as the result of the same commercial processes' (ibid.). Furthermore, as in any area of 'creative' endeavour, there is a constant process of reworking the common stock of the musical tradition, as continuity is self-consciously combined with change (Hatch and Millward 1987: intro.).

The auteur approach in cinema studies attempts to tease out the relationships among, and common elements evident in, a group of films, by locating the dominant personality, usually the director, in and across individual films. The status of auteur theory in cinema studies has been the subject of considerable debate (see Cook 1989), but provides a useful starting point to consider its value in relation to popular music. Indeed, at first sight, auteur theory would seem to be more applicable to popular music than film. While they are working within an industrial system, individual performers are, at least primarily, responsible for their recorded product. Further, as I have already suggested, a clear evaluative hierarchy of performers is held in the industry and among both musicians and fans. But how are we to identify the popular music auteur and confer such status? Critics and fans generally refer here to several interlocking criteria: the ability of the auteur to break new ground, innovating, crossing or blurring genre boundaries; the ability to perform their own 'original' material, especially by writing their own songs; the exercising of a fair measure of control over various facets of the production process; and the holding of some sense of personal overarching vision of the music and its relation to the canon. Auteurs are usually considered to maintain their high profile over a period of time. Those most frequently accorded major status – Dylan, the Beatles, James Brown, and U2, for example – have all enjoyed lengthy careers. While their status may have diminished, with most recent work largely being found wanting when placed against their earlier output (Dylan, Elvis, the Rolling Stones), such figures retain auteur status on the basis of their historical contribution, as do auteur figures whose careers were cut short, such as Buddy Holly, Jimi Hendrix, Janis Joplin, and Kurt Cobain.

In sum, such criteria combine to accord the auteur figure an iconic, near-mythic status in popular music. Interestingly, these criteria are similar to those utilised in the analysis of film auteurs. What needs to be added to the equation, however, is the crucial manner in which the concerns, preoccupations, and iconography of auteurs (and stars) resonate with the lives of those who avidly consume their work and follow their lives. While leading film directors may be well known, it is rare for them to attract the sort of attention from fans that is accorded to 'rock stars', including stalking and harassment.

There exists among both critics and consumers of rock 'n' roll and its later genre variations, a roll call of performers accorded the status of auteur. These include Elvis, primarily for fusing gospel, country and R&B at the birth of rock 'n' roll, the Beatles, the Rolling Stones, Bob Dylan, James Brown, Jimi Hendrix, David Bowie, and, more recently, REM, Michael Jackson, and Bruce Springsteen. The gender balance of this group (the absence of women performers) reflects the masculinist orientation of the music industry (see Chapter 12). These auteurs have all achieved commercial as well as critical recognition. There are also performers whose work has hardly dominated the sales charts, but who are regarded as having a distinctive style and *oeuvre* which has taken the music in new and innovative directions. This group includes Randy Newman, Tom Waites, Frank Zappa, and bands who have attempted to cross or redefine genre boundaries, such as Radiohead, The Orb, and My Bloody Valentine.

At this point of course, not only are my personal judgements (prejudices?) being revealed, but we are beginning to create a hierarchy within the concept of 'auteur', leading us into arguments as to the relative contributions of this range of performers, and the nature of creativity (see Chapter 6). Such judgements are in part social constructs: an individual is creative if the society of their time considers their work to be such; the value accorded particular auteurs can and does change over time. In the first edition of this book, I included Prince among my case studies of 'rock auteurs', on the strength of his innovative work during the 1980s and early 1990s. 'The Artist' was important as a black musician who achieved crossover success (i.e. sold well to both blacks and whites in the US), in the process 'breaking' MTV's neglect of black artists. His videos and films include several highly innovative efforts, most notably *Purple Rain*. As a performer, Prince pushed the boundaries of acceptability in the themes in his work, while providing one of the most fascinating and impressive amalgams of musical genres: a mix of pop, rock, funk, gospel, hip-hop, psychedelia, and disco. Since then, Prince has continued to be musically highly productive, but the results have been more mixed. In recent years, his critical stature has declined, and his music has been relatively neglected, with more attention paid to the adoption of a symbol as his 'name', his dispute with his record company, and his marriage and fatherhood. While his status as an auteur figure remains assured, he has been dropped here, as has Pete Townshend, to make way for more contemporary examples of authorship in popular music.

The above examples of auteurs are all musicians. But as suggested earlier (in Chapter 6), there is a strong case for according auteur status to other key figures involved in creating the music in its various forms: the songwriter(s), the producer, and music video directors (on the last, see Chapter 10). Indeed, in some cases, these figures, rather than the musicians, may even provide the dominant input. It can also be argued that, as with contemporary film-making, the creative process in rock is a 'team game' with various contributions melding together, even if a particular musician is providing the overall vision. Despite this multiple authorship, as Straw acutely observes, 'typically we evaluate a musical recording or concert as the output of a single individual or group' (1999: 200).

Phil Spector: behind the wall of sound

Spector started by writing songs, and achieved initial success with 'To Know Him Is To Love Him', sung by the Teddy Bears, a group he created. In 1960 Atlantic Records permitted him, at the age of nineteen, to produce some sessions. He created hits for Ray Peterson and Curtis Lee, wrote 'Spanish Harlem' for Ben E. King, and then founded his own label, Philles. Three years of whirlwind success followed, during which he produced a series of songs which became teen anthems: 'Then He Kissed Me', 'Be My Baby', 'You've Lost That Lovin' Feelin' ', 'Da Doo Ron Ron', and 'He's A Rebel'. Though these featured some great female vocalists, the performers were virtually interchangeable; the star was Spector. As a producer he celebrated the teen idol phenomenon of the 1960s while transcending it, using quality songs, first class arrangements, and leading session musicians. The noise he created, the so-called 'Spector sound', was overwhelming in its intensity.

> Through multitracking, he made his rhythm sections seem like armies, and turned the beat into a murderous mass cannonade. No question; his records were the loudest, fiercest, most magnificent explosions that rock had yet produced, or dreamed of. And Spector stood in the center, swamped by this mayhem, twiddling the knobs, controlling everything.
>
> (Cohn 1992: 153)

A millionaire at 21, Spector was hailed by the industry as a genius, but the impetus slackened in the mid-1960s. In 1966 Spector made his finest record, 'River Deep, Mountain High' with Ike and Tina Turner. When it failed commercially, he announced his retirement. A subsequent return from several years of self-imposed exile saw a few successes. He cut 'Imagine' with John Lennon and 'My Sweet Lord' with George Harrison and produced albums for both the former Beatles. But the dizzy earlier heights were not to be scaled again, in part because he no longer had total control, but was working as a hired hand. His presence alone was now insufficient to virtually guarantee a record's success. Writing his profile in 1979, Cohn painted a picture of a reclusive figure whose myth had swamped his present reality.

Spector's success can be attributed to a combination of two factors. First, he established the concept of business independence, seeking to control every aspect of his own enterprise: production, publicity, and distribution. Second, Spector was one of the first self-conscious rock artists, 'the first to rationalize, the first to comprehend precisely what he was up to. With him, there was immediately a totally new level of sophistication, complexity, musical range' (Cohn 1992: 154). Paradoxically, Spector managed to raid every musical source he could and still be completely original; to be strictly commercial while concerned with the records as art. He combined the two great rock 'n' roll romances – rebellion and teen dream – into one.

Spector's achievement remains impressive, and the positive response to the 1991 reprise of his work, the CD set *Back To Mono (1950–1969)*, was indicative of the continued interest in his work. Spector remastered sixty of his singles (plus his attempt to create an album as a total entity, *Christmas Gift to You*), retaining their original mono sound. Spector's claim to auteur status rests on a combination of initial musical innovation and the aura of mystery created by his 'star' lifestyle and subsequent reclusiveness. In this respect, he has much in common with those musicians considered here as auteurs.

Frank Zappa: 'We're Only In It For the Money'

Auteur status is not always dependent on chart success; indeed, the absence of 'significant market volume' is sometimes almost a necessary corollary of cult status and critical recognition. Frank Zappa is an example of such a cult figure. Zappa was a rock iconoclast whose career comprised over fifty albums (including many double and triple sets), three feature films, three feature length videos, and numerous side projects, including record labels and a merchandising operation. Zappa self-consciously played with a variety of musical traditions, mutating them into something unique, often with 'weird' and not easily accessible results. Although best known for his guitar playing, he was proficient on a range of instruments.

In the mid-1960s, with his group the Mothers of Invention, Zappa developed a musical style that was musically wildly eclectic, and thematically weighted to political debate and satire. His subsequent work included many milestones in rock. *Freak Out* in 1966 was the first rock double album, one of the first concept LPs, and an acknowledged influence on the Beatles' *Sergeant Pepper's Lonely Hearts Club Band*. *Freak Out* also introduced Zappa's brand of political parody and social commentary, with songs like 'Who Are the Brain Police?' The album reached *BillBoard*'s Top 200 album chart, and established Zappa and the Mothers as 'underground' figures. *Absolutely Free* (1967) is a contender for the first rock opera, and carried on Zappa's lampooning of American hypocrisy and conservatism: 'Plastic People' and 'America Drinks and Goes Home'. In the same year, the album *We're Only In It For The Money* satirised psychedelia and the hippy era, and sent up the Beatles' *Sergeant Pepper*.

In subsequent work, on solo albums and with the Mothers of Invention, Zappa continued to explore the same themes. He mixed satire and send-ups with 'serious' political commentary and dazzling musicianship, while milling a miscellany of musical genres and utilising the talents of well-known musicians, including violinist and composer Jean Luc Ponty, Little Feat's Lowell George, drummer Aynsley Dunbar, vocalists Mark Volman and Howard Kaplan (both ex-Turtles, later Flo and Eddie), and guitar virtuoso Steve Vai. The breadth of this group of performers is indicative of Zappa's range of musical interests. He formed his own labels, on which he recorded and promoted Alice Cooper (whose debut LP is on Straight), and Captain Beefheart, whose *Trout Mask Replica* Zappa also produced. Zappa's score for rock group and orchestra, *200 Motels*, was launched in 1970, while the London Symphony Orchestra recorded two albums of Zappa's work in 1983.

The keystones of Zappa's work were his control over this variety of projects, his composing skills, and his mastery of production technology. In his autobiography, Zappa recounts the problems the Mothers of Invention had with their record company, MGM, and industry sharp practices such as pressing plant overruns: 'We went through a major legal struggle with MGM over royalties on those first LPs. It took about eight years to resolve'. There were also problems caused by MGM censoring the Mothers' lyrics without their knowledge or consent. By 1984, Zappa had sued two industry giants, CBS and Warners, and had learned a lot more about 'creative accounting practices' (Zappa 1990: 83). Such experiences led Zappa to emphasise retaining control over all facets of his work. Indeed, Zappa's degree of control over the musicians in his bands, and the extent of his involvement in particular projects, became legendary.

Zappa was the most prominent rock musician to speak out against moves in the United States to censor rock. He argued for the basic right of free speech under the Constitution, seeing the PMRC (Parents' Music Resource Center) proposals for record ratings as 'ill-conceived nonsense' based on totally false notions of the effects of popular music (Zappa 1990; and see Chapter 12). Zappa, as always, injected a sense of humour into a serious message: his subsequent 1986 Grammy award-winning *Jazz From Hell* carried a sticker warning against offensive lyrics; the album is purely instrumental!

Though seen primarily as a cult figure, receiving critical acclaim from music critics and his fellow musicians, Zappa also achieved some commercial success: his 1974 solo album *Apostrophe (')* was certified gold in the US, making number 10 in the *Billboard* chart, while the single from it, 'Don't Eat the Yellow Snow', was Zappa's first in *Billboard*'s Hot 100 (even if only reaching number 86). His classical compositions, particularly *The Perfect Stranger and Other Works*, and his electronic recordings sold well. Interest in his work remains steady, even after his death in December 1993, as indicated by the current availability of the bulk of his albums on CD and the success of the compilation *Strictly Commercial* (1995). But commercialism is not what Zappa was primarily about. At times, he almost deliberately eschewed success by opting for 'bad taste' and its attendant lack of airplay. Rather he fulfilled the criteria of the genuinely creative artist – conceding the ultimate subjectivity and social construction of 'creativity' – and was concerned with exploring and extending the dimensions of the 'rock' form. Accordingly, although his output was variable in quality, Zappa's talent and auteur status in popular music is widely recognised.

Bruce Springsteen: The Boss

Bruce Springsteen is an example of a performer who enjoys both star and auteur status. Widely regarded as an outstanding songwriter, Springsteen is also a distinctive singer and a more than competent guitarist, and a respected band leader. Initially a cult figure, by 1985 'The Boss', as he became known to his fans, was the world's most successful white rock star since Elvis. Underpinning Springsteen's standing was his authenticity:

> if you want an artist whose work, both on record and onstage, compels a compassionate understanding of people's lives – their emotions and imaginings, their jobs and their play – you have nowhere to go in the realm of rock & roll but to Bruce Springsteen.
>
> (DeCurtis 1992: 619)

Springsteen worked in a number of local bands in the Asbury Park, New Jersey, area from the late 1960s, forming the E Street Band in 1972. The group's spirited live performances brought Springsteen to the attention of John Hammond, who signed him to CBS. *Greetings From Asbury Park, NJ* (1973) was a 'brash, invigorating debut' (Clarke 1990: 1108) but was almost swamped by the efforts of the media to make him the new Bob Dylan. Along with *The Wild, the Innocent and The E Street Shuffle* (1974), *Greetings* mapped out the themes of cultural continuity and community on which much of Springsteen's songwriting career was to be built. Critic Jon Landau saw Springsteen perform in 1974 and proclaimed him 'the future of rock 'n' roll', a tag which was to initially prove something of a millstone. The album *Born To Run* (1975) was hailed as a classic, and has retained its place as one of the key releases of the decade. The album features several powerful rock songs ('Thunder Road', 'Jungleland', 'Born to Run') which dealt with the lives of 'little people' in small-town America, reflecting Springsteen's New Jersey upbringing, and 'mining a vein of searing romanticism with the unshakeable integrity that quickly became his hallmark' (Sinclair 1992: 335). Springsteen appeared on the covers of *Time* and *Newsweek* in the same week, a case of media overkill given his still only cult following, and his first two albums finally charted.

However, management problems meant he did not record for three years, and instead he toured extensively. One consequence of this was a copious number of bootleg releases, further encouraging a cult interest in the singer's work. During this period, Springsteen's legendary stage shows, three to four-plus hour marathon concerts, consolidated his reputation. In these, he covered rock 'n' roll classics as well as his own songs. *Darkness On The Edge Of Town* (1978) was a starker, more sombre album, indicative of Springsteen's court struggles with former manager Mike Appel, and hinting at a new political sensibility in his work ('Factory'). The two-disc *The River* (1980) was Springsteen's first number one album, with a single from it, 'Hungry Heart', his first Top 10 hit. *The River* displayed Springsteen's narrative powers at their best, mixing up-tempo rockers with personal ballad-like statements which offered further glimpses of the everyday concerns and dreams of ordinary people, combined with a growing dose of social realism. A world tour during 1980–81 consolidated Springsteen's growing global commercial and artistic status.

Nebraska (1982) was a surprising departure: a solo acoustic LP made at home on a cassette deck, showing the singer's preparedness to take commercial risks rather than mining the familiar, profitable vein. A 'pensive consideration of the state of the nation – obliquely, not overtly political' (Clarke 1990: 1109), it still reached number 3 and charted for twenty-nine weeks. This deviation from what fans and critics had come to expect was indicative of Springsteen's determination to do what he wanted, and follow his musical inclinations. *Born in the USA* (1984) was a return to the earlier, more commercial approach. The ambiguous clenched-fist hyperbole of the title track, and the American flag imagery on the cover, fuelled controversy (see Chapter 8), and also fuelled market interest: the album was number 1 in the US for seven weeks, and included four hit singles (with 'Dancing In the Dark' reaching Number 2). After being one of the most bootlegged of artists, in 1986 Springsteen released his own live set, a five-disc retrospective *Bruce Springsteen and The E Street Band: Live, 1975–1985*. It entered the album charts at number 1 on the day of its release, something unprecedented for a multi-set. Ultimately about survival at all levels, and reflecting tensions in his own relationships, *Tunnel of Love* (1987) moved away from the stadium-filled hard rock sound of *Born in the USA* back once more to the concerns of ordinary lives.

Springsteen deals heavily in nostalgia and myth. A masterful songwriter, his work paints lyrical images of America. The characters on the early albums are socially marginalised – drifters, hustlers, and outlaws. His focus then moved to factory workers and mainstream working-class figures, but the spirit of the songs remained the same. Springsteen draws strongly on his own working-class background for songs like the exemplary 'Born To Run', and his music thus runs the gamut from nostalgia and melancholy to headlong idealism. In a 1992 *Rolling Stone* interview, on the eve of a summer tour of the United States, Springsteen observed:

All I try to do is to write music that feels meaningful to me, that has commitment and passion behind it. And I guess I feel that if what I'm writing about is real, and if there's emotion, then hey, there'll be somebody who wants to hear it.

(James Henke, *Rolling Stone*, October 1992: 52)

It was to be Springsteen's last album for five years, a period during which he remarried, became a father, and was prominent in supporting political causes, most notably by headlining the 1988 Amnesty International Human Rights Tour. He re-emerged with a double release in 1992 (*Human Touch* and *Lucky*, in which the singer 'traced an emotional movement from questioning and self-doubt to commitment and domestic fulfilment' (DeCurtis 1992: 165). Their relative lack of commercial success, however, raised questions about Springsteen's status and musical relevance in the 1990s, and his continued creativity. Such question marks were underlined by the release of an MTV *Unplugged* album in 1993 and a *Greatest Hits* album in 1995, suggesting the singer was out of fresh ideas.

Success is clearly a relative term in Springsteen's case. While not reaching the dizzy commercial heights achieved during the 1980s, his mid- and late 1990s recordings and tours have continued to sell well, chart highly, and be critically well received: the sobering *The Ghost of Tom Joad* (1995), which he supported with an acoustic tour; *Tracks* (1998) a four CD, sixty-six track history of his twenty-five year recording career, which showed his continuing development as a songwriter (available in scaled down form as *18 Tracks*). His 2000 tour, reuniting him with the E Street Band, was greeted by fans with all the fervour of a religious revival.

Springsteen has consciously used his position as performer to support causes he believes in. In his 1980s tours he promoted food banks and community groups, as well as personally donating. He also supported the Vietnam Veterans of America, played at the 1979 No Nukes concert, and contributed to the Amnesty International tour of 1988. While Springsteen helped to rejuvenate American populism, he firmly rejected President Reagan's attempts to harness the singer's popularity to his 1984 re-election campaign. During the 1990s, he continued to actively support a variety of broadly humanitarian and politically left causes.

'The Boss' has maintained a position of superstar with populist appeal, whose blue-collar bravado tempered with a broadly humanitarian sincerity appears to strike a universal chord. His success is linked to his vision and ideals, and his dedication to his audience and his music: 'You know what rock 'n' roll is?' asked Springsteen in 1978, 'It's me and my band going out to the audience tonight and growing older with that audience' (Sinclair 1992: 333). Over twenty years later, now aged fifty, Springsteen was still presenting an energetic three-hour show to sold out stadiums, seeking to 'reconnect with the audience that has sustained me since I was very young' (*Q*, May 1999: 66; interview). His songs continue to relate to people's lives, their work stresses, financial hassles, and emotional difficulties. As Pratt observes,

Springsteen has continued to address the alienation and critical distance from American society expressed by Bob Dylan, but has done so 'operating *within* the assumptions of the dominant, male-defined culture – hard work, patriotism, cars, girls, marriage, and the promise of the American dream. He proposes no war, no drugs to alter consciousness – just life in the USA for ordinary people' (Pratt 1990:188).

Madonna: material girl

The continued success of Madonna provides a fascinating case study of the nature of star appeal in popular music. By the end of the 1980s Madonna was a superstar, one of the best-known women in the world and certainly one of the most discussed and analysed figures in popular culture. By then there was virtually a 'Madonna industry', with a plethora of studies of widely varying quality; and both popular and academic interest in her remained high through the 1990s. (For insightful analyses see Schwichtenberg 1993; and Kellner 1995: chap. 8; a solid 'popular' account of Madonna's early career is Bego 1992). The multimedia contract she signed with Time Warner in 1992, said to be worth US$60 million, was indicative of her cultural impact.

The discourse surrounding Madonna provides a range of contradictory readings and evaluations. Madonna is a star whom many critics and fans love to hate, a performer who 'used a licentious image and a little-girl voice to keep at the pinnacle of pop for the better part of the eighties' (Shapiro 1991:156), and whose stage routine was described by a Vatican official as 'one of the most satanic shows in the history of humanity'. To many, her success rests on artifice and media manipulation, but 'manufactured sensation is usually short-lived, and contrived art is almost always conservative, while Madonna's career has been neither' (Considine 1992: 662). As Kellner concludes: 'Madonna pushes the most sensitive buttons of sexuality, gender, race, and class, offering challenging and provocative images and cultural artifacts, as well as ones that reinforce dominant conventions. The Madonna construct *is* a set of contradictions' (Kellner 1995: 263).

The bare facts of the career of this American 'superstar' Madonna Louise Ciccone, better known as simply Madonna, are straightforward enough. She trained briefly as a dancer at the University of Michigan, and became interested in music through the influence of drummer boyfriend Steve Bray. She moved to New York City, then briefly to Paris, where she was a backup singer for French disco singer Patrick Hernandez. Returning to NYC, Madonna performed with a series of new wave bands, graduating from drummer in the Breakfast Club to singer in Emmy; the latter group taking her name when they were joined by Bray. A demo tape got her a contract with Shire, and her first single 'Everybody' was produced and promoted by boyfriend DJ Mark Kamins. Her first album *Madonna 83* spawned several hit singles, including

'Holiday' which made the Top 20 in both the US and the UK. Most of the album tracks were produced by ex-Miles Davis sideman Reggie Lucas, though 'Holiday' itself was produced by a new boyfriend, John 'Jellybean' Benitez. Madonna's commercial breakthrough came with the LP, *Like a Virgin*, produced by Nile Rogers. Both single and album were number 1 hits in the US. The title track was a Number 3 UK single, with the album going to number 1 in the UK a year after its initial release, as Madonna's publicity gained momentum.

Madonna produced a series of music videos projecting a distinct image for a national audience, and emerged as one of the first MTV superstars (see O'Brien, L. 1995).

Film work (especially in *Desperately Seeking Susan*, a surprise success in 1985) assisted her career, promoting songs like 'Into the Groove', even if praise centred on her acting rather than her singing. In 1984 *Rolling Stone* magazine featured her in a glossy eight-page bathing suit spread, in which Madonna posed as her idol Marilyn Monroe. In Britain, a high-powered publicity campaign and increasing general interest in her saw Madonna appear on the front covers of publications as different as the men's magazine *Penthouse* and the elitist society monthly *Tatler*. Her brief marriage to actor Sean Penn turned into a media event, as did a series of subsequent relationships, including one with Warren Beattie when they worked together on the film *Dick Tracy* (1991).

By mid-1985 sales of her first two albums had topped 11 million worldwide. Subsequent recordings maintained and went way beyond even this level of success. In 1987 her personal fortune was estimated at over US$175 million. Her 1987 'Who's That Girl' world tour saw Madonna perform to 1.35 million fans in Japan, the United States and Europe; while her later 'Blonde Ambition' tour was an even bigger success. Her success owed a great deal to her performance style, through both concerts and video, and her ability to keep herself in the public eye. Controversy over videos such as 'Open Your Heart' (1987) and 'Justify My Love' (1990) merely increased media and fan interest. Indeed, Madonna turned a potentially hurtful MTV ban of the 'Justify' video into a media coup, as her appearance on America's serious nightly TV news-feature programme *Nightline* to discuss the ban, pulled in the show's biggest ever audience. Throughout her career, Madonna has retained a high degree of creative control over her work. She co-writes the majority of her songs, and has co-produced all her albums since *True Blue* in 1986. In October 1990 the respected *Forbes* financial magazine headlined her as 'America's Smartest Businesswoman'.

Somewhat cynically, it has been observed that, particularly earlier in her career, Madonna managed to choose the 'right' boyfriends at the right time to assist her efforts. Evaluations of Madonna's early success rarely gave much credit to her music, which was described as a form of disco/dance, characterised by a voice like that of 'Minnie Mouse on helium' (Clarke 1990: 754). This is an overstatement when applied to Madonna's meticulously crafted, if ultimately insubstantial, pop, but music critics largely concurred that 'it is still difficult to judge how much of her music is the product of real feelings and how much of it is a coolly calculated exercise in line with the latest marketing strategies' (Sinclair 1992: 200). In similar vein, Shapiro (1991: 156) saw Madonna's real achievement as her marketing prescience, 'her ability to understand the currency of combining the visual, the audio, and the slightly outrageous to rise to the top of the mediocre contemporary pop music scene'. These views, of course, were judging Madonna's work in terms of the problematic traditional rock criterion of 'authenticity'.

The Madonna phenomenon of the 1980s was underpinned by her charismatic personality and captivating stage presence, her sexuality appealed to young males, while her predominantly girl fans identified with her strong character and emphasis on being her 'own person', in control of her sexuality and her career. At the same time, 'Madonna's carnivalesque transgressions of gender and sexuality, the source of much pleasure for her fans, are extremely disturbing to her haters, and often this hate is focused on the body and expressed in a discourse about the body' (Schulze et al. 1993: 24; see also Fiske 1989). These teenage girl fans, Madonna 'wannabes', with peroxide hair, 1950s sunglasses, frilly pink dresses and clutching Madonna posters, were prominent among the 77,000 strong crowd which attended the singer's 1987 concert at London's Wembley stadium. In dressing like her, they took on the success and glamour Madonna symbolised, while identifying with her projected values of rebellion against parental authority, her combination of sexual freedom with personal responsibility – she preaches safe sex.

The musical dimensions of her work aside, Madonna has shown the ability to constantly reinvent her persona, moving through several distinct images, a process which is a necessary part of ensuring her enduring star status. Her public image has shifted from the early 'boy toy' vamp to screen siren, from raunchy charity shop dresser in the 1980s to the Marilyn Monroe glamorous persona of the early and mid-1990s. Her audience has arguably aged along with her in the process. Madonna has always let the media and her fans know just enough of her private life to whet their appetites but never enough to satisfy them. This was evident in the 'intimate portrayal of her world' which was ostensibly revealed in the film and video *Truth or Dare* (also released as *In Bed With Madonna*). Shot worldwide during the 1991 Blonde Ambition tour, it shows Madonna and her troupe as a close-knit family group with the singer as its matriarch. Director Alek Keshishian claimed of it: 'it's not a neatly wrapped up picture which offers conclusions about Madonna's life, but allows you to see her humanity and deal with the part of her that's more than just a star'. Yet the film conceals far more than it reveals. Stardom in popular music, as in other forms of popular culture, is arguably as much about illusion and appeal to the fantasies of the audience, as it is about talent and creativity.

Madonna must also be considered as much as an economic entity as a purely cultural phenomenon. By 1992, she had generated more than US$500 million in music sales for Time Warner, lending 'a certain added resonance to the notion that she's like the head of a corporation overseeing her image control' (Seigworth 1993: 305). Through the 1990s, Madonna's records, music videos, film work (*Evita*), and even a soft-core pornographic book (*Sex*, 1992), kept her in the public eye. And her albums continued to sell well: *Bedtime Stories* (1994) was her seventh album to go multi-platinum, and, as I write this, her latest release *Music* (September 2000) is rapidly climbing the *Billboard* chart). Madonna's critical status has moved beyond the earlier negative views: her collaboration with noted techno producer William Orbit on *Ray of Light* (1999) won the Grammy for the best album of that year. Madonna continues to possess one of the most recognisable 'star' names, a bankable image ready-made for the present era of media globalisation.

The Spice Girls

As with Madonna, The Spice Girls success story raises issues of the status of musical genres, image and representation, the commodification of popular music, and the nature and operation of celebrity in pop culture more generally.

The Spice Girls were originally put together by the management team of Bob Herbert and his son Chris. Chris drew up a flyer, which he distributed in London and the south-east of England: 'R.U. 18–23 with the ability to sing/dance. R.U. street-wise, outgoing, ambitious, and dedicated?' Four hundred showed up for the auditions at Danceworks studios, just off London's Oxford Street. The original five Spice Girls (including Michelle Stephenson, who dropped out and was replaced by Emma Bunton) met for the first time in March 1994. Victoria Adams, Melanie Brown, Emma Bunton, Melanie Chisholm, and Geri Halliwell came from varying backgrounds, and the combination of personalities to make up the group were chosen quite deliberately. The press, and their fans, later referred to them as Posh (Victoria), Sporty (Mel C), Baby (Emma), Scary (Melanie Brown), and Ginger (Geri); labels which became pervasive public signifiers, and helped consolidate the Girls' image.

Chris Herbert used Trinity, a dance/rehearsal/recording studio in Woking, Surrey as a base for the group, who spent almost a year there, working on their singing and developing embryonic songwriting skills, and beginning the process of selling themselves to the music industry. The Herberts had no official contract with the Girls, and were a relatively small company, and the band, now increasingly confident in their abilities, looked around for a deal that offered greater support to their increasing ambitions. In April 1995 they left manager Chris Herbert and signed with Simon Fuller's 19 Management. In 1996, they signed to Virgin Records for a reported £2 million advance.

Fuller commissioned three teams of songwriters, all of whom had considerable music industry experience, credits, and success, to work with/for the group, to develop their song ideas. Their input is shown on the group's debut album. Stannard and Rowe, who had previously written material/hits for East 17 and Take That, came up with three of the Girls' four number one singles: 'Wannabe', '2 Become 1', and 'Mama', and also wrote 'If U Can't Dance'. Absolute (Paul Wilson and Andy Watkins) provided 'Who Do You Think You Are', 'Something Kinda Funny', 'Naked', and 'Last Time Lover'. The remaining two songs on the first album, 'Say You'll Be There' and 'Love Thing' were written by Eliot Kennedy (one with Cary Bayliss). The Spice Girls get songwriting credit on all of the songs on the *Spice* album, but Davis (1997) claims that the Girls only get about one-twentieth of the composer's royalties apiece.

The debut single 'Wannabe' was released in July 1996. It went to number 1 in the UK within a few weeks and stayed there for two months – a record for a debut single by a UK girl group. Subsequently it reached the number 1 chart position in thirty-one countries, including the USA, selling four million copies worldwide. The Spice Girls next three singles also topped the UK charts, making them the only group to have had four UK number 1s with their four first singles, and already the most successful British girl group ever. The appeal of the group was enhanced by their videos and energetic dance routines and performances on leading music television show *Top of the Pops*. The *Spice* LP went triple platinum in the UK within three weeks of its release, and by mid-1997 had sold over ten million copies worldwide. The Girls' personal lives, notably earlier modelling efforts and personal relationships, came under intense scrutiny by first the British, then the international press, especially the tabloids. The group's slogan, 'Girl Power', 'a hybrid of 90s good-feel optimism and cheery fun-pub feminism which alienates no one' (Davis 1997: 35), attracted considerable debate.

During 1996 and into 1997, the Spice Girls solidified their success in Britain, and then tackled America. A carefully orchestrated marketing campaign was undertaken by Virgin in the US, partly to offset initial critical reception of the records. For example, the *Rolling Stone*'s negative March 1997 review of *Spice*, which labelled the music a watered down mix of hip-hop and pop, and accorded it only one and a half stars (on a five-star scale). 'Despite their pro-woman posing', wrote reviewer Christina Kelly, 'the Girls don't get bogged down by anything deeper than mugging for promo shots and giving out tips on getting boys into bed' (cited Dickerson 1998: 205). Virgin marketed the band with heavy emphasis on their videos and the Girls visual appeal, largely avoiding the more potentially awkward print media. This meant 'high profiles for MTV, short interviews for television, and staged events where cameras could only get passing glimpses of the Spice Girls in controlled situations'. MTV was crucial, 'showing the Girls' nipple-friendly video (for "Wannabe") at every opportunity' (Dickerson 1998: 205). In July 1997, *Spice* topped the *Billboard* album charts, and, *Rolling Stone* ran a cover story headlined 'Spice Girls Conquer the World', a nine-page article, which told readers everything they could possibly want to know about the Spice Girls (10 July 1997 issue). All this without playing a concert, and not playing live, except on the television show *Late Night with David Letterman*.

The Spice Girls filled a market niche. As Chris Herbert observed:

> The whole teen-band scene at that time was saturated by boy bands. I felt that if you could appeal to the boys as well, you'd be laughing. If you could put together a girl band which was both sassy, for the girls, and with obvious sex appeal, to attract the boys, you'd double your audience.
>
> (Davis 1997: 35)

The Spice Girls also provided an antidote to the 'laddish' culture of UK Brit pop in the early 1990s, associated with performers such as the Gallagher brothers (Oasis). The Spice Girls were the subject of considerable hostility from many 'rock' critics/fans, who saw them as a media artifact, a view underpinned by the historical denigration of dance pop as a genre.

Their success was made possible by a combination of their music, their marketing, and their personalities. The Spice Girls' music is 'a mixture of dance, hip-hop, R&B, and smooth-as-silk pop ballads. Technically solid. Middle of the road. Nothing extreme' (Dickerson 1998: 203). This is to overlook the appeal of the clever and catchy lyrics of songs such as 'Wannabe', with its catchphrase 'Zig-a-zig-ah' for sex, and the highlighting of ongoing friendship and a streetwise attitude toward relationships.

> Yo, I'll tell you what I want, what I really really want,
> So tell me what you want, what you really really want,
> I'll tell you what I want, what I really really want,
> So tell me what you want, what you really really want,
> I wanna, I wanna, I wanna, I wanna, I wanna really
> really really wanna zig-a-zig-ha.
>
> If you want my future forget my past,
> If you wanna get with me better make it fast,
> Now don't go wasting my precious time,
> Get your act together we could be just fine.
>
> If you wanna be my lover, you gotta get with my friends,
> Make it last forever friendship never ends,

If you wanna be my lover, you have got to give,
Taking is too easy, but that's the way it is.

What do you think about that now you know how I feel,
Say you can handle my love are you for real,
I won't be hasty, I'll give you a try
If you really bug me then I'll say goodbye.
                    (The Spice Girls, 'Wannabe', Virgin, 1996)

However, this well-crafted pop is not the foundation for their mega-success, which was due mainly to the band's public image, which they partly created for themselves through force of personality and an irreverent attitude to the music industry and the media. They were seen as five 'sassy' individuals who combined girl next door appeal with considerable sex appeal. 'They introduced the language of independence to a willing audience of pre-teen and teenage girls – girl power' (Whiteley 2000: 215). In a discourse reminiscent of Madonna's early career, critics pointed to a contradiction between the Spice Girls' self-expression and their subversion of standard 'feminine' images, and their incorporation into a male-dominated industry. The group themselves, and their defenders, in response claimed that this was of their own choosing and on their own terms.

The franchising (through product endorsements) of a huge range of Spice Girl products added to the Girls' ubiquitous presence through 1997 and 1998. In December 1997 Q magazine rated the Spice Girls the 'biggest rock band in the world', based on the amount of airplay they had received, total income from record sales, concert tickets, etc., and the number of appearances on national magazine covers (both music and 'general' titles). In 1998 the Spice Girls released their second album, *Spice World*, again topping the charts internationally, and a movie of the same name. In August 1998, 'Viva Forever' became their seventh UK number 1 single, and they sold out a forty date 'world' tour. During 1999 and into 2000 the group's momentum eased: Gerry departed, and was not replaced; the remaining members devoted themselves to individual projects (e.g. Mel C's *Northern Star*); and Victoria and Mel B became mothers. A third Spice Girls album was released in November 2000; its reception will indicate whether the Spice Girls are more than a passing phenomenon.

On her way: Shania Twain

Country emerged in the US as a major market force in popular music in the 1990s (see Sernoe 1998) and classic stereotypes associated with the genre (especially its maudlin themes and limited appeal) no longer hold up. *Billboard* placed Garth

Brooks as Top Country Album Artist *and* Top Pop Album Artist for the years 1990, 1991, and 1993. In 1993, all six of his albums were included among the 100 most popular albums of the year, with two – *No Fences* and *Ropin' the Wind* – having sold about ten million copies each. His crossover success opened the way on the pop charts for other country artists, often referred to as 'new country', with Billy Ray Cyrus, Dwight Yoakum, Mary Chapin Carpenter, and Reba McEntire among the best selling artists of the early to mid-1990s. This contributed to a general market dominance by women performers, who in 1996 and 1997 had approximately 60 per cent of the releases to make the top twenty in the *Billboard* album charts (Dickerson 1998). At the same time, country radio became the second most listened to music format in the United States, second only to adult contemporary, and video channel CMT (Country Music Television) achieved a significant market share. The success of Shania Twain during the late 1990s was in part made possible by this aggressive resurgence of country music, and the receptive context which it created. Her crossover to the commercial mainstream and massive success, however, lifted the 'country' tag from her, and by 1998 she was an international figure.

Shania Twain was born in Canada. Her life story has, slightly cynically, been compared to a fairy tale: 'A country girl from Timmins, Ontario, is raised dirt poor, starts performing in bars as a child, loses her parents at age 22 when their car collides with a logging truck, sings to support her three teenage siblings, then finds her prince – reclusive rock producer Robert John (Mutt) Lange – who gives her a studio kiss of stardom' (Brian Johnson, 'Shania Revealed'; cover story in *Maclean's*, Canada's leading magazine, 23 March 1998; Hager 1998, provides a detailed and balanced biography). Her success is based on a combination of her songwriting, her striking and attractive looks, her music videos, and, as Johnson suggests (above), the role of Mutt Lange in her recordings. The weighting variously accorded to these factors, illustrate the controversy that has surrounded her status as a star and a popular music 'auteur'.

Twain moved to Nashville in 1991 after signing a deal with Mercury Nashville, changing her name from Eileen to Shania, which means 'I'm on my way' in Ojibwa (the language of her foster father). Her self-titled debut album (1993) featured only one of her own compositions, her producers opting instead for songs from established songwriters, a common practice in Nashville. The debut was respectable, without making a major impact: it sold around a hundred thousand copies, two singles from it got to number 55 on the *Billboard* Hot Country Singles Chart, and Shania made *Billboard*'s 1993 list of promising new artists. The accompanying music video for 'What Made You Say That', her own composition, broke with country tradition, celebrating her 'wholesome' sexuality, as she frolicked on a tropical beach with a male 'hunk'. It featured her bared navel, which became a 'trademark' on later videos and magazine covers. Screened on CMT Europe, the video also brought Shania to the attention of leading English producer Mutt Lange. The two started collaborating on songwriting, became close friends, and were married in December 1993.

Shania's second album, *The Woman in Me* (1995), was produced by Lange, who also partially financed it. Featuring a number of the songs turned down for the first album. *The Woman in Me* took a year and a half and more than half a million dollars to complete, a recording effort which stunned Nashville, where budgets of one-tenth of that amount were standard (Hager 1998: 54). It sold twelve million copies by the end of 1998. Of the twelve songs, ten were co-written by Shania and Mutt, and there was a solo contribution from each. As Hager describes it, this was a creative collaboration, with each contributing from their strengths and complementing the other. In producing *The Woman in Me*, Lange drew on the 'rock' style which he had used for very successful records with Def Leppard, AC/DC, and Bryan Adams. The album was a combination of 'Irresistible songs, sassy lyrics, all backed by Lange's onion-skin production, which reveals more of each song with each play' (*Q* review, November 1999).

Her third album, *Come on Over* (1998) sold 4.2 million during its first five months of release. The first single from it, 'You're Still the One', topped the *Billboard* country chart in May 1998, and went on to reach number 1 on the pop chart. Both the album and the several singles from it topped charts internationally.

This success was achieved, her critics observed, without Twain performing 'live'. This claim conveniently overlooking the fact that she had been performing in public from the age of three, but really referred to the singer not initially undertaking a concert tour to promote her albums. Instead, Shania did a series of promotional appearances, in shopping centres, on talk shows, and at industry showcases. This led to claims that her songs were largely the product of the recording studio, and raised questions about her ability to present them in performance. Twain was also frequently accused of being a 'packaged' artist, created by her high-powered management (Jon Landau, who also represents Bruce Springsteen). The success of her extensive touring in 1998 and into 1999, and the quality of her stage performance, erased these questions. The tour also enabled the production of a best-selling concert video.

Cover stories (for example, *Rolling Stone*, 3 September 1998; *Q*, November 1999) accentuate Shania's 'natural' physical appeal, particularly her bare midriff, a feature of several of her early videos. In her songs and videos, Twain combines a flirtatious glamour and self-empowerment: 'a country singer who looks like a supermodel' who 'on camera projects a playful allure that is part come-on, part come-off-it' (Johnson, *Maclean's*, 23 March 1998: 50). This is feminism very much in the mould of the Spice Girls.

Her songs, mainly co-written with Lange, reinvigorate tired county formats. They range from ballads of domestic bliss ('You're Still the One'), and feisty reassurance

('Don't Be Stupid. You Know I Love You'), to clever assertions of women's rights ('Honey I'm Home', is a neat role reversal). Within its pop ballad format and catchy tune, 'Black Eyes, Blue Tears' alerts listeners to domestic violence:

Black eyes, I don't need 'em
Blue tears, gimme freedom

Positively never goin' back
I won't live where things are out of whack
No more rollin' with the punches
No more usin' or abusin'

I'd rather die standing
Than live on my knees
Beggin' please – no more

Black eyes, I don't need 'em
Blue tears, gimme freedom
Black eyes – all behind me
Blue tears'll never find me now
   (Shania Twain, 'Black Eyes, Blue Tears',
         from album *Come On Over*,
          Mercury/Polygram, 1998)

Shania Twain is a popular music auteur whose work and marketable image have made her a star, although her success illustrates the frequent contribution of others to musical authorship.

Fat Boy Slim: multiple authorship

One factor common to the auteur and star figures I have considered so far is the value attached to the retaining of a consistent identity across time, the creation of a 'brand name' persona, through ongoing changes of style and genre. Straw makes a persuasive case that such a view of authorship has been challenged by the manner in which 'so much popular music now unfolds within highly specialized cultural niches – complex clusters of influence and cross-fertilization marked by tiny moves ahead or to the side' (Straw 1999: 206). The dance music scene and the work of Norman Cook, provide an example of a different style of 'career'. (The following draws on Stuart Hutchins' Profile of Cook, in *Juice Magazine*, March 1999; and Reynolds 1998.)

Cook first came to public notice in the UK, when he played bass with the indie pop band the Housemartins, who had some chart success in the mid-1980s; 'Caravan of Love' was a UK number 1 in December 1986. When they broke up in the late 1980s, Cook formed Beats International, and had another British number one with 'Dub Be Good to Me'. But Beats International were castigated for 'trying to play black music', Cook's marriage ended, he declared bankruptcy, and was diagnosed as clinically depressed. A dance floor epiphany, aided by 'E' (the drug ecstasy), led him to form Freakpower, a retro-funk band, who had a top five hit in Britain when 'Turn On Tune In Drop Out' was used for a Levi's ad. Cook also started releasing records as Pizzaman and the Mighty Dub Katz. Inspired by the Chemical Brothers and London clubs such as Heavenly Social, he became a leading DJ and recording figure in the scene that became known as big beat (Reynolds 1998: 384–6). His first album as Fat Boy Slim, *Better Living Through Chemistry* (1996), and a series of singles during 1997–98 made him an international figure, especially in the dance music community. His remixes of Cornershop's 'Brimful of Asha' and Wildchild's 'Renegade Master' both reached number 1 in the UK, and his own 'The Rockafeller Skank' and 'Gangsta Trippin' also charted. Both the last were on his commercially highly successful album *You've Come a Long Way Baby* (1998), while another single from this, 'Praise You', also went to number 1. The Fat Boy Slim sound has been described as 'a mix of speeded up hip-hop beats, (Roland) 303 driven basslines and big sampled hooks', and by Norman himself as 'big dumb music for drunken students' (Stuart Hutchins, *Juice Magazine*, March 1999: 46).

Norman Cook has kept up a bewildering array of aliases (indeed, Norman Cook is itself a pseudonym), in part because he believes his musical past meant that some people would not approach his music with an open mind. This failure to let each stylistic change add to his musical persona over time, as it has with Madonna for example, is 'strategically appropriate' in the field of contemporary dance music, where 'such changes are read as signs that the individual's origins in (or commitment to) any one style are not genuine, that the individual's participation in that genre's unfolding history is merely a momentary visit' (Straw 1999: 206).

The auteurs and stars I have considered here share a number of characteristics. At a fairly self-evident level, in their musical careers they all exercise considerable control over their artistic lives, perhaps because this has often been hard won. All have an ability to retain an audience across time, either through reinventing their persona/image, or through exploring new avenues in their music. They all have produced a substantial body of work, often multimedia in form; and they have all been, to varying degrees, seeking new ways of reinterpreting or reaffirming popular music styles. These characteristics apply to both auteurs and stars, but the latter go beyond them, to function as mythic constructs, related to their audiences collective and individual relationship to the music and performer (Marshall 1997: 163). Popular music stars and auteurs also represent economic entities, a unique commodity form which is both a labour process and product. The continuity of their careers contributes to stability in the marketplace, thereby enhancing the cultural and potential commercial value of their musical 'texts', to which I now turn.

Chapter 8

'Message understood'

Musicology and genre

Textual analysis is concerned with identifying and 'unpacking' the formal qualities of texts. It is primarily concerned with the underpinning structures of texts and their constituent characteristics; as such, it has become closely associated with semiotic analysis, often linked to psychoanalytical concepts. In the case of popular music, this means examining the musical constituents of recordings of songs, with particular attention to their lyrics, and with their audiovisual format: the music video (see Chapter 9). Space precludes dealing with record and CD sleeve covers, which can also be considered a form of text.

I begin this chapter with an examination of the nature and value of textual analysis as an approach to establishing meaning in popular music, with particular attention to musicology and lyric analysis. Three examples of lyric analysis illustrate the difficulties of such an approach: Tammy Wynette's 'Stand By Your Man', Willie Dixon's 'Spoonful', and Bruce Springsteen's 'Born in the USA'. Second, the examples of the development of heavy metal and techno/dance music in the 1990s show how genre study usefully moves us beyond the music as pure text, alerting us once again to the value of context and consumption.

Musicology

The study of the formal properties of music *qua* music is termed musicology. In broad terms, musicology is:

> the whole body of systematized knowledge about music which results from the application of a scientific method of investigation or research, or of

philosophical speculation and rational systematization to the facts, the processes and development of musical art, and to the relation of man in general.

(*Harvard Dictionary of Music*; cited Middleton 1990: 103)

A major debate in popular music studies has been constructed around the value of a musicological approach to music texts. Indeed, there is an argument as to whether popular music even merits such a 'serious' analysis, a question related to the high culture and mass society critiques of popular music. As I observed in Chapter 1, until recently, academic musicologists have generally neglected rock/pop music, in part out of an unwillingness to engage with a form of music which is accorded low cultural value in comparison with 'serious' music. At the same time, many sociologists writing on popular music have been wary of musicology. Frith (1983) saw 'rock critics' as essentially preoccupied with sociology rather than sound, and too ready to dismiss musicology as having little relevance to the study of rock. The arguments here were well rehearsed through the 1980s: traditional musicology neglects the social context, emphasises the transcription of music (the score), and elevates harmonic and rhythmic structure to pride of place as an evaluative criterion. Popular music, on the other hand, emphasises interpretation through performance, and is received primarily in terms of the body and emotions rather than as pure text. Many 'rock' musicians observed that classical music operated according to a different set of musical criteria, which has little validity for their own efforts (e.g. Pete Townshend; in Palmer 1970: 131).

More recently, there are signs that the largely negative attitude toward musicology (in relation to popular music) is changing. Several musicologists have engaged with popular music, while popular music scholars have accorded musicology more weight (e.g. Walser 1993; McClary 1991; Middleton 1990; Covach and Boone 1997; Tagg 1990). This work varies in the degree to which such analysis simply takes as a given the concepts/tools of traditional (i.e. more classical music oriented) musicology (e.g. Mellers 1974, 1986), or modifies these in relation to popular music (e.g. Moore 1993). Unfortunately, even these few efforts illustrate the central problem of terminology, which erects barriers to the musically non-literate. Consider Mellers description of Vera Hall's unaccompanied field holler, 'Trouble so hard': 'By omitting degrees of the diatonic scale, she makes a "gapped" pentatonic mode, achieving maximum expressivity from the sorrow-burdened words by distonations of pitch and vagaries of rhythm, in a timbre pure yet harshly penetrating' (Mellers 1986: 5). While the author provides a glossary, this frequently creates its own difficulties; for example, the description of the diatonic scale involving necessary reference to the concepts of tonality and dominant, subordinate and relative notes. This is not so much to fault Mellers' treatment of popular female singers, but to simply illustrate the initial difficulties facing attempts to apply any more sophisticated musical analysis to popular forms, such as rock. These difficulties become particularly evident when classroom attempts to analyse particular pieces of popular music founder on pupils' (and teachers'!) general lack of knowledge of even basic musical terminology.

A number of these authors have argued, with reference to detailed examples, that musical analysis of selected compositions is a workable approach to studying the nature and evolution of popular music, with such analysis presupposing a basic knowledge of the elements of music: melody, rhythm, harmony, lyrics, and performance (for a useful and accessible introduction to these elements, see Brown 1994). However, it can be argued that some of this work demonstrates that the traditional conception of musicology remains inadequate when applied to popular music in any straightforward manner (equating the two forms). For example, a concentration on technical textual aspects alone – the score – is inadequate, since it fails to deal with how the effects listeners celebrate are constructed, what McLary and Walser (1990: 287) term 'the dimensions of music that are most compelling and yet most threatening to rationality'. This takes into consideration the role of pleasure, the relationship of the body, feelings and emotions, and sexuality in constructing responses to rock music. It needs extension into the more affective domains of the relationship between the text and its listeners, and into the generic and historical locations of the text and its performer(s). Genre study usefully moves us beyond the music as pure text, alerting us once again to the value of context and consumption. So too does the study of narrative structures and representations in popular music, particularly the ideological and contextual aspects of these.

Ideally, what is needed is an approach embracing both traditional musicology and these affective aspects of music. It is worth remembering that people are more 'musical' than is usually credited. Radio listening – switching stations in search of something recognisable or engaging – and selecting which music to play on one's stereo involves an ability to distinguish between different types of music. This is to utilise a more extended definition of 'musical' (Tagg 1990: 104), where what is crucial is the link between musical structures and people's use of them.

Why do songs have words?

Even when there has been a concern to address popular music genres such as 'rock' as music, this has largely concentrated on its lyrical component. In his insightful historical discussion, 'Why Do Songs Have Words?', Frith shows how through the 1950s and 1960s the sociology of popular music was dominated by the analysis of the words of songs. This was largely because such an approach was grounded in a familiar research methodology – content analysis. It did make a certain amount of sense given the dominance of popular music by the 'bland, universal well-made song'

(Whitcomb 1972) of Tin Pan Alley, but assumed, however, 'that it was possible to read back from lyrics to the social forces that produced them' (Frith 1988b: 106).

Such an approach is evident in the extensive efforts of Cooper, who demonstrates the use of lyrics to approach social, political and personal issues: 'The attitudes and values portrayed in modern tunes demand the reflective consideration of students because they strike at the heart of the major social and political issues of our time: ecology, women's liberation, political cynicism, militarism, drug abuse, and others' (Cooper 1981: 8; see also Cooper 1990). This assumes that the words of the songs indeed express general social attitudes, and, given that songwriters are social beings and presumably conscious of changing cultural norms etc., this view does have some validity. As Frith points out, however, content analysis treats lyrics too simply:

> The words of all songs are given equal value, their meaning is taken to be transparent; no account is given of their actual performance or their musical setting. This enables us to code lyrics statistically, but it involves a questionable theoretical judgement: content codes refer to what the words describe – situations and states of mind – but not to how they describe, to their significance as language. Even more problematically, these analysts tend to equate a song's popularity to public agreement with its message.
>
> (Frith 1988b: 107)

Let us consider some instructive examples of such difficulties.

Stand by your lyric

'Stand By Your Man', co-written (with Billy Sherrill) and sung by Tammy Wynette. A number 1 hit upon its release in 1968, the song remains one of the best-selling records by a woman in the history of country music. Wynette adopted it as her theme song, performing it in all her concerts, and using it as the title for both her autobiography and the television movie about her life. The song even sparked a number 1 hit response: Ronnie Milsap's Grammy-winning '(I'm A) Stand By My Woman Man' (1976). The popularity of 'Stand By Your Man' was matched by the controversy and critical response it created. This focused on the song's apparently sexist message:

> Stand by your man
> Give him two arms to cling to
> And something warm to come to
> On nights he's cold and lonely
> Stand by your man
> And tell the world you love him

Keep giving all the love you can
Stand by your man.

This chorus was generally interpreted as a simple clarion call for women to subserviently support their male partners, reducing the woman's role essentially to a physical one, providing 'arms' and 'something warm'. *Newsweek* headlined a 1971 article on Wynette's music: 'Songs of Non-Liberation', while other reviewers labelled her work 'pre-feminist' and equated it with traditional views of women's 'allegiance to the stronger sex'. But while the dynamics of the song emphasise the chorus, the lyrics to its only verse make its interpretation more problematic:

Sometimes it's hard to be a woman
Giving all your love to just one man
You'll have bad times
And he'll have good times
Doin' things you don't understand
But if you love him
You'll forgive him
Even though he's hard to understand
And if you love him
Be proud of him
'Cause after all he's just a man.

The verse is presenting the hardships women face in their relationships with men, with the last line a neatly condescending assertion of women's superior gender status. Another dimension which reinforces this emphasis is Tammy Wynette's personal life. Then a twice-divorced mother of three, several of her previous hits had asserted the views of 'a wronged and righteous' single woman: especially her song 'D-I-V-O-R-C-E'. Furthermore, her subsequent tortured personal life (she died in 1998), including three additional marriages, and further songs elaborating the earlier pro-woman themes, suggest Wynette was using 'Stand By Your Man' to make an ironic statement about the contradictory dimensions of women's experience of relationships. The verse and chorus of the song represent the dilemma women face of meeting their gender obligations, while anticipating their ideal achievement. Accordingly, the song must be understood as a totality (Morris 1992).

The Sherrill–Wynette songwriting partnership was mirrored in the song, with the male mandated chorus providing the main theme, which is countered by the female-authored verse. It is also significant that Wynette disassociated herself from the interpretations of the song as sexist: 'I never did understand all the commotion over the lyrics of that song. I don't see anything in that song that implies that a woman is supposed to sit home and raise babies while a man goes out and raises hell' (Wynette 1980: 193). To validate this interpretation of 'Stand By Your Man', it would be necessary to ask women (and men?) how they respond to and interpret the song, given that listeners respond in a variety of ways to the same musical text. This simple but essential point is further illustrated by the song 'Spoonful'.

A spoonful of drugs?

Hatch and Millward (1987) use the term 'song families' for songs which are revived and reworked, as succeeding musical generations of musicians give them new rhythms. Willie Dixon's 'Spoonful' (based on Charlie Patton's 'A Spoonful of Blues', 1929), recorded by a number of artists, illustrates this process, musically and in terms of the social meanings ascribed to various renditions of the song.

> Could fill spoons full of diamonds,
> Could fill spoons full of gold,
> Just a little spoon of your precious love
> Satisfies my soul
> (chorus) That spoon that spoon that spoonful (repeats)
>   ('Spoonful', Willie Dixon, composer)

Many listeners, myself included, have interpreted the song as being about drug use, a view reflecting our initial exposure to the song in the mid-1960s as part of the counter culture. Dixon rejects this as simply incorrect, but it again shows how meaning is ultimately dependent on what associations listeners attach to any particular work, and the period in which particular renditions of it are situated. Dixon describes the idea behind the song:

> The idea of 'Spoonful' was that it doesn't take a large amount of anything to be good. If you have a little money when you need it, you're right there in the right spot, that'll buy you a lot. If a doctor give you less than a spoonful of some kind of medicine that can kill you, he can give you less than a spoonful of another one that will make you well.
>
> (Dixon 1989)

In the UK in the late 1950s and early 1960s, a number of musicians became intensely interested in Black American performers, including those whose work provided the antecedents of rock 'n' roll. Groups began playing covers or reworked versions of the American R&B and blues (e.g. the Rolling Stones, the Yardbirds, the Animals), gradually transforming the music into what became known as 'rock'. A significant audience emerged for this music, stimulated by tours of England by several leading American bluesmen, including Howlin Wolf and Muddy Waters (see Hatch and Millward 1987: 94–107). Guitarist Eric Clapton (formerly with the Yardbirds and John Mayall's Bluesbreakers) was prominent among those reaching back beyond 1950s rock 'n' roll to country and electric blues for inspiration and musical texts. In 1966, with two other key figures in the British rhythm and blues movement, Ginger Baker (drums) and Jack Bruce (bass), both from the Graham Bond Organisation, Clapton formed Cream. The trio came together in a conscious attempt to push the boundaries of rock through developing the potential of blues-based music (Headlam 1997, provides an excellent discussion of this project, tracing Cream's versions of blues classics back to their original sources in Chicago and Delta blues).

While Howling Wolf, for whom Dixon originally wrote the song, was the first to record 'Spoonful', the best-known subsequent version is that performed by Cream (initially on their album *Fresh Cream*, 1966, and subsequently in an extended live form on the double album *Wheels of Fire*, 1968, Cream's approach to 'Spoonful', and the drug associations listeners attributed to it, reflected the context of the British 'underground' scene of the late 1960s, with its drug use and preference for 'progressive' music and extended pieces (Willis 1978).

Patriotism and irony in the USA

Songs create identification through their emotional appeal, but this does not necessarily mean that they can be reduced to a simple slogan or message, although some listeners may do just that. This is evident in Bruce Springsteen's song 'Born in the USA'. As we saw in Chapter 7, Springsteen was a dominant figure in 1980s rock music. His song 'Born in the USA' represents one of his most powerful political statements, reflecting the self-consciously political stance evident in his work, and his view that 'I don't think people are being taught to think hard enough about things in general, whether its about their own lives, politics, the situation in Nicaragua, or whatever' (1987 interview; cited Pratt 1990: 177).

'Born in the USA' is a bitter narrative of life in the American underclass. The first person singer-narrator, Springsteen, joins the army to avoid 'a little hometown jam', fights in Vietnam, where his brother is killed, and returns to unemployment, seemingly with no hope or future.

> Born down in a dead man's town,
> The first kick I took was when I hit the ground
> You end up like a dog that's been beat too much
> Til you spend half your life just covering up.
> > (Bruce Springsteen, 'Born in the USA')

The music has a militaristic flavour, especially in the upbeat chorus sections, with the anthemic refrain:

BORN IN THE USA
I was BORN IN THE USA
I was BORN IN THE USA
BORN IN THE USA

It is an open question to what extent Springsteen's listeners appreciate the song as a resigned and ironic comment on the United States. Springsteen himself was highly conscious of this:

> I opened the paper one day and saw where they had quizzed kids on what different songs meant to them and they asked them what 'Born in the USA' meant. 'Well, its about my country', they answered. Well, that is what it's about – that's certainly one of the things it's about – but if that's as far in as you go, you're going to miss it, you know?
>
> (Pratt 1990: 177)

Casually listening to the song, many of my own students regard it simply as a homage to America, picking up on the celebratory anthem-like chorus, rather than the verse narrative. A provocative comparison with the original recorded version of the song, is provided by Springsteen's live acoustic version, which appears on *Tracks*, 1999. Here, due to Springsteen's vocal and guitar being fairly constant throughout, the verses 'compete' on an equal footing with the chorus, and listeners are more conscious of the song's ironic celebration of the United States.

As with Wynette's 'Stand By Your Man' and 'Spoonful', this again demonstrates that listeners use songs for their own purposes, and the popularity of particular performers is only in part derived from the substantive content of their work.

'The poetry of rock'

Lyric analysis also tends to valorise certain forms of popular music, most notably blues, soul, country, and some varieties of rock and pop, notably those featuring singer-songwriters, such as Bob Dylan, Randy Newman, and Tracy Chapman. These are seen as 'the authentic expression of popular experiences and needs', whereas mainstream popular music song lyrics are largely seen in terms of mass culture arguments, and criticised for their banality and lack of depth (Hoggart 1957). In a leftist version of this critique, Dave Harker (1980) reads off Tin Pan Alley lyrics as straightforward statements of bourgeois hegemony, equating pop's central themes of love and romance with the 'sentimental ideology' of capitalist society. Conversely, Harker argues for 'authentic' lyrics as the expression of 'authentic' relationships, with both reflecting direct experience, unmediated by ideology. (His approach is demonstrated in his comparison of the Beatles 'She Loves You', with Bob Dylan's parody of that song, 'It Aint Me Babe'; Harker 1980: 129.)

This brings us back to the question of the significance of song lyrics. More importantly, and echoing the debate in literary studies, it illustrates the difficulties of 'preferred readings'. Harker imposes his own ideological presuppositions on the work of the two artists. Accordingly, the Beatles' song is seen as trite and politically compromised, while Dylan's response is judged as 'a critique of bourgeois sensibility' (ibid.: 130). The listening audiences of each of the songs may well see things rather differently, as indeed do other critics and the songs' composers.

Part of the argument for 1960s rock's superiority over pop and earlier forms of popular music rested on the claim that its major songwriters were poets. Richard Goldstein's *The Poetry of Rock* (1969) and similar anthologies helped to popularise this view. As Frith (1988b: 117) points out, this work has emphasised a particular form of rock lyrics – those akin to romantic poetry with lots of covert and obscure allusions. This is to attempt to validate 'rock' in terms of established 'art' forms, elevating the role of the songwriter to that of an auteur figure with the ability to work in a recognisable high cultural mode (an approach linked to the early years of *Rolling Stone* magazine; see Chapter 4). An extension of this position is the relegation of mainstream commercial rock/pop lyrics to banality and worthlessness. Yet clearly such lyrics do in some sense matter to their listeners: *Smash Hits*, focusing on the words of the latest chart entries, has been one of Britain's biggest selling music magazines. Frith (1988b: 121) suggests that a critical question here is 'how do words and voices work differently for different types of pop and audience?' This necessitates addressing how song lyrics work as ordinary language.

Song and social realism

One of the issues here is the realism of song. A notion of lyrical realism asserts 'a direct relationship between a lyric and the social or emotional condition it describes and represents' (Frith 1988b: 112). This is evident in the study of folk song and the analysis of blues lyrics. For example, Charles Keil read American post-war urban blues lyrics as expressing their black singers' personal adjustment to urban ghettoisation: 'a more detailed analysis of blues lyrics might make it possible to describe with greater insight the changes in male roles within the Negro community as defined by Negroes at various levels of socio-economic status and mobility within the lower class' (Keil 1966: 74). The lyric content of city, urban and soul blues also reflects varying sorts of adjustment to urban conditions generally, as does Jamaican music (see Jones 1988; Hebdige 1990).

Even if blues lyrics and reggae do reflect social realities, is their role to confirm oppression or do they encourage struggle? And why do we still enjoy them, even while identifying with the singer's sadness? Garon (1975) compares blues to poetry, arguing that the blues convey pleasure 'through its use of images, convulsive images, images of the fantastic and of the marvellous, images of desire'. An alternative answer to the latter question is that most listeners simply don't listen too carefully to the lyrics. As Frith later observed, in his influential *The Sociology of Rock* he went so far as to ignore lyric analysis altogether, and 'simply assumed that the meaning of music could be deduced from its users' characteristics' (Frith 1988a: 119). As I have demonstrated, the same popular culture texts are interpreted in varying ways and for different purposes by different audiences. My own students' responses to particular songs support the view that popular music audiences listen primarily to the beat and the melody – the sound of the record – and make their own sense of songs; accordingly, meaning cannot be simply read off from the lyrics. Indeed, it is not uncommon for lyrics to be misconstrued, sometimes with comic results (e.g. in the 1960s Bob Dylan heard the Beatles 'I get by with a little help from my friends' as 'I get high etc.', assuming they were already 'turned on' to marijuana).

These difficulties aside, there is much to be said for utilising musicology, provided that such analysis is kept easily accessible to those who have never encountered music theory, and that its ambit is extended. To begin with, it is necessary for students to get a grasp of the meaning of basic musical terms: rhythm, beat, etc. (see Brown 1994). Once this is established, students can move on to the examination of individual pieces. This involves identifying those formal properties which 'stand out' for the listener, i.e. whether or not the piece has a strong rhythm, the nature of its vocals, the use of particular instruments, and so on. Second, the emotional and physical response of the listeners to each piece must be identified and discussed. This is to emphasise the individual's reaction to popular culture, essentially at the affective, personalised level. Third, and most important, these first two aspects must be brought together by considering how particular stylistic and musical techniques serve to encourage certain responses from their listeners, and the role of genre in determining musical meaning.

For most listeners, their response to popular music is 'a gut thing'; their response is at the level of the affective rather than the intellectual. While fans do intellectualise about the music, their attempts to do so are very much in terms of their physical and emotional response to it. Here students can be encouraged to interrogate the process of their listening: the foot-tapping or finger drumming response to the beat; the singing along with the chorus of well-known songs; the air guitar; and the abandonment of restraint through various modes of dance. Emotional associations, the links forged between people, places, moods, and particular songs means the experience of the song becomes polymorphous. Nor should the importance of the listening context be forgotten here. One of the major problems of classroom analysis of popular music, is that the relatively sterile environment and the anchoring of the physical body in place are far removed from the normal contexts in which the music is consumed – the pub, the club, the concert hall, and the home. The interrelationship of these aspects is demonstrated in the case studies at the end of this chapter. At this point, it is necessary to situate them in terms of the crucial concept of genre.

GENRE

Genre can be basically defined as a category or type. A key component of textual analysis, genre is widely used to analyse popular culture texts, most notably in films and novels (e.g. thrillers, science fiction, and horror). The various encyclopedias, the standard histories, and academic analyses of popular music all use genre as a central organising element. Some accounts tend to use style and genre as overlapping terms, or prefer style to genre (e.g. Moore 1993). The layout of stock in music retail outlets, and in mail order record clubs, also suggests that there are clearly identifiable genres of popular music, which are understood as such by consumers. Indeed, fans will frequently identify themselves with particular genres, often demonstrating considerable knowledge of the complexities of their preferences (sub-genres). Similarly, musicians will frequently situate their work by reference to genres and musical styles.

The usual approach to defining musical genres is 'to follow the distinctions made by the music industry which, in turn, reflect both musical history and marketing categories' (Frith 1987; see also his discussion in Frith 1996). Another approach, suggested by Frith, is to 'classify them according to their ideological effects, the way they sell themselves as art, community or emotion'. He gives the example of a form of 'rock' termed 'authentic', exemplified by Bruce Springsteen: 'The whole point of this genre is to develop musical conventions which are, in themselves, measures of "truth". As listeners we are drawn into a certain form of reality: this is what it is like to live in America, this is what it is like to love or hurt. The resulting work is the pop equivalent of film theorists' "classic realist text"' (1987: 147). Against and in interplay with authentic genres can be placed a tradition of artifice, with surface images and transitory sounds predominant, e.g. in glam rock.

Critical analysis of popular music genres has concentrated on the question of their fluidity. Chambers in the mid-1980s correctly observed that there were by then quite rigid boundaries between genres, as exemplified by 'art rock'. A major trend since then has been the continued splintering of popular music into an increasingly varied range of genres and sub-genres. For example, Reynolds (1998) identifies over forty distinct sub-genres within dance music (see also the sixty or so genre entries in

Shuker, 1998). Currently, while musical genres continue to function as marketing categories and reference points for musicians, critics, and fans, particular examples clearly demonstrate that genre divisions must be regarded as highly fluid. No style is totally independent of those that have preceded it, and musicians borrow elements from existing styles and incorporate them into new forms. Performers have always absorbed influences across genre (and ethnic) lines. In the 1920s, country pioneer Jimmie Rogers drew extensively from existing blues and popular music traditions, just as, in the 1990s, Oasis reworked the imagery and sounds of British 1960s rock. Further, many performers can fit under more than one classification, or shift between and across genres during their careers. There is also considerable genre bending: subverting or playing with the conventions of existing musical genres, or adopting an ironic distance from those same conventions. This process is strongly present in hybrid genres, where different styles inform and engage with each other (e.g. jazz rock, rap metal).

It is useful to distinguish between meta-genres, which are rather loose amalgams of various styles (e.g. alternative rock, world music), and genres, which arguably exist in a purer, more easily understood and specified form (e.g. disco). It is also important to acknowledge the significance of sub-genres, which are particularly evident in well-established and developed styles/genres, and qualify any simplistic depiction of a genre; the blues, heavy metal and techno/dance provide good examples of strongly differentiated genres.

'Mainstream' musical genres are operating within a commercial system of record companies, contracts, marketing, publicity, management, support staff and so on; within this context performers tour and perform, make recordings, and create an image. As Breen (1991: 193) observed, moving into the 1990s every genre and sub-genre of popular music shared a location on 'the totalized map of popular music culture, where the bridges that form the industrial crossovers from one domain of the popular music industry to the next are increasingly interconnected'.

In the light of the above, several general characteristics of popular music genres can be identified. First, there are the stylistic traits present in the music: their musical characteristics, 'a code of sonic requirements ... a certain sound, which is produced according to conventions of composition, instrumentation and performance' (Weinstein 1991a: 6). These may vary in terms of their coherence and sustainability (as examples such as Christian rock, and glam rock clearly demonstrate), particularly in meta-genres. Along with other aspects of genre, particular musical characteristics can be situated within the general historical evolution of popular music. Of particular significance here is the role of technology, which establishes both constraints and possibilities in relation to the nature of performance, and the recording, distribution, and reception of the music. Second, there are other, essentially non-musical, stylistic attributes, most notably image and its associated visual style. This includes standard iconography and record cover format; the locale and structure of performances, especially in concert, and the dress, make-up, and hair styles adopted by both the performers and their listeners and fans. Musical and visual stylistic aspects combine in terms of how they operate to produce particular ideological effects, a set of associations which situate the genre within the broader musical constituency.

Third, there is the primary audience for particular styles. The relationship between fans and their genre preferences is a form of transaction, mediated by the forms of delivery, creating specific cultural forms with sets of expectations (see Weinstein 1991a). Genres are accorded specific places in a musical hierarchy by both critics and fans, and by many performers. This hierarchy is loosely based around the notions of authenticity, sincerity, and commercialism. Dance pop (e.g. Steps, Kylie Minogue) is often dismissed as all froth and no substance, an evaluation based on its musical qualities, and therefore overlooking the real basis of its appeal in fan–performer identification and style. Likewise, genres seen as commercial manufactures, such as 'bubblegum' in the late 1960s, and much of disco in the 1980s. The ultimately subjective nature of these concepts, and the shifting constituency of genres, can be illustrated by the case of heavy metal.

'Born to be wild': heavy metal

Heavy metal (HM) began in the late 1960s, its origins variously being traced to several key recordings: Blue Cheer's 1968 reworking of Eddie Cochran's 1950s hit 'Summertime Blues', which turned Cochran's great acoustic guitar riff into distorted metallic sounding electric guitar chords, accompanied by a thumping percussion; Steppenwolf's 'Born To Be Wild' (1967) with its reference to 'heavy metal thunder' (from the William Burroughs' novel *Naked Lunch*) in the song's second verse; and the release of British metallers Black Sabbath's eponymous debut album (1970), which reached number 8 in the UK album chart and spent three months on the US album chart.

HM was a logical progression from the power trios of 1960s groups such as the Jimi Hendrix Experience and Cream, who played blues-based rock with heavily amplified guitar and bass reinforcing each other. The commercial success of the British bands Black Sabbath, Deep Purple and, above all, Led Zeppelin, and Grand Funk and Mountain in the US – despite the general critical 'thumbs down' for their efforts – consolidated heavy metal as a market force in the early 1970s, and established a heavy metal youth subculture. Even this short list of performers demonstrates the difficulties of bounding the genre. Led Zeppelin performed more traditional blues-based material and combined acoustic outings with electric guitars, yet are accorded the HM tag chiefly because they were played at a very loud volume.

Although Deep Purple and their American counterparts may be considered HM bands, they can just as easily be classified as 'hard' or 'heavy' rock. In the 1980s, there was a clear distinction possible between the more overtly, commercially oriented, MTV friendly HM bands, such as Bon Jovi and Poison with their glam rock images, and mainstream HM bands, whose styles merge into hard rock, such as Guns 'n' Roses, and Aerosmith. These were joined by thrash or speed metal, labels which are a journalistic convenience for guitar-based, non-mainstream metal, usually played faster and louder. This metal sub-genre initially developed in the San Francisco Bay area in the late 1980s, with groups like Metallica drawing their inspiration from British HM bands such as Def Leppard and Iron Maiden. Other bands emerged in other centres, most notably Suicidal Tendencies and Slayer in Los Angeles, and Anthrax in New York. During the 1990s, these established sub-genres of HM were joined by new variants (e.g. death metal) and hybrid forms (e.g. funk metal; rap metal).

Consequently, the musical parameters of heavy metal (HM) as a diverse genre cannot be comfortably reduced to formulaic terms. It is usually louder, 'harder' and faster-paced than conventional rock music, and remains predominantly guitar oriented. The main instruments are electric guitars (lead and bass) drums and electronic keyboards, but there are numerous variants within this basic framework.

HM is frequently criticised as incorporating the worst excesses of popular music, notably its perceived narcissism and sexism, and it is also often musically dismissed. Even Lester Bangs, one of the few rock critics to favourably view the emergence of HM, wrote of the genre:

> As its detractors have always claimed, heavy-metal rock is nothing more than a bunch of noise; it is not music, it's distortion – and that is precisely why its adherents find it appealing. Of all contemporary rock, it is the genre most closely identified with violence and aggression, rapine and carnage. Heavy metal orchestrates technological nihilism.
>
> (Bangs 1992)

HM was one of the main targets of moves to censor popular music in the 1980s (see Chapter 12).

Until the publication of Weinstein's comprehensive sociological study (1991a), and Walser's more musically grounded treatment (1993), there were few attempts to seriously discuss the genre. Yet HM displays a musical cogency and enjoys a mass appeal, existing within a set of social relations. Some forms of the genre have enjoyed enormous commercial success, and have a large fan base; other, 'harder' sub-genres have a cult following. Many HM fans are working class, white, young and male, identifying with the phallic imagery of guitars and the general muscularity and oppositional orientation of the form (there is some debate here: see Walser 1993). The symbols associated with HM, which include Nazi insignia and Egyptian and biblical symbols, provide a signature of identification with the genre, being widely adopted by metal's youth cult following (see Arnett 1996). The genre has maintained its high market profile into the 1990s, despite critical derision and a negative public image. Its latest variant, rap metal, has breathed new life into the genre, achieving considerable commercial and critical success (e.g. Rage Against the Machine).

The interesting question is why a genre generally panned by the critics (and many other music fans) as formulaic noise, associated with a negative social stance and consequent public controversy, is so popular? What is the basis of HM's appeal? As Breen argues, the rise of HM in the 1980s was linked to 'firstly, a search for substance and authenticity in rock music and, secondly, to advanced methods of marketing music for mass consumption' (Breen 1991: 194; see also Weinstein 1991a: chap. 4). The theatrical aspects of HM, plus its musical accessibility, are part of its commercial appeal and success. The genre's performers present an achievable image of flounced hair and torn jeans, a rock lifestyle whose surface aspects at least are affordable to its followers. Marketing has played a major part: 'No niche market anywhere is left alone and every niche is reinforced by others' (Breen 1991: 196). The impact of heavy metal on MTV has been significant here (see Chapter 10).

Techno, dance, and beyond

Techno emerged as a musical style and meta-genre in the 1980s, partly associated with new, computer-generated, sound/composition technologies available to musicians. Techno is often conflated with house and ambient music, or used contiguously with the whole corpus of contemporary dance music. Techno became closely associated with a particular social setting, being the staple music at large-scale parties, or 'raves'. Along with the use of the drug ecstasy, these generated considerable controversy (and moral panic) in the early to mid-1990s in the UK and internationally (see Thornton 1995).

The defining musical characteristics of techno are, in most cases: a slavish devotion to the beat, and the use of rhythm as a hypnotic tool (usually 115–160 bpm); these are primarily, and often entirely, created by electronic means; a lack of vocals; and a significant use of samples (e.g. Prodigy, *Fat of the Land*, 1997). A number of variants, or sub-genres quickly emerged within techno, often linked with particular record labels/regional scenes (see Garratt 1999; Reynolds 1998 provides an extensive musical 'map'). The 'proto-techno' of the original Detroit (US) creators of the genre revealed a mixture of influences, especially the German electronic band Kraftwerk's 'assembly line technopop', and the funk of George Clinton and Parliament. From this basis came 'Detroit techno', a stripped-down, aggressive funk sound, played mostly on analogue instruments and characterised by a severe, pounding rhythm, and 'hardcore techno', speed metal tunes played on Detroit techno instrumentation. Subsequent variants included the more accessible and commercial 'techno-rave'; 'breakbeat', a style using sped-up hip-hop beat samples; and 'tribal', with rhythm patterns and sounds drawing on Native American and world music. Some techno performers have moved progressively with and through a number of these styles; e.g. the Shamen's initial recordings combined psychedelic rock with hardcore rap rhythms, while their later work makes greater use of samples, drum machines and heavily amplified guitar sounds (the Shamen, *Boss Drum*, 1992).

Contemporary dance music is a prominent meta-genre, closely associated with the club music scene, with substantial sales and its own charts. It is strongest in the United Kingdom, but is increasingly evident internationally, although most of the major British performers have only attained cult status in the US market. In Britain and Europe, dance has become part of mainstream popular music, embraced by the music industry as a possible antidote to the declining sales in the highly fragmented rock/pop market. While the contemporary music market is volatile and unclear, dance has overtaken alternative/grunge as the major commercial force (along with hip-hop) internationally.

Into the 1990s techno became practically synonymous with contemporary dance music, mutating into a bewildering and volatile mix of different musical styles (and associated scenes and loose subcultures); most notably jungle, house, trip-hop, and drum 'n' bass. These were broadly characterised by their use of state of the art technology, extensive use of samples, musical eclecticism, and links to dance/club scenes. As music press reviews and articles, and marketing hype indicate, there is considerable overlap between the various forms, with shifting and unclear boundaries present, and sub-genres splintering off, including jungle, house, trip-hop, and drum 'n' bass, often with national variants , for example 'Italo house' (Mitchell 1996: chap. 4). Each in turn has mutated, for example, house into Chicago, acid, and deep house. These are linked to various scenes, record labels, and performers.

'Trip-hop', for example, began to circulate as a term in the British music press during 1995, referring to a Bristol-based 'movement' led by Massive Attack, Portishead, and Tricky (Johnson 1996). Stylistically, trip-hop was 'a dark, seductive combination of hip-hop beats, atmospheric reverb-laden guitars and samples, soul hooks, deep bass grooves and ethereal melodies' (AMG 1995: 506). The style had actually been around for several years, in various forms of slowed down hip-hop.

These two brief genre studies, heavy metal and dance music, illustrate the need to go beyond popular music as pure text, alerting us once again to the value of context and consumption. Along with the concepts of star and auteur, musicology and genre provide a basis for the consideration of particular musical texts, both recordings and music videos, to which I now turn.

Chapter 9

'Sweet dreams (are made of this)'
Musical texts

Building on the discussion in the previous chapter, I turn now to specific texts ,
particularly the ideological and contextual aspects of these. A range of specific songs
provide examples of such analysis, chosen to represent particular genres and historical moments: the classic Delta blues of Robert Johnson, 'Love In Vain' (1936); the
Who's power-pop, mod anthem, 'My Generation' (1966); the Sex Pistols' seminal
punk statement, 'Anarchy in the UK' (1976); Grandmaster Flash and the Furious
Five's urban rap, 'The Message' (1982); Kylie Minogue's chart-topping pop cover,
'Locomotion' (1987); and S Club 7s 'Bring It All Back' (1999). I then consider a key
form of audio-visual text, music videos (MVs), identifying some basic considerations
which usefully inform specific 'textual' readings of MV, and the difficulties endemic
in constructing a classificatory typology of music videos. These intentions are in part
addressed through two case studies of music video: Duran Duran's 'Hungry Like the
Wolf', and Madonna's 'Open Your Heart'.

An important starting question here is how do you 'justify' a particular genre and
song as worthy of attention? The majority of the songs and music videos included
here were selected for their innovative break with, or reworking of, established traditions and conventions. They generally exemplify two central aspects of a popular
music aesthetic: first, extending the traditional form; and second, working within the
form itself, breaking it up and subverting its conventions. But, as the examples here
demonstrate, we must go beyond simple aesthetics to explain why particular songs
'work' in terms of creating an audience. Accordingly, while attention is given to the
musical qualities of each example, they are also situated in terms of genre,
the personal history of the performer(s) and their place in rock, and the audience

reception of the song. The examples chosen represent a range of genres or styles of popular music, located at different historical moments.

Robert Johnson, 'Love In Vain Blues' (1936–37)

(On *King of the Delta Blues Singers, volume 2*, CBS Records UK, 1970; also available on the boxed set *Robert Johnson: The Complete Recordings*, Columbia, 1990)

Robert Johnson is regarded as 'the key transitional figure working within the Mississippi Delta's blues culture. He bridged the gap between the music's rural beginnings and its modern urban manifestations' (Barlow 1989: 45; the following is based on Barlow 1989 and Guralnick 1989).

Born in 1911, Johnson was raised by his mother, who routinely moved from place to place in the mid-South. His own adulthood was similarly restless, and provided a recurring message in his work. Fellow bluesman and travelling companion, Johnny Shines said of Johnson: 'People might consider him wild because he didn't think nothing of just taking off from wherever he was, just pack up and go. He had that about travelling'. Robert Johnson's only recording sessions were held in San Antonio late in 1936 and in Dallas in early 1937, and he recorded a total of only twenty-nine blues tracks. This small output was to have an influence out of all proportion to its size, not only on the blues, but also on the development of 'rock' in the 1960s, as British bands like the Rolling Stones and Cream covered songs by Johnson (see Headlam 1997, and the references therein). The singer was murdered in Greenwood, Mississippi in 1938, poisoned by a jealous lover, aged only 27. Johnson was widely thought to have sold his soul to the devil in return for the ability to be an outstanding blues singer and guitarist, since he disappeared for a short period and returned amazingly proficient. This, along with his early death and the lack of details about his life, created a mythic figure in the history of popular music.

While Johnson started out in the blues as a harmonica player, he switched to guitar. He was strongly influenced by Son House's bottleneck slide technique, which formed the core of his own playing style, and by other contemporary Delta bluesmen such as Charley Patton and Willie Brown. But Johnson assimilated a range of other influences, incorporating them into his own distinctive style: 'His guitar work was also influenced by the recordings of Kokomo Arnold, Willie Newbern, and Lonnie Johnson, who also influenced many of his vocal inflections, along with Leroy Carr, Peetie Wheatstraw, and Skip James' (Barlow 1989: 45–6). Contemporaries commented on the breadth of Johnson's musical tastes, marvelled at his ability to:

pick a song right out of the air. He'd hear it being played on the radio and play it right back note for note. He could do it with blues, spirituals, hillbilly music, popular stuff. You name it he could play it.

(Robert Jr. Lockwood, cited Barlow 1989: 46)

He'd be sitting there listening to the radio – and you wouldn't even know he was paying any attention to it – and later that evening maybe, he'd walk out on the streets and play the same songs that were played over the radio, four or five songs he'd liked out of the whole session over the radio and he'd play them all evening, and he'd continue to play them.

(Johnny Shines, cited Barlow 1989: 46)

Johnson was influential in three areas. First, through his guitar playing:

As a guitarist he almost completely turned the blues around. His tightening of the rhythmic line was the basis for the instrumental blues scene that followed him in Chicago – letting the upper strings play a free melodic part, but using the thumb for a hard rhythm in the lower strings that was also a drum part.

(Samuel Charters, blues historian; cited Barlow 1989: 47)

Robert Palmer notes how Johnson made his guitar:

sound uncannily like a full band, furnishing a heavy beat with his feet, chording innovative shuffle rhythms and picking out high treble-string lead with his slider, all at the same time. Fellow guitarists would watch him with unabashed, open mouth wonder. They were watching the Delta's first modern bluesman at work.

(cited Barlow 1989: 47)

Second, Johnson recorded a number of strikingly original songs, which captured a timeless feeling of desperation and intensity. In songs like 'Ramblin' On My Mind', 'Dust My Broom' and 'Sweet Home Chicago' Johnson celebrated mobility and personal freedom; double entendres and sexual metaphors abound in 'I'm A Steady Rollin' Man', 'Terraplane Blues', and 'Traveling Riverside Blues'; and in 'Cross Road Blues' and 'Hell Hound On My Trail' Johnson encouraged the legend that he had flirted with the devil.

I've got to keep moving, I've got to keep moving
Blues falling down like hail, Blues falling down like hail

And the days keeps on 'minding me
There's a hell hound on my trail
    ('Hell Hound On My Trail')

Third, Johnson's voice is particularly effective at conveying a fatalistic sense of the social and spiritual forces he saw arrayed against him. His vocal intonation is especially compelling in his poignant 'Love In Vain Blues', with its themes of painful departure and separation:

I followed her to the station with her suitcase in my hand
And I followed her to the station with her suitcase in my hand
Well its hard to tell, its hard to tell when all your love's in vain
All my love's in vain.
    ('Love In Vain Blues', first verse)

An analysis based on the song lyrics would not convey the emotional impact of Johnson's voice and its interplay with guitar in the recorded version of the song. In performance, the song is stripped down to its bare essentials, making it almost minimalist in contemporary terms. Obviously, if judged by the standards of traditional, classical musicology, it would be found wanting. The vocal is weak and wavering, and the singer does not project well. Yet Johnson's voice has an edge of desperation and hints at depths of experience. This is abetted by the use of repetition, and the interplay between the miked acoustic guitar and the voice. The piece also exemplifies the role of improvisation and performance in much rock music. It retains the ability to affect listeners today, though its impact is limited by the primitive recording technology of its day. My own students regard it as somewhat maudlin, yet remain conscious of its force. They also find Johnson's original an interesting comparison with the Rolling Stones 'cover' version (on the album *Let It Bleed*) which they are more familiar with. Certainly they concede that their 'appreciation' of the song is greatly enhanced by locating it as a key text in the development of post-1950s 'rock'. This is to emphasise the point that a knowledge of the performer and their influence on 'the popular music canon' adds dimensions beyond simple listening to the piece purely on its own terms.

The Who: 'My Generation' (Brunswick/Decca, 1965)

The Who's songwriter, Pete Townshend was very self-reflexive in his attitude towards 'rock', which he was concerned to promote as an art form, capable of inspiring and promoting social change. Townshend wrote a string of hits dealing with the frustrations of youth: 'musical acid bombs, uniquely summing up that Sixties teenage attitude which compounded swaggering confidence with spluttering frustration', and which 'are still touched by a magic that has rarely been duplicated in English rock' (Sinclair 1992: 381–2). 'My Generation' was the most outstanding of these.

'My Generation' was released in the UK in November, 1965. Entering the *NME* chart at number 16, it went on to peak at number 2. In the United States, where the Who had yet to perform, and receiving only limited promotion, it only reached number 74 on the *Billboard* chart. The Who as a group had already established themselves in the UK with two previous charting singles, and had become closely associated with the style of an emergent British youth subculture – the mods. The record established the Who as one of the most innovative of the new British rock groups in the wake of the Beatles; it became the endpiece of the band's concerts, and provided the title song on their first album (on Brunswick in the UK): 'Suddenly the Who went from being one, albeit the most promising, of a mass of beat groups to spokesmen, stuttering on behalf of an entire generation' (Perry 1998: 30). While the song had a very spontaneous sound to it, 'My Generation' had actually been laboriously developed by Townshend, through a number of intermediate stages (see Perry 1998).

'My Generation' was associated with the mod subculture which emerged in the UK in the mid-1960s (see Hebdige 1979: chap. 4): 'it epitomises everything that Mod meant to the mods themselves and to a whole generation of kids for whom mod was the only adequate expression of their feelings' (Herman 1971: 62). The song presents a picture of a confused and inarticulate adolescent, with lead singer Roger Daltrey singing the vocal in a stuttering fashion that mimics the speed-induced verbal stoppages associated with mod methedrine use.

> People try to put us down
> (Talkin' 'bout my generation)
> Just because we get around
> (Talkin' 'bout my generation)
> Things they do look awful cold
> (Talkin' 'bout my generation)
> Hope I die before I get old
> (Talkin' 'bout my generation)
>   (The Who,
>   'My Generation', first verse)

Amusingly, the BBC actually initially banned the song from its playlists for ridiculing those with speech handicaps! The song itself employs what Townshend called 'the Who brag form', with its self-assertive aggressiveness concealing a basic insecurity. Its pace is fast and frantic. It is a combination of bravado and inarticulateness; the stuttering conveys a mix of rage and frustration – as if the singer can't get the words out.

'My Generation' was a logical progression from the earlier Who singles, 'I Can't Explain' and 'Anyway, Anyhow, Anywhere'. Like them, it opened with a series of power chords and rustling drums, which Keith Moon subsequently develops into a slashing attack on his kit, and John Entwistle's rumbling bass ('perhaps the most prominently recorded electric bass in rock up to that time', Marsh 1983: 186). This style had developed because the Who had no rhythm guitarist, accordingly Townshend's lead guitar is strongly rhythmic, emphasising chord structures rather than melodic lines: 'The fast, chunky and complex backing of the first two verses gives way to a dialogue between bass and lead guitar in which the bass plays a melody to which the lead "replies" with rhythmic chords' (Herman 1971). This is partly counterbalanced by the highly amplified bass and drums to a degree playing the melody. The ability of a small number of players to produce such a sound was made possible by amplification.

A series of simple chord changes keep the momentum going. The song builds in intensity, with a crescendo of feedback, climaxing with sounds reminiscent of the demolishing of lead guitar and drum kit which formed part of the Who's auto-destructive stage act. But what was most revolutionary about the song was its use of feedback. Rather than being used 'as a gimmick separate from the basic flow of the music', 'My Generation' uses feedback 'for the first time as an integral part of a rock composition – without it, the song would be incomplete' (Marsh 1983).

Today's youth still find 'My Generation' of interest. It is seen as having clear links with the later 'three chord thrash' of late 1970s punk, which many students listen to contemporary variants of, while the mod association acts as a nostalgic prompt to further investigation of the song and the Who.

Sex Pistols, 'Anarchy in the UK' (EMI, UK, 1976)

Evaluation then and since gives 'Anarchy in the UK' and the Sex Pistols debut album, which for many listeners was their first exposure to the song, a key place in the advent of punk rock in 1977–78 in the UK and accords it a lasting influence. For Marsh, it illustrates the musical fracture presented by punk in the late 1970s: 'somebody had figured out how to make artistically and commercially viable pop music based on a rhythmic process outside R&B, a feat unequalled since the advent of Elvis Presley; consequently, things were fundamentally different thereafter. It was a true historic disjuncture' (Marsh 1989: 72). For Savage (1991), it was 'an index of their increasing ambition ... a call to arms, delivered in language that was as explosive as the group's name'. For Greil Marcus (1992: 594ff.), it was part of the Sex Pistols' rupturing of rock 'n' roll, as they 'broke the story of rock & roll in half', turning it back on itself, and recasting key questions as to its cultural weight (see also Sabin 1999; and the contemporary reviews collected in Heylin 1998: 137ff.).

Savage traces the genesis and impact of 'Anarchy', giving it a definite political intent, and accusing John Lydon (Johnny Rotten) of 'deliberately using inflammatory imagery' particularly the terms 'antichrist' and 'anarchist', both conveying images of apocalypse, the second coming, and social chaos: 'there seems little doubt that Lydon was fed material by Vivienne Westwood (McLaren's designer partner) and Jamie Reid (the Pistol's graphic artist), which he then converted to his own lyric' (Savage 1991: 204).

The raw sound of the song is hardly accidental, as it went through a number of versions and recording sessions. 'Anarchy in the UK' was one of seven songs recorded by the group in July 1976, and it was these tapes that their manager Malcom McLaren took to the recording companies. With a stagnant music industry largely reacting to trends rather than initiating them, the Pistols material at first created little interest.

> When production values were complex and smooth, the Goodman (producer, Dave Goodman) tapes capture the group's live sound 'of broken glass and rusty razor blades'. In 1976, they must have sounded to the uninitiated like a rougher, more inept version of the new wave of Pub Rock bands, none of whom had reached the attention of the industry.
>
> (Savage 1991: 206; see also Heylin 1998)

Two days after they signed for EMI, the Sex Pistols again recorded 'Anarchy in the UK', which was to be their first single. The initial attempt 'to get the spirit of live performance' (bass player Glen Matlock) proved unsatisfactory, and it was eventually re-recorded with a different producer, Chris Thomas replacing Dave Goodman. On 26 November, the single was finally released: 'A much cleaner, more mainstream version, it was by that stage so loaded with expectation that it was difficult to listen objectively' (Savage 1991: 255). Following the infamous Grundy interview on Thames Television on 2 December, and the subsequent controversy and distribution problems, the single climbed to number 43 on the *NME* British chart and eventually reached number 27 in late December; it never charted in the United States.

The ingredients of 'Anarchy in the UK' typify punk rock (the following discussion is based primarily on Laing 1988). First, punk bands relied on live shows to establish an identity and build a reputation, consequently 'techniques of recording and of arrangement were adopted which were intended to signify the "live" commitment of the disc' (Laing 1988: 74). In short, punk records generally sound 'live', as if the studio had not come between the intentions of the musicians and their listening audience. Second, the use of the voice is in an identifiably punk mode, blurring the lyric with the singer's aggressive vocal, which lies between ordinary speech and singing. This makes the sound of the recording (voice plus instruments) more important than the actual identifiable lyric. Thus, for Laing 'any hope for the pure message, vocals as reflector of meaning, is doomed', which makes it 'possible (if difficult) to find pleasure in this celebrated punk rock song without the necessity of agreeing with the message' (Laing 1988: 75–6, 78). This is rather at odds with Savage's view of 'Anarchy' as a political text, but is the dominant impression of the song retained by most casual listeners. Yet how 'seriously' are we to take punk lyrics like 'Anarchy'? The ideology of sincerity was central to punk; in interviews, 'the stated beliefs of musicians, and their congruence with the perceived messages of their lyrics, became routine topics' (ibid.: 90). But, as various analyses demonstrate, in many cases punk lyrics are like collages, a series of often fractured images, with no necessarily correct reading (Sabin 1999).

Third, there is punk's mode of address. Compared with much popular music, the confidential stance is rare in punk rock, and 'Anarchy' is strongly in a sardonic declamatory mode. As with other punk songs, there is also an emphasis on addressing individuals other than 'lovers', and a 'plural specific' address. Fourth, the tempo of punk is usually described as 'basic' and 'primitive'. As a minimalist genre, punk rock eschewed the growing use of electronic instruments associated with 'progressive' rock, and featured a strict guitar and drums instrumental line-up: 'this was a sound best suited to expressing anger and frustration, focusing chaos, dramatizing the last days as daily life and ramming all emotions into the narrow gap between a blank stare and a sardonic grin' (Marcus 1992: 595). The lack of importance of virtuosity in instrumental solos, reflected punk's frequent association of skill with glibness. The frequently alleged musical incompetence of punk bands, however, was largely a myth, often fuelled by the bands themselves (on this point, see McNeil and McCain 1996; and Marcus Gray's study of the Clash, *Last Gang in Town*, 1995, which takes issue with much of the received wisdom regarding punk's supposed values).

'More crucial to punk's sense of difference from other musics is its attitude to rhythm' (Laing 1988: 85). It tended to submerge syncopation in its rhythmic patterns – the main reason for the 'undanceability' of much punk rock. This 'provided a feeling of unbroken rhythmic flow, enhanced by the breakneck eight to the bar rhythm of much punk rock' (ibid.), adding to the urgency which the voice and aggressive vocals evoked.

As even this abbreviated discussion indicates, 'Anarchy' indicates the congruence between punk as music and the social location and values of the associated punk subculture (see Hebdige 1979: 114ff.). Music here exists very much within a broader set of social relations.

Grandmaster Flash and the Furious 5: 'The Message' (Sugar Hill, 1982)

'The Message' was significant for ushering in rap, initially a dance fad which began in the late 1970s among black and Hispanic teenagers in New York's outer boroughs (on the development of rap, and the associated hip-hop, see Potter 1995). Its exponents made their own mixes, borrowing from a range of musical sources – sampling – and talking over the music – rapping – in a form of improvised street poetry. This was commercially significant, as black kids were 'doing their own thing' and bypassing the retail outlets: 'By taping bits of funk off air and recycling it, the break-dancers were setting up a direct line to their culture heroes. They were cutting out the middlemen' (Hebdige 1990: 140). Many of the early rappers recorded on independent labels, most prominently Sugar Hill in New York, but the trend was soon taken up by both white artists and the majors.

'The Message' is rap's greatest statement of contemporary urban despair, epitomised by the refrain in the chorus: 'Sometimes I wonder how I keep from goin' under'. As Marsh puts it, 'the words were abetted by the music: melody stretched by synthesizer, pulse provided by funk bass and glowering drums, comment aided by scratchy rhythm guitar' (Marsh 1989: 61–2). Like much subsequent rap, while 'The Message' is lyrically negative it is set to a compelling dance beat. The song opens with a mix of handclaps and sharp, pared down percussion (drum beats and cymbals), establishing a fast foot-tapping beat. This is quickly joined by a synthesizer, which moves up and down the scales in time to the beat: four beats up, four straight beats, four beats down, four straight beats. This interplay of synth and sharp percussion initially sounds merely bouncy and quietly unobtrusive, but as it goes on and on throughout the song – some seven minutes in length in its extended play release version – it starts to have a more disturbing and irritating quality, becoming a metaphor for being trapped in the ghetto and tenement life.

The song's lyric is a syncopated rap on the theme of ghetto living and on being poor and black in America, presenting a series of vivid and negative images: tenement slum blocks with broken glass everywhere, people urinating in the stairwells, rats and cockroaches, junkie muggers and bag ladies, people living off welfare and watching too much television. A series of stories are presented within this context, including a horribly inevitable life 'in the ghetto', reminiscent of Elvis Presley's song of that title. A child is born, drops out of school into unemployment and crime. Prison and sexual abuse follow, and he is found hanged in his cell. There is a didactic message here, telling young blacks not to get involved with gangsters and crime. The song ends with the use of ambient sounds of ghetto life and language.

'The Message' remains compelling listening, and evidence of rap's vitality despite its subsequent commercialisation and frequent critical denigration: in 1987 four million copies of white middle-class trio the Beastie Boys album *Licensed To Ill* 'were sold to 13-year-olds who don't know any better, giving new credence to the question "do you spell rap with a big or a small c?"' (Clarke 1990: 959). However, the commercialisation of rap, with performers like MC Hammer and Vanilla Ice, is only one side of the story; on the other is the hard-edged social commentary, chart success and controversy of NWA, Public Enemy, and Ice-T (see Chapter 12: Politics). Public Enemy's Chick D describes rap as 'black America's CNN', a way for a national community without access to the mainstream media to communicate and share its politics, style and language (Light 1991: 688).

Kylie Minogue, 'The Loco-motion' (single 1987; on album *Kylie*, 1988)

Australian singer Kylie Minogue has had to fight for serious recognition, beginning her music career to almost universal critical disapproval. Minogue's first record and chart success, was a cover of Gerry Goffin and Carol King's 'Locomotion' (a hit for Little Eva in 1962). The song's up-tempo dance beat was retained, along with what became the characteristic formula of Kylie's records: verve, bounce, and an inoffensive singing tone. This firmly located her in the dance pop/disco genre, and she was accordingly considered ephemeral pop. The denigration of dance pop and disco is related to their being predominantly 'female musics', which carry little weight in male-dominated 'rock' discourse. The criticism of Minogue was also based on a perception of her not having 'paid her dues' in terms of the dominant Australian pub rock performance tradition and an emphasis on live performance (see Turner 1992). Linked to this was a view of Kylie as a manufactured pop star, who had capitalised on a bankable image (as a star in the Australian TV, soap *Neighbours*), by her move into popular music. Critics also pointed to the role of producers Stock, Aitken, Waterman, who wrote (with the exception of 'Loco-motion'), produced, and arranged all the tracks on Minogue's first album.

The success of Kylie Minogue illustrated a number of trends in the music industry in the 1980s, trends which were to be confirmed in the 1990s: the emerging primacy of stars over auteurs; cross-media fertilisation; the increased prominence of women in the charts; and the successful recycling of old songs. As the example of Madonna amply demonstrates (Chapter 7), stars were figures whose cultural and commercial currency extended well beyond their musical talents. In Minogue's case, she had 'paid her artistic dues' and established her face and name as a star in *Neighbours*, and extended that success into pop. Her ability as a consummate camera performer, a result of her grounding in television, was central to the successful use of music video to promote Minogue's music: 'Minogue makes the camera (and by extension her audience) a "friend", and interacts with it accordingly. To have a star for a friend is irresistible to an audience such as Kylie's' (Rex 1992: 156). In her role of Charlene in *Neighbours*, Minogue was 'the girl next door', whose world was a fun place which struck a resonant chord with the soap's largely teenage audience. The star process created Kylie as authorised to 'speak' for this youthful constituency, and this cultural authority was transferable from the television screen to the dance pop record.

Kylie Minogue was one of a number of women performers to make an impact on the charts in the 1980s: including Madonna, Cyndi Lauper, Whitney Houston, Paula Abdul, Gloria Estefan, and Janet Jackson (Schlattman 1991). This new level of success for female artists was frequently associated with the view that these 1980s female performers had much more control over their music and careers than their 1970s peers. While this view has some validity, such control was usually exercised later in their careers, as commercial success and an increased knowledge of the industry encouraged greater artistic independence. This is clearly the case with Kylie Minogue: 'I was very much a puppet in the beginning. I was blinkered by my record company. I was unable to look left or right' (Q interview, October 1992).

Kylie Minogue has continued to record, and her longevity was demonstrated in 2000 with her number 1 record in the UK, 'Spinning Around', making her one of few performers to have number 1 hits in each of three decades.

S Club 7, 'Bring it All Back' (1999)

The critical response to Kylie Minogue in the 1980s was echoed by the hostile response from 'rock' fans and critics to dance pop in the late 1990s. As we have seen, in the case of the Spice Girls, the merits of their music were often pushed to one side in the preoccupation with the personas and private lives of the group (Chapter 7). In similar fashion, S Club 7 are frequently seen as 'just another manufactured pop group'. While this charge is in a sense correct, it overlooks the talent that led those particular performers to be chosen for the group, the basis of their appeal to their young fans, and the nature of contemporary celebrity in pop music.

Reflecting their name, S Club 7 consists of seven members, whose public image (via their television show) is very much that of a supportive friendship group. Initial TV and 19 Management (who manage the Spice Girls) conducted a nationwide search in the UK to develop a group to star in a teen-oriented television show for BBC1. The television show, 'S Club 7 in Miami', débuted in the UK during 1999, and went on to be screened internationally. Its success led to the show being re-screened (on BBC2 in January 2000), and to its marketing as two 'sell through' video compilations of several episodes. A follow-up series, 'S Club 7 in LA', first screened in the UK on BBC1 in early 2000, was also sold overseas (it began screening in New Zealand in August 2000). The group's debut single 'Bring It All Back' topped the UK chart, and enjoyed modest success when it was released in the United States. A second single, 'S Club Party', also charted, as did the groups self-titled first album. In August 2000, a second album and the first single from it ('Reach') charted in the UK, and overseas.

Television exposure and recording success meant S Club have appeared frequently in the teen music magazines, with several cover stories (e.g. *Smash Hits*, 5 April 2000), and on shows such as *Top of the Pops*. They also have an impressive official web site (www.sclub7.co.uk), which introduces visitors to 'the s club experience' in an interactive and engaging manner. The site enables fans to find out personal details about each member of the group, the recordings and television shows, and their other activities. Fans can register to receive advance information about all of these, and can leave messages for the groups' members. The web site consolidates S Club 7's fan base, and provides a valuable adjunct to more traditional forms of music marketing. This fan base appears to largely consist of young girls, and some boys, aged between eight and twelve, a significant 'demographic' with considerable spending power.

The range of personalities in the group provide someone and something for most fans; e.g. 'Hannah is my favourite person in the band. She is cool and has a nice voice, and does very good dancing' (Emma, 9). The four girls and three boys in S Club are a very photogenic and physically appealing group, who range in age from 16 to 22 years. To quote New Zealand teen magazine *Tearaway* (January 2000) they are 'loud, fresh and wild, with a "we can do it" attitude'. Their song lyrics are a factor here, with many young fans able to relate to the positive messages in songs such as 'You're My Number 1' and 'Bring It All Back':

> Hold on to what you try to be: your individuality
> When the world is on your shoulders
> Just smile and let it go
> If people try to put you down
> Just walk on by don't turn around
> You only have to answer to yourself
>
> Don't you know its true what they say
> In life it aint easy
> But your time's coming around
> So don't you stop tryin
>
> Don't stop never give up
> Hold your head high and reach the top

Let the world see what you have got
Bring it all back for you for (to) you.
(S Club 7, 'Bring It All Back', 1999)

S Club's success can be attributed to a combination of their infectious dance pop, the emphasis on supportive friendship in the television shows, and the youthful members' appeal to young fans. And all of this has been astutely marketed, with each market niche reinforcing the others.

The examples of textual analysis included here illustrate the need to extend the traditional musicological approach to popular music, into the relationships between texts and listeners, and the generic and historical location of texts and their performers. The production of meaning in the music is, once again, situated in the nexus between industry economics and rock history, musicians and their audience. A further example of this process is music video, which is now of such stature that it merits separate consideration.

READING MUSIC VIDEOS

The primary focus in the study of music video (MV) has been on their nature as audio-visual texts. Various attempts to read music videos have necessarily adopted the insights and concepts of film (and television) studies, although these have had to be modified in the light of the different functions they often play in MVs, particularly in relation to the music. There is also some recognition, at times rather belated, of the point that MVs are not self-contained texts, but reflective of their nature as industrial and commercial products (see Chapter 10).

The main intention here is to sketch some basic considerations which usefully inform specific 'textual' readings of MV, and, with particular reference to the work of Anne Kaplan, to examine the difficulties endemic in constructing a classificatory typology of music videos. These intentions are in part addressed through two case studies of music video: Madonna's 'Justify My Love' and Duran Duran's 'Hungry Like the Wolf'. These are chosen for their familiarity, though the ephemeral nature of most MVs must be conceded. Further, the difficulty of prose analysis of a visual text, in the absence of that same text, is painfully obvious. (My discussion can only be a preliminary and highly abbreviated one; for extended discussion of music videos as texts and examples of close readings, see Goodwin 1993; Vernallis 1998; Roberts 1996).

Two general points frequently made about MVs as individual texts are their preoccupation with visual style, and, associated with this, their status as key exemplars of 'postmodern' texts. Music videos were clearly pioneers in video expression, but their visual emphasis raises problems for their musical dimensions. As some three-quarters of sensory information comes in through the eye, the video viewer concentrates on the images, arguably at the expense of the soundtrack. This combination has been accused of fuelling performers' preoccupation with visual style, which can dominate over content. MV has become a crucial marketing tool, with the music often merely part of an overall style package offered to consumers.

Cultural historian and theorist Jameson (1984) saw music videos as 'meta entertainments' that embody the postmodern condition. It is certainly clear that MVs do indeed merge commercial and artistic image production and abolish traditional boundaries between an image and its real life referent. In this respect, their most obvious characteristic is their similarity to adverts, making them a part of a blatantly consumerist culture. Kaplan (1987) goes as far as to suggest that the MV spectator has become decentred and fragmented, unable any longer to distinguish 'fiction' from 'reality', part of postmodern culture. This conflation of MV and postmodernism is, however, difficult to sustain. While many MVs display considerable evidence of pastiche, intertextuality and eclecticism, this does not in itself make them postmodern (for an insightful discussion of this point, see Goodwin 1993). Further, the nature of MVs as a whole is arguably becoming more traditional and clichéd, as is evident from just a few hours watching MTV.

Considering music videos as texts means applying some stock topics and questions. These are derived partly from film studies, and include cinematic aspects, such as camera techniques, lighting, use of colour, and editing. Different styles of video utilise different conventions; heavy metal videos, for example, make considerable use of wide-angle lens and zoom shots in keeping with their emphasis on a 'live concert' format. A major focus of MV analysis which follows film studies, is the nature of the gaze in MV – who is looking at who, how, and what do these conventions convey in terms of power relations, gender stereotypes, and the social construction of self?

In more general thematic terms, there is a need to also consider:

1   The mood of the video – the way in which the music, the words and the visuals combine to produce a general feeling of nostalgia, romanticism, nihilism, or whatever.
2   The narrative structure – the extent to which the video tells a clear time-sequenced story, or is a non-linear pastiche of images, flashbacks, etc.
3   The degree of realism or fantasy of the settings or environments in the video, and the relationship between genres and particular settings (e.g. rap and the street).
4   The standard themes evident; for example, the treatment of authority, love and sex, 'growing up' and the loss of childhood innocence, political and social consciousness.
5   The importance of performance; why does this format fit particular genres such as heavy metal?

6   Different modes of sexuality – the female as mother/whore figure; androgyny and the blurring of dress codes; and homoeroticism.

7   The nature of MVs as a star text, centred on the role played by the central performer(s) in the video and the interrelationship of this to their star persona in rock more generally.

8   The music – what we hear and how it relates to what we see. This is often a critical absence from visual-oriented readings of MV. Goodwin goes so far as to argue that:

> a musicology of the music video image is the basis for understanding how to undertake a credible textual study. Issues relating to the sound–vision relation, the formal organization of music videos, questions of pleasure and so on, need to be related to the musical portion of the text.
>
> (Goodwin 1993: intro.)

These are not simply signposts to reading individual MVs, they are also factors which can be utilised to categorise them. Although much criticised, the most thorough initial attempt to categorise MVs remains that developed by Kaplan, in her study *Rocking Around the Clock: Music Television, Postmodernism, and Consumer Culture* (1987). While Kaplan is primarily concerned with analysing MTV, she also constructs an interesting typology of individual MVs. Her five categories here are derived from combining a reading of rock history with theoretical tools taken from psychoanalytic and film theory, a combination that at times sits awkwardly. Her five typical video forms are: the romantic, the socially conscious, the nihilist, the classical, and the postmodern. Critics have found this categorisation 'confusing and ultimately not very helpful' (Goodwin 1987: 42; see also Cubitt 1991: 52f.), as have my students and myself when attempting to apply the typology to particular videos.

As Goodwin (1993) observes, Kaplan's schema is weak partly because it mixes the bases for each category: the first three are situated in pop history – the romantic clips drawing from 1960s soft rock; the socially conscious from 1970s rock, and the nihilist from 1980s new wave and heavy metal music. But then the remaining two categories are based in film theory (with the classical category related to realist film texts), and the postmodern in some sort of catch-all residual category in which postmodern motifs, evident in practically all MVs, are simply more plentiful. The result is that clips placed in one category might just as easily be located in another. It is also questionable to collapse the history of pop/rock music into a series of decades, each dominated by and identified with a certain style of music. Further, the schema ignores the significance of genre and auteurship in the music industry, both of which sit awkwardly with it.

What would be a viable alternative schema? Perhaps the eclectic nature of music video makes impossible anything other than a basic distinction between performance and fictional narrative MVs? Let us consider this question in the light of two classic examples.

Duran Duran, 'Hungry Like the Wolf' (music video, director: Russell Mulcahy, 1981)

This Duran Duran MV illustrates the need to consider music videos as promotional devices as much as mini visual texts. Formed in 1978, UK pop quartet Duran Duran achieved considerable early commercial success with several hits in the British top 20 in 1981, but initially failed to dent the US market. Despite intensive touring in North America and the photogenic group's considerable exposure in the teen music press, their self-titled debut album on Capitol/EMI failed to yield a hit single and had only risen to number 150 on the album charts. Exposure on MTV changed this dramatically.

The group had already attracted attention with their first video: 'Girls On Film' (1980) directed by leading video auteurs Godley and Creme. The group barely appear in the MV, which features a series of soft-core porn style scenes, including attractive, scantily clad (nude in the uncensored version) women pillow-fighting on a whipped cream-covered phallic pole! Kevin Godley acknowledges the sexism of the video, but explains:

> Look, we just did our job. We were very explicitly told by Duran Duran's management to make a very sensational, erotic piece that would be for clubs, where it would get shown uncensored, just to make people take notice and talk about it.
>
> (cited Shore 1985: 86)

That bands were increasingly making two versions of their videos, one for mainstream television shows and MTV, and one for more adult cable outlets and clubs, demonstrates the market-driven nature of the video text, and any reading of MV must take this intention into account.

The 'Hungry Like the Wolf' video also raises the issue of authorship in MVs. While it is customary to refer to MVs as being the product of the particular performer featured, and some artists take a major role in determining the nature of their MVs, 'the directors most often are responsible for the concepts, the vision, the imagery, and the editing rhythm that coalesce into a look that keeps people watching' (Shore 1985: 97). This is still the case, particularly with 'new' performers unfamiliar with the medium. There are a number of MV directors who can be considered 'auteurs' in the field, including Godley and Creme, Russell Mulcahy, David Mallet, Brian Grant, and Julian Temple. Several, most notably Mulcahy and Temple, have gone on to directing major feature films.

In August 1981, as MTV began broadcasting in North America, EMI invested $200,000 to send Duran Duran to Sri Lanka to shoot three video clips with director Russell Mulcahy. One of them, 'Hungry Like the Wolf', became an MTV favourite. Less than two months after the two-week shoot, the clip was in heavy rotation on MTV, was getting heavy radio airplay, and this exposure helped propel the single into the top 10 and Duran Duran's second album, *Rio*, into the upper reaches of the album charts. MTV confirmed Duran Duran as a teenage sensation (Hill 1986). In 1983, in conjunction with Sony which was promoting its new video 45s (which included the Duran's 'Girls On Film' – in an uncensored version – and 'Hungry'), along with Duran Duran's long-form video cassette, the group undertook a highly successful video tour of major clubs across North America; 'Each date on the video tour sold out, and in every city the video tour hit, Duran Duran's records sold out within days' (Shore 1985: 93–4).

In 'Hungry like the Wolf' Singer Simon LeBon's head rises in slow motion out of a river as rain pours down. He then chases a beautiful Indian woman, clad only in an animal skin (?) through a Sri Lankan tropical jungle and open air market. During the chase, he has his brow mopped by a young Indian (boy?) and overturns a bar room table. When he catches the beast/woman they have an encounter suggestive of both sex and violence:

> Mulcahy's ravenously tracking and panning camera, insinuating erotic ambiguity, and editing wizardry (frames slide in from the left or right, double and split-screen edits on and around the beat, etc) which have been the real stars of the show all along, come into full play ... we've been dazzled seduced and abandoned.
>
> (Shore 1985: 178)

The nature of the narrative is almost irrelevant here, serving merely to showcase LeBon, and add an aura of exotic appeal and sexuality to the song.

Any satisfactory analysis of 'Hungry' as a text must acknowledge this 'focus on the star' aspect of it. Duran Duran were the pin-up band of the mid-1980s, particularly among young girls. Watching the video even now, young women students focus on the physical appeal of the singer, who is variously described as 'delicious', a 'hunk', and 'sexy'. Young male viewers acknowledge that LeBon is 'conventionally handsome' and some even tentatively point to his rather androgynous appeal. The star appeal of LeBon is fed on and enhanced by the technical virtuosity of the director, already then recognised as a leading auteur of the music video form. Mulcahy is arguably the star as much as LeBon – though not, of course, to the young fans of Duran Duran in the mid-1980s.

Even purely at the level of text, 'Hungry like the Wolf' is difficult to categorise in Kaplan's terms. It has elements of the 'classical', with the male as subject and the woman as object: 'I'm on the hunt I'm after you' sings LeBon – though there is a case for reversing this distinction. Further, the video's narrative structure is a mini-drama, based loosely around LeBon's chase while his friends are being enticed by lithe beauties back in the town, a narrative which never fully realises closure. But in Kaplan's terms, the video also has strongly 'postmodernist' features. The rapid editing creates a series of disjointed images, which disrupt linear time and leave the viewer uncertain about the sequence of the events and even if there is indeed a 'plot' to follow.

Kaplan pays little attention to the music in her analysis of music video, an absence that is significant in the case of 'Hungry' (even if it is admittedly not one of the MVs she analyses). The sharp rhythm and strong beat of the song, along with the single male voice, match the rapid editing and sheer physical aggression of the video. It is the music that links and 'makes sense of' the images, which would not have the same impact on their own.

Madonna, 'Justify My Love' (music video, director Jean-Baptiste Mondino, 1990)

Madonna is a central example of the significance of the star image in the construction and appeal of MVs:

> Singled out for identification, but also for homo- as well as heteroerotic and narcissistic pleasures, the star takes on the role of originator of the work, the absent centre of its production, the core of the economy of desire established in the tape or the body of work mapped out by the artist as *auteur*.
>
> (Cubitt 1991: 57)

In the case of star performers, their specific videos do not stand alone, but are intimately related to their established public persona.

Madonna's MVs have been the subject of considerable public controversy and academic analysis (see Roberts 1996: chap. 3; Cubitt 1991; Schwichtenberg 1993). In December 1990, her 'Justify My Love' video was rejected by American MTV even though it was shown in its entirety on ABC's *Nightline*, and promptly generated the programme's largest audience of the year. In the UK, 'Justify My Love' was screened only on a late night MV show on Channel 4, and the video was accorded similar treatment internationally.

The MV features Madonna in bra and garter belt in an erotic encounter with a lover, played by her then real-life boyfriend Tony Ward, along with several other androgynous figures, in a Paris hotel (for a full description, see Henderson 1993). The video portrays a series of fantasies: bisexuality, voyeurism, group sex, cross-dressing and mild sado-masochism, and icons abound: chains, black leather, and crucifixes. As Henderson observes, the video was almost revolutionary:

> In its sexual stances, 'Justify My Love' defies some of music videos' worst cliches, opening up an aesthetic and political corner for other ways of envisaging sex in popular culture. Unlike most MTV clips (ZZ Top's come to mind), it eroticizes all its characters – female, male, and those in between, black and white – fondly entangling them in a collective fantasy even as it foregrounds its star. Madonna's voice, *her* voice, orchestrate that fantasy, whose polymorphism slips and slides around conventional video images of sensation and arousal.
>
> (Henderson 1993: 111–12)

Madonna herself defended the video as being 'about honesty and the celebration of sex. There's nothing wrong with that'.

Primarily at issue in the public and academic debates during the 1980s and into the 1990s over MVs such as 'Justify My Love' was whether Madonna was simply appealing, through the sexual 'explicitness' of her videos, to male (and female) voyeurism, or was in fact a proto-feminist. Madonna herself adopted the latter position: 'I may be dressing like the typical bimbo, or whatever, but I'm in charge of my fantasies. I put myself in these situations with men' (press report, December 1990). Several academic commentators identified with this claim: Frith argues that 'selling women as stars means showing them in charge of their femininity (and its construction as a way of looking)', not just as available objects for the male gaze (Frith 1988a: 217); and Kaplan regarded Madonna as 'the female star who perhaps more than any other embodies the new postmodern feminist heroine in her odd combination of seductiveness and a gutsy sort of independence' (Kaplan 1987: 117).

Similar arguments surround Madonna's use of religiously charged icons. To some it was simply read as blasphemy, and another facet of the performer's deliberately courting controversy to gain increased public exposure; this was part of a wider body of public criticism which constructed Madonna as 'Low-Other' (see Schulze *et al.* 1993). Conversely, while offering a semiotic analysis sympathetic to Madonna, Fiske writes:

> Combining the crucifix with the signs of pornography is a carnivalesque profanity, but the new combination does not 'mean' anything specific, all it signifies is her power over discourse, her ability to use the already written signifiers of

patriarchal Christianity, and to tear them away from their signifieds is a moment of empowerment.

(Fiske 1989: 252–3)

Although analyses which present readings of Madonna and 'Justify My Love' (and her other videos) as potentially empowering for women viewers are plausible, they tend to assume that this removes her from the patriarchal gaze. Rather, observation of, and discussions with, male viewers suggest that her early videos do still function as voyeuristic texts, albeit in a complex fashion. While boys enjoyed looking at Madonna as an object of sexual desire, they were perturbed by the confidence she expressed in her own sexuality, and as such labelled her a 'tart'. Analysing Madonna's equally controversial video 'Open Your Heart', Bordo (1993) concluded that the dominant position in the video is in fact still that of the objectifying gaze. This gaze, however, is hardly a unitary 'male' one. Madonna's videos are variously read off by particular ethnic groups, by different sections of the gay community, and by both differentially socially located fans and critics of the singer (see the essays in Schwichtenberg 1993; also Brown and Schulze 1990).

The videos examined here are arguably typical of the MV form, and illustrative of the difficulties of textual classification. As we have seen, to explain the nature of their appeal it is necessary to go beyond their purely textual aspects, and consider their function as polysemic narratives and images of viewer fantasy and desire. As are other popular culture texts, MVs present a semiotic terrain open to cultural struggles over meaning. This illustrates the general point that meanings and pleasures are not purely embedded 'in' MV texts, but are produced in the act of viewing. Music videos are indicative of the general importance of the visual (re)presentation of popular music, the subject of Chapter 10.

Chapter 10

'U got the look'
Film and television, music video and MTV

This chapter deals with the visual (re-)presentation of popular music, examining the relationship between popular music and film, television, and, in particular, music video and MTV. As was shown in Chapter 2, 'music became a thing' (Eisenberg 1988) with the advent of recording technology in the late nineteenth century enabling its development in commodity form, independent of its 'live' performance aspects. Until its twentieth-century reproduction on disc and dissemination on radio, music was not purely an aural experience but one also involving the pleasure of seeing the performance. While 'live' performance continued to be important, music was now often mediated by the new visual media.

The cinema was central to the historical development of the marketing of music, with the key place of music in 'silent' movies, and the popularity of musicals in the 1930s and 1940s. The youth-oriented films of the 1950s, most notably *Rock Around the Clock*, along with appearances of performers like Elvis on the new medium of television, watched by 40 million viewers on the *Ed Sullivan Show*, helped establish rock 'n' roll as a major form of popular culture. Television soon developed programmes for the teenage audiences who became demographically important in the late 1950s. Music videos, along with the introduction of compact discs, helped rescue a flagging record industry in the early 1980s. In so doing, they established visual style – never of course totally out of style – as a pre-eminent aspect of performance. At the same time, feature film continues to use popular music for both its narrative themes and characters, and for sound tracks.

POPULAR MUSIC ON THE SILVER SCREEN

Film has had an important relationship to popular music. Early silent films often had a live musical accompaniment, usually piano. With the 'talkies', musicals became a major genre in the 1930s, and continued to be important into the 1960s (see Millard 1995; Kalinak 1992). Composers and musicians, primarily stars, provided a source of material for these films, as did Broadway musicals. The various genres of popular music, its fans and performers acted as a rich vein of colourful, tragic and salutary stories for film-makers. A new form of musical, the 'rock musical', played an important part in establishing rock 'n' roll in the mid-1950s. Allied with such musicals were youth movies, with a range of sub-genres, and 'rockumentaries'. Over the past thirty years or so, considerable synergy has been created between the music and film industries. Film soundtracks represent another avenue of revenue for recordings, including the back catalogue, and help promote contemporary releases.

'Rock musicals'

Films dealing in some way with popular music, or drawing on it for their soundtrack, are frequently treated as a generic group. Szatz calls them 'popular musicals', although this term could apply equally to their historical predecessors, and they are also accorded the label 'rock film'. There is now a substantial body of such films, including a number of identifiable sub-genres, with a considerable literature on them (see the bibliography in Cooper 1992; for a useful filmography, see Romney and Wootton 1995) and the discussion here is highly selective.

During the 1950s, the decline of the Hollywood studio system and dwindling cinema audiences, led to the need to more systematically target particular audiences. Hollywood linked up with the record industry to target youth, with a spate of teenage musicals helping popularise emergent stars such as Elvis (e.g. *Jail House Rock*, 1957). *Blackboard Jungle* (1954) used the new genre of rock 'n' roll to symbolise adolescent rebellion against the authority of the school. Most early popular musicals had basic plots involving the career of a young rock performer; for example *Rock Around the Clock* (1955), *Don't Knock the Rock* (1956), and *The Girl Can't Help It* (1957). These were frequently combined with the other stock form, films serving purely as contrived vehicles for their real-life stars. Most of Elvis Presley's movies, from *Love Me Tender* (1956) onward, were of this order, while British examples include Cliff Richard in *The Young Ones*, and Tommy Steele in *Six-Five Special* (1958).

Any interest such films retain is largely due to their participant's music rather than their acting talents, though they did function as star vehicles for figures like Presley. In helping establish an identity for rock 'n' roll, the teenage musicals placed youth in opposition to adult authority, and for conservatives confirmed the 'folk devil' image of fans of the new genre, associating them with juvenile delinquency, a major concern internationally through the 1950s (see Doherty 1988: chap. 3). Thematically, however, the popular musicals actually stressed reconciliation between generations and classes, with this acting as a point of narrative closure at the film's ending. Such musicals also helped create an audience and a market for the new musical form, particularly in countries distant from the initial developments. These related roles continued to be in evidence in the subsequent development of the popular/rock musical.

An early example of the power of cinema is provided by 'Rock Around the Clock', by Bill Haley and the Comets. Originally released in May 1954, it barely dented the *Billboard* chart, peaking at number 23, where it stayed for only one week. Greater success came when the song was prominently used on the soundtrack for *Blackboard Jungle*, one of the most successful and controversial films of 1955. Re-released in May 1955, 'Rock Around the Clock' went to number 1 in the UK and the USA. By the end of 1955 it had become the most popular recording in the US since 'The Tennessee Waltz', selling 6 million copies (Miller 1999: 91).

The impact of Merseybeat in the early 1960s was consolidated by a number of films. Gerry and the Pacemakers brought a taste of the emergent Liverpool scene to a broader audience with their 1964 film *Ferry Across the Mersey*. This stuck to what had already become a standard formula – struggling young band makes good after initial setbacks – which was only shaken when the Beatles enlisted director Richard Lester to produce the innovative and pseudo-biographical *A Hard Day's Night* (1964). Along with *Help* (1965), this consolidated the Beatle's market dominance, and extended the rock film genre into new and more interesting anarchic forms. In the mid–late 1960s, with the emergence of the counterculture, popular music was a necessary backdrop and a cachet of cultural authenticity for films such as *Easy Rider* (1969) and *The Graduate* (1967). Both fused effective popular music soundtracks with the search for a personal and cultural identity in contemporary America.

During the 1970s and 1980s there was a profusion of popular musicals: the realist Jamaican film *The Harder They Come* (1972); the flower power and religious fantasy of *Godspell* (1973); *Jesus Christ Superstar* (1973) and *Hair* (1979); the disco-dance musicals of *Saturday Night Fever* (1977), *Grease* (1978), and *Staying Alive* (1983); and the dance fantasies of *Flashdance* (1983), and *Dirty Dancing* (1987). The 'rock lifestyle' was the focus of *That'll Be The Day* (1973), and Ken Russell's version of *Tommy* (1975). Nostalgia was at the core of *American Graffitti* (1973), *The Blues Brothers* (1978), *Quadrophenia* (1979), and *The Buddy Holly Story* (1978). The success of these popular musicals prepared the ground for the success of MTV, launched in 1981, by redefining the political economy of rock, moving the emphasis from sound to images (Grossberg 1992).

The Rocky Horror Picture Show (1975) created a new sub-genre: the cult musical. Following its first New York midnight screening in 1976, over the next six years the film played to over five thousand people each week, only at midnight, in over 200 cinemas throughout the United States. People started coming dressed in some of the costumes shown in the film, and began singing and talking back to the screen. The audience became an integral part of the cinematic experience, an indulgence in fantasy and catharsis. The film went on to became the king of the 'midnight movies' – cult films shown at midnight on weekends (see Samuels 1983).

Dance narratives

An important sub-genre were dance narratives, such as *Saturday Night Fever* (1977), *Strictly Ballroom* (1992), and *Dirty Dancing* (1987). The attraction of these dance narratives, lies in 'the fantasies of achievement they afford their subjects' (McRobbie 1991: 201); they exemplify Grant's observation that, more generally, thematically 'musicals have been concerned with articulating a sense of community and defining the parameters of sexual desire, the two themes of course being intimately related' (Grant 1986: 196). *Dirty Dancing* (1987), directed by Emile Ardolino, is an example of this process. It also exemplified the way in which the film and music industries by the 1980s were working together to maximise the potential of both mediums, with carefully chosen music for the associated soundtrack album (see Frith 1988b: 97–8). The film features many of the stock ingredients of 'youth films' aimed at a teenage market: a 1960s setting, sexual attraction and rock 'n' roll, and stereotyped adults out to spoil the kids fun, but it stands out from the genre through its serious treatment of a young woman's sexual 'coming of age'. College-bound Baby, played by diminutive Jennifer Grey, is on holiday with her parents at a hotel resort. She comes across a party where the resort's resident dance partners, played by Patrick Swayze and Cynthia Rhodes, and their friends, are dancing in an intimate and very suggestive manner: 'dirty dancing'. Rhodes drops out to have an abortion, involving a side plot about Swayze's credibility as a 'responsible' lover, leaving Swayze without a dance partner. Baby steps into the role, becomes a professional-level dancer in a few sessions, and the two fall in love and into bed. The narrative is resolved in a satisfying (at least from the audience's viewpoint), if improbable happy ending.

As with *Flashdance* (see McRobbie 1991), young female viewers of *Dirty Dancing* were attracted to its narrative of romance, while the eroticism of the visual subtext appealed to young males. Both aspects are present in a dynamic visual style which owed much to music videos, featuring a series of dynamic dancing routines, choreographed to a strong rock soundtrack. They represent the collapsing of class and gender distinctions between the two principals: Swayze's combination of macho and sensitive working-class male 'hunk', and Grey's slightly hesitant middle-class female integrity. As McRobbie observed of similar films: 'Dance operates as a metaphor for an external reality which is unconstrained by the limits and expectations of gender identity and which successfully and relatively painlessly transports its subjects from a passive to a more active psychic position' (McRobbie 1991: 201). Here, Baby is an active and willing partner in the loss of her virginity, and ultimately wins her father over to Swayze's virtues. Gender, class and generational conflicts are all collapsed through the power of the dance to create a temporary emotional community of interest in the ending of the film. *Dirty Dancing* works for its audience by involving them in this fantasy resolution.

Popular musical films have continued to mine the themes of youth subcultures (*Rivers Edge*, 1987), adolescent and young adult sexuality and gender relations (*Singles*, 1992); generational conflict; nostalgia (*Velvet Goldmine*, 1999; *The Last Days of Disco*, 1998); stardom and the 'rock lifestyle'; (e.g. *Purple Rain*, 1984; *The Doors*, 1990; *Sid and Nancy*, 1986; *Why Do Fools Fool in Love?*, 1998); and fandom (*High Fidelity*, 2000). The story lines of these films involve popular music to varying extents, ranging from its centrality to the narrative theme, to its use as a contextualising soundtrack. The films articulate with the hopes and dreams, and fantasy lives, which popular music brings to people everywhere. Where an actual artist is drawn on, or featured, such films help the process of mythologising them, as with Elvis Presley, the Janis Joplin character in *The Rose* (1979), the reprise of the Beatle's pre-fame days in Hamburg, *Backbeat* (1995), and director Julian Temple's re-examination of the Sex Pistols and punk rock in *The Filth and the Fury* (2000). An underpinning theme is often youth/adolescence as a rite of passage, frequently characterised by storm and stress, and the search for independence and identity. Given such themes are ones identified in the literature as central adolescent 'tasks' and preoccupations, they clearly appeal to youthful cinema audiences, and to film-makers looking for box-office appeal.

The 'rock musicals' discussed above are frequently based on the quest for the success sought by popular musicians. In the highly successful realist *The Commitments* (1991), directed by Alan Parker, the lead character, Jimmy Rabbitte, attempts to bring soul to the Irish by forming an R&B band in Dublin. His unlikely collection of individuals, the Commitments, argue constantly, have problems acquiring gear and gigs, and, after one great pub performance, the band disintegrates. This process is also part of cinema's 'rockumentary'.

Rockumentaries

Rockumentaries include films and television programmes/series documenting music festivals, concerts, tours, local music scenes, and the history of popular music. Films of music festivals have consolidated the mythic status of events like Woodstock; and the 1970 film was a major box office success. A number of other concert and concert tour films have had a similar but more limited commercial and ideological impact;

e.g. *The Last Waltz* (1978), a record of The Band's final concert; *Hail, Hail Rock and Roll* (1987), featuring Chuck Berry and other early rock 'n' roll performers; *Stop Making Sense* (1984), featuring Talking Heads; and Prince's *Sign of the Times* (1987). Such films capture particular moments in 'rock history', while validating particular musical styles and performers. The problem for film makers with such projects is that there are only so many things you can do with concert performances, given their restricted ambit, and many of the conventions they rely on have become cinematic cliché; e.g. *Rattle and Hum* (1988), the film of U2's American tour.

Stop Making Sense, directed by Jonathon Demme, won the 1984 Best Documentary Award from the US National Society of Film Critics. A record of new wave band Talking Heads in concert, the film used material from three Hollywood shows in December 1983. The documentary is shot in a cool, almost classical style, with the unobtrusive camera subservient to the performances. Instead of stage histrionics and overpowering light shows, director Demme used 'minimalist' staging, lighting and presentation. The film helped bring a moderately successful 'cult' band to a broader audience. The ongoing interest in *Stop Making Sense* saw the soundtrack being re-released in 1999 to mark the fifteenth anniversary of the film, using the CD format to include for the first time all sixteen songs featured in the concert.

Documentaries have also been important in exposing particular scenes and sounds to a wider audience; e.g. *The Decline of Western Civilization, Part One* (1981) on the Los Angeles punk/hardcore scene circa 1981, featuring Black Flag, the Circle Jerks, X, and the Germs; its 'sequel', *The Decline of Western Civilization, Part Two: the Metal Years* (1988), which included Metallica, and Motorhead; *Hype* (1996) on the Seattle grunge scene; and *Buena Vista Social Club* (1999), which, along with the earlier Grammy-winning album (of the same title, 1996) brought Cuban music into the mainstream. Other popular music documentaries have celebrated major performers; e.g. the Who in *The Kids Are Alright* (1979). As with any genre, the ultimate accolade is parody, represented by *This is Spinal Tap* (1984). There is also an important body of documentaries examining the history of popular music, most notably the joint BBC–PBS series *Dancing in the Street*, accompanied by a lavishly illustrated book (Palmer 1995), and VH1's series of performer profiles, *Behind the Music*, which now number over a hundred. These reframe the past, by privileging particular moments, styles, and performers over others.

The various rockumentary forms of popular musical have served a number of economic and ideological functions. While celebrating 'youth' and the mythic status of stars, they also confirm their status as 'the other' for critics of these sounds and their performers. They validate and confirm particular musical styles and historical moments in the history of popular music as somehow worthy of more 'serious' attention.

Soundtracks

Mainstream narrative cinema has used two types of musical soundtrack to compliment the filmic text: (1) theme music, usually composed specifically for the film (e.g. *Star Wars*, *Jaws*); (2) a soundtrack consisting of selected popular music, usually contemporary with the temporal and physical setting of the film, or representative of the period evoked (e.g. *The Big Chill*, *Singles*, *American Graffiti*). The emphasis here is on the second of these forms, although occasionally there may be two 'soundtracks' released, or the two approaches are sometimes combined (e.g. *Dead Man Walking*, 1996; *Batman*, 1989).

Rock Around the Clock (1956) and many of the films featuring Elvis Presley demonstrated the market appeal of popular musical soundtracks, as had many Hollywood musicals before them. Mainstream narrative cinema has increasingly used popular music soundtracks to great effect, with accompanying commercial success for both film and record. This occurred with the soundtrack to *The Commitments* (1991); featuring some impressive covers of soul classics and the powerful voice of Andrew Strong (who plays the part of the lead singer Deco), it charted internationally, reaching number 1 in a several countries.

Such soundtracks feature popular music composed specifically for the film, or previously recorded work which is thematically or temporally related to the film: e.g. *The Big Chill* (1983); *Boyz N The Hood* (1991). This enables multimedia marketing, with accompanying commercial success for both film and record. Prince's soundtrack for the film *Batman* (1989) was part of a carefully orchestrated marketing campaign, which successfully created interest in the film and helped break Prince to a wider audience, primarily through exposure (of the promotional video clip) on MTV (Shuker 1994). Several musicians better known for their band recordings have followed Ry Cooder's example and moved into composing music for such films; e.g. Trent Razor (Nine Inch Nails) for *Natural Born Killers* (1994), and Kirk Hammet (Metallica) and Orbital for *Spawn* (1999). Films aimed at children (and the parents who take them to the movies) have had some of the biggest selling soundtrack albums in recent years: *The Lion King*, and *Tarzan*.

THE SMALL SCREEN

A contradictory relationship has traditionally existed between television and popular music. Television is traditionally a medium of family entertainment, collapsing class, gender, ethnic, and generational differences in order to construct a homogeneous audience held together by the ideology of the nuclear family. Since it emerged in the 1950s, 'rock' in contrast has traditionally presented itself as being about 'difference', emphasising individual tastes and preferences.

In spite of these differences – or arguably because of them – television was quick to seize the commercial opportunities offered by the emergent youth culture market of the 1950s. 'Television became devoted, at least in part, to the feature of televisual musical products for an audience that spent much of its leisure time and money in the consumption of pop music goods' (Burnett 1990: 23). This led to a proliferation of television popular music shows. On American television these included Paul Whiteman's *TV Teen Club* (which ran from 1949 to 1954), and *American Bandstand*, one of the longest running shows in television history which started in 1952 and is still screening. Britain had *Juke Box Jury* and *Top of the Pops*, both starting in the late 1950s. In 1963 *Ready Steady Go!* (RSG) began showcasing new talent, who usually performed live, compared to the *Top of The Pops* which presented staid studio lip-synchs with backing from a house orchestra. The American show *Shindig!*, débuting in 1964, adopted *RSG*'s format. In the UK, *Top of the Pops* and *The Old Grey Whistle Test* historically established the power of musical television to shape tastes. Television's presentation of pop and rock music prior to the advent of music video was generally uninspiring. Performers either straightforwardly performed, even if at times in an impressively frenetic manner (as with the Who's début effort on *RSG*) or mimed to their recordings in a pseudo-live setting.

In addition to regular programmes, one-off shows became showcases for performers and genres, helping to launch new material (e.g. the *Top of the Pops* Robbie Williams special, which helped the singer's new album to the top of the charts when it was screened in New Zealand in August 2000). Such shows can be crucial historical moments. Michael Jackson's performance of his number one single 'Billie Jean' on the TV special *Motown 25: Yesterday, Today, and Forever*, before nearly 50 million viewers, 'would energize the music scene once again and set in motion all the forces that would go on to shape the popular culture of the 1980s' (DeCurtis 1991: 638–9). Drawing on the video he had made for 'Billie Jean', Jackson lip-synched to a recorded track, leaving him free to execute his outstanding dance steps, including the début of the 'Moonwalk'. Jackson's performance indicated the power of such mass exposure in the marketplace. His album *Thriller*, released on 1 December 1982, had already reached number 1 over the Christmas period, and looked like emulating the success of Jackson's previous solo album *Off the Wall* (which sold 6 million copies). But the singer's charismatic and electrifying performance of 'Billie Jean' boosted the sales of *Thriller*, which went on to sell 40 million copies, the best-selling album in history.

The 1980s success of MTV boosted televised music videos (MV) and reshaped the form. In the United States and Canada, nearly every major city soon had its own televised music video show. As with their historical forerunners, these were significant partly because of their importance to advertisers, drawing a young audience whose consuming habits and brand allegiance are not set. Along with MTV (see below), popular music on television helps construct a global teenage consumer.

Several nationally syndicated MV programmes have continued to be a stock part of TV channel viewing schedules in the United Kingdom and Western Europe, and New Zealand and Australia. Currently, *The Pepsi Chart Show* screens in twenty-five countries, reaching in excess of 40 million viewers, making it 'the biggest terrestrial TV music franchise on the planet' (Danielsen 2000). Some cultural critics are suspicious of this conflation of a leading multinational corporation and an Anglo-American dominated international pop culture, a triumph of global branding. However, the show's various national versions are at pains to reflect local markets and accommodate local-content regulations.

The kiwi experience

The New Zealand ('kiwi') experience illustrates further the factors at work in the emergence and nature of regular MV-based programmes on commercial television, particularly the place of such programmes within scheduling practices. This localised example at first sight appears remote from the experience of MV programmes in countries such as the United States, Canada, and the United Kingdom, since the majority of New Zealand TV viewers do not have access to cable television or Sky's music channel 'Juice'. However, New Zealand TV usefully demonstrates the problems and practices common with respect to MV on mainstream television channels, particularly the nature and size of the MV audience, and the links between MV programmes, advertising, and record sales. Of particular interest, linking up with our earlier discussion of cultural imperialism, is the status of local MV compared with its imported counterparts competing for space on such programmes.

When introducing popular music programmes to broadcast television in the 1960s, New Zealand followed British formats (as did Australia: see Stockbridge 1992). New Zealand's first such programmes, *Happen Inn* and *C'mon*, were presented by a dapperly dressed host, popular radio DJ Peter Sinclair, who introduced local artists performing hits by overseas stars. While original material was scarce, the shows helped establish MV on New Zealand television. Their orientation was firmly towards chart material, and their audience were largely teenagers.

Since it succeeded *C'mon* in 1985, the leading chart-based popular music programme has been *RTR Countdown*. Its brief was to 'support the best New Zealand talent', along with featured overseas artists, new releases and a countdown of the country's top 20 singles. Originally called *Ready To Roll*, the show followed the earlier practice of bringing in local artists to perform live cover versions of overseas hits. In the early 1980s, with MTV and the emergence of the music video into its own, cover versions became outmoded. While this 'authentic' content made for more interesting viewing, the downside was less work for local artists. In 1988, in line with its format as a chart-based show and reputation as a chart leader, it changed its title to *RTR*

Countdown; currently it is the *Coca-Cola RTR 2000* show. Throughout its history, the various versions of the programme have enjoyed particularly high ratings, and market surveys indicate that its viewers remain very much a teenage audience.

In March 1978 *Radio With Pictures* began, breaking the top 20 format by featuring original local material and non-mainstream artists. Oriented towards older fans, and screened later at night, the show indicated television's recognition of the segmented nature of its rock/pop viewing audience. *Radio With Pictures* (RWP) was originally hosted by Dr Rock, Barry Jenkin, a DJ from the former 'pirate' station, Radio Hauraki in Auckland. Jenkin, who was openly supportive of 'alternative' styles of music, became something of a cult figure, and *RWP* developed into the most important promotional vehicle available to local bands. The show went through several manifestations and presenters, firmly establishing itself as something of a local music institution in the process. In 1980 a new frontperson replaced Jenkin, whose championing of punk and new wave bands was considered too daring in programming circles. *RWP* now emphasised more middle-of-the-road acts like Fleetwood Mac, with the deciding factor now being not the degree of 'hipness' but 'the quality of the video'. In 1988, despite considerable outcry from its supporters, *RWP* was axed, as its non-commercial bias had become out of step in a deregulated television industry. It returned in the 1990s, albeit in a new format and without a 'live' host.

Television programmers face considerable difficulties in scheduling such shows for the varied audiences who comprise the general category of 'music fans'. This difficulty was compounded with the entry of two further broadcast television channels into the New Zealand market in the 1990s, and the subscription service offered by Sky television . The commercial logic of such a competitive situation means that if programme scheduling and advertising revenue demand particular types of television music shows, e.g. a top 20 singles show, then that is what must be delivered. The recent corporatising of Television New Zealand to make it more responsive to competition and the demands of advertisers, has led to a duplication of music video programmes across the various channels. Currently the various broadcasters screen similar music video programmes in approximately the same weekend time slots.

These programmes are important as a source of advertising revenue. They also raise questions of local content, cultural imperialism, and the globalisation of popular music. In 1986 a dispute flared up between Television New Zealand and the record industry. Previously, MVs were shown on the various music television shows on the basis that both sides got something out of it. TVNZ did not have to pay to make the videos that provided the bulk of programming material for *Ready to Roll*, *RWP*, etc., nor did it usually pay for screening rights. The record companies, on the other hand got free and often highly effective advertising: Bruce Springsteen's double album *The River* sold a respectable 15,000 copies in New Zealand, but *Born in the USA*, boosted by heavy exposure for two video clips, sold some 200,000. Even allowing for considerations such as the relative cost of double and single albums, and the arguably greater commercial accessibility of *Born in the USA*, it seems clear that the associated MVs played a major role in the album's success.

In April 1986 the major record companies asked TVNZ to pay for their music videos, at the then standard rate (approximately US$27 per minute) paid for overseas programmes; TVNZ refused and the companies stopped supplying the overseas MVs. The effect on the popularity of the television MV programmes was dramatic, with heavy audience losses. This decline threatened a lucrative source of advertising income for TVNZ. Not surprisingly, the record companies and TVNZ soon reached a compromise, and imported music video once again dominated local television. While the absence of imported material gave local artists' MV efforts greater exposure, local viewers generally associated 'quality' MVs with those made overseas. Such a preference is partly explained by fans' identification with international stars rather than homegrown product, but also reflected the inability of local musicians to budget for MVs on the scale of their foreign counterparts. This situation eventually led New Zealand On Air, who distribute the income from the broadcasting licensing fee, to finance MVs made by local performers (see Chapter 4). This support, plus the people from the film industry being prepared to undertake MV projects at much cheaper rates than usual, has seen an increase in the availability of local product. But there is still the problem of getting it screened. In 2000 there was a combined total of only seven hours of MV programming on the free-to-air TV channels. Although content analysis of the various programmes showed an increase in the proportion of local clips, this remained relatively low despite the NZ On Air scheme.

This raises the question of how MVs are selected for inclusion in such shows, a subject on which little information exists. Currently, all New Zealand television channels use the audience research practices of commercial radio to identify which newly released songs are most likely to be successful and appeal to the most viewers, a practice that also appears to be common internationally. Consequently, competing music video-based programmes often have almost identical playlists. The logic of commercial television competition for music video viewers, as a market to be sold to advertisers, is more of the same, and an emphasis on commercial 'mainstream' popular music.

MUSIC VIDEO

When I was writing the first edition of this book, in 1992–93, the analysis of music video had become one of the major growth areas in both television studies and the study of popular music, with several books, special journal issues, and a multitude of articles on music video. This level of interest has continued (see the references in Shepherd *et al.* 1997). Frith had suggested that 'Pop video is now more heavily theorized than pop music, and has generated more scholarly nonsense than anything since punk' (Frith 1988a: 205). This view, which I shared, reflected the preoccupations in much of this early literature. The majority of commentators on music video concentrated on their visual aspect, their perceived violence and sexuality/sexism, and their significance as a central postmodern cultural artifact. Situating themselves in film studies rather than music studies, these analyses focused on music videos as discrete, self-contained, essentially visual texts. They thereby largely ignored MV's industrial and commercial dimensions, their placement in the flow of TV programming, their music as opposed to their imagery, and the links between MVs and the construction of stardom in popular music.

These dimensions have been accorded greater consideration in subsequent studies (notably those by Goodwin 1993; and Banks 1996). For a fuller reading of MVs it remains necessary to consider their production process and their commercial function for the music industry, the institutional practices of channels such as MTV, and their reception as polysemic texts, open to varying audience interpretations. In other words, it is the interaction of context, text, and consumption which are determining the cultural meaning of music video. Music video is both an industrial, commercial product and a cultural form.

Visual radio or musical television?

The term 'music video' is actually used in a loose fashion for a number of distinctive televisual viewing formats and experiences. At the same time, there is uncertainty about whether MV should be considered and analysed as a predominantly aural, visual, or hybrid form. Is music video best thought of as a form of television, or as a distinctive spin off from popular music, an extension of the radio dial? We must also acknowledge the broader cultural influence of music video style and format. There is its presence in feature films (e.g. *The Crow*; *Seven*) and television programmes (e.g. *Ally McBeal*), with the use of MV-style film trailers acting as promotional vehicles for the movie and fuelling chart success for the associated songs (e.g. 'You Take My Breath Away' from *Top Gun*). There is also the increasing use of the MV format in television advertising, along with 'classic' rock and pop songs, as in Levi's use of the Clash's 'Should I Stay or Should I Go?' This exposure facilitated the successful re-release of the song, thus at the same time providing us with yet another case of the incorporation of the punk ethic into consumerist culture. The fact that MVs have 'arrived' as a cultural form was also signalled through the 1990s by the music press reviewing long-form MVs, national music awards including a 'best video' category, and the annual MTV Awards.

It can be argued that MV is more music than television, a perspective which underpins the view of MVs as a form of advertising which, as such, should not be paid for by the broadcasters. Roe and Lofgren (1988) see MV as 'visual radio', observing that many in its audience turn to MVs for much the same reasons they turn to the radio or record players, with a visual bonus added. However, a number of features suggest that MV can actually be legitimately considered as a television programme genre, similar to sitcoms and soaps: its reliance on visuals, and the impact of these; its basic similarity to advertisements, with MV's standardised length and conventions, etc.; its production as a commercial form or product; and its mass dissemination via network, cable, and video. That said, the nature of the MV audience distinguishes it from the majority of television genre. Music video programmes and MTV are watched largely by older teenagers and young adults, who are otherwise traditionally among the most infrequent television viewers, and watching MVs is a different experience from viewing other programmes. MV consumption is characterised by more active viewing, often in a peer group, whose reasons for viewing go beyond simply the appeal of the MVs to more social considerations (Shuker 1994).

It seems most appropriate to consider MV as a hybrid cultural form, encompassing elements of television and radio. Further, it is important to distinguish between several distinct yet overlapping meanings of the term 'music video'. First, there are individual MV programmes within general broadcast television channel schedules (considered earlier); second, there is the long-form music video cassette, available for hire or purchase (see Shuker 1998); third, there is MTV and similar cable or satellite music channels.

Individual music video clips follow the conventions of the traditional 45 single. Usually about three minutes long, they function, in the industry's own terms, as 'promotional devices', encouraging record sales and chart action. (The analysis of MVs as individual audio-visual texts is considered in Chapter 9.) While these clips are the staple component in each of the three categories, their place in each case is different, as are their associated patterns of consumption. All three forms, and the video clips that are their staple ingredient, are part of the culture industry. Accordingly, we turn next to historically situating MVs as commercial products, formed at the intersections of the music and television industries, and the rise of MTV.

Visual 45s

A historical perspective on MV suggests that it is not as innovative as is often claimed. As the earlier discussion of film and television suggests, MV represented 'a new phase of development for sound recording as a cultural form', rather than a dramatic break with tradition (Laing 1985: 78). There were visual jukeboxes in the early 1940s, the 'Soundies', short, three-minute films available for viewing in road-houses and bars across North America. They featured country music, jazz, and pop performers, along with dancers, comedians, vaudeville acts, and an array of pin-ups. While music video is simply the latest innovation in the visual development of popular music, 'rock video' did represent a major break with previous convention (see Shore 1985; Cubitt 1991). Historically, with a few exceptions like the 'Soundies', music soundtracks were generally created after, or at best concurrently with, the story and the visuals. This changed with music videos' use of the visuals and story to complement the music, though the relative importance of sound and visuals remained problematic. If putting music and television together was hardly new, the combination took off in the 1980s fuelled by two developments: the advent of cable television, and dramatic advances in what was technically possible in television and video.

In the late 1980s, the MV became an essential part of music industry promotional strategy, selling records and helping build public identification with an artist. Virtually every single released, by both majors and independent labels alike, was supported by a video. The video to accompany The Communards' 1986 single 'Don't Leave Me This Way', cost London Recordings £75,000, the most expensive clip in the label's history. This paid off when sales skyrocketed the day after the video was first shown on TV, and the record went on to top the charts. Examples abound of performers whose commercial success was tied to their videos, particularly through high-rotation screening on MTV. According to Virgin Records executive Jeff Ayeroff, video took Talking Heads from a group that could sell maybe 700,000 albums each time, to a group that sold 3 million each time out.

While the MV has maintained its influence in the music industry, its vitality has flagged during the 1990s. In June 1992, UK-based magazine VOX posed the question: 'Is the pop promo in permanent decline?' Writer Chas de Whalley argued that despite MTV's increasing penetration of UK screen-time, the recession in the recording industry, particularly the dwindling singles market, had forced record companies to cut back on the number of videos commissioned, and to slash the budgets of those they do. This saw several leading music video production companies folding, and a decline in the standard of the average pop video. More recently, according to video director Dani Jacobs of Swivel Films (who shot the Corrs' 'Dreams' video), 'there is a growing trend for record labels to make a very few big budget promos of over 100,000 pounds for a handful of priority acts and make the rest as cheaply as possible' (cited in Q, December 1998: 40).

I WANT MY MTV

In North America, the 24-hour, non-stop commercial cable channel, 'MTV: Music Television', founded in 1981, has made its logo synonymous with the music video form. Originally owned by the Warner Amex Satellite Company, but subsequently sold to Viacom International, the channel became enormously popular, and was credited with boosting a flagging music industry in the 1980s. MTV is also highly profitable. Not only did it eventually capture a considerable share of the advertising directed at the youth and young adult/yuppie market, as Goodwin observes, MTV solved the perennial problem of cable television – how to generate enough revenue for new programming – by having the record companies largely pay for the 'programmes' by financing the video clips (Goodwin 1993). In the late 1980s it was reaching nearly 20 million American homes, and was regularly watched by 85 per cent of 18 to 34-year-olds (Kaplan 1987). In 1992, Viacom launched a share float that gave MTV the economic clout of the three main networks in the USA (*Business Week*, 18 May 1992).

In November 1991, *MTV 10*, an hour-long celebration of MTV's tenth anniversary, was screened in prime-time on the North American ABC TV network. The show asserted the cultural centrality of MTV over the networks, opening with a performance of 'Freedom 90' by George Michael: 'We won the race/Got out of the place/Went back home/Got a brand new face/For the boys on MTV'. Performers on the show included Michael Jackson, Madonna, and REM, and *MTV 10* was subsequently screened worldwide, while the 1992 MTV Music Awards were seen in 139 countries.

By the early 1990s, MTV had 28 million subscribers, and was adding 1–3 million new subscribers every year. MTV's success spawned a host of imitators in the United States, and a number of national franchises and imitations around the globe. After an initial struggle to untangle cable and satellite regulations in dozens of countries, MTV Europe, launched in 1988, broke even for the first time in February 1993, and became the continent's fastest growing satellite channel. By 1993, its 24-hours-a-day MV programming was available in more than 44 million homes, and it was adding subscribers at the rate of almost a million a month (*Time*, 29 March 1993: 36). Of its airtime, 30 per cent is reserved for European performers, and while the programme format is similar to that of its parent station, 'a genuine effort appears to have been made to play a substantial number of "European" music videos' (Burnett 1990). MTV-Asia began broadcasting in late 1991, and its signal covers more than thirty countries from Japan to the Middle East. The channel's English-language broadcasts reached more than 3 million households with a programme dominated by MVs by Western stars, but with an approximately 20 per cent quota of Asian performers (*Time*, 30 November 1992: 57; on MTV in Latin America see Hanke 1998). While MVs are the staple of such channel's programming, they also screen concerts, interviews, and rock-oriented news and gossip items, acting as a visual radio channel.

The influence of MTV on the North American music industry during the 1980s – and, therefore, by association, globally – was enormous. By 1991, 80 per cent of the songs on *Billboard*'s Hot 100 were represented by a video (Riordan 1991: 310). MTV became the most effective way to 'break' a new artist, and to take an emerging artist into star status. Performers who received considerable exposure on MTV before they were picked up by radio include Madonna, Duran Duran, the Thompson Twins, and Paula Abdul. Rimmer argues that the new 'invasion' of the American charts by British groups in the 1980s was directly attributable to MTV (Rimmer 1985).

Given their crucial role in determining commercial success, a key question is how particular MVs are chosen for the MTV playlist. Evidence on this point is sparse, and it is clearly an area for further inquiry. Surprisingly, Kaplan's (1987) study of the channel ignores the selection issue, as do most commentators preoccupied with the videos as texts. Rubey (1991) noted that MTV's top 20 lists are compiled from national album sales, video airplay, and the channel's own research and requests, building circularity and subjectivity into the process. In his thorough study of the operation of MTV, Banks (1996: chap. 9) looks at the gatekeeper role of the American MTV channel, the operation of its Acquisitions Committee and the standards, both stated and unstated, which they apply. He concludes that major companies willingly edit videos on a regular basis to conform to MTV's standards, even coercing artists into making changes to song lyrics, while smaller, independent companies cannot usually get their videos on MTV.

Despite the heady growth of the 1980s, the American MTV channel began the 1990s by retrenching. MTV executives claimed that the format had lost its freshness and was becoming clichéd, that the clips submitted to them 'are often simplistic to a fault. They're too literal, depriving viewers of their own interpretations' (press report, 15 January 1990). The channel initiated a programme overhaul designed to lessen its reliance on videos; new shows included Unplugged, a 30-minute Sunday programme featuring live acoustic performances by bands such as Crowded House. Unplugged has proven highly successful, particularly through associated chart-topping album releases (Eric Clapton, Mariah Carey). These programme changes were a direct response to research on viewership patterns, which indicated, not surprisingly, that people tuned in to MTV for only as long as they enjoy the clips. With MVs making up some 90 per cent of the channel's broadcast day, negative reaction to a few clips can spell problems for audience retention and the sale of advertising time. This is a situation MTV shares with 'mainstream' television and radio, which have always been in the business of delivering audiences to advertisers in a highly competitive market.

As Kaplan observes, 'MTV functions like one continuous ad in that nearly all of its short segments are indeed ads of one kind or another. It is for this reason that MTV, more than any other television, may be said to be about consumption' (Kaplan 1987:12). Given advertisers' need for data, especially demographic and psychological information about programme audiences, some attention has been paid to identifying, classifying and describing MTV viewers' lifestyle characteristics (see Shuker

1994, for a summary of earlier studies). Some of the most interesting work on MV has been undertaken by feminist researchers interested in the relationship of girls to the medium. Stockbridge (1990) has reformulated notions of spectatorship and the gaze in relation to male and female performance in and around music videos. She challenges Kaplan's conception of the male gaze as given, and raises the possibility of voyeurism on the part of the female viewer, a possibility confirmed by Henderson's (1993) analysis of gay readings of Madonna's 'Justify My Love'. Viewer fantasy plays a key role here, allowing for 'the possibility of multiple and not gender specific spectator positions' (Stockbridge 1990: 107). Music videos and their star images 'address girl audiences by textually making reference to consumer girl culture, a gendered cultural experience engaged in by American middle-class girls' (Lewis 1990: 89). Again, this is a dynamic relationship, and raises the possibility of such videos being interpreted by the girls as 'textual strategies of opposition' (Lewis 1990: 96). Both commentators illustrate the general point that we must be careful about making 'preferred readings' of particular videos, and be aware of the diversity of audience responses to them.

This chapter has dealt with the visual (re-)presentation of popular music, examining the relationship between popular music and film, television, and, in particular, music video and MTV. While textual analysis has formed part of the discussion, my emphasis has been rather on the industrial aspects of these audio-visual texts. Up to this point, I have examined the production of popular music, its creators and their work, and the manner in which these are disseminated. I turn finally to consider more fully the reception and consumption of the music, especially the political nature of these processes.

Chapter 11

'My generation'
Audiences and fans, scenes and subcultures

The chapter begins with the changing demographics of popular music consumption, and the related development of a 'sociology of youth', with music as a key part of this. I then turn to particular consumption practices: dance; concert-going, and record collecting. The second part of the chapter examines the study of subcultures in relation to youth and popular music, the concept of musical 'scenes' and fandom as a social practice.

Studies of the consumption of popular music examine the place of music in the lives of 'youth' as a general social category, various musical styles as a central component of the 'style' of youth subcultures, and the social identity of fans. These different consumer groups, and the studies associated with them, are treated discretely here, but there is obviously considerable overlap and movement between them. An individual will be part of 'youth' in general, but at the same time may also be a member of a subculture/a local scene, and/or display a knowledge of the music and an adherence to it at the fan or aficionado level. Three factors underpin the musical consumption of all these audiences: the role of popular music as a form of cultural capital, as a source for the construction of identity, and as a source of audience pleasure. To emphasise these is to privilege the personal and social uses of music in people's lives, an emphasis which places the consumption of music within the now dominant paradigm of audience studies, which stresses the *active* nature of media audiences, while also recognising that such consumption is, at the same time, shaped by social contexts.

TOO OLD TO ROCK 'N' ROLL: THE DEMOGRAPHICS OF MUSIC

The study of audiences in popular music focuses largely on 'youth'. As an age cohort, seen usually as around 13–24 years of age, youth were historically major consumers of rock 'n' roll in the 1950s, and the wide range of genres it subsequently splintered into, and will be treated as such here. The straightforward association of genres such as 'rock' and 'pop' with youth, however, needs qualifying. Certainly, the music was initially aimed at the youth market in the 1950s, and young people have continued to be major consumers of it, and for the leisure industries in general. At the same time, the market has extended to those who grew up with the music in the 1950s and 1960s, and who have continued to follow it, ageing along with their favoured surviving performers of the 1960s. As Dave Marsh puts it:

> Rock and soul-based music has become more sustaining, not less, as I've aged. It may be true that young people were the first people to realize that rock and soul had a serious message to convey, but that message has little or nothing to do with youth *per se*.
>
> (Marsh 1989: xxiii)

Accordingly, attempts to locate the audience for popular music primarily among 'youth', once historically correct, no longer apply with the same force. The head of Polygram Records, Rick Dobbis, observed in 1993: 'The lament in the industry a few years ago was that older buyers are listening to news radio and not buying records anymore. But research shows that they're actually spending a lot of money on a wide variety of music. They make multiple purchases and buy boxed sets' (New Zealand Press Association report, July 1993). This was then confirmed by surveys undertaken by the Recording Industry Association of America: in the past five years, the music-buying power of thirty-somethings has risen 6.4 per cent, while purchases by those under twenty-four have fallen by 12.1 per cent; music consumers over thirty now make up 42 per cent of the American market (ibid.). These trends have continued through the rest of the 1990s, and demographics are partly responsible for the continued success of performers as diverse as the Rolling Stones, Bonnie Raitt, and Bob Dylan. Older consumers, in part at least, also account for the present predominance of 'golden oldies' radio formats, though their tastes do not remain fixed purely at the nostalgic level. Throughout 1994 and 1995 'nostalgia rock' was prominent in popular music, with the release of 'new' Beatles material (*Live at the BBC*, etc.); the launch of *MOJO* magazine, placing rock history firmly at its core and with 35 per cent of its readers aged 35-plus; and successful tours by the Rolling Stones, Pink Floyd and the Eagles, among other ageing performers. The changing nature of the 'rock' audience has implications for musical styles: turned-off by rap metal, techno, and hip-hop, older listeners return to the familiar styles and artists of their own adolescence, or contemporary music that is 'easy on the ear', such as the work of Celine Dion and Shania Twain.

Given that relative generational size is an important explanatory variable of generational experience, the demographic significance of 'youth' in the overall age structure influences their importance socially, economically, and politically. In most Western societies, following the peaking of the post-war 'baby boom', the absolute numbers of young people entering the labour market for the first time declined during the 1980s, and continued to fall until the end of the century. In the United States, for example, in July 1983, the number of Americans over the age of sixty-five surpassed the number of teenagers (Dychtwald 1989: 8). As Frith argued, a key explanation for what he perceived as the rock genre's lack of vitality by the late 1980s, was the decline of the youth market: 'In material terms, the traditional rock consumer – the "rebellious" teenager – is no longer the central market figure' (Frith 1988b: 127). This decline in youth as a market force – both as consumers and as producers – has significantly altered youth's social visibility. The consequent clash with established expectations is increasingly evident, as is youth's relative political powerlessness.

That said, the demographic decline of youth must not be exaggerated. As marketing analysts continue to observe, young people remain a major consumer group with considerable discretionary income for the leisure industries to tap. *Time* magazine noted in a 1997 cover story on 'Generation X', that there were 45 million Xers born in the United States between 1965 and 1977, and this group now represented annual purchasing power of some $125 billion a year (*Time*, 9 June 1997). Younger listeners are also a substantial market, as the marketing of the Spice Girls showed.

Youth culture

The blanket term 'youth' conceals more than simple age divisions, as a social category it embraces a wide variety of taste groups, subcultures, and fandom; all audience segments themselves differentiated by class, ethnicity, age, and gender. These differentiations, and their significance to popular music, have historically been addressed by a now considerable literature on the sociology of youth.

The concept of youth culture developed in the 1950s. It assumed that all teenagers shared similar leisure interests and pursuits and are involved in some form of revolt against their elders. The emergence of a distinctive youth culture was linked to the growing autonomy of youth (particularly working-class youth) because of their increased incomes. Greater spending power gave youth the means to express their own distinct values and separate ideals, and large markets were developed for teenage interests, most notably music and clothes. Advertising analyst Mark Abrams, in a pamphlet aptly titled *The Teenage Consumer* (1959), estimated that in Britain there was available 'a grand total of 900 million pounds a year to be spent by teenagers at their own discretion'. In real terms, this was twice the pre-war figure. In the US, the

195

consumer potential of the new teenagers outstripped that of any other segment of the population, as between 1946 and 1958, teenage buying potential grew to an esti-mated $10 billion. A further explanation for the prominence of this youth or teenage culture was the dramatic growth of secondary and university education in Western countries, as young people spending longer periods in educational institutions encouraged youth separateness and solidarity (Coleman 1961).

While academic sociology now began to display considerable interest in 'youth' as a social group, it was slower to more specifically explore the relationship between music and its adolescent audience. Initially, youth were seen as a relatively passive consumer group, with 'youth culture' shaped by the burgeoning leisure industries. Hall and Whannell reflected British anxiety about the effects of the emergent teenage culture, especially in its imported American forms: 'Teenage culture is a contradictory mixture of the authentic and the manufactured: it is an area of self-expression for the young and a lush grazing ground for the commercial providers' (Hall and Whannell 1964; see also Hoggart 1957). Similarly, in the United States the work of Riesman (1950) acknowledged the varied bases for American youth's musical tastes, but still saw the majority of adolescents as fodder for commercial interests.

The 1960s saw the growth of a youth counterculture, with youth protests in the universities and on the streets against the Establishment and the war in Vietnam. It seemed to some that a major division in society was the so-called 'generation gap', usually believed to be reached between the age of twenty-five and thirty. Youth were now viewed as a definite social block, belonging to a generational culture which tran-scended class, status, and occupation. Popular music, particularly emergent genres such as psychedelic or acid rock, was regarded as an age-specific means of cultural expression, uniting young people and confirming their radical potential (Reich 1967).

By the 1970s, this view of a homogeneous youth culture, offering a radical chal-lenge to the established social order, was obviously untenable. The radicalism of the 1960s' protest movement had become defused through its commercialisation, including the marketing of 'alternative rock' by major recording companies, and the counterculture's continued identification with middle-class rather than working-class youth. The emphasis on an age-based youth culture had obscured the key fact that a major shaper of adolescents' values and attitudes was the social class back-ground of those involved. Rather than being part of a coherent youth culture, it became clear that youth consisted of a 'mainstream' majority, and minority subcul-tures whose distinctiveness was shaped largely by the social class and ethnic background of their members. Sociological interest now concentrated on the various youth subcultures, whose members were seen to rely on leisure and style as a means of winning their own cultural space, and thus represented cultural oppositional politics at the symbolic level.

By the 1990s, the preoccupation with subcultures was being strongly challenged. Steve Redhead's detailed reading of post-punk events in the United Kingdom suggested that the very notion of 'subculture', and the emphasis on it as part of a tradition of rock 'authenticity' and opposition at the level of cultural politics required revision: 'Such notions are not capable of capturing the changes in youth culture and rock culture from at least the late 1970s onwards. They are, moreover, unsatisfactory as accounts of pop history and youth culture in general' (Redhead 1990: 41–2; see also Gelder and Thornton 1997).

Interest turned more to the majority of youth, those who do not join or identify with subcultures, the nature of fandom, and the study of local musical scenes. While the commercial orientation of the musical tastes of 'mainstream' youth are still, as with Riesman fifty years earlier, taken as given, this consumption is seen in more active and creative terms. Further, it is by no means a homogeneous situation, as, like the various subcultures, the 'mainstream' is revealed as a varied audience with different tastes and allegiances informed by factors such as class, ethnicity, and gender. Similarly, the phenomenon of pop/rock fandom, previously largely ignored, has been redefined and subjected to serious scrutiny.

Against this brief synopsis of developments in the sociology of youth and popular music, we can situate a fuller consideration of these differing audiences and the studies and theories associated with them.

SURVEYING TASTE: PROFILING CONSUMPTION

Studies of youth consumption of popular music are usually reliant on questionnaire-based surveys, case studies utilising indepth interviews and intensive participant observation, or some combination of these. The questionnaire and survey approach supplies useful data, but becomes at times too simply empiricist, since it is unable to do little more than speculate about the relationship between various patterns of responses. Conversely, a reliance on more qualitative methodologies alone, although providing rich qualitative information about consumption, can all too easily become totally individualised and even anecdotalised.

What is needed is an approach that combines the two methodologies, and which is situated in terms of theories about cultural consumption. The following discussion draws on various studies in both the quantitative and qualitative modes, in order to address a number of questions about the consumption of popular music. At one level, these are strictly empirical questions: the level of consumption, the formats which it occurs in, and the relative significance of preferred genres. Beyond these, although derived in part from them, are more complex questions about the *nature* of this consumption and its broader relationship to taste cultures. Accordingly, the discussion which follows moves from 'youth' to youth subcultures and fandom, and on to the shared role of music as pleasure and cultural capital in all three audiences. We begin with the music consumption of youth in general.

As a general social category, one factor youth have in common is an interest in music:

> young people's musical activities, whatever their cultural background or social position, rest on a substantial and sophisticated body of knowledge about popular music. Most young people have a clear understanding of its different genres, and an ability to hear and place sounds in terms of their histories, influences and sources. Young musicians and audiences have no hesitation about making and justifying judgements of meaning and value.
>
> (Willis *et al.* 1990: 59)

Cultural surveys in North America, the United Kingdom, Australia and New Zealand all indicate high levels of music consumption, a term embracing the purchase of recorded music, attending live performances, watching music videos and MTV, listening to the radio, making tape compilations, and downloading music from the net. Although not entirely restricted to them, this consumption is most evident among youth. In New Zealand, for example, my ongoing surveys show that 'listening to music' is secondary-school pupils' most preferred leisure activity, particularly among girls, and this remained the case with the 16–24 year age group. Similarly, on average American adolescents spend four to five hours a day listening to music and watching music videos. This involvement extends beyond sheer time spent: 'Music alters and intensifies their moods, furnishes much of their slang, dominates their conversations, and provides the ambience at their social gatherings. Music styles define the crowds and cliques they run in. Music personalities provide models for how they act and dress' (Christenson and Roberts 1998: 8, their study gives considerable supportive evidence for this claim). The great majority of this music is popular music, with its range of genre styles. Only a minority of students identify classical music as one of their interests, a situation which stands in sharp contrast to the classical music orientation of most school music syllabus prescriptions.

Such general quantitative data provides only one narrow aspect of the story. To further explore the relationship between music and its audience, it is necessary to examine factors that might affect consumer's responses to popular music, and the connection between particular genres and styles and social and cultural formations. It is now clear that popular music preferences follow discernible trends in terms of gender, age, ethnicity, and class. Accordingly, for the more specific cultural significance of rock we must look to studies which relate general consumption to these indices, and then go beyond these, to qualitative investigations at the level of the individual record buyer, concert-goer, and clubber.

In a pioneering study, Murdoch and Phelps (1973) established that English adolescents' pop music preferences were strongly differentiated by social class, a finding replicated in similar studies, in a number of countries since (see Shuker 1994). In studies of music consumption in ethnically mixed or diverse populations, black adolescents are demonstrably more likely (then their white or Asian counterparts) to favour black music genres, most notably soul, R&B, blues, reggae, and rap. For example, such differences are clear in New Zealand, a multicultural society, with almost 15 per cent of the population being either descendants of the indigenous Maori people or Pacific (Polynesian) Islanders, and the majority population descendants of the British and European immigrants ('Pakeha'). Strong Maori and Polynesian support for reggae, soul, and rap music is hardly surprising, since these categories (along with the blues) have become virtually synonymous with 'black music' and black culture.

Reggae does not simply describe an experience, but it politicises it through creating symbols for listeners to identify with. Many Maori and Polynesian youth are knowledgeable about rasta, and familiar with some of the metaphors in the music (Babylon, Jah, etc.). They regard reggae as relevant to the structural location of Maori and Polynesian as a major part of New Zealand's socially dispossessed working class. Such views are also expressed by black youth in England and North America. Rap has emerged as a major genre preference among black youth internationally (Spencer 1991). It has established a strong following in Auckland, New Zealand's main concentration of Polynesians, with several prominent rap performers (Che Fu), and specialised record labels and radio stations catering for the genre and its audience. Rap's appeal is in part through its links to dance and street culture, but adherents are also frequently conscious of the politicised work of performers such as Public Enemy and Ice-T (Zemke-White 2000).

The various attempts to profile music consumption also show a clear pattern of age and gender-based genre preferences. Younger adolescents, particularly girls, prefer 'commercial pop' (e.g. Britney Spears, S Club 7); older adolescents express greater interest in more 'progressive' forms and artists (U2, Hole). That girls enjoy chart pop music more than boys reflects the segmented nature of the market, with performers such as Kylie Minogue in the 1980s and New Kids on the Block in the early 1990s oriented toward younger listeners, particularly girls, and being marketed as such (Marshall 1997). As we saw in Chapter 4, music magazines such as *Smash Hits*, are aimed at the young adolescent market. The majority of their readers are girls, who buy them partly for their pin-up posters, reflecting their frequent obsession with particular stars and what has been termed 'teenybopper' bedroom culture (McRobbie and Garber 1976).

Many listeners in their late teens and early twenties are more interested in 'minority' genre tastes, and less interested in more overtly commercial popular music genres. In part, this is a deliberate distancing from adolescence. New Zealand university students I have interviewed during the 1990s speak of 'growing out of' mainstream or commercial music, and diversifying their musical preferences. Some identified strongly with 'alternative/progressive' music (their labels), favouring groups such as NOFX and Rage Against the Machine; others were 'into' thrash metal and still retained an affinity with the 'Seattle grunge bands' (Nirvana, Pearl Jam). As consumers get older, their tastes in music often become more open to exploring new genres and less commercial forms of popular music. For example, the market for 'world music' appears to be primarily middle-class listeners, in their thirties and forties. Such patterns reflect the dominant forms of musical cultural capital within particular peer groups. On the other hand, many adults' popular music tastes remain fixed at the commercial level, focused primarily on the back catalogue, or they largely stop purchasing recordings or going to clubs and concerts.

MODES OF CONSUMPTION

Beyond patterns of genre and demographic and social preferences in relation to popular music, there exists a complex pattern of modes of consumption. These include buying recorded music, viewing MTV and music videos, listening to the radio, home taping, and downloading music from the net. To these could be added the various 'secondary' levels of involvement – reading the music press, and decorating your bedroom walls with its posters; dancing and clubbing; and concert-going – and the relation of these to the social use and interpretation of music texts. Several of these have been dealt with elsewhere in this study; here I want to examine how we actually access music texts in their various modes, and the associated social practices, through three examples: record collecting, dancing, and attending concerts.

Record collecting

Buying recorded music in its various formats is central to the consumption of popular music. Most people purchase sound recordings in a limited and generally unsystematic fashion, but record collectors represent a more extreme version of this practice. The term 'record collecting' is shorthand for a variety of related practices. Foremost is the collection of sound recordings in various formats, although with a marked preference for vinyl, by individuals. This is the dimension of record collecting focused on here. (Although both individual and institutional record collecting will frequently embrace the collection of related literature and memorabilia; e.g. the Hard Rock Café chain).

While fan accounts and a recent best-selling novel provide some insights (Aizlewood 1994; Smith 1995: 133–45; Hornby 1995), more extended critical discussion of record collecting is sparse. (Although collecting generally has been the subject of considerable theoretical speculation and empirical study; see Pearce 1998, for a useful overview of the literature.) Drawing on some of the considerable general literature on collecting and collectors, Straw (1997) usefully speculates on the psychology of record collecting as a social practice, especially its largely male character, but his analysis lacks any embedding in the views of collectors themselves. Building on Straw, and the extensive writing of Pearce (1995, 1998) on collecting, during 1999 I interviewed a number of self-identified record collectors, to provide more empirical support for speculations about the nature and psychology of the activity.

As Straw observes, record collecting can be regarded as 'either structures of control or the by-products of irrational and fetishistic obsession: as material evidence of the homosocial information-mongering which is one underpinning of male power and compensatory undertakings by those unable to wield that power' (Straw 1997: 4). In common with other forms of collecting, record collecting can represent a public display of power and knowledge, serving as a form of cultural capital within the peer group. Collecting also provides a private refuge from the wider world and the immediate domestic environment. In *High Fidelity*, Rob Fleming in times of stress re-catalogues his album collection:

> Is it so wrong, wanting to be at home with your record collection? It's not like collecting records is like collecting stamps, or beer mats, or antique thimbles. There's a whole world in here, a nicer, dirtier, more violent, more colourful, sleazier, more dangerous, more loving world than the world I live in.
>
> (Hornby 1995: 73)

Muesterberger (1994) has theorised that collecting is a way of overcoming childhood anxiety by creating a sense of order and completion. This can border on the obsessional: Eisenberg describes the case of 'Clarence', a New York record collector crippled with arthritis and now on welfare, living in an unlit, unheated fourteen-room house 'so crammed with trash that the door wouldn't open – and with three-quarters of a million (vinyl) records'. 'Clarence' had inherited the house from his parents, along with a considerable inheritance, now gone, which enabled him to pursue his dream of owning a complete collection of jazz, pop, and rock recordings, along with ethnomusicological field recordings and various recorded ephemera (Eisenberg 1988: 1ff.).

Record collecting is a male-dominated practice. My own opportunity sample of twenty-one collectors included only three women, and none of their collecting was on the scale of a number of the men. A Canadian documentary on record collectors, referred to by Straw (1997), included only five females among its 100 subjects. The huge success, especially with male readers, of Nick Hornby's novel *High Fidelity*, suggested considerable empathy for the protagonist, a London record shop owner who is a committed record collector. And Fleming's shop Championship Vinyl, 'for the serious record collector', gets by 'because of the people who make a special effort to shop here Saturdays – young men – always young men' (Hornby 1995: 37). For male collectors, the social role of collecting appears to be a significant part of masculinity. As Straw suggests,

> record collections, like sports statistics, provide the raw materials around which the rituals of homosocial interaction take shape. Just as ongoing conversation between men shapes the composition and extension of each man's collection, so each man finds, in the similarity of his points of reference to his peers, confirmation of a shared universe of critical judgement.
>
> (Straw 1997: 5)

The process of collecting can take on the nature of a ritual. Frequently it is the search itself that provides gratification, although the anticipation of 'a find' is central to this. Buying recorded music in its various formats 'is a process that involves clear symbolic work: complex and careful exercises of choice from the point of view of initial listening to seeking out and scrutinizing records' (Willis et al. 1990: 61). This is brought out by my interviewees, who constantly referred to both the effort and the pleasure involved in systematically gathering information from peers, older siblings, the music press, especially collector magazines, discographies, price guides, and the back catalogue, and then searching for particular recordings. This search will frequently embrace specialist and second-hand record shops, mail order and Internet shopping, record fairs, and the bargain bins at mainstream record and general retail stores. Once items are acquired, they must then be ordered and classified, an ongoing process.

As yet another example of the intersection of production and consumption, record collecting can both stimulate and, possibly, ossify particular musical genres. Small record labels have historically served a collectors' market, since they were willing to release (or re-release) material in smaller pressings which larger companies considered uncommercial. This practice had long been evident in the jazz and blues fields, and was part of the advent of rock and roll in the 1950s. More recently, labels such as Rhino and Charlie have established their commercial success through catering to a collector's market with well-packaged compilations and re-issues.

Radio and home taping

In addition to directly purchasing recordings, there are other significant ways of gaining access to music, both live and in commodity form. Radio remains the major source for most people's engagement with music, with surveys indicating that young people in particular frequently 'listen to the radio'. Although this is generally 'listening' at an unfocused level, with the radio acting as a companion and as background to other activities, at times listening to the radio is deliberately undertaken in order to hear and tape new music. This is frequently done in relation to particular specialist shows or DJs. As with other aspects of rock consumption, preferences for particular radio stations or formats are related to factors such as age and ethnicity. For example, Maori and Polynesian youth in Auckland choose to listen to Mai FM88, a 'dance-oriented Urban Contemporary music' station, rather than the several local stations broadcasting classic hits and contemporary rock. Mai FM88 is one of eighteen 'iwi' (tribal community) radio stations to be funded by New Zealand On Air to promote Maori language and culture, adding a cultural politics dimension to its appeal.

Making their own personal audio tape compilations is a significant aspect of people's acquisition of popular music. Aside from the convenience of ensuring access to preferred texts, selected (particularly with albums) to avoid any 'dross' or material not liked sufficiently to warrant inclusion, home taping of music is cheap, making it a very suitable strategy for those on limited incomes. Home taping is primarily from the radio, but 'Young people frequently rely on friends, with larger record collections to make tapes for them. There is something of an informal hierarchy of taste operating here' (Willis *et al.* 1990: 63). Even younger consumers, who are often seen as relatively undiscriminating and easily swayed by the influence of market forces, see their music preferences as the product of a more complex set of influences, with the views of their friends being of paramount importance. Home taping is also significant as an aspect of consumption which is largely beyond the ability of the music industry to influence, although it has traditionally been anxious to do so. Much the same can be said of 'burning' your own CDs by downloading music from the Internet, via Napster and MP3, although this involves more expensive hardware and technological expertise.

These forms of accessing popular music concentrate on accessing the musical text, the recording. They may be pursued in the public sphere – shopping – but are primarily domestic activities, often undertaken individually and usually in a physically passive manner. On the other hand, music is more actively consumed when it is danced to, or experienced 'live', through concerts.

Dancing the night away

Dancing is a significant aspect of the consumption of popular music. Various styles of music have historically been associated with particular dance styles: 'jitter bugging' in the 1940s; rock 'n' roll in the 1950s; the twist, the shake, and the jerk in the 1960s; punk and the 'pogo' in the 1970s; the Northern soul style of athletic, acrobatic dance, and rap's break-dancing and body-popping through the 1980s and 1990s. In more general terms, dance is central to the general experience of adolescence (especially school dances), the leisure lives of young adults (parties, discos, and pub 'rave ups'), and as part of courtship.

Dancers break free of their bodies in a combination of 'socialised pleasures and individualised desires', and its significance lies primarily in its 'extremely strong, almost symbiotic relationship with its audience', particularly for girls and young women (McRobbie 1991: 194, 192). Dance also acts as a marker of significant points in the daily routine, punctuating it with what Chambers (1985) labels the 'freedom of Saturday night'. Dance also carries connotations as a pleasure of the physical rather than the intellectual, the body rather than the mind, and at times the associated sexual display has aroused anxiety to regulate dance, or at least control who is dancing with who.

Dancing is associated with some popular music genres to a greater extent than others, for example, disco, rap and dance music. There are also forms of dance which are genre specific; for example, the energetic aerobics of contemporary pop performers such as S Club 7 and the Vengaboys. These are a central part of their appeal, and it is common to see young girls imitating the dance routines, both at the groups' live appearances and at home playing the records or watching the videos.

The dance practices associated with alternative music provide an example of the intersection of musical genres, dance styles, and subcultural values (I am relying here largely on the fascinating discussion in Tsitsos 1999, based on his participant observation study in San Francisco in 1995). Three dance styles are involved : slamdancing, moshing, and stage diving. Slamdancing originated in the punk subculture of the late 1970s as a modification of the 'pogo', and moshing emerged in the 1980s as a variation on slamdancing. Both are aggressive dances performed mostly by males in the 'pit', an informally bounded, roughly circular area near the front of the stage. Moshing is a form of circle dance: 'a hard skipping, more or less in time to the music, in a circular, counterclockwise pattern. Elbows are often extended and used as bumpers, along with the shoulders' (Weinstein 1991a: 228), and arms are frequently swinging. With slam dancing, while movement may still be counter clockwise, dancers move in a more 'run and collide' fashion, slamming into each other. Stage diving is a form of theatrical choreography , which originated in heavy metal concerts:

> Members of the audience climb up to the stage, touch or imitate the band members for a moment, and then dive back into the audience. The style of the dive is the belly flop, but instead of water the divers land on the outstretched hands of the audience. That they are caught, and prevented from crashing to the hard floor, is a sign of audience solidarity.
>
> (Breen 1991: 229–30)

The variant styles are linked to identifiable subgroups within the alternative scene. Slamdancing mirrors an 'apolitical punk ideology of rebellion' in the breakdown of symbolic order which seems to occur in the pit, with its 'assertions of individual presence and autonomy'. At the same time, it creates and reinforces unity through concern for the welfare of others (with practices such as the picking up of fallen dancers; Tsitsos 1999: 407). Moshing, in contrast, lacks the elements, such as circular motion, which promote unity in the pit, and is identified with a 'straight edge ideology of rebellion' (ibid.: 410). 'Through their participation in (and rejection of) these dances, members of the scene pledge allegiance to the rules which govern their rebellion' (ibid.: 413). There is also a process of gender discrimination at work in the maintenance of such male-dominated dance practices, which stress male bonding rather then male–female pairing.

Dance music and club culture provide a further example of the social complexity of dance (see Thornton 1995; Bennett 2000: chap. 4), tied to controversies around drug use/abuse and attempts to regulate this and the associated venues, as with the UK's 1994 Criminal Justice and Public Order Act (see Redhead 1997; Homan 2000).

Concerts

Concerts are a ritual for both performers and their audience, and reflect different musical styles. The traditional 'rock' concert illustrates the nature of the concert experience. Small sees symphony orchestra concerts as celebrating 'the power holding class in our society' (Small 1987). In a similar fashion, 'rock' concerts celebrate youth. Such celebration is not purely of youth as a demographic group, but rather of the idea of 'youth'. Some of those who have grown up with 'rock', in what was arguably its heyday in the 1960s, now in their late forties, recapture youthful memories and vitality by still attending concerts. While the enjoyment of the performer(s) and the music is still there, that enjoyment is linked to this vicarious pleasure, a reprise of one's youth. This concert attendance is usually to 'revisit' the surviving performers – and their music – of the ageing fans' own generation: witness the audiences at Paul McCartney's 1993 world tour concerts, who received his post-Beatles work with polite respect, reserving their enthusiasm and delight primarily for the 'covers' of Beatles' classics. In similar fashion, the concert song set list of 'reunion' tours by bands such as the Eagles and Fleetwood Mac rarely stray from their now familiar original repertoire.

Part of the ritual of attending is 'getting pumped up for the concert', a process which can include spending hours in queues, or 'on hold' to ensure tickets (many concerts by top acts sell out in a matter of hours); listening again to the band's albums; talking with other fans about the coming event (especially where expectations have been generated by previous concerts by the performer); travelling, often over long distances, to the concert venue; possible pre-concert drug use; and 'dressing up' for the concert. These all become part of the celebratory experience. At 'rock' concerts, the audience are outgoing, loud, and more demonstrative. This is especially so during the performance, with shouting, clapping, and the stamping of feet throughout. Often there are verbal exchanges between the performers and their audience, usually good humoured but sometimes more confrontational. Again, this is consistent with the essential physicality of much of the genre, especially in live performance.

General consumption patterns and modes demonstrate a structural homology between the audience and various social indicators. Such homology is evident at its most extreme in youth subcultures, to which I now turn.

Subcultures and style

Music is one of a complex of elements making up subcultural style. Its role in terms of pleasure and cultural capital is similar to that played out among more mainstream youth, albeit in an accentuated form. As indicated in my earlier sketch of the sociology of youth, the relationship between popular music and youth subcultures was comprehensively explored in a number of studies during the 1970s and early 1980s. Collectively, these confirmed what became a frequently asserted thesis: that youth subcultures appropriate and innovate musical forms and styles as a basis for their identity, and, in so doing, assert a countercultural politics. This perspective was primarily associated with writers linked to the influential Birmingham (UK) Centre for Contemporary Cultural Studies (Hall and Jefferson 1976; Willis 1978; Hebdige 1979), whose views initially became conventional wisdom in the study of youth subcultures (see Bennett 2000 for a succinct but comprehensive overview).

For the writers associated with the BCCCS, subcultures were regarded as 'meaning systems, modes of expression or life styles developed by groups in subordinate structural positions in response to dominant meaning systems, and which reflect their attempt to solve structural contradictions rising from the wider societal context' (Brake 1985: 8). Hebdige's classic text starts from the premise that style in subculture is 'pregnant with significance', and illustrates this through a comprehensive analysis of various spectacular subcultural styles: beats and hipsters in the 1950s, Teddy boys in the 1950s and 1970s, mods in the early 1960s, skinheads in the late 1960s, rastas in the 1970s, glam rockers in the early to mid-1970s, and, most visible of all, punks in the mid-1970s. Subcultures rely on leisure and style as a means of making their values visible in a society saturated by the codes and symbols of the dominant culture. The significance of subcultures for their participants is that they offer a solution, albeit at a 'magical' level, to structural dislocations through the establishment of an 'achieved identity' – the selection of certain elements of style outside of those associated with the ascribed identity offered by work, home, or school (Hebdige 1979: 132).

Clearly, the majority of youth pass through life without any significant involvement in 'deviant' subcultures. Associated aspects of subcultural fashion and musical tastes may be adopted, but for 'respectable' youth these are essentially divorced from subcultural lifestyles and values. Members of youth subcultures, on the other hand, utilise symbolic elements to construct an identity outside the restraints of class and education, an identity which places them squarely outside of conservative mainstream society: 'The attraction of subculture is its rebelliousness, its hedonism, its escape from the restrictions of work and home. It offers a place to explore fun, heterosexuality, masculinity and by definition femininity' (Brake 1985: 19).

Youth subcultures in the 1970s and early 1980s were an international phenomenon. Subcultural styles in both Britain and the United States essentially developed naturally out of their immediate context, reworking commercial popular culture into a subculture which reflected and made sense of their structural social location. Membership of a subculture was seen necessarily to involve membership of a class culture and could be either an extension of, or in opposition to, the parent class culture (see Clarke, in Hall and Jefferson 1976, on the skinheads). This process was not, however, so clear-cut in more culturally dependent societies. In Canada the situation was confused by the nation's historical links with Britain and France and the marked contemporary influence of its close proximity to the United States, a situation contributing to Canada's problem of finding a sense of national identity. Canadian youth cultures were consequently largely derivative and any potential oppositional force in them was highly muted (Brake 1985).

Youth subcultures in New Zealand were also imitative of overseas styles, and only spasmodically (as with the bodgies of the late 1950s – see Chapter 12) sufficiently visible to provoke a sense of moral outrage. New Zealand youth largely accept the dominant ethos of liberal egalitarianism in a society where class as a dividing factor has, in the popular view at least, been muted. Ethnic divisions and large-scale youth unemployment, both clearly evident in the 1990s, suggest the possibility of increasingly visible oppositional youth subcultures forming, but as yet this has occurred only in the most limited and fragmentary manner. Local variants of punk, heavy metal, hip-hop, and rasta subcultures largely draw on imported styles, rather than attempt to develop indigenous forms based on local traditions.

The BCCCS writers' socio-cultural analyses represented an original and imaginative contribution to the sociology of youth cultures, but displayed common weaknesses: a tendency to overemphasise the symbolic 'resistance' of subcultures, and to imbue this with an unwarranted political significance; the romanticising of working-class subcultures; the neglect of ordinary or conformist youth; and a masculine emphasis, with little attention paid to the subcultural experiences of girls ('correctives' to the masculinist view of subcultures have been offered by McRobbie 1988, 1991, and Gilbert and Taylor 1991; for examples and critiques of the BCCCS studies, see the reader edited by Gelder and Thornton 1997, and Redhead 1990).

What about the music?

For the subcultural analysts of the 1970s, homology was central to the consideration of the place of music in youth subcultures. This was between the 'focal concerns, activities, group structure and the collective self-image' of the subculture, and the cultural artifacts and practices adopted by the members of the subculture. The latter were seen as 'objects in which they could see their central values held and reflected' (Hall and Jefferson 1976: 56), including music.

The most developed applications of the concept of homology to the preferred music of specific subcultures are Willis' study of bike boys and hippies, *Profane Culture* (1978), and Hebdige's various case studies in his hugely influential study *Subculture: The Meaning of Style* (1979). Willis argued that there existed a 'fit' between certain styles and fashions, cultural values, and group identity; for example, between the intense activism, physical prowess, love of machines and taboo on introspection, of motorbike boys, and their preference for 1950s rock 'n' roll. For Hebdige, the punks best illustrated the principle:

> The subculture was nothing if not consistent. There was a homological relation between the trashy cut-up clothes and spiky hair, the pogo and the amphetamines, the spitting, the vomiting, the format of the fanzines, the insurrectionary poses and the 'soulless', frantically driven music.
>
> (Hebdige 1979: 114–15)

However, the 'Birmingham' treatment of music in subcultures had serious limitations. As Middleton (1990: 156–64) points out, music is absent from the accounts in Hall and Jefferson (1976) of skinheads and teds, perhaps because it is in fact difficult precisely to locate the place of music in either subculture. In the case of the skinheads, their preferred music changed over time, making problematic any argument for its homological role in skinhead culture. As Hebdige observed, the 'early' skinheads preference for elements of black style, including reggae and ska music, is contradictory considering their racial stance. But Hebdige's own use of homology to analyse the mods and their music is too quick to attribute stylistic attributes to a specifically subcultural influence, rather than recognising their generalisability (see Middleton 1990, and the discussion in Chapter 8). Middleton similarly interrogates Willis' case study of the rockers' preferences for rock 'n' roll, seeing it as too simplistic a rendering down of the music, producing an ideal form in the place of what was, in reality, a more complex picture. In sum, in these studies the connection between music and subculture is drawn much too tightly, the analysis 'flawed above all by the uncompromising drive to homology' (Middleton 1990: 161).

A convergence between music and cultural group values continued to be evident in youth subcultures through the 1990s, most notably in heavy metal (Arnett 1996), hip-hop, Goth, and various strands of punk. However, subsequent theoretical discussions and case studies suggest that the degree of homology between subcultures and music had been overstated. Furthermore, the very value of the concept 'subcultures', and particularly its conflation with oppositional cultural politics, became seriously questioned (Grossberg 1992; Redhead 1990). Even Dick Hebdige, one of the central figures of 1970s subcultural theory, concluded that 'theoretical models are as tied to their own times as the human bodies that produce them. The idea of subculture-as-negation grew up alongside punk, remained inextricably linked to it and died when it died' (Hebdige 1988: 8: the essay 'Young Lives' is presented as 'my attempt at a farewell to youth studies'). Through the 1990s, the concepts of 'clubcultures' and a global youth formation challenged (and arguably now supplanted) 'subculture' as the key to the analysis of youth culture.

The cultural studies preoccupation with youth subcultures obscured the significance of subcultural affiliations held by older music fans. A case in point is the academically neglected example of northern soul, a regional cult in the UK Midlands, based around ballroom/club culture and all-night dancing to 1960s Motown and independent label (e.g. Cameo, Parkway, Verve) soul records chosen for their 'danceability'; (e.g. The Exciters). Northern soul became prominent in the early 1970s, with the Wigan Casino, a First World War dance hall, being declared by American *Billboard* to be the world's best discotheque. The subculture has maintained itself, with fanzines, continued all-nighters, and record compilations. Rarity and exclusivity of records, and commodity exchange are integral to the northern soul scene.

Hollows and Milestone's case study of northern soul challenges orthodox subcultural theory, and its preoccupation with music as symbol and the homology between musical style and subcultural values. Northern soul produces a sense of identity and belonging based on the consumption of 'music as music', based around a club scene. Here the records have value both as commodities and as bearers of musical meaning. The exchange, buying and selling of records is an important part of the northern soul scene. Indeed, the use of 'white labels' represents a unique form of fetishisation of black musical culture by white consumers (Hollows and Milestone 1998). The example of northern soul illustrates how the preoccupation with subculturalist analysis has been partly supplanted in popular music studies by an interest in music scenes and the role of locality, and by studies of fandom.

SCENES AND SOUNDS: THE MUSIC OF PLACE

The intersection of music and its physical location has been a developing field of inquiry, with a number of distinct and original contributions to the critical examination of space and scale as significant aspects in the production and consumption of sound recordings. Cultural geographers have been doing research on music since the late 1960s, seeking to establish 'the nexus between the social, cultural, economic and political in musical analysis' (Kong, 1995: 273). Traditionally, the geographical analysis of music emphasised the dynamics and consequences of the geographical distribution of recorded music around the world, and how particular musical sounds have become associated with particular places. This work was largely characterised by the use of a narrow range of methods and theories, and focused on only a few musical styles, notably blues, folk, and country. Studies of rock and pop music, and their various genres, were notably absent from the majority of this work. Only in the 1990s have these musical forms and their locales been deemed worthy of serious study and accorded greater attention by cultural geographers and popular music scholars (see Leyshon *et al.* 1998; McLeay 1998; Stokes 1994; Straw 1992; Bennett 2000).

While the cohesion of their 'common' musical signatures is frequently exaggerated, local sounds provide marketing possibilities by providing a 'brand name' which consumers can identify with. Interest in particular sounds has concentrated on the significance of locality, and how music may serve as a marker of identity. Many histories of popular music refer to particular geographic locales, usually cities or regions, as being identified at a specific historical juncture with a sound. Examples include the Liverpool 'Merseybeat' sound associated with the Beatles, Gerry and the Pacemakers, and the Searchers in the early 1960s, San Franciso and the psychedelic rock of the Jefferson Airplane, Moby Grape, and the Grateful Dead in the later 1960s, and the various punk scenes of the 1970s. Somewhat contiguous with this usage, is the application of scene, for example, Athens, Georgia in the late 1980s, Manchester (see below). This implies a range of activities, loosely centred around and aligned to a particular style of music and its associated performers (see Olson 1998, for a useful theoretical discussion of the concept of scenes).

A New Zealand example of this is the emergence of the 'Dunedin sound' associated with the now internationally recognised Flying Nun label. In the late 1970s, a number of bands in Dunedin, a university city of then only just over 100,000 people, established a local cult following through their appearances at various pubs and university venues. National exposure and critical and commercial success followed, and several bands (the Chills, the Bats, the JPS) went on to establish international reputations, largely on the 'indie' college circuit in the UK and North America. The 'Dunedin Sound' and 'the Flying Nun Sound' became shorthand for these bands, despite the clear differentiation among the Flying Nun label's recorded output. The sound itself, at least in its original evocation, was largely equated with a 'jangly' guitar-driven sound, a distinctive New Zealand accent on the vocals, and 'low-tech' recording and production, all serving to produce a specifically identifiable local product (see Mitchell 1996).

More recently, Manchester provides an instructive example of the role of geography in forging a distinctive orientation to localised alternative music. The notion of a Manchester sound/scene was a loose label, popularised by the British music press in the early 1990s. Since the late 1970s, Manchester has been associated with several styles of indie/alternative music: in the late 1970s and early 1980s, the post-punk sound of Joy Division, which mutated into New Order; 'bedsit blues' in the mid-1980s with the Smiths and James; and the tempo and mood was revived around 1988, in the wake of 'Acid House', with the arrival of the club-and-Ecstasy sounds of 'Madchester', led by the Happy Mondays, the Stone Roses and Oldham's Inspiral Carpets. All three periods and styles fed off the association with Manchester: the songs often had included clear geographical references and reflected localised feelings and experiences; record covers and other promotional imagery incorporated place-related references; and a network of alternative record labels (especially Factory Records), venues, and an active local press created a supportive network for the bands and their followers (Halfacree and Kitchen 1996)

The recent edited volume *Music and Place* exemplifies the type of work being undertaken on the significance of locality, place, and space. Its editors argue for:

> study that recognises the simultaneously material and imaginal qualities of musical production, through processes that both localise and give form. It is a focus that gives a central role for the spatial processes by which sounds are differentiated, and through which the economic, social, and aesthetic geographies forged through musical practices are intimately bound up with the production of space and place.
>
> (Leyshon *et al.* 1998: 2)

Locality and youth culture are fruitfully brought together in the work of Bennett (2000), who uses a series of ethnographic studies to interrogate the significance of place and associated youth cultures in framing popular music consumption. For example, his study of the urban dance music forms (such as house, techno, and jungle) in Newcastle upon Tyne, England, illustrates how, through their participation in club events and 'house' parties, 'the members of this scene celebrate a shared underground sensibility that is designed to challenge the perceived oppression and archaism of Newcastle's official night-time economy and the coercive practices of the local police force' (Bennett 2000: 68).

These studies interrogate the nature of soundscapes; definitions of music and cultural value; the geographies of different musical genres; and the place of music in local, national and global cultures.

FANDOM

In the introduction to her edited study of fan culture and popular media, Lisa Lewis observes that while fans are 'the most visible and identifiable of audiences', they 'have been overlooked or not taken seriously as research subjects by critics and scholars' and 'maligned and sensationalized by the popular press, mistrusted by the public' (Lewis 1992: 1). This situation reflected the traditional view of fandom, which situates it in terms of pathology and deviance, and reserves the label 'fans' for teenagers who are generally presented as avidly and uncritically following the latest pop sensation. These fans have been unfairly denigrated in most writing on popular music, and, indeed, by many other consumers. Their behaviour is often described as a form of pathology, and the terms applied to it have clear connotations of condemnation and undesirability: 'Beatlemania', 'teenyboppers', and 'groupies'. The last can be considered an extreme form of fan, moving beyond vicarious identification and using their sexuality to get close to the stars – even if the encounter is usually a fleeting one.

The contributors to Lewis' volume, along with several edited collections (Aizelwood 1994; Smith 1995), collectively rescue fandom from its former neglect. These writers show fandom is a complex phenomenon, related to the formation of social identities, especially sexuality. They recognise fandom as an active process, which offers its participants membership of a community not defined in traditional terms of status, etc.

Attempts to more satisfactorily define fandom are various. Fiske sees it as the register of a subordinate system of cultural taste:

> Fandom is typically associated with cultural forms that the dominant value system denigrates – pop music, romance novels, comics, Hollywood mass-appeal stars (sport, probably because of its appeal to masculinity is an exception). It is thus associated with the cultural tastes of subordinate formations of the people, particularly with those disempowered by any combination of gender, age, class, and race.
>
> (Fiske 1992: 30)

This is plausible, but not all fans, in the extended sense I want to use the term here, occupy such social positions.

Grossberg, more acutely, defines fandom as a distinct 'sensibility', in which the fan's relation to cultural texts 'operates in the domain of affect or mood' (1992: 56).

Taking this notion, we can usefully extend the term fan to embrace those who see themselves as 'serious' devotees or *aficionados* of particular musical styles or performers. These are fans in terms of the word's origins in 'fanatic', but their fanaticism is usually at more of an intellectual level and focused on the music *per se* rather than on the persona of the performer(s). Accordingly, unlike the 'teenyboppers', such fans tend to be lauded as representatives of the 'serious' side of popular music. Indeed, such individuals would not usually describe themselves as 'fans', preferring instead to describe themselves as 'into' particular performers or genres.

I want to use this distinction between fans in the traditional sense, and fans as *aficionados*, to more closely examine the nature of fandom. I must stress that this is not to perpetuate an aesthetically based, discriminatory view of the former group. Both categories of fan engage in fandom as an active process, and both often display impressive knowledge of their preferred genres or performers. My argument is that their emotional and physical investments are different, as are the social consumption situations in which their fandom operates.

The 'serious fans' are characterised by what can be termed 'secondary involvement' in music (Straw 1990: 104): the seeking out of rare releases, such as the picture discs and bootlegs; the reading of fanzines in addition to commercial music magazines; concert going; and an interest in record labels and producers as well as performers. Such people frequently become record collectors on a large scale, underpinning an infrastructure of specialist record shops and, of key importance, second-hand record shops (see above). Serious fans may also be involved in music-oriented subcultures (e.g. heavy metal), though the situation here seems more complex (see Weinstein 1991a: chap. 4).

A typical example of such involvement is Julian, a 21-year-old student. Julian 'liked to have a rattle on the drums' (his father had been a drummer and retained his kit) and considered himself reasonably proficient – 'I can keep time' – but was 'into music' primarily as a consumer. While at school, he had followed Queen intensely: 'I got a lot of picture disks, and kept in touch with specialist and second-hand record shops for limited editions, bootlegs, and suchlike'. He was now more interested in less commercial forms of music, 'particularly industrial hip hop – Ministry, Nine Inch Nails – and dub'. As the production manager for the campus student radio station, Julian had access to a lot of new music, with one of 'the perks' being able to retain some for his own collection. He regularly attended concerts, even when he did not necessarily buy the artist's records. Julian read a range of music magazines, with a preference for *Vox*, 'always' watched television's music video shows – 'my link to commercial music', and 'constantly' listened to music on the radio, or, more frequently, on CD or tape. He wanted to extend his broad interest in music vocationally, and was planning to enrol in a broadcasting course (and subsequently did so). Shared musical tastes were a basis for most of his friendships (author interview). This configuration of interests, characterised by an intensive interest in particular performers or genres, is typical of university students and other young adults (see also Willis *et al.* 1990; Christenson and Roberts 1998).

'Fans', in the more widely accepted pejorative sense of the term, will collect the records put out by their favoured 'star' performers, but these are only one aspect of an interest focused rather on the image and persona of the star. Rimmer saw fans as the foundation of the post-punk British 'New Pop' of the 1980s. Groups and performers like Culture Club, Duran Duran, Wham!, Spandau Ballet, Nick Kershaw, and Howard Jones had a fanatical female following:

> fans so devoted they wear their clothes and copy their hair-dos, fans who chase them around in taxis and hound them to their hotels, fans appearing in droves anywhere they know they might show up, fans ferreting out their ex-directory phone numbers and showering them with preposterously lavish presents, fans waving banners and screaming their lungs out at concerts, fans rioting at airports.
>
> (Rimmer 1985: 104–5)

Such fans are a merchandising dream, buying up practically anything associated with the group, with their support in extreme cases bordering on the pathological. The story is one that can be related to each new teen phenomenon since Rimmer wrote, from New Kids on the Block in the early 1990s (see Marshall 1997) to Take That, Boyzone, and the Spice Girls.

Yet Rimmer is, quite correctly, also anxious to defend these fans: 'Pop fans aren't stupid. They know what they want. And ultimately, all the media manipulation in the world isn't going to sell them something they haven't got any use for' (Rimmer 1985: 108). Fred and Judy Vermorel's book *Starlust* (1985), and the essays in *Love is the Drug* (Aizelwood 1994), suggest that, whatever the press of 'context' – the intentions of the industry, the pop press, and musicians themselves – meaning in the music is ultimately created by the consumers. Fans of performers such as David Bowie, Barry Manilow, Marc Bolan, and Jon Bon Jovi speak of them almost as religious touchstones, helping them to get through their lives even if it antagonises their jealous partners. The artists provide emotional and even physical comfort to such fans: 'I'm an only child, and earlier this year my father died. I still haven't got over it but I only have to look at my posters or play Nick's records to feel a little better' (Julie, age 16, Nick Kershaw fan, Vermorel and Vermorel 1985).

Such strong identification with the star becomes a source of pleasure here. The discomfort or even pain involved is an important part of this, since it is its resolution – or, at least, the possibility of resolution – which provides the pleasure.

Empowerment, pleasure and cultural capital

Fandom has a good deal in common with subcultures, as both are central to identity.

> By participating in fandom, fans construct coherent identities for themselves. In the process, they enter a domain of cultural activity of their own making which is, potentially, a source of empowerment in struggles against oppressive ideologies and the unsatisfactory circumstances of everyday life.
>
> (Lewis 1992: 3; summarising Grossberg's contribution)

Beyond possible empowerment, fandom as a form of cultural activity has a number of pleasurable dimensions common to both types of fan identified here: dance and its associated rituals of display and restraint; verisimilitude – the anticipatory pleasure of attending a concert or playing a new purchase; the sheer physical pleasure of handling records, tapes or CDs; the pleasure of finding that rare item in a second-hand store bin; and the intellectual and emotional pleasures associated with 'knowing' about particular artists and genres valued by one's peers and associates. This last is a form of cultural capital, and is central to the understanding of popular consumption.

As shown earlier, musical tastes and styles followed or adopted by particular groups of consumers are affected by a number of social factors, especially class, gender, ethnicity, and age. This situation suggests that the designation of popular music genres is more of a sociological than a musical one, a point reinforced by the varied reception of specific music texts (see Chapter 9). Consumption is not simply a matter of 'personal' preference, but is, in part, socially constructed. Linked to this process, is the manner in which popular music serves as a form of symbolic or cultural capital.

Following Bourdieu (1984) we can see 'taste' as both conceived and maintained in social groups' efforts to differentiate and distance themselves from others, and underpinning varying social status positions. Music has traditionally been a crucial dimension of this process. Writing in 1950, Riesman astutely distinguished between two teenage audiences for popular music. First, a majority group with 'an undiscriminating taste in popular music, [who] seldom express articulate preferences', and for whom the functions of music were predominantly social. This group consumed 'mainstream', commercial music, following the stars and the hit parade. Second, Riesman identified a minority group of 'the more active listeners', who had a more rebellious attitude towards popular music, indicated by:

> an insistence on rigorous standards of judgement and taste in a relativist culture; a preference for the uncommercialized, unadvertized small bands rather than

name bands; the development of a private language ... (and) a profound resent-
ment of the commercialization of radio and musicians.

(Riesman 1950: 412)

Among Swedish youth in the 1980s, argued Trondmam, rock was split between two
major genres: a mature 'artistic' rock, and a commercial 'idol rock' (Trondman 1990).
In such a distinction, one form of rock – the mature – is identified with what
Bourdieu refers to as legitimate culture, while the other expresses distance from legitimate culture. Trondman, utilising data from a large-scale Swedish survey, teases out
the more precise functioning of this core distinction. The adherents of artistic rock
were found primarily among university students and graduates, people who have
good prospects of becoming part of the legitimate culture. For them, there is an
emphasis on music that satisfies demands of 'intellectuality', 'aesthetic appeal', and
'association with tradition'. Linking these qualities to 'legitimate culture', Trondman
(1990: 81) argues that the acquisition of such musical culture capital can assist its
holders in becoming assimilated into the dominant social elite. This process and the
distinctions upon which it is based, is very similar to the operation of fandom within
contemporary popular music genres, especially the various forms of 'alternative'
music.

Acquiring any form of popular music cultural capital involves developing a
knowledge of selected musical traditions, their history, and their associated
performers. With this background, an individual can knowledgeably discuss such
details as styles, trends, record companies, and the biographies of artists, and even
nuances such as associated record producers and session musicians. Such cultural
capital does not necessarily have to be part of the dominant, generally accepted tradition, but can instead function to distance its adherents from that tradition, asserting
their own oppositional stance. As we saw, this is the pattern with many youth subcultures, which appropriate and innovate musical styles and forms as a basis for their
identity.

A major theoretical issue is the relationship between popular culture and market
forces, especially the extent to which styles and tastes are synthetically produced for a
deliberately stimulated mass market. Popular music is an example of this process,
which exemplifies the debate between culturalism and structuralism in the analysis
of popular culture. As I have previously argued (Chapter 1), we need to see culture as
a reciprocal concept, an active practice which shapes and conditions economic and
political processes, as well as being conditioned and shaped by them. The various
types of consumers of popular music genres considered here illustrate this reciprocity,
occupying a critical social space in the process whereby the music acquires cultural
meaning and significance.

Chapter 12

'Pushin' too hard'
Popular music and cultural politics

Particular genres of popular music have sparked controversy and opposition, both upon their emergence and sporadically since: rock 'n' roll in the mid-1950s, psychedelic rock in the late 1960s, disco and punk in the 1970s, heavy metal and gangsta rap in the 1980s, and rave culture in the 1990s, to name only the better-known examples (see Martin and Seagrave 1988; Cloonan 1996; Winfield and Davidson 1999; Cohen 1997). Criticism has centred variously on the influence of such genres on youthful values, attitudes and behaviour through the music's (perceived) sexuality and sexism, nihilism and violence, obscenity, black magic and anti-Christian nature. The political edge of popular music has been partly the result of this hostile reaction often accorded to the music and its associated causes and followers, helping to politicise the musicians and their fans.

While such episodes are a standard part of the history of popular music – music hall, jazz, and other new forms of popular music were also all stigmatised in their day – rarely are their nature and cultural significance more fully teased out. The first part of this chapter argues that they have constituted a form of moral panic – the social concern generated by them was greatly exaggerated, and the perceived threat to social harmony was by no means as ominous as many regarded it. Attempts to control and regulate popular music genres such as rock and rap are significant as part of the ongoing contestation of cultural hegemony, particularly with the emergence of the New Right.

In addition to ongoing debates over the 'effects' and influence of popular music, there have always been attempts to harness the music to social and political ends, and arguments around the validity of notions of music as an empowering and political force. The second part of this chapter considers several examples: gender and sexual politics, particularly the Riot Grrrl 'movement', and the phenomenon of 'conscience rock'. The main issue here is the influence of such cultural interventions.

MORAL PANIC AND REGULATION

The episodes dealt with here have been chosen for their value in illuminating different facets of the reaction to popular music, at particular historical moments. First, the New Zealand reaction to rock 'n' roll in the 1950s exemplifies the characteristic concerns displayed internationally towards the new form of popular music: antipathy towards it as music, the anti-social behaviour linked to concerts and rock movies, and, most importantly, the associations with juvenile delinquency. Second, the issues of obscenity and free speech are examined in the light of the establishment of the PMRC and the celebrated court action against American band the Dead Kennedys in 1986–87, and controversies surrounding the lyrics of songs by 2 Live Crew (1990) and Ice-T (1992). Third, attempts to link the Columbine massacre of 1999 to the influence of Marilyn Manson illustrate the ongoing tendency to blame 'rock' for deeper social problems. These case studies illustrate the utility of the concept of moral panic to examine how music, as a central form of popular culture, becomes invested with ideological significance.

To place such opposition to popular music in context, it is important to acknowledge that popular culture in general has historically been the target of censure, condemnation and regulation (for detailed discussion, see Gilbert 1986; Shuker and Openshaw 1991). In the 1950s, for example, psychologist Frederic Wertham's influential bestseller, *Seduction of the Innocent*, argued for a direct causal connection between comic books and juvenile delinquency. Concern over new media and the activities of their youthful consumers seems to periodically reach a peak, frequently associated with 'boundary crises', periods of ambiguity and strain in society, which lead to attempts to more clearly establish moral boundaries. In many instances, such boundary crises are forms of 'moral panic', a concept popularised by sociologist Stanley Cohen's now classic study of mods and rockers in the United Kingdom, *Folk Devils and Moral Panics*. Cohen states that a period of moral panic occurs when:

> A condition, episode, person or group of persons emerges to become defined as a threat to societal values and interests; its nature is presented in a stylised and stereotypical fashion by the mass media; the moral barricades are manned by editors, bishops, politicians and other right-thinking people; socially accredited experts pronounce their diagnoses and solutions; ways of coping are evolved or

(more often) resorted to; the condition then disappears, submerges or deterio-
rates and becomes more visible.

(Cohen 1980: 9)

The second stage of Cohen's view of moral panic is particularly significant, involving
as it does the repudiation of the 'common-sense' view that the media simply report
what happens. Cohen's own case study of the 1960s clashes between mods and
rockers in the UK (the 'folk devils' of his title), showed up just such a process of the
selection and presentation of news. The media coverage of the clashes simplified
their causes, labelled and stigmatised the youth involved, whipped up public feeling,
and encouraged a retributive, deterrent approach by those in authority.

Examining the historical relationship between youth, 'antisocial' attitudes and
behaviours, and popular music means, once again, to consider culture as a political issue.
At a deeper level, moral panics around new media are episodes in cultural politics and
the continual reconstitution and contestation of cultural hegemony. Underpinning
debates over popular fiction, comics, film, television, video and popular music genres
and performers are a series of assumptions about popular or 'mass' culture, which is
frequently seen as diametrically opposed to a 'high' culture tradition. As already argued
(Chapter 1), this dichotomy is a doubtful basis for evaluating particular forms of culture,
and such a distinction is increasingly difficult to sustain in practice. The whole notion of
a 'high–low' culture distinction must be regarded as a social construct, resting on class-
based value judgements. It is more appropriate to view particular cultural forms in terms
of both their formal qualities and their social function for consumers, while keeping in
mind the salient point that any evaluation must be primarily in terms relevant to the
group that produces and appreciates it. This is particularly the case with popular music
(Shepherd et al. 1977). With these general points in mind, we can turn to our examples of
music and moral panics.

Rock 'n' roll: the devil's music

As we saw in Chapter 2, both the music industry and the social context of the early
1950s were ready for rock 'n' roll. With fuller employment, general economic pros-
perity, and their emergence as an important consumer group, teenagers began to
demand their own music and clothes, and to develop a generational-based identity.
Before 1956, popular music was dominated by American sounds, epitomised by the
recurrent image of the 'crooner'. The music was largely safe, solid stuff, what Cohn
terms 'the palais age – the golden era of the big bands, when everything was soft,
warm, sentimental, when everything was make believe' (Cohn 1970: 11). There was
little here for young people to identify with, though riot-provoking performers like
Johnny Ray represented prototypes for rock.

Although rock music began with rock 'n' roll in the mid-1950s, as Tosches (1984) documents, it had been evolving well prior to this, and was hardly the sole creation of Elvis Presley and Alan Freed. The phrase 'rock 'n' roll' itself was popularised with its sexual connotations in the music of the 1920s. In 1922, blues singer Trixie Smith recorded 'My Daddy Rocks Me (With One Steady Roll)' for Black Swan Records, and various lyrical elaborations followed from other artists through the 1930s and 1940s (Tosches 1984: 5–6). Rock 'n' roll was basically 'a mixture of two traditions: Negro rhythm and blues and white romantic crooning, coloured beat and white sentiment' (Cohn 1970: 11). Negro rhythm and blues was good-time music, dance-able and unpretentious. While highly popular on rhythm and blues charts and radio stations, it received little airplay on white radio stations, and was frequently banned because of the explicit sexual content of songs such as Hank Ballard's 'Work With Me Annie', Billy Ward's 'Sixty Minute Man', and the Penguin's 'Baby Let Me Bang Your Box'. It is this link between sex and rock 'n' roll – the devil's music – which underpinned the moral reaction to its popularisation in the 1950s.

In April 1954, Bill Haley made 'Rock Around the Clock'. The record was a hit in America, then worldwide; eventually selling 15 million copies. While it did not start rock 'n' roll, it did represent a critical symbol in the popularisation of the new musical form. 'Rock Around the Clock' was featured in the MGM movie *Blackboard Jungle*, the story of a young teacher at a tough New York school. The success of the film with teenage audiences, and the popularity of Haley's song (see Miller 1999: 87–94), led to Haley being signed to make a film of his own. *Rock Around the Clock* (1956) told how Bill Haley and his band popularised rock 'n' roll, but the thin story was really a show-case for the rock acts on the soundtrack. The film proved enormously popular internationally, but attracted controversy over its effect on audiences. In Britain, for example, local councils banned showings of the film following riots in some cinemas. According to contemporary press reports, in the Gaiety Cinema, Manchester,

> gangs of teenage youths and their girlfriends danced in the aisles, vaulted up on to the stage, and turned fire hoses on the manager when he tried to restore order. After the programme, they surged into city streets in a wild stampede, bringing traffic to a standstill in the centre of town and pounding a rock 'n' roll rhythm on buses and cars with their fists.

Haley was an unlikely hero for youth to emulate, since his image (old, balding, and chubby) hardly matched the music, but others were waiting in the wings. In this brief overview, complex developments must be reduced to their key moments. The success of Haley was one, the emergence of Chuck Berry and Little Richard another. Elvis Presley's was the biggest yet:

His big contribution was that he brought it home just how economically powerful teenagers could really be. Before Elvis, rock had been a feature of vague rebellion. Once he'd happened, it immediately became solid, self-contained, and then it spawned its own style in clothes and language and sex, a total independence in almost everything – all the things that are now taken for granted.

(Cohn 1970: 23)

Cohn is overly enthusiastic about teenagers' independence, but by the end of 1957 Elvis had grown into an annual $20 million industry, and the process of homogenisation of both 'the King' and the music had begun.

The new music provoked considerable criticism, with many older musicians contemptuous of rock 'n' roll, and conservative commentators regarding it as a moral threat.

Viewed as a social phenomenon, the current craze for rock 'n' roll material is one of the most terrifying things ever to have happened to popular music. Musically speaking, of course, the whole thing is laughable. It is a monstrous threat, both to the moral acceptance and the artistic emancipation of jazz. Let us oppose it to the end.

(British jazzman Steve Race, in Rogers 1982: 18)

Rock 'n' roll 'down under'

Although necessarily brief, this capsule view of the early history of rock 'n' roll is apposite, since the New Zealand experience we now turn to closely followed developments overseas, illustrating the rapid establishment of rock as an international phenomenon. This can be seen through New Zealand's response to the film *Rock Around the Clock*, and the emergence of the antipodean folk devil, the bodgie (for a fuller discussion of these, see Shuker and Openshaw 1991; the quotes here are from contemporary press reports). The local reaction in each case contained elements of a moral panic, with youth once again being constructed as posing a social problem.

As with their overseas counterparts, by the mid-1950s New Zealand youth were more visible and more affluent. Contemporary press advertising reflected increased awareness of youth as a distinctive market, particularly for clothes and records. Dances and concerts catering for youth increased, and the nationally broadcast Lever Hit Parade began in November 1955.

In late 1956 *Rock Around the Clock* arrived in New Zealand, and was approved for general exhibition by the Film Censor, who noted that 'a somewhat compulsive rhythm pervaded the film but otherwise there was nothing unusual about it'. Anticipation of similar scenes in New Zealand to the riots accompanying screenings

221

of the film overseas were rarely met. Despite press headlines such as 'Larrikins Take Over After Film', and 'Rock 'n' Roll Addicts in Minor Disturbance', the crowds attending screenings were in fact generally restrained. Indeed, there was almost an air of disappointment. The police, prepared for trouble, were present at and following some screenings, but were rarely needed. In Auckland, the country's main centre,

> in spite of a few policemen standing by, and the expectancy that had booked the cinema out, the first night's showing passed off with nothing more rowdy than some adolescent hand-clapping, some whistling and stamping, a little squealing in the rain after the show, and one charge of obstruction.

This was in spite of the cinema's provocative publicity for the film, which included a foyer display of press cuttings of the riots produced by the film overseas!

For most observers, rock 'n' roll was at worst a safety valve, and a passing craze: 'It does invite one to dance with hypnotic abandon and self-display, but to listen to it is more monotonous than boogie-woogie'! As occurred overseas, there was a tendency to see rock 'n' roll as 'not a very attractive art form for those whose tastes have made any progress towards maturity. Prime requisites appear to be that the words – or sounds – should be meaningless and repetitive, while any semblance of melody is hastily and noisily murdered'. Generally, however, the press ignored the new phenomenon, while popular music on the radio remained largely confined to the numerous Maori show bands of the day, supplemented by a bit of jazz.

New Zealand's first real rock 'n' roll hero emerged in 1957: Johnny Devlin, an 18-year-old bank clerk. Devlin was a self-conscious Presley imitator, a natural singer and showman. His first record, 'Lawdy Miss Clawdy' became the most successful local single of the 1950s. Successful tours, including a hugely successful five-month national tour during 1958, saw sell-out houses, Devlin mobbed by screaming girls, and several incidents of damage to theatres and injuries to the police protecting the singer. While the tour subsequently assumed almost mythic proportions in the history of rock 'n' roll in New Zealand, there was clearly an element of media promotional hype present. Devlin, for example, wore lightly stitched clothing to facilitate the incidents where the fans 'ripped the clothes from his back'.

If both *Rock Around the Clock* and Johnny Devlin's concerts failed to measure up as local moral panics, the bodgies represented New Zealand's very own folk devils of the 1950s. Bodgies and widgies, their female companions, were the local equivalent of the English Teddy Boys, adopting similar styles:

> The males wore unusual and exaggerated haircuts. All went to extremes in the

style of suits worn. The trousers were all much tighter in the legs than usual. Some favoured extreme shortness of leg exposing garishly coloured socks. Coats, when worn, were fuller in cut and much longer than is normal by conservative standards, while all favoured brightly coloured shirts, pullovers or wind-breakers, and neckerchiefs.

(Manning 1958: 9)

Although Manning makes little reference to the leisure pursuits of the group, other sources indicate that as in Britain rock 'n' roll was the musical style the bodgies most strongly identified with: Buddy Holly, Gene Vincent and Eddie Cochrane joining earlier heroes like Haley.

Manning's was an openly hostile study; it is subtitled 'A Study in Psychological Abnormality' . The New Zealand public and press largely shared his view of bodgies as juvenile delinquents who posed a social threat. The bodgie soon became a national bogey man, with alarmist newspaper reports about bodgie behaviour. During 1958, one Wellington paper reported that 'the parade of brutality' by bodgies and widgies had reached such a peak that many parents were 'fearful of allowing their children out at night'. Gender inscribed these discourses: the hysteria provoked by Devlin was a predominantly female phenomenon, which received little serious criticism; the male bodgie was a different matter: 'When they are not feeling in too violent a mood they confine their activities to pushing people off footpaths. When looking for thrills, they fight among themselves, often with knives and bicycle chains' (press reports). Bodgies became identified with hooliganism or vandalism, and Parliament debated the problem. Young compulsory military trainees on leave harassed and beat up bodgies, forcibly taking over bodgie milk bars in central Auckland, while incoming trainees with bodgie haircuts were initially left unshorn, resulting in harassment.

The bodgie threat was clearly an exaggerated one. In conformist New Zealand of the late 1950s, bodgies and widgies stood out. The surprising fact was not that New Zealand had young delinquents, 'but that they are relatively such a small group' (NZ *Listener*, editorial, 18 April 1958).

ROCK, FREE SPEECH, AND THE NEW RIGHT

During the mid-1980s, a general trend towards censorship emerged in the United States:

an attack on the right of free speech, spearheaded by well-organized and well-financed pressure groups from the New Right. This anti-rock, pro-censorship campaign represents a power play by the New Right, particularly the religious right, to impose censorship, via ratings and arrests, on musicians, filmmakers and writers whose points of view they do not agree with or approve of.

(Sluka 1991)

While the 'New Right' is a complex network of political, secular and religious organisations rather than a unified grouping, it exerts considerable influence through its letter writing and petition campaigns, its television and radio programmes, and the publications of its ideological think-tanks. The various New Right groups recognised that shared public concerns with social issues can be successfully mobilised to achieve and maintain political support and solidarity.

Such conservative groups have historically targeted youth subcultures, most notably punk, and rock music as a threat to traditional 'family' values (Martin and Seagrave 1988: chap. 21; Cloonan 1996). The music is perceived as embodying a range of negative influences, which need to be regulated and controlled. It is claimed that rock is:

the single most powerful tool with which Satan communicates his evil message. MURDER MUSIC has led millions of young people into alcoholism, abortion, crime, drug addiction, incest, prostitution, sadomasochism, satanic worshipping, sexual promiscuity, suicide and much more. MURDER MUSIC has to be STOPPED NOW! The moral fiber of our country and young lives are at stake!

('Rock deprogrammer', Pastor Fletcher Brothers, abridged from Denselow 1990: 264)

Initially the anti-rock campaign was spearheaded by fundamentalist Christian groups, aligned with powerful right-wing pressure groups sponsored by television evangelists, such as the Reverend Jerry Falwell's 'Moral Majority' and 'Clean Up America Crusade'. While pushing for stricter censorship legislation, such groups enjoyed more success through pressure on the music producers and distributors. Tele-evangelist Jimmy Swaggart, after equating rock with 'pornography and degenerative filth which denigrates all the values we hold sacred and is destructive to youth', met with company representatives of the Wal-Mart discount chain, whose 800 outlets subsequently stopped stocking rock and teen magazines and albums by a number of bands, including Ozzy Osbourne and Motley Crue, because of their alleged 'satanic' and 'pornographic' content (Kennedy 1990: 135).

The PMRC

The New Right attack on rock and free speech was boosted by the formation, in 1985, of the Parent's Music Resource Center (PMRC). Headed by a group of

'Washington wives' – most were married to Senators or Congressmen – who were also 'born again' Christians, the PMRC dedicated themselves to 'cleaning up' rock music, which they saw as potentially harmful to young people, terming it 'secondary child abuse'. One of the founding members, Tipper Gore, became involved because she had bought her 8-year-old daughter a copy of Prince's album *Purple Rain* and found that one of its songs, 'Darling Nicki', referred to masturbation ('I met her in a hotel lobby, masturbating with a magazine').

The PMRC published a *Rock Music Report*, condemning what they claimed to be the five major themes in the music: rebellion, substance abuse, sexual promiscuity and perversion, violence-nihilism, and the occult. They started a highly organised letter-writing campaign, and began arguing for the implementation of a ratings system for records, similar to that used in the cinema. The PMRC also sent copies of lyrics of songs they saw as objectionable to programme directors at radio and television stations, to be screened for 'offensive material', and pressed record companies to reassess the contracts of artists who featured violence, substance abuse, or explicit sexuality in their recorded work or concerts.

All these measures were aimed at encouraging self-censorship in the music industry, and the group's tactics met with considerable success. The high point of their efforts was the 1985 US Senate Commerce Committee hearings on the influence of music (see Denselow 1990: chap. 10). No legislation came out of the hearings, but the Record Industry Association of America voluntarily responded by introducing a generic 'Parents Advisory Explicit Lyrics' label to appear on albums deemed to warrant it, a practice that became widespread during the 1990s. The next major focus for the PMRC was the Dead Kennedys obscenity trial during 1986–87.

Penis Landscape

In December 1985 a 13-year-old girl bought a copy of the Dead Kennedys' album *Frankenchrist* from a record shop in the San Fernando Valley in California. The record contained a poster entitled 'Penis Landscape' by Swiss surrealist artist H.R. Giger, best known for his Oscar-winning work on the sets of the film *Alien*. The work was a detail from a larger painting, *Landscape #20, Where Are We Coming From?* and depicted male appendages arranged in neat rows. Jello Biafra, the Dead Kennedys' lead singer, explained that he had included the print because 'The painting portrayed to me a vortex of exploitation and I realised that the same theme ran through the album'. The band put an 'alternative' warning sticker on the album: 'WARNING; the fold-out to this album contains a work of art by H.R. Giger that some people may find shocking, repulsive or offensive. Life can sometimes be that way' (Kennedy 1990: 132). The girl's parents saw it differently, and complained to the State Attorney General's Office that it was 'pornographic'. In April 1986 police raided

225

Jello Biafra's home and the office of Alternative Tentacles Records, the label founded by the Dead Kennedys, looking for obscene material. None was found, but in June Biafra was eventually charged with distributing harmful material to minors, and the case finally went to trial in August 1987.

The Dead Kennedys had been the subject of controversy and the target of New Right censorship before. Formed in San Francisco in 1978, the band played a form of punk thrash music with politically hard-edged lyrics. Their first single 'California Uber Alles' was a satirical attack on State Governor Jerry Brown, and included lines like 'Your kids will meditate in school' and 'You will jog for the master race'. Later work included 'Holiday in Cambodia' about the horrors of the Pol Pot regime, and the anti-alcohol warning 'Too Drunk To Fuck', which gained chart success despite its title and the subsequent lack of radio airplay. Shunned by the mainstream record companies, the group began their own label, Alternative Tentacles, which also promoted similarly ostracised groups. While their name alone practically ensured commercial failure in the US, the Dead Kennedys' records enjoyed considerable success in the European 'indie' charts. Albums such as *Bedtime for Democracy* tackled political subjects like Reagan's foreign policy and the US censorship lobby, satirised MTV, and attacked American business involvement in South Africa. While the groups punk thrash backing and Biafra's breakneck lyrics often made the lyrics almost unintelligible, this was hardly work to endear the band to the establishment.

Jello's trial in Los Angeles in 1987 was seen as a major test case for the censorship of popular music. Support from Frank Zappa and Little Steven, and a series of benefit shows from European punk bands, helped raise the $70,000 needed for defence costs, and Biafra defended himself, and was articulate in his opposition to censorship, and his support for free speech. He argued that there was a danger that the US was returning to the climate of the 1950s, when anti-communist witchhunts led to the banning of an earlier political songwriter, Pete Seeger. The case ran for two weeks. The jury deadlocked (7 to 5) in Jello's favour, but could make no further progress, and the judge finally declared a mistrial (Kennedy 1990: 144).

Even if it was a victory for free speech, the case had finished the Dead Kennedys. Already having internal problems, with Biafra tied up in the litigation process, and prevented from performing, the group broke up in December 1986. Biafra went on to a career as a 'political performance artist', doing monologue style presentations such as 'Ollie North for President'; the PMRC remained active, and went on to new targets.

Rap

In the early 1990s, rap music became the main target of the 'anti-rock, pro-censorship' lobby. The new genre had already been attacked from the left for its sexism and homophobia, and was now criticised for its profanity and obscenity. A judge in Florida declared the rap group 2 Live Crew's album *As Nasty as they Want to Be* to be obscene, the first such ruling for a recorded work in United States history. Following this, a record store owner was arrested when he sold the album to an undercover police officer, and three members of the band were arrested for performing material from the album at a concert with an 'adults only' rating. The band members were eventually acquitted of the obscenity charge, but the conviction of the store owner was upheld (Gilmore 1990: 14).

The anti-authority political attitudes and values in some rap music also attracted the attention of the New Right. The Los Angeles rap group Niggers With Attitude (NWA) song 'Fuck the Police' and Ice-T's song 'Cop Killer' both caused considerable controversy and calls to ban their performers' concerts and records. In the United Kingdom, in October 1990, gangsta rappers Niggers With Attitude (NWA) released a single with a B-side 'She Swallowed It', dealing with oral sex. Many of the major department store chains, and some music retailers, refused to stock the record, conscious of the lack of clarity surrounding the 1959 Obscene Publications Act, and fearing prosecution. In June 1991, NWA released their second album, *Efil4zaggin* (Niggaz 4 life, backwards) in the UK, after it had already topped the American *Billboard* chart and sold nearly a million copies in its first week of release. The album contained a number of tracks featuring sexual degradation and extreme violence toward women, along with considerable swearing. The police raided the premises of Polygram, the record's UK distributor, and seized some 12,000 copies of the album, and shops withdrew the album from sale. A prosecution followed, using the Obscene Publications Act's definition of an 'obscene article' as one which 'tend(s) to deprave and corrupt'. The high profile court case revolved around free speech arguments versus claims that the record was obscene, especially in its portrayal of women. The magistrates who judged the case ruled that the album was not obscene under the terms of the Act; the seized stock was returned and the album went back on sale (see Cloonan 1995, for a detailed treatment of this episode, and the associated issues).

Cop Killer

Ice-T's 'Cop Killer' is a revenge fantasy of the disempowered, in which the singer recounts getting ready to 'dust some cops off'.

> I got my black shirt on,
> I got my black gloves on,
> I got my ski mask on,
> This shit's been too long.
> I got my twelve-gauge sawed off,

I got my headlights turned off,
I'm 'bout to dust some shots off,
I'm 'bout to dust some cops off.
(Ice-T, 'Copkiller', WB, 1992)

The warning sticker on the tape cassette version of the album *Body Count*, which includes 'Cop Killer', hardly appeased critics of the record: 'Warning: This tape contains material that may be offensive to someone out there!' It was claimed that the song glorified the murder of police, and both President Bush and Vice President Dan Quayle sided with law-enforcement groups in protesting Time Warner's release of the record. Several US national record-store chains stopped selling *Body Count*, and in July 1992 Time Warner pulled the song at Ice-T's request after police groups picketed the media conglomerate's shareholders meeting in Beverley Hills. Anxious to avoid governmental regulation, in September, Warner Music Group executives met with several of the rappers on the label, including Ice-T, and warned them to change their lyrics on some songs or find another label for their work (*Los Angeles Times*, 10 December 1992). Time Warner's Sire Records delayed the release of Ice-T's *Home Invasion* album; the performer eventually changed labels, and the album was released on Rhyme Syndicate/Virgin in 1993.

In New Zealand, in July 1992, the Police Commissioner unsuccessfully attempted to prevent an Ice-T concert in Auckland, arguing that 'Anyone who comes to this country preaching in obscene terms the killing of police, should not be welcome here'. Several record shop owners refused to stock the album containing the song. The local music industry, student radio stations, and several leading music journalists responded by defending the song as a piece of 'role play', linking it with the singer's recent performance in the film *New Jack City* and the right to free speech. Undeterred, the police took *Body Count* and the song's publishers and distributors, Warners, to the Indecent Publications Tribunal, in an effort to get it banned under New Zealand's Indecent Publications Act. This was the first time in twenty years that a sound recording had come before this censorship body, and the first ever case involving popular music (previous sound recording cases before the Tribunal were 'readings' from erotic novels or memoirs!). As such, it created considerable interest, not least due to the appeal of rap among the country's Polynesian and Maori youth (see Chapter 11).

The case rehearsed familiar arguments around the influence of song lyrics. The police contended that:

given the content of the songs, it is possible that people could be corrupted by hearing the sound recording, and in the case of the song 'Cop Killer' that some individuals may be exhorted to act with violence towards the Police. The course of conduct advocated in the song 'Cop Killer' is a direct threat to law enforcement personnel generally and causes grave concern to the police.

(Mr H. Woods, Senior Legal Adviser for the New Zealand Police; cited in Indecent Publications Tribunal Decision No.100/92)

Defence submissions argued that the album offered a powerful treatment of the:

sense of disenfranchisement and hopelessness that a large segment of American youth are faced with, and the violence that is bred in such an environment. It is a social commentary that we would like to believe is far removed from our society here in New Zealand. But whether this is so or not, the album has a validity and topicality as a reflection of the disenfranchised segment of our society.

(Ms Karen Soich, Warner Brothers counsel; ibid.)

After reviewing the various submissions, and listening carefully to the album, the Tribunal concluded that 'the dominant effect of the album is complex'. While 'its lyrics are repugnant to most New Zealanders, it is a much bigger step to link those lyrics to subsequent anti-social behaviour' (ibid.). It found the song 'Cop Killer' to be 'not exhortatory', saw the album as displaying 'an honest purpose', and found *Body Count* not indecent.

These moral panics around popular music can be situated against the global emergence of a New Right, embracing free market politics and a moral cultural conservatism. Grossberg observes of this trend in the United States:

The new conservatism is, in a certain sense, a matter of public language, of what can be said, of the limits of the allowable. This has made culture into a crucial terrain on which struggles over power, and the politics of the nation, are waged.

(Grossberg 1992: 162)

As he concludes, this struggle involves a new form of regulation: 'a variety of attacks become tokens of a broader attack, not so much on the freedom of expression as on the freedom of distribution and circulation' (ibid.: 163). The earlier debates have been reprised through the 1990s, in the controversy surrounding the work of performers such as Eminem, Dr Dre, and Marilyn Manson.

In such a climate, the music industry has moved further toward self-regulation. In 2000, white rapper Eminem's U.S. chart-topping album, *The Marshall Mathers LP*, was heavily criticised for its homophobic and misogynist lyrics. In what has become routine industry practice, the record label (Interscope/Universal) excised entire tracks to create an alternative album that parents can buy for their children, while extensively editing the lyrics in the remaining songs to eliminate references to drugs, violence, profanity and hate (*The New York Times on the Web*, 1 August 2000).

Columbine and Marilyn Manson

The massacre at Columbine High School in Littleton, Colorado, on 29 April 1999, resulted in fifteen deaths and twenty-three injuries, some severe. The two young men responsible were students at the school, and killed themselves at the end of their bloody rampage. News coverage of the shootings was intense. Speculation about its causes referred to the negative influence of violent media on youth, especially video games; neo-Nazi ideology; and rock music (see the special forum in *Popular Music and Society*, 23, 3, Fall 1999). When it was revealed that the two boys who killed their classmates were Marilyn Manson fans, the band cancelled their American tour. (Ironically, at the same time, the National Rifle Association went ahead with their national meeting in Denver.) For some commentators, Marilyn Manson became the 'designated demon' for the Columbine massacre. Manson responded with an articulate statement in *Rolling Stone* ('Columbine: Whose Fault Is It?', 24 June 1999: 23–4), observing that such simplistic associations missed the deeper reasons for the tragedy, which lay in youth disenchantment and alienation.

The latest in a succession of entertainers whose career is based on confrontation and shock value, Marilyn Manson (formerly Brian Warner) was accustomed to controversy. He and his band members play under aliases combining a famous woman's name with the last name of a serial killer; in Warner's case the well-known star Marilyn Monroe, and Charles Manson. The self-appointed 'Antichrist Superstar' (the title of the band's second album), has been termed 'one of rock's biggest personalities and smartest social commentators' (*Q*, January 2000: 118). In songs such as 'The Dope Show' and 'Beautiful People', he examined the underbelly of American life and popular culture. Their highly theatrical act, reminiscent of Alice Cooper, was designed to shock audiences. Along with the songs, it gained the group a cult following in the mid-1990s, mainly among the Goth subculture. During 1997–98 *Antichrist Superstar* pushed them into the commercial mainstream, while Manson hit the headlines with his proclamations against organised religion. Their third album, *Mechanical Animals* (1998), topped the charts in a number of countries, but caused outrage when Manson appeared as a naked, sexless android on the cover and in the video for the single 'The Dope Show' (D. Dalton, 'Pleased to Meet You', *MOJO*, September 1999, provides an insightful analysis of Marilyn Manson's career and persona).

The debates around its influence and the associated calls for the censorship of popular music and its performers are a reminder of the force of music as symbolic politics, operating in the cultural arena. In related fashion, and arguably even more strongly demonstrating its cultural power, is the use of popular music to assert and support political views and causes. Many artists have used their music to make political statements on a variety of issues, including racism, class, gender politics, sexuality, and the environment. At times, such concerns have prompted organised interventions, as with Live Aid, Lilith Fair, and various conscience concerts. There has been considerable debate around the role of music in these initiatives. One of the most significant aspects of music's cultural politics, is the contribution it makes to the shaping of social identities.

MUSIC AND GENDER POLITICS

Writing in 1977, Chapple and Garofalo describe a situation which has been slow to change:

> The absence of women as creators in pop music can be called sexist. Sexism is the systematic discrimination against and degradation of women, and the denial of equal power to women in human affairs. Sexism is as pervasive in rock music as in any other form of music. It pervades the structure of the music industry along with the lyrics and instrumentation of the music itself.
>
> (1977: 269)

This volume, and Steward and Garratt's *Signed, Sealed, and Delivered* (1984), provided numerous examples of the difficult struggle experienced by women in all phases of the music business. Through the 1980 and into the 1990s, analyses of the treatment of girls and women in popular music and youth subcultures continued to see them as absent, 'invisible' or socially insignificant (see McRobbie 1991; Frith 1983; Chambers 1985). In addition, critics could point to the male-dominated musical canon in musicology (McClary 1991); and the manner in which girl fans and their musical tastes are often denigrated (teenyboppers).

The tendency to marginalise women performers/genres in the history of popular music was also critiqued. Compare, for example, the status accorded contemporaries Jim Morrison (heroic, romantic 'rock icon'), and Janis Joplin ('a sad figure'), despite her critical and commercial success, which more than matched his in the late 1960s. Gaar (1992) provides a revisionist account placing gender to the fore, correctly contending that popular culture analysts and rock journalists have continued largely to ignore the contributions of women to rock. She includes 'girl' groups, individual women artists, singer-songwriters, and women involved in the rock press and record companies (see also O'Brien, L. 1995).

Also at issue is the perceived masculine or feminine nature of particular genres/styles. Dance pop is generally seen as 'a girls' genre', while hard rock and heavy metal are regarded as primarily male-oriented genres (see under sexuality, below). Women performers predominate in a cappella and gospel music, and are prominent in folk and country, and among singer-songwriters. Male DJs are the norm in the contemporary dance music scene. How 'natural' are such associations, and in what ways are they social constructs?

There is now a body of work seeking to understand and explain how and why rock (and many other popular music genres) is 'actively produced as male' (Cohen 1997; see also Whiteley 2000). The term 'women in rock' emerged as a media concept in the early 1970s, and has persisted despite being criticised as a 'generic mushy lump' (O'Brien, L. 1995: 3), unrelated to the wide variation among female performers, even those within the rock genre. There are two main dimensions: women as performers, and women in the music industry, with women being marginalised and stereotyped in both. There is a lack of women in the male-dominated music industry, with the majority in stereotypically 'female' roles (e.g. press, office personnel, and there are few women working in A&R, or as producers, managers, and sound mixers, Negus 1992).

Cohen found that, in the Liverpool music scene she studied, women were not simply absent, but were actively excluded. All-male bands tended to preserve the music as their domain, keeping the involvement of wives and girlfriends at a distance.

> On several occasions I was informed that two things split up a band: women and money. Many complained that women were a distraction at rehearsals because they created tension within the band and pressured the band's members to talk to them or take them home.
>
> (Cohen 1991: 209)

This situation reflects the more restricted social position of women, with greater domestic commitments and less physical freedom; the lack of encouragement given to girls to learn rock instruments; and rock sexuality as predominantly masculine. Consequently, there are few women bands in rock, or women instrumentalists, and, most women rock performers are 'packaged as traditional, stereotyped, male images of women' (Cohen 1991: 203). Paradoxically, of course, the success of many bands depended upon their appeal to female consumers, and male band members appreciated the fact that band membership helped make them attractive to women.

Bayton's discussion of 'women and the electric guitar' is a good example of the social processes at work here (Bayton 1997). Her Oxford (UK) study showed only between 2 and 4 per cent of instrumentalists in local bands were women, and 'the reasons for women's absence are entirely social'. Gender socialisation teaches girls how to be 'feminine' and not to engage in 'masculine' activities: 'Playing the flute, violin, and piano is traditionally "feminine", playing electric guitar is "masculine". On TV and in magazines, young women are presented with repeated images of men playing electric guitar; there are few female role models to inspire them' (Bayton 1997: 39). Further, compared to boys, teenage women lack money, time, space, transport and access to equipment. Even if a girl does take up the electric guitar, they have difficulty gaining access to the informal friendship groups within rock-music making, which are crucial learning environments. Guitar shops are 'male terrain' and nearly all of Bayton's interviewees regarded them as alien territory. The technology associated with the electric guitar – leads, amplifiers, plug boards – is strongly categorised as 'masculine', and presents another hurdle to female performers. The association of guitar playing with masculine prowess, with the 'axe' as an extension of the male body, and playing it a pseudo-masturbatory act, consolidate its status as :an exclusively 'masculine' idiom.

Riot Grrrl

In the early 1990s this gendered soundscape was challenged by the Riot Grrrl movement. Initially based in Washington DC, and Olympia, Washington, Riot Grrrl quickly became the focus of considerable media attention. Through fanzines and sympathetic role models among female musicians, riot grrrls asserted the need to break down the masculine camaraderie of the alternative and hardcore music scenes, which marginalised girls and young women. They drew on feminism and punk DIY ideology to question conventional ideas of femininity; and rejected rockist ideas of cool and mystique, challenging the view that enhanced technical virtuosity is necessary to create music. Some writers referred to them as 'punk feminists' (see Leonard 1997). Riot grrrls aimed to create a cultural space for young women in which they could express themselves without being subject to male scrutiny. They played with conflicting images and stereotyped conventions; e.g. the appropriation of 'girl' and their assertive use of the term 'slut'. Musically, the performers linked to the riot grrrl movement (e.g. L7, Bikini Kill) sounded very like traditional hardcore and late 1970s punk bands, but their emphasis was on the process rather than the product.

Sexuality

Popular music is also a significant area of culture in which sexual politics are struggled over. Sexuality refers to the expression of sexual identity, through sexual activity, or the projection of sexual desire and attraction. Sexuality and desire are central human emotions, or drives, which have been an essential part of the appeal of the culture/entertainment industries, including popular music, and the social processes whereby performers and their texts operate in the public arena.

233

Sexuality is central to discussions of how male and, more frequently, female performers are conceived of – socially constructed – as sex objects or symbols of desire. Here certain forms of subjectivity and identity are projected as 'normal', traditionally white, male heterosexuality. The operation of this process is a major focus in studies of music video and stardom, and in relation to particular genres of music. It involves considerations of the nature of spectatorship and the (gendered) gaze, utilising conventions primarily developed in film studies (see the discussion of music videos in Chapter 10).

Sexual ambiguity is central to many forms of popular music, which has frequently subverted the dominant sexuality constructed around male–female binaries. Discussion has concentrated on exploring the relationship between sexual orientation, public personas, and a performer's music. Some performers openly represent or subvert and 'play with' a range of sexualities. Others constitute themselves, at times very self-consciously, as objects of heterosexual desire, or as icons for different ('deviant'?) sexualities and their constituencies. Several 1950s male stars were 'adored objects', catering to both homosexual desire and female consumption; e.g. Elvis Presley, Fabian. Later performers include representations of the homoerotic (e.g. Madonna, Morrissey); androgyny (Bowie during the Ziggy period), the effeminate (the Cure), and asexuality (Boy George); bi-sexuality (Morrissey again, Suede); and gay and lesbian (The Village People; Freddie Mercury; k.d.lang). The application of such labels, their connotations, and their relationship to actual gay communities have been at times strongly contested (see Geyrhalter 1996).

Some genres/performers are linked to particular sexualities/communities; e.g. disco generally celebrates the pleasure of the body and physicality, and is linked to the gay community and specific club scenes; heavy metal (HM) has traditionally been associated with overt masculinity, as have some forms of rock (hard rock/cock rock; see Frith and McRobbie 1990). Heavy metal illustrates this. Walser argues that HM has historically been actively *made* as male, and acts to 'reproduce and reflect patriarchal assumptions and ideologies' which underpin Western society (1993: 111). He suggests that HM bands promote male bonding and legitimate male power through a combination of misogyny (in song lyrics, videos) and exscription: the creation through the music, album covers, and videos of fantasy worlds without women, where male heroes battle against monsters and superhuman villains (ibid.: 110). Arnett observes that even though some HM fans are women, their involvement is often through a boyfriend, or due to the sexual attraction they feel toward the performers or fans; consequently they struggle 'to reconcile their enthusiasm for Heavy Metal with their sense of being not quite welcome in that world' (Arnett 1996: 140).

The lyrics of many mainstream pop songs deal with heterosexual love, desire, longing, and lust. Others deal with other sexual orientations and sexual practices; for example the Kinks, 'Lola', 1970; Little Richard, 'Tutti Frutti', 1956; and Frankie Goes to Hollywood, 'Relax', 1984. Songs can openly support or express solidarity with particular sexualities, as with Lou Reed's, 'Walk on the Wild Side', 1973; and Tom Robinson's 'Glad to be Gay', 1979. Other songs criticise non-heterosexuality or openly express homophobic or misogynist views. There is considerable argument over how the lyrics and the associated cultural values in these musical texts are understood and responded to by their listeners, audiences, and fans. Are the artists intended or preferred readings, embedded in the text, acknowledged, let alone assimilated into individual and social values and meanings? (see Press and Reynolds 1995; Negus 1996: 123–33; Savage 1988).

RAISING CONSCIOUSNESS, RAISING MONEY

As I discussed in Chapter 1, there are observers who regard popular music as essentially manipulated by the market and consequently devoid of oppositional cultural possibilities. These pessimistic analyses are the heirs to the Frankfurt School and traditional forms of political economy. In support of their stance, they emphasise the market domination exercised by the major record companies, with its associated incorporation and homogenisation of new styles, and the desire to avoid controversy – unless of course it sells! At its most extreme this can include dropping artists whose controversial material has become too extreme for corporate sensitivities, as occurred with the Sex Pistols and several rappers. Ranged against this point of view, are the obvious uses of music as a form of political expression, its use by music oriented youth subcultures to create a cultural space, and as a powerful means of raising both consciousness about, and funds for, political causes.

There is disagreement as to the cultural significance and force of such statements. For Grossberg, 'on the one hand, so much activity is attempting to explicitly articulate rock to political activism; on the other hand, this activity seems to have little impact on the rock formation, its various audiences or its relations to larger social struggles' (Grossberg 1992: 168). This argument rests on a perceived 'radical disassociation' of the political content of the music of bands such as U2, REM and Midnight Oil 'from their emotionally and affectively powerful appeals' (ibid.). Grossberg's view relies largely on the commonplace observation that many listeners can derive pleasure from such performers without either subscribing to their politics, or, indeed, even being aware of them.

Against this, however, a variety of examples can be adduced to illustrate that many listeners *do* have their ideological horizons both confirmed and extended by association with political rock, which can also have practical benefits. In the United Kingdom in the 1970s, Rock Against Racism mobilised support against the National Front (Widgery 1986; Street 1986; Shuker 1994). The Amnesty International tours of 1988 are estimated to have added some 200,000 new members to the organisation in the USA alone (see Garofalo 1992b; Denselow 1990). In a sense, these constitute the flip side of attempts to censure and control the medium.

Frith and Street (1992) suggest that the history of such attempts to use popular music to forge mass movements will always face two problems. First, the time-scale, as 'The power of popular music is by its nature momentary', novelty and shock value have a short life-span, and routinisation and disempowering follows'. Second, the confused nature of musical power's 'collectivity': 'The power of mass music certainly comes from its mobilization of an audience; a series of individual choices (to buy this record, this concert ticket) becomes the means to a shared experience and identity. The question, though, is whether this identity has any political substance' (Frith and Street 1992: 80). A further dimension of this question, is the tendency of many commentators to incorrectly assume that 'youth' represent some sort of 'natural left' political constituency.

Before moving to examples of 'conscience rock', it is worth noting that popular music is hardly the preserve of the political left and broadly progressive politics. It can, and has been, used to support a broad range of political positions. American presidential candidates regularly use well-known artists for performances at their rallies. White supremacist organisations like the National Front in the UK have used 'alternative' music (such as 'oi') to attract new recruits, and Resistance Records in West Virginia is the world's largest neo-Nazi record label, with over 250 titles, mainly 'hate core'. And anti-abortion activists have co-opted 'We Shall Overcome' to maintain solidarity at sit-ins outside abortion clinics.

Conscience rock

In the 1980s, these questions about the viability of music in the direct service of organised political movements were addressed by a different style of cultural politics: the 'mega-events' (Garofalo 1992b), or what I term 'conscience rock'. This new phenomenon of political rock emerged in the mid-1980s, with popular musicians joining and reinforcing international concern at the grim effects of mass famine in Africa, and taking up anti-nuclear, environmental, and other international causes. By the end of the 1990s the list of causes here is a long one, and includes Live Aid, Sun City, Farm Aid, the Nelson Mandela tribute concerts, several Amnesty International tours, numerous Greenpeace concerts, and Music for Tibet. Such efforts are not purely political: Rock Against AIDS has raised awareness about the epidemic, and funds to help combat it.

Here I want to consider Live Aid in the 1980s as an example of what I term 'conscience rock', opening up the question of the political potential of popular music to raise consciousness and money for social interventions. Band-Aid's 'Do they know it's Christmas?' was the first of a number of singles to raise public consciousness and funds to aid famine relief in Africa, and established the pattern and format for those that followed. While the very name of the effort conceded its limitations given the scale of the problem, Band-Aid proved far more successful than any of those involved had anticipated. Recorded by thirty-seven English pop stars in London in late November 1984, the record was perfectly timed for the British Christmas market; it sold about 10 million copies and raised about £8 million (Rijven and Straw 1989: 200; see also Denselow 1990: 244ff.).

The record cover contrasted the well-to-do children of the West and the poverty of their Ethiopian counterparts. The back of the cover sleeve constructed and celebrated a brotherhood of rock, in contrast to the music press' usual stressing of the individual image of performers. USA (United Support of Artists) for Africa followed with 'We are the world'. The song title neatly suggested global interdependence, while its lyrics reaffirmed nineteenth-century charity: 'Its time to lend a hand to life, so lets start giving', adding an echo of the Beatles' idealism with 'and the truth, you know, love is all we need'. The single became CBS's fastest seller ever. Together with an album, videos and the sales of posters and T-shirts, United Support of Artists grossed $50 million dollars; the bulk of this went to famine relief and longer-term aid in Africa, with 10 per cent going to the hungry and homeless in the USA. A number of similar regional and national Band-Aid singles followed.

On 13 July 1985 Live Aid was broadcast worldwide via television, directly from Sydney, Australia, Wembley Stadium in London, and the JFK stadium in Philadelphia. The performers included David Bowie, Queen, U2, and Paul McCartney in London; Eric Clapton, Duran Duran, and Bob Dylan in Philadelphia. With the assistance of Concorde, Phil Collins performed at both shows. Seven telecommunications satellites beamed the event live to an estimated one billion viewers in some 150 countries, including the Soviet Union and China. Viewers were encouraged to phone in to their national contact and pledge their contribution. The records and concerts shared an air of patriotism; the notion of each nation doing its bit for the common cause – 'donationalism', and collectively they emphasised a sense of community and togetherness.

The Band-Aid phenomenon raised a host of questions about the motives of the celebrities involved, marketing politics, and the reasons for the overwhelming public response to charity rock in the mid-1980s. Much analysis was critical, finding 'the various charity projects tasteless, self-serving for those involved, symptomatic of existing geopolitical relations and politically inappropriate' (Rijven and Straw 1989: 206). There was also criticism that the line-up of artists performing at the two main Live Aid concerts consisted primarily of white stars, and the majority of the recordings reflected 'the same muzak characteristics, transparent frameworks built on the conventions of pop song writing that only sell because of the Band-Aid connotation' (ibid.: 203). Pragmatic rock politics, observed Straw, were now taking on the crasser aspects of the pop music industry.

Such criticism reflected a tendency on the part of the political left to claim the moral high ground, and was rooted in a 'rock ideology' preoccupied with notions of sincerity and authenticity. This rather misses the point that Band-Aid was not about music, and popular music as a focal point for youth, but rather about raising money and consciousness. The critics' preoccupation with credibility and ideological purity is accordingly misplaced. As Rijven goes on to observe, somewhat cynically, the Band-Aid projects showed 'a high media sensibility that feeds on itself – charity opens all doors' (ibid.). This is to acknowledge the multimedia nature of such high-profile public events, which became a feature of them in the 1990s.

Rijven concludes by critiquing Band-Aid for 'a naive political attitude combined with a moral superiority' (ibid.: 204). This was certainly evident, though to go beyond it was expecting too much of the musicians involved. After all, how many people are aware of the international dynamics of the international economy and their contribution to the Ethiopian situation? At least charity/aid is a first step, even if based initially on a simple apolitical humanitarianism. Political sophistication comes later, as Bob Geldof himself found when investigating the use of the funds the Live Aid concert generated:

> he was inevitably involved in a crash course in food aid politics, the realities of the African scene, the problems of debt, and an understanding of the strings often attached to aid offers from West or East, and the amounts Africa spends, and is encouraged to spend, on armaments.
>
> (Denselow 1990: 246; see also Geldof 1986)

As Straw puts it, 'rock's discourse on politics is primarily concerned with nudging people rather than instances of political intervention'. He makes the point, usually overlooked, 'that the participation of artists in the various Ethiopia records is in many ways less significant than the involvement of the music industries: 'The waiving of record label, distributor and retail profits is much more unprecedented and spectacular than the gathering of artists for charity purposes' (Rijven and Straw 1989: 208, 204). Since this industry concession provided the bulk of the money to the cause, it rendered irrelevant the debates over the credibility, motives and sincerity of the artists involved. The cultural significance of Live Aid's 'We are the World' lay in its commercial form as much as in its political focus.

The examples in this chapter show that the issue of the political role of popular music is hardly an 'either–or' argument. For every case of a performer, genre, text, or consumer constrained and regulated by gender expectations, capital, pressure groups, and the State, there are counter-examples of the successful use of the music to raise political consciousness and finance for political issues, causes, and movements. In terms of cultural politics, popular music is a site of cultural struggle, with constant attempts to establish dominance, exploit cultural contradictions, and negotiate hegemony.

Conclusion: 'wrap it up'
Popular music and cultural meaning

This book began with an outline of the main approaches to the study of popular culture and the mass media, relating these to the study of popular music. Popular music studies have reflected the general field of cultural studies, in that they have tended to privilege one aspect of the matrix of factors which determine meaning: the production context; the creators of musical texts, primarily but not exclusively musicians; the texts themselves, including music video; and the consumers of the music. I have included these various aspects here, in some cases broadening them to include previously neglected topics, most notably the music press. My central argument has been that the nature of meaning in cultural products and practices must be located within the dynamic interrelationship of the production context, the texts and their creators, and the audience. Of course, to facilitate discussion, the very organisation of this text has tended to perpetuate the notion that these are indeed discrete aspects, although I have stressed throughout the links between them.

It is not possible to baldly state a model of the interrelationship between these aspects, or to claim primacy for any one of them in *every case* of the process whereby meaning is determined in rock. The reading, listening and thinking undertaken while writing this second edition of *Understanding Popular Music* have again convinced me that an argument can be made for the overarching influence of considerations of political economy and the significance of the production context, including its technological aspects. But, while this is persuasive and indeed widely accepted, even this position must be qualified. The commodity form which music takes, and the capitalist relations of mass industrial production under which most commercial music is created, significantly affect the availability of particular texts and the meanings which they produce. However, such determination is never absolute: meanings are mediated, the dominant meanings of texts subverted, and 'alternatives' to 'mainstream', commercial music are always present. Accordingly, popular music must be seen as a site of symbolic struggle in the cultural sphere. It then becomes a question of the specificity of particular sites of production, texts, and consumption, and the changing nature and relative importance of these.

My own location in pop culture, as a post-war 'baby boomer', illustrates the point that our response to popular music, and the various attempts to document and analyse it, is far from a purely intellectual one. Analysis and documentation cannot be divorced from the volatile and contested area of emotions and popular memory. My own emotional ties to the music and artists of the late 1960s, to subsequent styles and performers reminiscent of these, and to the notion of popular music as a politically significant cultural force, are clearly discernible in this account. Hence, when I was completing the first edition, my sense of loss at the death of Frank Zappa (in December 1993). And despite some concessions to the appeal of contemporary performers such as Gomez and Pearl Jam, the greater susceptibility of my dollar to recent retrospective compilations by The Flying Burrito Brothers and the Neville Brothers, and the current work of artists such as Neil Young, Bruce Springsteen, and Van Morrison. Here we are 'talkin' about my generation', and those who continue to mine its musical legacy.

This is not to suggest, however, that the audience is the primary determinant of cultural meaning. While the case studies of music texts and their consumers here demonstrate that meaning in cultural texts is polysemic, as already argued, such meanings are constrained and shaped by the dynamics of the music industry, including the technologies utilised in the production and dissemination of texts, the intentions of the performers, and the social location of their listeners.

The value of historically locating the nature of meaning in popular music is important here, operating at two main levels. First, the accretion of meanings generated by the very fact of the music *having* a history, a series of reference points for music industry personnel, musicians, critics and fans. Second, the utility of reconsidering this history to interrogate dominant myths about the development of the music; for example, the advent of rock 'n' roll is revealed not as purely the interaction of an outburst of creativity and the post-war baby boom, but also as a consequence of the reorientation of the music industry in the early 1950s.

With the exception of a few studies of music policy, cultural imperialism, and the globalisation of culture, the majority of academic – or, for that matter, journalistic – popular music studies concentrate their analysis on one national context, or the Anglo-American nexus of popular music. I have demonstrated the utility of a variety of local and national examples to more adequately explain the development and nature of popular music as a cultural form. Although rock and its associated genres have been an international phenomenon, and are increasingly so, local variants remain important, particularly for illustrating the utility of notions such as the Anglo-American 'rock hegemony', cultural imperialism, and globalisation. Expressions of the national within the global context of popular music remain both marginal and contested, as the Canadian and New Zealand situations illustrate.

Appendix 1
Chapter/song titles

It was my initial intention to use the particular song titles chosen as chapter headings without providing their 'discography', as a challenge to reader's musical cultural capital. Upon reflection, I decided that this was unfair to the composers and performers concerned – and several of the releases are fairly obscure! So, using US labels and release dates:

1   'What's Goin' On?' Marvin Gaye, Tamla, 1967. Produced by Marvin Gaye; written by Al Cleveland, Marvin Gaye, and Renaldo Benson.
2   'Every 1's a Winner'. Hot Chocolate, Infinity, 1978. Produced by Mickie Most; written by Errol Brown.
3   'Pump Up the Volume'. M/A/R/R/S, Fourth and Broadway, 1987. Produced by Martyn Young; written by Martyn and Steve Young.
4   'We Are the World'. USA for Africa, Columbia, 1985. Produced by Quincy Jones; written by Michael Jackson and Lionel Richie.
5   'On the Cover of the Rolling Stone'. Dr Hook and the Medicine Show, Columbia, 1972. Written by Shel Silverstein.
6   'I'm just a singer (in a rock 'n' roll band)'. The Moody Blues, Threshold, 1973
7   'So You Want to be a Rock 'n' Roll Star?' The Byrds, Columbia, 1967. Produced by Gary Usher; written by Roger McGuinn and Chris Hillman.
8   'Message Understood'. Sandie Shaw, Pye, 1965.
9   'Sweet Dreams (Are Made of This)'. The Eurythmics, RCA, 1983.
10 'U Got the Look'. Prince, Paisley Park, 1987. Written and produced by Prince.
11 'My Generation'. The Who, Decca, 1966. Produced by Shel Talmy; written by Pete Townshend.

12 'Pushin' Too Hard'. The Seeds, GNP Crescendo, 1966. Producer not credited; written by
     Sky Saxon.
     Conclusion: 'Wrap it Up'. Sam and Dave, Stax, 1968. Written and produced by Isaac
     Hayes and David Porter.

Appendix 2
Discography

For convenience, I have included only albums currently available on CD. The listing is obviously highly selective, and represents those artists/work I feel are representative of the popular music discussed in this volume; i.e., largely Anglo-American and post Second World War. For convenience, and following a common approach, presentation is primarily by 'decades'.

For fuller discographies, and details of particular releases, I recommend the following sources, which I have drawn on here:

Juice Magazine, Number 75, March 1999: 'The 100 Greatest Albums of the 90s'.

Muzik, Issue No. 50, July 1999: 'The 50 Most Influential Records of all Time' (a dance music perspective).

Rolling Stone, July 1997: 'The Rolling Stone 200. The definitive library of the best albums ever made (plus the must-have collections and anthologies)'.

MOJO, August 1995: '100 Classic Albums of the Rock Era' (reproduced in Mark Cunningham, *Good Vibrations*, 1996: Appendix 1).

MC Strong (1996) *The Wee Rock Discography*, Canongate Books, Edinburgh.

Also useful are the annual 'best of' lists in music magazines; e.g. MOJO, *Rolling Stone* (the Yearbook), *Juice*; the volumes from 'rock critics'; e.g. Christgau, Gilmore, DeCurtis; and the general record guides; e.g. The Rough Guide series; AMG.

The antecedents of rock 'n' roll

Blues

Robert Johnson, *The Complete Recordings*, Columbia, 1990.

247

Bessie Smith, *The Complete Recordings*, Columbia/Legacy, 1991.
Muddy Waters, *His Best 1947 to 1955*, Chess, Legendary Masters Series, 1997.
Howlin' Wolf, *Howlin' Wolf*, Chess/MCA, 1984.

R&B; Gospel

Atlantic R&B 1947–1974, Atlantic, 1991.
Ruth Brown, *Rockin' in Rhythm: The Best of Ruth Brown*, Rhino, 1996.
Louis Jordan, *The Best of Lewis Jordan*, MCA, 1989.
Big Joe Turner, *Big Bad and Blue*, Rhino, 1994.

Country; Bluegrass

The Carter Family, *The Carter Family: Country Music Hall of Fame Series*, MCA, 1991.
Hank Williams, *40 Greatest Hits*, Polydor, 1988.
Rob Willis and his Texas Playboys, Anthology 1935–1973, Rhino, 1991.

The 1950s

Chuck Berry, *The Great Twenty-eight*, Chess, 1984.
Johny Cash, *The Sun Years*, Rhino, 1991.
Ray Charles, *The Birth of Soul*, Atlanta, 1991.
The Everly Brothers, *Cadence Classics*, Rhino, 1985.
Buddy Holly, *20 Golden Greats*, MCA, 1978.
Jerry Lee Lewis, *Anthology: All Killer No Filler*, Rhino, 1993.
Little Richard, *18 Greatest Hits*, Rhino, 1985.
Elvis Presley, *The Complete Sun Sessions*, RCA, 1987.
Elvis Golden Records, RCA, 1984.
Various Artists, *Loud, Fast & Out of Control: The Wild Sounds of '50s Rock*, Rhino, 1998 (4CD
  Boxed Set).

The 1960s

The Animals, *The Best of the Animals*, MGM, 1966 (reissued on Abko).
The Band, *The Band*, Capital, 1969.
The Beach Boys, *Pet Sounds*, Capital, 1966.
The Beatles, *The Beatles/1962–1966*, Capital, 1973.
—— *Sgt. Pepper's Lonely Hearts Club Band*, 1967.
James Brown, *20 All-Time Greatest Hits!*, Polydor, 1991.
The Byrds, *The Byrds Greatest Hits*, Columbia, 1967.
Cream, *Wheels of Fire*, Polydor, 1968.
Creedence Clearwater Revival, *Creedence Gold*, Fantasy, 1972.
The Doors, *The Best of the Doors*, Elektra, 1991.

Bob Dylan, *Highway 61 Revisited*, Columbia, 1965.

Aretha Franklin, *I Never Loved a Man the Way I Love You*, Atlanta, 1962.

The Grateful Dead, *American Beauty*, Warner Brothers, 1970.

The Jimi Hendrix Experience, *Electric Ladyland*, Reprise, 1968.

Led Zeppelin, *Led Zeppelin II*, Atlantic, 1969.

Joni Mitchell, *Blue*, Reprise, 1971.

Pink Floyd, *Dark Side of the Moon*, Capital, 1973.

Otis Redding, *Otis: The Definitive Otis Redding*, Atlantic/Rhino, 1993.

The Rolling Stones, *Big Hits (High Tide and Green Grass)*, ABKO, 1966.

Phil Spector, *Back to Mono* (1958–1969), ABKO, 1991.

Dusty Springfield, *Dusty in Memphis*, Rhino, 1969.

The Supremes, *Anthology*, Motown, 1974.

Various Artists, *The Best of the Girl Groups, Vol. 1&2*, Rhino, 1990.

The Who, *Meaty, Beaty, Big & Bouncy*, MCA, 1971.

The 1970s

Aerosmith, *Rocks*, Columbia, 1976.

The Allman Brothers, *At Fillmore East*, Capricorn, 1971.

Black Sabbath, *Paranoid*, Warner Brothers, 1971.

Blondie, *Parallel Lines*, Chrysalis, 1978.

David Bowie, *Hunky Dory*, REC, 1971.

Jackson Browne, *Jackson Browne*, Asylum, 1972.

The Clash, *London Calling*, Epic, 1979.

The Eagles, *Hotel California*, Elektra/Asylum, 1976.

Fleetwood Mac, *Rumours*, Warner Brothers, 1977.

Marvin Gaye, *What's Goin' On*, Tamla, 1971.

Al Green, *Greatest Hits*, Hi, 1972.

The Harder They Come (Film Soundtrack), Mango/Island, 1972.

Elton John, *Greatest Hits*, MCA, 1974.

Carole King, *Tapestry*, ODE/CBS, 1971.

Kraftwerk, *Trans-Europe Express*, Capital, 1977.

Bob Marley and the Wailers, *Burnin'*, Tuff Gong/Island, 1973.

Van Morrison, *Moondance*, Warner Brothers, 1970.

Randy Newman, *12 Songs*, Reprise, 1970.

Ramones, *Ramones*, Sire, 1976.

The Rolling Stones, *Exile on Main Street*, Virgin, 1972.

Saturday Night Fever (Film Soundtrack), RSO/Ploygram, 1977.

The Sex Pistols, *Never Mind the Bollocks Here's the Sex Pistols*, Warner Bros., 1977.

Rod Stewart, *Every Picture Tells a Story*, Mercury, 1971.

Stevie Wonder, *Innervisions*, Tamla/Motown, 1973.

Neil Young, *After the Gold Rush*, Reprise, 1970.

The 1980s

Abba, *Abba Gold, Greatest Hits*, Polydor, 1992.

Afrika Bambaata and the Soulsonic Force, *Planet Rock*, Tommy Boy, 1986.

Bon Jovi, *Slippery When Wet*, Mercury, 1986.

De La Soul, *Three Feet High and Rising*, Tommy Boy, 1989.

Eurythmics, *Greatest Hits*, Warner, 1991.

Guns 'N' Roses, *Appetite For Destruction*, Uzi Suicide/Geffen, 1987.

Michael Jackson, *Thriller*, Epic, 1982.

Joy Division, *Closer*, Factory, 1980 (reissued on Qwest).

Madonna, *Like a Prayer*, Sire, 1989.

Prince, *Purple Rain*, Warner Bros., 1984.

Public Enemy, *It Takes A Nation Of Millions to Hold Us Back*, Def Jam, 1989.

REM, *Document*, IRS, 1987.

The Smiths, *The Smiths*, Rough Trade/Sire, 1984.

Bruce Springsteen, *Born in the USA*, Columbia, 1984.

The Stone Roses, *Complete Stone Roses*, Geffen/Silverstone, 1995.

Talking Heads, *Stop Making Sense*, Sire, 1984.

U2, *The Joshua Tree*, Island, 1987.

The 1990s

Beck, *Odelay*, Geffen/DCG, 1996.

Bjork, *Post*, Polydor, 1995.

Garth Brooks, *No Fences*, Capital, 1990.

Jeff Buckley, *Grace*, 1994.

Celine Dion, *Falling Into You*, Epic, 1996.

Bob Dylan, *Time Out of Mind*, Columbia, 1998.

The Fugees, *The Score*, Columbia, 1996.

Hole, *Live Through This*, DGC, 1994.

Madonna, *Ray of Light*, Maverick/Warner, 1998.

Massive Attack, *Blue Lines*, Virgin, 1991.

Sara McLachlan, *Fumbling Towards Ecstasy*, Arista, 1994.

Alanis Morissette, *Jagged Little Pill*, Maverick/Warner, 1995.

My Bloody Valentine, *Loveless*, Sire, 1991.

Nine Inch Nails, *Pretty Hate Machine*, TVT, 1989.

Nirvana, *Nevermind*, Sub Pop/DGC, 1991.

Oasis, *What's The Story Morning Glory?*, Creation/Eic, 1995.

Liz Phair, *Exile in Guyville*, Matador/Shock, 1993.
Pearl Jam, *VS*, Epic, 1993.
Rage Against The Machine, *Los Angeles*, 1999.
REM, *Automatic for the People*, Warner, 1992.
Roni Size/Reprazent, *New Forms*, Talkin Loud, 1998.
The Smashing Pumpkins, *Siamese Dream*, Virgin, 1993.
The Spice Girls, *Spice World*, Virgin, 1997.
Shania Twain, *Come On Over*, 1999.
U2, *Achtung Baby*, Island, 1991.

Further resources and bibliography

In addition to the books and articles listed here, I have made extensive use of music magazines and the Internet. These provide current and often extensive information on particular music scenes, genres, and performers, and the activities of record companies.

Music magazines

ICE, *The CD News Authority*; *Rolling Stone* (US and Australian editions; especially the annual Yearbook); *Billboard, Music Week, VOX, MOJO, Pavement, Rip It Up, Q,* and *Guitar Player*. In addition to their print version, several of these have web sites. *Addicted to Noise* is on-line only (see below)

Selected Internet world wide web sites

Note that these are subject to change; in accessing them you use only the section within the <>. An enormous number of other sites can be accessed through these.

Addicted to Noise, excellent current reviews and column: <http://www.addict.com>
Internet Undergound Music Archive, an excellent starting point: <http://www.iuma.com/index.html>
Perfect Beat. The Pacific Journal of Research Into Contemporary Music and Popular Culture: <http://www.elm.mq.edu.au/pbeat/pbeat.htm>
Rolling Stone, Australia: <http://www.rstone.com.au/>
The RoJaRo Index, a bibliographic guide to the music press: <http://www.notam.uio.no/rojaro/>
Rough Guides to Rock, Reggae, and World Music: <http://www.roughguides.com/music/index.html>

BIBLIOGRAPHY

The International Association for the Study of Popular Music (IASPM): <http://www.iaspm.net>
Internet Music Resource Guide: <http://www.teleport.com/~celinec/music.shtml>
All Music Guide, a very comprehensive data base, constantly updating its print equivalent. You can search by artist, album, song titles, styles, and labels: <http://www.allmusic.com/>

Bibliography

Abbs, P. (1975) *Reclamations: Essays on Culture, Mass-Culture and the Curriculum*, London: Heinemann.

Abrams, N. (1995) 'Antonio's B-Boys: Rap, Rappers, and Gramsci's Intellectuals', *Popular Music and Society*, 19, 4: 1–20.

Adorno, T. with the assistance of Simpson, G. (1941) 'On Popular Music', in Frith, S. and Goodwin, A. (eds), *On Record: Rock, Pop, and The Written Word*, New York: Pantheon Books.

—— (1976) 'Perennial Fashions: Jazz', in *Prisms*, London; first published in 1955.

—— (1991) *The Culture Industry: Selected Essays on Mass Culture*, edited by Bernstein J., London: Routledge.

Agger, B. (1992) *Cultural Studies as Critical Theory*, London: Falmer Press.

Aizlewood, J. (ed.) (1994) *Love is the Drug*, London: Penguin.

AMG (1995) *All Music Guide to Rock*, Erlewine, M., Bogdanov, V. and Woodstra, C. (eds), San Francisco, CA: Miller Freeman.

Ang, I. (1991) *Desperately Seeking the Audience*, London and New York: Routledge.

Arnett, J. (1996) *Metalheads: Heavy Metal Music and Adolescent Alienation*, Boulder, CO: Westview Press.

Arnold, M. (1869) *Culture and Anarchy*, Cambridge: Cambridge University Press, 1986.

Bagdikian, B.H. (1997) *The Media Monopoly*, Boston, MA: Beacon Press.

Bangs, L. (1990) *Psychotic Reactions & Carburetor Dung*, Marcus, G. (ed.), London: Minerva.

—— (1992) 'Heavy Metal', in DeCurtis, A. and Henke, J. (eds), *The Rolling Stone Illustrated History of Rock 'n' Roll*, 3rd edn, New York: Random House, pp. 452–4.

Banks, J. (1996) *Monopoly Television. MTV's Quest to Control the Music*, Boulder, CO: Westview Press.

Barlow, W. (1989) *Looking Up At Down: The Emergence of Blues Culture*, Philadelphia, PA: Temple University Press.

Barnard, S. (1989) *On the Radio: Music Radio in Britain*, Milton Keynes: Open University Press.

Barnes, K. (1988) 'Top 40 Radio: A Fragment of the Imagination', in Frith, S. (ed.), *Facing the Music*, New York: Pantheon, pp.51–87.

Barnes, Richard (1979) *Mods*, London: Eel Pie Publishing.

Barnett, R.J. and Cavanagh, J. (1994) *Global Dreams: Imperial Corporations and the New World Order*, New York: Simon & Schuster.

Barrow, S. and Dalton, P. (1997) *Reggae: The Rough Guide*, edited by Buckley, J,.London: The Rough Guides.

254

Barrow, T. and Newby, J. (1996) *Inside the Music Business*, London and New York: Routledge.

Bayton, M. (1997) 'Women and the Electric Guitar', in Whiteley, S. (ed.), *Sexing the Groove: Popular Music and Gender*, London and New York: Routledge, pp.37–49.

Beadle, J. (1993) *Will Pop Eat Itself?: Pop Music in the Soundbite Era*, London: Faber & Faber.

Becker, H. (1997) 'The Culture of a Deviant Group: The "Jazz" Musician', in Gelder, K. and Thornton, S. (eds), *The Subcultures Reader*, London and New York: Routledge (first published 1963).

Bego, M. (1992) *Madonna: Blonde Ambition*, Melbourne: Bookman Press.

Bennett, A. (2000) *Popular Music and Youth Culture: Music, Identity and Place*, London: Macmillan.

Bennett, H.S. (1990) 'The Realities of Practice', in Frith, S. and Goodwin, A. (eds), *On Record: Rock, Pop, and the Written Word*, New York: Pantheon Books, pp.221–37.

Bennett, T., Frith, S., Grossberg, L., Shepherd, J. and Turner, G. (1993) *Rock and Popular Music: Politics, Policies, Institutions*, London: Routledge.

Berkenstadt, J. and Cross, C.R. (1998) *Nevermind: Nirvana*, New York: Schirmer Books.

Berland, J. (1988) 'Locating Listening: Technological Space, Popular Music, Canadian Mediations', *Cultural Studies*, 2, 3, October.

—— (1991) 'Free Trade and Canadian Music: Level Playing Field or Scorched Earth?', *Cultural Studies*, 5, 3: 317–25.

Bishton, D. (1986) *Black Heart Man*, London: Chatto & Windus.

Blake, A. (1992) *The Music Business*, London: Batsford.

Bliss, K. (1999) 'Canada: Busting Out All Over', in *Billboard*, 16 January: 50.

Bloom, A. (1987) *The Closing of the American Mind*, New York: Simon & Schuster.

Bloustien, G. (ed.) (1999) *Musical Visions*, Sydney: Wakefield Press.

Bordo, S. (1993) '"Material Girl": The Effacements of Postmodern Culture', in Schwichtenberg, C. (ed.), *The Madonna Connection: Representational Politics, Subcultural Identities, and Cultural Theory*, St Leonards, NSW: Allen & Unwin, pp.265–90.

Bourdieu, P. (1984) *Distinction: A Social Critique of the Judgement of Taste*, London: Routledge & Kegan Paul.

Boyd, Todd (1994) 'Check Yo Self, Before You Wreck Yo Self: Variations on a Political Theme in Rap Music and Popular Culture', *Public Culture*, 7: 289–312.

Boyd-Barrett, O. and Newbold, C. (1995) *Approaches to Media: A Reader*, London and New York: Arnold and St Martin's Press.

Brackett, D. (1995) *Interpreting Popular Music*, Cambridge: Cambridge University Press.

Brake, M. (1985) *Comparative Youth Culture*, London: Routledge & Kegan Paul.

Brantlinger, P. (1990) *Crusoe's Footprints: Cultural Studies in Britain and America*, New York: Routledge.

Breen, M. (1991) 'A Stairway To Heaven Or A Highway To Hell?: Heavy Metal Rock Music In The 1990s', *Cultural Studies*, 5, 2 (May): 191–203.

—— (1995) 'The End of the World as We Know it: Popular Music's Cultural Mobility', *Cultural Studies*, 9, 3 (October): 486–504.

—— (1999) *Rock Dogs*, London: Pluto Press.

Broughton, S., Ellingham, M., Muddyman, D. and Trillo, R. (eds) (1994) *World Music. The Rough Guide*, London: The Rough Guides.

Brown, C.T. (1994) *The Art of Rock and Roll*, 3rd edn, New Jersey: Prentice Hall.

Brown, J. and Schulze, L. (1990) 'The Effects of Race, Gender and Fandom on Audiences: Interpretations of Madonna's Music Videos', *Journal of Communication*, 40, 2.

Brown, M.E. (ed.) (1990) *Television and Women's Culture*, London: Sage.

Burnett, R. (1990) 'From a Whisper to a Scream: Music Video and Cultural Form', in Roe, K, and Carlsson, V. (eds), *Popular Music Research*, an anthology from NORDICOM-Sweden, NORDICOM, University of Goteborg.

—— (1996) *The Global Jukebox: The International Music Industry*, London: Routledge.

Cantin, P. (1997) *Alanis Morissette Jagged*, London: Bloomsbury.

Carnoy, G. (1990) 'Geography of Music: Inventory and Prospect', *Journal of Cultural Geography*, 10, 2: 35–48.

Cawelti, J. (1971) 'Notes Toward an Aesthetic of Popular Culture', *Journal of Popular Culture*, 5, 2 (Fall): 255–68.

Chambers, I. (1985) *Urban Rhythms: Pop Music and Popular Culture*, London: Macmillan.

—— (1986) *Popular Culture: The Metropolitan Experience*, London: Methuen.

Chanan, M. (1995) *Repeated Takes: A Short History of Recording and its Effects on Music*, London: Verso.

Chapman, R. (1992) *Selling the Sixties: The Pirates and Pop Music Radio*, London and New York: Routledge.

Chapple, S. and Garofalo, R. (1977) *Rock 'n' Roll Is Here To Pay*, Chicago, IL: Nelson-Hall.

Charlton, K. (1994) *Rock Music Styles: A History*, 2nd edn, Madison, WI: Brown & Benchmark.

Chauncey, Sarah (1999) 'The Artists', *Canadian Musician*, 20th Anniversary Issue, 21, 2 (March/April): 48–58.

Christenson, P.G. and Roberts, D.F. (1998) *It's Not Only Rock & Roll: Popular Music in the Lives of Adolescents*, Cresskill, NJ: Hampton Press, Inc.

Christgau, R. (1982) *Christgau's Guide. Rock Albums of the 70s*, London: Vermilion.

—— (1990) *Christgau's Record Guide: The '80s*, London: Vermilion.

—— (1998) *Grown Up All Wrong: 75 Great Rock and Pop Artists from Vaudeville to Techno*, Cambridge and London: Harvard University Press.

Christianen, M. (1995) 'Cycles of Symbolic Production? A New Model to Explain Concentration, Diversity and Innovation in the Music Industry', *Popular Music*, 14, 1: 55–93.

Clarke, D. (ed.) (1990) *Penguin Encyclopedia of Popular Music*, London and New York: Penguin.

—— (1995) *The Rise and Fall of Popular Music*, London: Viking/The Penguin Group.

Clayson, A. (1995) *Beat Merchants*, London: Blandford.

Cline, C. (1992) 'Essays from Bitch: The Women's Rock Newsletter with Bite', in Lewis, L. (ed.), *The Adoring Audience: Fan Culture and the Popular Media*, London: Routledge.

Cloonan, M. (1995) 'I Fought the Law: Popular Music and British Obscenity Law', *Popular Music*, 14, 3 (October): 349–63.

—— (1996) *Banned! Censorship of Popular Music in Britain: 1967–92*, Aldershot: Arena.

Cohen, Sara (1991) *Rock Culture in Liverpool: Popular Music in the Making*, Oxford: Clarendon Press.

—— (1997) 'Men Making a Scene: Rock Music and the Production of Gender', in Whiteley, S. (ed.), *Sexing the Groove: Popular Music and Gender*, London and New York: Routledge, pp. 17–36.

—— (1998) 'Sounding Out the City: Music and the Sensuous Production of Place', in Leyshon, A., Matless, D. and Revill, G. (eds), *The Place of Music*, New York: The Guilford Press, pp. 269–90.

—— (1999) 'Scenes', in Horner, B. and Swiss, T. (eds), *Key Terms in Popular Music and Culture*, Oxford: Blackwell, pp.239–50.

Cohen, Stanley (1980) *Folk Devils and Moral Panics*, Oxford: Robertson.

Cohn, N. (1970) *WopBopaLooBopLupBamBoom: Pop From the Beginning*, St Albans: Paldin, Granada.

—— (1992) 'Phil Spector', in DeCurtis, A. and Henke, J. (eds), *The Rolling Stone Illustrated History of Rock 'n' Roll*, 3rd edn, New York: Random House, pp.177–88.

Coleman, J. (1961) *The Adolescent Society*, New York: Free Press.

Considine, J.D. (1992) 'Madonna', in DeCurtis, A. and Henke, J. (eds), *The Rolling Stone Illustrated History of Rock and Roll*, 3rd edn, New York: Random House, pp.656–62.

Cook, P. (ed.) (1989) *The Film Book*, London: British Film Institute.

Cooper, B.L. (1981) 'A Popular Music Perspective: Challenging Sexism in the Social Studies Classroom', *The Social Studies*, 71: 71ff.

—— (1990) *Popular Music Perspectives: Ideas, Themes, and Patterns in Contemporary Lyrics*, Bowling Green, OH: Bowling Green State University Press.

—— (1992) 'A Review Essay and Bibliography of Studies on Rock 'n' Roll Movies, 1955–1963', *Popular Music and Society*, 16, 1: 85–92.

Cope, N. (1990) 'Walkmen's Global Stride', *Business*, March.

Covach, J. and Boone, G.M. (eds) (1997) *Understanding Rock. Essays in Musical Analysis*, New York: Oxford University Press.

Crafts, S.D., Cavicchi, D. and Keil, C. and the Music in Daily Life Project (1993) *My Music*, Hanover and London: Wesleyan University Press.

Crisell, A. (1994) *Understanding Radio*, 2nd edn, London and New York: Routledge.

Cross, B. (1993) *It's Not About a Salary: Rap, Race and Resistance in Los Angeles*, New York: Verso.

Cubitt, S. (1991) *Timeshift: On Video Culture*, London: Routledge.

Cunningham, M. (1996) *Good Vibrations: A History of Record Production*, Chessington: Castle Communications.

Cupit, M., Ramsay, G. and Shelton, L. (1995) *Music, New Music and All That: Teenage Radio in the 90s*, Sydney: Australian Broadcasting Authority.

Curran, J., Morley, D. and Walkerdine, V. (eds) (1996) *Cultural Studies and Communications*, London and New York: Arnold.

Curtis, J. (1987) *Rock Eras: Interpretations of Music and Society 1954–1984*, Bowling Green, OH: Bowling Green State University Press.

Cusic, D. (1996) *Music in the Market*, Bowling Green, OH: Bowling Green State University Press.

Dancing in the Street, PBS/BBC 10 part series on the history of rock (and see Palmer, R. 1995).

Danielsen, S. (2000) 'Hitting the Right Mix', *The Australian*, 6 April–12 April: 16.

Dannen, F. (1991) *Hit Men. Power Brokers and Fast Money Inside the Music Business*, New York: Vintage Books.

Davis, A. (1997) 'Spice Invaders!', *Record Collector*, 213 (May): 34–9.

DeCurtis, A. (ed.) (1991) 'Rock and Roll Culture', *South Atlantic Quarterly*, Special Issue, 90, 4 (Fall).

—— (1992) 'Bruce Springsteen', in DeCurtis, A. and Henke, K. (eds), *The Rolling Stone Illustrated History of Rock and Roll*, 3rd edn, New York: Random House, pp.619–25.

DeCurtis, A. and Henke, J. (1992) *The Rolling Stone Illustrated History of Rock and Roll*, 3rd edn, New York: Random House.

Denisoff, R.S. (1986) *Tarnished Gold: The Record Industry Revisited*, New Jersey: Transaction.

Denselow, R. (1990) *When The Music's Over: The Story of Political Pop*, London: Faber.

DeRogatis, J. (1996) *Kaleidoscope Eyes: Psychedelic Rock from the '60s to the '90s*, New Jersey: Citadel Press.

DFSP (1999) 'The Canadian Recording Industry', Presentation prepared by DFSP, Ottawa: Department of Canadian Heritage, 5 January.

Dickerson, J. (1998) *Women On Top: The Quiet Revolution That's Rocking the American Music Industry*, New York: Billboard Books.

Dixon, W. with Snowden, D. (1989) *I Am The Blues: The Willie Dixon Story*, London: Quartet Books.

Doggett, P. (1997) 'Rock Books', *Record Collector*, 212 (April): 35–57.

Doherty, T. (1988) *Teenagers & Teenpics: The Juvenilization of American Movies in the 1950s*, Boston, MA: Unwin Hyman.

Donnelly, K.J. (1998) 'The Classical Film Forever: Batman, Batman Returns and Post Classical Film Music', in Neale, S. and Smith, M. (eds), *Contemporary Hollywood*, London: Routledge, pp.142–55.

Dorland, M. (ed.) (1996) *The Cultural Industries in Canada: Problems, Policies and Prospects*, Toronto: James Lorimer & Company.

Draper, R. (1990) *Rolling Stone Magazine: The Uncensored History*, New York: Doubleday.

Dychtwald, K. (1989) *Age Wave*, Los Angeles, CA: Tarcher.

Dyer, R. (1990) 'In Defence of Disco', in Frith, S. and Goodwin, A. (eds), *On Record: Rock, Pop, and the Written Word*, New York: Pantheon Books.

Edgar, A. and Sedgwick, P. (eds) (1999) *Key Concepts in Cultural Theory*, London and New York: Routledge.

Ehrlich, D. (1997) *Inside the Music: Conversations with Contemporary Musicians About Spirituality, Creativity, and Consciousness*, Boston , MA and London: Shambhala.

Eisenberg, E. (1988) *The Recording Angel: Music, Records and Culture From Aristotle to Zappa*, London: Pan Books.

Elderen, P.L. van (1989) 'Pop and Government Policy in the Netherlands (1985)', in Frith, S. (ed.), *World Music, Politics and Social Change*, Manchester: Manchester University Press.

Eliot, M. (1989) *Rockonomics: The Money Behind the Music*, New York/Toronto: Franklin Watts.

Ennis, P.H. (1992) *The Seventh Stream: The Emergence of Rock n Roll in American Popular Music*, Hanover and London: Wesleyan University Press.

Epstein, J.S. (ed.) (1994) *Adolescents and Their Music. If It's Too Loud, You're Too Old*, New York and London: Garland Publishing.

Escott, C. with Hawkins, M. (1991) *Good Rockin' Tonight: Sun Records and the Birth of Rock 'n' Roll*, New York: St. Martins Press.

Evans, L. (1994) *Women, Sex and Rock 'n' Roll. In Their Own Words*, London: Pandora/HarperCollins.

Evans, M. (1998) 'Quality Criticism – Music Reviewing in Australian Rock Magazines', *Perfect Beat*, 3, 4 (January): 38–50.

Ewbank, A.J. and Papageorgiou, F.T. (eds) (1997) *Whose Master's Voice? The Development of Popular Music in Thirteen Cultures*, Westport, CT: Greenwood Press.

Ewen, S. (1988) *All Consuming Images: The Politics of Style in Contemporary Culture*, New York: Basic Books.

Eyerman, R. and Jamison, A. (1995) 'Social Movements and Cultural Transformation: Popular Music in the 1960s', *Media, Culture & Society*, 17: 449–68.

Fairchild, C. (1995) '"Alternative" Music and the Politics of Cultural Autonomy: The Case of Fugazi and the D.C. Scene', *Popular Music and Society*, 19, 1: 17–36.

Farrell, G. (1998) 'The Early Days of the Gramophone Industry in India: Historical, Social, and Musical Perspectives', in Leyshon, A., Matless, D. and Revill, G. (eds), *The Place of Music*, New York: The Guilford Press, pp.57–82.

Fink, M. (1989) *Inside the Music Business. Music in Contemporary Life*, New York: Schirmer/Macmillan.

Finnegan, R. (1989) *The Hidden Musicians. Music-Making in an English Town*, Cambridge: Cambridge University Press.

Fiske, J. (1989) *Understanding Popular Culture*, Boston, MA: Unwin Hyman.

—— (1992) 'The Cultural Economy of Fandom', in Lewis, L. (ed.), *The Adoring Audience: Fan Culture and the Popular Media*, London: Routledge.

Flohel, R. (1990) 'The Canadian Music Industry: A Quick Guide', in Baskerville, D. (ed.), *Music Business Handbook and Career Guide*, New York: Sherwood, pp.495–503.

Fonarow, W. (1995) 'The Spatial Organization of the Indie Music Gig', in Gelder, K. and Thornton, S. (eds), *The Subcultures Reader*, London: Routledge, pp.360–9.

Friedlander, P. (1996) *Rock And Roll: A Social History*, Boulder, CO: Westview Press.

Frith, S. (1978) *The Sociology of Rock*, London: Constable.

—— (1983) *Sound Effects: Youth, Leisure and the Politics of Rock 'n' Roll*, London: Constable.

—— (1987) 'Towards an Aesthetic of Popular Music', in Leppert, R. and McClary, S. (eds), *Music and Society*, Cambridge: Cambridge University Press, pp.133–49.

—— (ed.) (1988a) *Facing the Music*, New York: Pantheon.

—— (1988b) *Music for Pleasure: Essays in the Sociology of Pop*, Cambridge: Polity Press.

—— (1988c) 'Video Pop: Picking Up The Pieces', in Frith, S. (ed.), *Facing the Music*, New York: Pantheon Books, pp.88–130.

—— (ed.) (1989) *World Music, Politics and Social Change*, Manchester: Manchester University Press.

—— (1996) *Performing Rites: On the Value of Popular Music*, Cambridge, MA: Harvard University Press.

Frith, S. and Goodwin, A. (eds) (1990) *On Record: Rock, Pop, and The Written Word*, New York: Pantheon Books.

Frith, S. and Horne, H. (1987) *Art Into Pop*, London: Methuen.

Frith, S. and McRobbie, A. (1990) 'Rock and Sexuality', in Frith, S. and Goodwin, A. (eds), *On Record: Rock, Pop, and the Written Word*, New York: Pantheon Books, pp.371–89.

Frith, S. and Street, J. (1992) 'Rock Against Racism and Red Wedge', in Garofalo, R. (ed.), *Rockin' the Boat: Mass Music and Mass Movements*, Boston, MA: South End Press.

Gaar, G. (1992) *She's A Rebel: The History of Women in Rock and Roll*, Seattle, WA: Seal Press.

Gaines, D. (1991) *Teenage Wasteland. Suburbia's Dead End Kids*, New York: HarperCollins.

Gambaccini, P., Rice, T. and Rice, J. (1987) *British Hit Singles. Edition 6: Every Hit Single Since 1952*, Enfield: Guinness Superlatives.

Gamman, L. and Marshment, M. (1988) *The Female Gaze, Women As Viewers of Popular Culture*, London: The Women's Press.

Gammond, P. (ed.) (1991) *The Oxford Companion to Popular Music*, Oxford: Oxford University Press.

Garnham, N. (1987) 'Concepts of Culture: Public Policy and the Cultural Industries', in *Cultural Studies*, 1, 1 (January): 23–7.

Garofalo, R. (1987) 'How Autonomous is Relative: Popular Music, the Social Formation and Cultural Struggle', *Popular Music*, 6, 1 (January): 77–92.

—— (1991) 'The Internationalization of the US Music Industry and its Impact on Canada', *Cultural Studies*, 5, 3: 326–31.

—— (ed.) (1992a) *Rockin' the Boat. Mass Music and Mass Movements*, Boston, MA: South End Press.

—— (1992b) 'Understanding Mega-Events', in Garofalo, R. (ed.), *Rockin' the Boat: Mass Music and Mass Movements*, Boston, MA: South End Press.

—— (1993) 'Whose World, What Beat: The Transnational Music Industry, Identity, and Cultural Imperialism', *The World of Music*, 35, 2: 16–32.

—— (1994) 'Culture versus Commerce: The Marketing of Black Popular Music', *Public Culture*, 7: 275–87.

—— (1997) *Rockin' Out: Popular Music in the USA*, Neeham Heights, MA: Allyn & Bacon.

Garon, P. (1975) *Blues and the Poetic Spirit*, London: Eddison.

Garratt, S. (1999) *Adventures in Wonderland: A Decade of Club Culture*, London: Headline.

Gatten, J. (1995) *Rock Music Scholarship An Interdisciplinary Bibliography*, Westport, CT: Greenwood Press.

Gay, P. du and Negus, K. (1994) 'The Changing Sites of Sound: Music Retailing and the Composition of Consumers', *Media, Culture and Society*, 16, 3: 395–413.

Gelatt, R. (1977) *The Fabulous Phonograph, 1877–1977*, New York: Macmillan.

Gelder, K. and Thornton, S. (eds) (1997) *The Subcultures Reader*, London and New York: Routledge.

Geldof, B. (1986) *Is That It?*, London: Penguin Books.

Gendron, B. (1986) 'Theodor Adorno Meets the Cadillacs', in Modleski, T. (ed.), *Studies in Entertainment*, Bloomington, IN: Indiana University Press, pp.18–36.

George, N. (1989) *The Death of Rhythm & Blues*, New York: Pantheon.

Geyrhalter, T. (1996) 'Effeminacy, Camp and Sexual Subversion in Rock: The Cure and Suede', *Popular Music*, 15, 2: 217–24.

Gilbert, J. (1986) *A Cycle of Outrage: America's Reaction to the Juvenile Delinquent in the 1950s*, New York: Oxford University Press.

Gilbert, J. and Pearson, E. (1999) *Discographies: Dance Music, Culture and the Politics of Sound*, London and New York: Routledge.

Gilbert, P. and Taylor, S. (1991) *Fashioning The Feminine: Girls, Popular Culture and Schooling*, Sydney: Allen & Unwin.

Gillet, C. (1983) *The Sound of the City: The Rise of Rock and Roll*, rev. edn, London: Souvenir Press.

Gilmore, M. (1990) 'The Season of the Witch Hunt', in *Rolling Stone, 1990 Yearbook*, Surrey Hills, NSW: Rolling Stone Australia.

Gilroy, P. (1993) *The Black Atlantic: Modernity and Double Consciousness*, Cambridge, MA: Harvard University Press.

—— (1997) 'Diaspora, Utopia, and the Critique of Capitalism', in Gelder, K. and Thornton, S. (eds), *The Subcultures Reader*, London and New York: Routledge.

Golden, A.L. (1997) *The Spice Girls: The Uncensored Story Behind Pop's Biggest Phenomenon*, New York: Ballantine Books.

Golding, P. and Murdoch, G. (1991) 'Culture, Communications and Political Economy', in Curran, J. and Gurevitch, M. (eds), *Mass Media and Communications*, London: Edward Arnold, pp.15–32.

Goldstein, R. (1969) *The Poetry of Rock*, New York: Bantam Books.

Goodman, F. (1997) *The Mansion on the Hill: Dylan, Young, Geffen, Springsteen, and the Head-On Collision of Rock and Commerce*, New York: Time Books/Random House.

Goodwin, A. (1987) 'Music Video in the (Post) Modern World', *Screen*, 28, 3: 36–55.

—— (1990) 'Sample and Hold: Pop Music in the Digital Age of Reproduction', in Frith, S. and Goodwin, A. (eds), *On Record: Rock, Pop, and the Written Word*, New York: Pantheon Books, pp.258–74.

—— (1991) 'Popular Music and Postmodern Theory', *Cultural Studies*, 5, 2 (May): 174–90.

—— (1993) *Dancing in the Distraction Factory Music Television and Popular Culture*, Oxford, MN: University of Minnesota Press.

—— (1998) 'Drumming and Memory: Scholarship, Technology, and Music-Making', in Swiss, T., Sloop, J. and Herman, A. (eds), *Mapping the Beat: Popular Music and Contemporary Theory*, Malden, MA and Oxford: Blackwell, pp.121–36.

Grant, B. (1986) 'The Classic Hollywood Musical and the "Problem" of Rock 'n' Roll', *Journal of Popular Film and Television*, 13, 4 (Winter): 195–205.

Gratten, Jeffrey N. (1995) *Rock Music Scholarship: An Interdisciplinary Bibliography*, Westport, CT: Greenwood Press.

Gray, M. (1995) *Last Gang in Town: The Story and Myth of the Clash*, New York: Henry Golt.

Grayck, T. (1996) *Rhythm and Noise: An Aesthetics of Rock*, Durham, NC and London: Duke University Press.

Greco, A.N. (ed.) (2000) *The Media and Entertainment Industries. Readings in Mass Communications*, Boston, MA: Allyn & Bacon.

Grenier, L. (1993) 'Policing French-Language Music on Canadian Radio', in Bennett, T. *et al.*, *Rock and Popular Music*, pp.119–41.

Grixti, J. (2000) *Young People and the Broadcasting Media. The Maltese Experience. A Report on Qualitative Research Undertaken for the Malta Broadcasting Authority*, Hamrun, Malta: Offset Press Ltd.

Gross, R.L. (1990) 'Heavy Metal Music: A New Subculture in American Society', *Journal of Popular Culture*, 24, 1 (Summer): 119–30.

Grossberg, L. (1992) *We Gotta Get Out of This Place: Popular Conservatism and Postmodern Culture*, New York: Routledge.

Grossberg, L., Nelson, C. and Treichler, P. (eds) (1992) *Cultural Studies*, New York and London: Routledge.

Guilbault, J. (1993) *Zouk: World Music in the West Indies*, Chicago, IL: University of Chicago Press.

Guralnick, P. (1989) *Feel Like Going Home*, London: Omnibus Press.

—— (1991) *Sweet Soul Music: Rhythm and Blues and the Southern Dream of Freedom*, London: Penguin.

Gurley, T. and Pfefferle, W. (1996) *Plug In: The Guide to Music on the Net*, New Jersey: Prentice Hall.

Hager, B. (1998) *On Her Way: The Life and Music of Shania Twain*, New York: Berkley Boulevard Books.

Haggerty. G. (1995) *A Guide to Popular Music Reference Books An Annotated Bibliography*, Westport, CT: Greenwood Press.

Halfacree, K. and Kitchin, R. (1996) '"Madchester Rave On": Placing the Fragments of Popular Music', *Area*, 28, 1: 47–55.

Hall, S. (1980) 'Cultural Studies: Two Paradigms', *Media, Culture and Society*, 2: 57–72.

—— (1981) 'Notes on Deconstructing "the Popular"', in Samuel, R. (ed.), *People's History and Socialist Theory*, London: Routledge & Kegan Paul.

Hall, S., Critcher, C., Jefferson, T., Clarke, J. and Roberts, R. (1978) *Policing the Crisis*, London: Macmillan.

Hall, S. and Jefferson, T. (eds) (1976) *Resistance Through Rituals: Youth Subcultures in Post-War Britain*, London: Hutchinson.

Hall, S. and Whannell, P. (1964) *The Popular Arts*, London: Hutchinson.

Hanke, R. (1998) '"Yo Quiero Mi MTV!": Making Music Television for Latin America', in Swiss, T., Sloop, J. and Herman, A. (eds), *Mapping the Beat: Popular Music and Contemporary Theory*, Malden, MA and Oxford: Blackwell, pp.219–46.

Hansen, B. (1992) 'Doo-Wop', in DeCurtis, A. and Henke, J. (eds), *The Rolling Stone Illustrated History of Rock and Roll*, 3rd edn, New York: Random House, pp.92–101.

Hardy, P. and Laing, D. (eds) (1991) *The Faber Companion to Twentieth Century Popular Music*, London: Faber & Faber.

Harker, D. (1980) *One For The Money: Politics and Popular Song*, London: Hutchinson.

—— (1997) 'The Wonderful World of IFPI: Music Industry Rhetoric, the Critics and the Classical Marxist Critique', *Popular Music*, 16, 1 (January): 45–79.

Haslam, D. (2000) 'What the Twist Did for the Peppermint Lounge', *London Review of Books*, 6 January: 27.

Hatch, D. and Millward, S. (1987) *From Blues to Rock: An Analytical History of Rock Music*, Manchester: Manchester University Press.

Hayward, P. (ed.) (1992) *From Pop to Punk to Postmodernism. Popular Music and Australian Culture from the 1960s to the 1990s*, Sydney: Allen & Unwin.

—— (1995) 'Enterprise on the New Frontier: Music, Industry and the Internet', *Convergence*, 1, 2.

Hayward, P., Mitchell, T. and Shuker, R. (eds) (1994) *North Meets South: Popular Music in Aotearoa/New Zealand*, Sydney: Perfect Beat Publications.

Hayward, S. (1996) *Key Concepts in Cinema Studies*, London and New York: Routledge.

Headlam, D. (1997) 'Blues Transformation in the Music of Cream', in Covach, J. and Boone, G.M. (eds), *Understanding Rock: Essays in Musical Analysis*, New York: Oxford University Press, pp.59–89.

Hebdige, D. (1979) *Subculture: The Meaning of Style*, London: Methuen.

—— (1988) *Hiding In The Light: On Images and Things*, London: Comedia/Routledge.

—— (1990) *Cut 'N' Mix: Culture, Identity, and Caribbean Music*, London: Comedia/Routledge.

Henderson, L. (1993) 'Justify Our Love: Madonna and the Politics of Queer Sex', in Schwichtenberg, C. (ed.), *The Madonna Connection: Representational Politics, Subcultural Identities, and Cultural Theory*, St. Leonards, NSW: Allen & Unwin, pp.107–28.

Herbert, T. (1998) 'Victorian Brass Bands: Class, Taste, and Space', in Leyshon, A., Matless, D. and Revill, G. (eds), *The Place of Music*, New York: The Guilford Press, pp.104–28.

Herman, E. and McChesney, R. (1997) *The Global Media: The New Missionaries of Global Capitalism*, London: Cassell.

Herman, G. (1971) *The Who*, London: November Books.

Herman, G. and Hoare, I. (1979) 'The Struggle for Song: A Reply to Leon Rosselson', in Gardner, C. (ed.), *Media, Politics and Culture*, London: Macmillan.

Hesmondhalgh, D. (1996a) 'Rethinking Popular Music after Rock and Soul', in Curran, J., Morley, D. and Walkerdine, V. (eds), *Cultural Studies and Communications*, London and New York: Arnold.

—— (1996b) 'Flexibility, Post-Fordism and the Music Industries', *Media, Culture and Society*, 18, 3: 469–88.

—— (1997) 'Post-Punk's Attempt to Democratise the Music Industry: the Success and Failure of Rough Trade', *Popular Music*, 16, 3, October: 255–92.

Heylin, C. (ed.) (1992) *The Penguin Book of Rock and Roll Writing*, London: Penguin.

—— (1993) *From the Velvets to the Voidoids: A Pre-Punk History for a Post-Punk World*, London: Penguin.

—— (1998) *Never Mind the Bollocks, Here's the Sex Pistols: The Sex Pistols*, New York: Schirmer Books.

Hill, D. (1986) *Designer Boys and Material Girls: Manufacturing the 80's Pop Dream*, Dorset: Blandford Press.

Hoggart, R. (1957) *The Uses of Literacy*, London: Penguin.

Hollows, J. and Milestone, K. (1998) 'Welcome to Dreamsville: A History and Geography of Northern Soul', in Leyshon, A., Matless, D. and Revill, G. (eds), *The Place of Music*, New York: The Guilford Press, pp.83–103.

Homan, S. (1999) 'Displaced Rhythms: Evicting Rock and Roll', in Bloustien, G. (ed.), *Musical Visions*, Syndey: Wakefield Press.

—— (2000) 'Losing the Local: Sydney and the Oz Rock Tradition', *Popular Music*, 19, 1 (January): 31–50.

Hornby, N. (1995) *High Fidelity*, New York: Riverheads Books.

Horner, B. and Swiss, T. (eds) (1999) *Key Terms in Popular Music and Culture*, Malden, MA: Blackwell.

Hull, G.P. (2000) 'The Structure of the Recorded Music Industry', in Greco, A.N. (ed.), *The Media and Entertainment Industries: Readings in Mass Communications*, Boston, MA: Allyn & Bacon, pp.76–98.

IFPI (1990) *World Record Sales 1969–1990: A Statistical History of the Recording Industry*, ed. and compiled Hung, M. and Morencos, E.G., London: International Federation of the Phonographic Industry.

Jameson, F. (1984) 'Postmodernism, or the Cultural Logic of Late Capitalism', *New Left Review*, 146 (July/August): 53–93.

Jipson, A. (1994) 'Why Athens?', *Popular Music & Society*, 18, 3: 19–31.

Johnson, B. (2000) *The Inaudible Music: Jazz, Gender and Australian Modernity*, Sydney: Currency Press.

Johnson, L. (1979) *The Cultural Critics*, London: Routledge.

Johnson, P. (1996) *Straight Outa Bristol: Massive Attack, Portishead, Tricky and the Roots of Hip Hop*, London: Sceptre (Hodder & Stoughton).

Jones, A. and Kantonen, J. (1999) *Saturday Night Forever. The Story of Disco*, Edinburgh and London: Mainstream Publishing.

Jones, M. (1999) 'Changing Slides – Labour's Music Industry Policy Under the Microscrope', *CQ: Critical Quarterly*, 41, 1: 22–31.

Jones, Simon (1988) *Black Culture, White Youth. The Reggae Tradition from JA to UK*, London: Macmillan.

Jones, Simon and Schumacher, T. (1992) 'Muzak: On Functional Music and Power', *Critical Studies in Mass Communications*, 9: 156–69.

Jones, Steve (1992) *Rock Formation: Music, Technology, and Mass Communication*, Newbury Park, CA: Sage.

—— (1995a) 'Recasting Popular Music Studies' Conceptions of the Authentic and the Local in Light of Bell's Theorem', in Straw, W. *et al.* (eds), *Popular Music – Style and Identity*, Montreal: Centre for Research on Canadian Cultural Industries and Institutions.

—— (1995b) 'Covering Cobain: Narrative Patterns in Journalism and Rock Criticism', *Popular Music & Society*, 19, 2: 103–18.

Kalinak, K. (1992) *Setting the Score: Music and the Classical Hollywood Film*, Madison, WI: University of Wisconsin Press.

Kaplan, E.A. (1987) *Rocking Around the Clock. Music Television, Postmodernism, and Consumer Culture*, New York: Methuen.

Karlen, N. (1994) *Babes in Toyland: The Making and Selling of a Rock and Roll Band*, New York: Avon Books.

Kassabian, A. (1999) 'Popular', in Horner, B. and Swiss, T. (eds), *Key Terms in Popular Music and Culture*, Oxford: Blackwell, pp.113–23.

Kealy, E. (1979) 'From Craft to Art: The Case of Sound Mixers and Popular Music', in Frith, S. and Goodwin, A. (eds), *On Record: Rock, Pop, and the Written Word*, New York: Pantheon, pp.207–20, first published 1978.

Keil, C. (1966) *Urban Blues*, Chicago, IL: University of Chicago Press.

Keil, C. and Field, S. (1994) *Music Grooves*, Chicago, IL and London: University of Chicago Press.

Kellner, D. (1995) *Media Culture: Cultural Studies, Identity and Politics Between the Modern and the Postmodern*, London and New York: Routledge.

Kelly, K. and McDonnel, E. (1999) *Stars Don't Stand Still in the Sky*, London: Routledge.

Kennedy, D. (1990) 'Frankenchrist Versus the State: The New Right, Rock Music and the Case of Jello Biafra', *Journal of Popular Culture*, 24: 1: 131–48.

Kennedy, R. and McNutt, R. (1999) *Little Labels – Big Sound: Small Record Companies and the Rise of American Music*, Bloomington and Indianapolis, IN: Indiana University Press.

Kibby, M.D. (2000) 'Home on the Page: A Virtual Place of Music Community', *Popular Music*, 19, 1 (January): 91–100.

Kirschner, T. (1994) 'The Lalapalooziation of American Youth', *Popular Music and Society*, 18, 1: 69–89.

—— (1998) 'Studying Rock: Towards a Materialist Ethnography', in Swiss, T., Sloop, J., and Herman, A. (eds), *Mapping the Beat: Popular Music and Contemporary Theory*, Malden, MA and Oxford: Blackwell, pp.247–68.

Kong, L. (1995) 'Popular Music in Singapore: Exploring Local Culture, Global Resources, and Regional Identities', *Environment and Planning D: Society and Space*, 14, 3 (June): 273–92.

Kruse, H. (1993) 'Subcultural Identity in Alternative Music Culture', *Popular Music*, 12, 1: 33–41.

Laing, D. (1985) 'Music Video: Industrial Product, Cultural Form', *Screen*, 26, 2: 78–83.

—— (1986) 'The Music Industry and the "Cultural Imperialism" Thesis', *Media, Culture and Society*, 8: 331–41.

—— (1988) 'The Grain of Punk: An Analysis of the Lyrics', in McRobbie, A. (ed.), *Zoot Suits and Second Hand Dresses: An Anthology of Fashion and Music*, Boston, MA: Unwin Hyman, pp.74–101.

—— (1990) 'Record Sales in the 1980s', *Popular Music*, 9, 2.

—— (1992) '"Sadeness", Scorpions and Single Markets: National and Transnational Trends in European Popular Music', *Popular Music*, 11, 2: 127–40.

Lanza, J. (1995) *Elevator Music: A Surreal History of Muzak Easy-Listening, and Other Moodsong*, New York: Picador.

Larkin, C. (ed.) (1993) *The Guinness Encyclopedia of Popular Music*, concise edn, London: Guinness Press.

—— (ed.) (1995) *The Guinness Who's Who of Indie New Wave*, 2nd edn, London: Guinness Press.

Lealand, G. (1988) *A Foreign Egg in Our Nest? American Popular Culture in New Zealand*, Wellington: Victoria University Press.

LeBlanc, L. (1999) 'CANADA: They're Never Home Anymore!', *Billboard*, 16 January: 49, 58.

Lee, S. (1995) 'An Examination of Industrial Practice: The Case of Wax Trax! Records', in Straw, W. *et al.* (eds), *Popular Music – Style and Identify*, Montreal: Centre for Research on Canadian Cultural Industries and Institutions.

Leonard, M. (1997) 'Rebel Girl, You are the Queen of My World: Feminism, "Subculture" and Grrrl Power', in Whiteley, S. (ed.), *Sexing the Groove. Popular Music and Gender*, London and New York: Routledge, pp.230–56.

Leonard, M. and Strachan, R. (2002) 'Music Press', 'Music Journalism', entries in Shepherd, J., Horn, D., Laing, D., Oliver, P. and Wicke, P. (eds), *The Encyclopedia of Popular Music of the World, Volume 1: The Industry, Contexts and Musical Practices*, London: Cassell.

Lewis, G.H. (ed.) (1993) *All That Glitters: Country Music in America*, Bowling Green, OH: Bowling Green State University Press.

Lewis, L.A. (1990) *Gender Politics and MTV: Voicing the Difference*, Philadelphia, PA: Temple University Press.

—— (ed.) (1992) *The Adoring Audience: Fan Culture and the Popular Media*, London: Routledge.

Leyser, B. (1994) *Rock Stars/Pop Stars. A Comprehensive Bibliography 1955–1994*, Westport, CT: Greenwood Press.

Leyshon, A., Matless, D. and Revill, G. (eds) (1998) *The Place of Music*, New York and London: The Guilford Press.

Light, A. (1991) 'About a Salary or a Reality? – Rap's Recurrent Conflict', in DeCurtis, A. (ed.), 'Rock and Roll Culture', *South Atlantic Quarterly*, special issue, 90, 4, (Fall).

Lipsitz, G. (1994) *Dangerous Crossroads. Popular Music, Postmodernism and the Poetics of Place*, London and New York: Verso.

Livingston, S. and Bovill, M. (1999) *Young People New Media*, London: London School of Economics.

Longhurst, B. (1995) *Popular Music and Society*, Cambridge: Polity Press.

Lopes, Paul (1992) 'Aspects of Production and Consumption in the Music Industry, 1967–1990', *American Sociological Review*, 57, 1: 46–71.

Malone, Bill C. (1985) *Country Music USA*, Austin, TX: University of Texas Press.

Mann, B. (2000) *I Want My MP3! How to Download, Rip, & Play Digital Music*, New York: McGraw-Hill.

Manning, A.E. (1958) *The Bodgie: A Study in Psychological Abnormality*, Sydney: Angus & Robertson.

Marcus, G. (1991a) *Mystery Train*, 4th edn, New York: Penguin (originally published, 1977).

—— (1991b) *Dead Elvis: A Chronicle of a Cultural Obsession*, New York: Penguin.

—— (1992) 'Anarchy in the UK', in DeCurtis, A. and Henke, J. (eds), *The Rolling Stone Illustrated History of Rock and Roll*, 3rd edn, New York: Random House, pp.594–608.

Marsh, D. (1983) *Before I Get Old: The Story of the Who*, New York: St Martin's Press.

—— (1987) *Glory Days: A Biography of Bruce Springsteen*, New York: Pantheon.

—— (1989) *The Heart of Rock and Soul: The 1001 Greatest Singles Ever Made*, New York: Plume/Penguin.

—— (1992) 'The Who', in DeCurtis, A. and Henke, J. (eds), *The Rolling Stone Illustrated History of Rock 'n' Roll*, 3rd edn, New York: Random House, pp.395–406.

Marsh, D., with Swenson, J. (eds) (1984) *The Rolling Stone Record Guide*, New York: Random House/Rolling Stone Press.

Marshall, P.D. (1997) *Celebrity and Power: Fame in Contemporary Culture*, Minneapolis, MN/London: University of Minnesota Press.

Martin, L. and Seagrave, K. (1988) *Anti-Rock: The Opposition to Rock 'n' Roll*, Hamden, CT: Archon Books.

Masterman, L. (1989) *Teaching The Media*, London: Routledge.

McClary, S. (1991) *Feminine Endings: Music, Gender, and Sexuality*, Minnesota, MN and Oxford: University of Minnesota Press.

McClary, S. and Walser, R. (1990) 'Start Making Sense! Musicology Wrestles with Rock', in Frith, S. and Goodwin, A. (eds), *On Record: Rock, Pop, and the Written Word*, New York: Pantheon, pp.277–92.

McLeay, C. (1994) 'The "Dunedin Sound" – New Zealand Rock and Cultural Geography', in *Perfect Beat*, 2, 1 (July): 38–50.

—— (1998) 'The Circuit of Popular Music', unpublished Ph.D. thesis, Human Geography, School of Earth Sciences, Macquarie University.

McNeil, L. and McCain, G. (1996) *Please Kill Me: The Uncensored Oral History of Punk*, New York: Grove Press.

McRobbie, A. (ed.) (1988) *Zoot Suits and Second Hand Dresses: An Anthology of Fashion and Music*, Boston, MA: Unwin/Hyman.

—— (1991) *Feminism and Youth Culture: From 'Jackie' to 'Just Seventeen'*, Houndmills: Macmillan.

McRobbie, A. and Garber, J. (1976) 'Girls and Subcultures: An Exploration', in Hall, S. and Jefferson, T. (eds), *Resistance Through Rituals*, London: Hutchinson/BCCCS.

Melhuish, Martin (1999) 'The Business', *Canadian Musician*, 20th anniversary issue, 21, 2 (March/April): 67–80.

Mellers, W. (1974) *Twilight of the Gods: The Beatles in Retrospect*, New York: The Viking Press.

—— (1986) *Angels of the Night: Popular Female Singers of Our Time*, Oxford: Blackwell.

Melly, G. (1970) *Revolt Into Style*, London: Penguin.

Middleton, R. (1990) *Studying Popular Music*, Milton Keynes: Open University Press.

Miles, B. (1997) *Paul McCartney: Many Years From Now*, London: Vintage.

Millard, A.J. (1995) *America on Record: A History of Recorded Sound*, Cambridge: Cambridge University Press.

Miller, J. (ed.) (1980) *The Rolling Stone Illustrated History of Rock 'n' Roll*, New York: Random House.

—— (1999) *Flowers in the Dustbin: The Rise of Rock and Roll, 1947–1977*, New York: Simon & Schuster.

Milner, A. (1991) *Contemporary Cultural Theory: An Introduction*, Sydney: Allen & Unwin.

Mitchell, T. (1996) *Popular Music and Local Identity*, London and New York: Leicester University Press.

Moore, A.F. (1993) *Rock: The Primary Text. Developing a Musicology of Rock*, Buckingham and Philadelphia, PA: Open University Press.

Morris, K. (1992) 'Sometimes It's Hard to be a Woman: Reinterpreting a Country Music Classic', *Popular Music and Society*, 16, 1 (Spring): 1–12.

Muesterberger, W. (1994) *Collecting: An Unruly Passion: Psychological Perspectives*, Princeton, NJ: Princeton University Press.

Murdoch, G. and Phelps, G. (1973) *Mass Media and the Secondary School*, London: Schools Council/Macmillan.

Murray, C.S. (1989) *Crosstown Traffic: Jimi Hendrix and Post-War Pop*, London: Faber & Faber.

—— (1991) *Shots From The Hip*, London: Penguin.

Music Central 96, CD-ROM, Microsoft.

Neal, M. (1999) *What the Music Said: Black Popular Music and Black Public Culture*, New York and London: Routledge.

Negus, K. (1992) *Producing Pop: Culture and Conflict in the Popular Music Industry*, London: Edward Arnold.

—— (1996) *Popular Music in Theory*, Cambridge: Polity Press.

—— (1999) *Music Genres and Corporate Cultures*, London and New York: Routledge.

Neuenfeldt, K. (ed.) (1997) *The Didjeridu: From Arnham Land to Internet*, London and Sydney: John Libby/Perfect Beat Publications.

O'Brien, K. (1995) *Hymn To Her Women Musicians Talk*, London: Virago Press.

O'Brien, L. (1995) *She Bop: The Definitive History of Women in Rock, Pop and Soul*, London: Penguin.

O'Sullivan, T., Hartley, J., Saunders, D., Montgomery, M. and Fiske, J. (1994) *Key Concepts in Communications*, London: Methuen.

Oliver, P. (ed.) (1990) *Black Music in Britain*, Buckingham: Open University Press.

Olson, M.J.V. (1998) '"Everybody Loves Our Town": Scenes, Spatiality, Migrancy', in Swiss, T., Sloop, J. and Herman, A. (eds), *Mapping the Beat: Popular Music and Contemporary Theory*, Malden, MA and Oxford: Blackwell, pp.269–90.

Ontario Ministry of Education (1989) *Media Literacy*, Toronto: Resource Guide.

Palmer, R. (1995) *Rock & Roll: An Unruly History*, New York: Harmony Books. This is a companion to the PBS/BBC 10-part television series, *Dancing in the Street*.

Palmer, T. (1970) *Born Under a Bad Sign*, London: William Kimber.

Pearce, S.M. (1995) *On Collecting*, London: Routledge.

—— (1998) *Collecting in Contemporary Practice*, London: Sage.

Pease, E. and Dennis, E. (eds) (1995) *Radio – The Forgotten Medium*, New Brunswick and London: Transaction Publishers.

Perry, J. (1998) *Meaty, Beaty, Big & Bouncy: The Who*, New York: Schirmer Books.

Peterson, R.A. (1990) 'Why 1955? Explaining the Advent of Rock Music', *Popular Music*, 9, 1: 97–116.

Peterson, R.A. and Berger, D.G. (1975) 'Cycles in Symbolic Production: The Case of Popular Music', *American Sociological Review*, 40; republished in Frith, S. and Goodwin, A. (eds), *On Record: Rock, Pop, and the Written Word*, New York: Pantheon, pp.140–59.

Plasketes, G. (1992) 'Romancing the Record: The Vinyl De-Evolution and Subcultural Evolution', *Journal of Popular Culture*, 26, 1, pp.109–22.

Potter, R. (1995) *Spectacular Vernaculars: Hip-Hop and the Politics of Postmodernism*, Albany, NY: SUNY Press.

Pratt, R. (1990) *Rhythm and Resistance: Explorations in the Political Use of Popular Music*, New York: Praeger.

Press, J. and Reynolds, S. (1995) *The Sex Revolts, Gender, Rebellion and Rock 'n' Roll*, London: Serpents Tail.

Read, O. and Welch, W.L. (1977) *From Tin Foil to Stereo: The Evolution of the Phonograph*, Indianapolis, IN: Howard Sams.

Reader, A. and Baxter, J. (1999) *Listen to This: Leading Musicians Recommend Their Favorite Recordings*, New York: Hyperion.

Redhead, S. (1990) *The End-Of-The-Century Party: Youth and Pop Towards 2000*, Manchester: Manchester University Press.

—— (1997) *Subculture to Clubcultures: An Introduction to Popular Cultural Studies*, Oxford: Blackwell.

Reich, C. (1967) *The Greening of America*, New York: Penguin.

Rex, I. (1992) 'Kylie: The Making of a Star', in Hayward, P. (ed.), *From Pop to Punk to Postmodernism: Popular Music and Australian Culture from the 1960s to the 1990s*, Sydney: Allen & Unwin, pp.149–59.

Reynolds, S. (1990) 'Return of the Inkies', *New Statesman and Society*, 31 (August): 26–7.

—— (1998) *Generation Ecstasy: Into the World of Techno and Rave Culture*, Boston, MA: Little, Brown & Company.

Riesman, D. (1950) 'Listening to Popular Music', *American Quarterly*, 2; republished in Frith, S. and Goodwin, A. (eds), *On Record: Rock, Pop, and the Written Word*, New York: Pantheon Books.

Rijven, S. and Straw, W. (1989) 'Rock for Ethiopia (1985)', in Frith, S. (ed.), *World Music, Politics and Social Change*, Manchester: Manchester University Press.

Rimmer, D. (1985) *Like Punk Never Happened: Culture Club and the New Pop*, London: Faber.

Riordan, J. (1991) *Making It In The New Music Business*, Cincinnati, OH: Writer's Digest Book.

Roach, C. (1997) 'Cultural Imperialism and Resistance in Media Theory and Literary Theory', *Media, Culture and Society*, 19: 47–66.

Roberts, R. (1996) *Ladies First: Women in Music Videos*, Jackson, MI: University of Mississippi.

Robinson, D., Buck, E., Cuthbert, M., *et al.* (1991) *Music At The Margins: Popular Music and Global Diversity*, Newbury Park, CA: Sage.

Roe, K. (1990) 'Adolescent's Music Use: A Structural–Cultural Approach', in Roe, K. and Carlsson, U. (eds), *Popular Music Research*, an anthology from NORDICOM-SWEDEN, NORDICOM, University of Goteborg.

Roe, K. and Carlsson, U. (eds) (1990) *Popular Music Research*, an anthology from NORDICOM-Sweden, NORDICOM, University of Goteborg.

Roe, K. and Lofgren, M. (1988) 'Music Video Use and Educational Achievement: A Swedish Study', *Popular Music*, 7, 3: 297–308.

Rogers, D. (1982) *Rock 'n' Roll*, London: Routledge & Kegan Paul.

Romanowski, W.D. and Denisoff, R.S. (1987) 'Money for Nothin' and the Charts for Free: Rock and the Movies', *Journal of Popular Culture*, 21, 3 (Winter): 63–78.

Romney, J. and Wootton, A. (1995) *Celluloid Jukebox: Popular Music and the Movies Since the 50s*, London: British Film Institute.

Rose, Tricia (1994) *Black Noise*, Hanover: Wesleyan University Press.

Ross, A. and Rose, T. (eds) (1995) *Microphone Fiends*, London and New York: Routledge.

Rosselson, L. (1979) 'Pop Music: Mobiliser or Opiate?', in Gardner, C. (ed.), *Media, Politics and Culture*, London: Macmillan.

Rothenbuhler, E. and Dimmick, J. (1982) 'Popular Music: Concentration and Diversity in the Industry, 1974–1980', *Journal of Communications*, 32 (Winter): 143–9.

Rubey, D. (1991) 'Voguing at the Carnival: Desire and Pleasure on MTV', in DeCurtis, A. (ed.), 'Rock and Roll Culture', *South Atlantic Quarterly*, Special Issue, 90, 4 (Fall).

Rutten, P. (1991) 'Local Popular Music on the National and International Markets', *Cultural Studies*, 5, 3 (October): 294–305.

Ryan, B. (1992) *Making Capital from Culture: The Corporate Form of Capitalist Production*, Berlin and New York: Walter de Gruyter.

Sabin, R. (ed.) (1999) *Punk Rock: So What? The Cultural Legacy of Punk*, London and New York: Routledge.

Samuels, S. (1983) *Midnight Movies*, New York: Collier/Macmillan.

Sanjek, R. (1988) *American Popular Music and Its Business. The First Four Hundred Years. Volume III: From 1900 to 1984*, New York: Oxford University Press.

—— (1997) 'Funkentelechy vs. the Stockholm Syndrome: The Place of Industrial Analysis in Popular Music Studies', *Popular Music and Society*, 21, 1, Spring: 73–92.

Santelli, R. (1993) *The Big Book of the Blues: A Biographical Encyclopedia*, New York: Penguin.

Savage, J. (1988) 'The Enemy Within: Sex, Rock and Identity', in Frith, S. (ed.), *Facing the Music*, New York: Pantheon Books.

—— (1991) *England's Dreaming: Sex Pistols and Punk Rock*, London: Faber & Faber.

Schiller, D. (1999) *Digital Capitalism: Networking the Global Market System*, Cambridge, MA: MIT Press.

Schlattman, T. (1991) 'From Disco Divas to the Material Girls: Who's Ruling the Charts?', *Popular Music and Society*, 14, 4: 1–14.

Schulze, L., White, A. and Brown, J. (1993) '"A Sacred Monster in Her Prime": Audience Construction of Madonna as Low-Other', in Schwichtenberg, C. (ed.), *The Madonna Connection: Representational Politics, Subcultural Identities, and Cultural Theory*, St Leonards, NSW: Allen & Unwin, pp.15–38.

Schwichtenberg, C. (ed.) (1993) *The Madonna Connection. Representational Politics, Subcultural Identities, and Cultural Theory*, St Leonards, NSW: Allen & Unwin.

Scovell, T.A. (2000) 'Sounds Promising', *NZ Net Guide*, 37 (March): 35–8.

Seigworth, G. (1993) 'The Distance Between Me and You: Madonna and Celestial Navigation', in Schwichtenberg, C. (ed.), *The Madonna Connection: Representation Politics, Subcultural Identities, and Cultural Theory*, St Leonards, NSW: Allen & Unwin, pp.291–318.

Sernoe, J. (1998) '"Here You Come Again": Country Music's Performance on the Pop Singles Charts from 1955 to 1966', *Popular Music and Society*, 22, 1 (Spring): 17–40.

Shapiro, B. (1991) *Rock and Roll Review: A Guide to Good Rock on CD*, Kansas City: Andrews and McMeel.

Shapiro, H. (1992) *Eric Clapton: Lost In The Blues*, London: Guinness Publishing.

Shaw, G. (1992) 'Brill Building Pop', in DeCurtis, A. and Henke, J. (eds), *The Rolling Stone Illustrated History of Rock and Roll*, 3rd edn, New York: Random House, pp.143–52.

Shepherd, J. (1986) 'Music Consumption and Cultural Self-Identities', *Media, Culture and Society*, 8, 3: 305–30.

—— (1991) *Music as Social Text*, Cambridge: Polity Press.

Shepherd, J., Horn, D., Laing, D., Oliver, P., Wicke, P., Tagg, P. and Wilson, J. (eds) (1997) *Popular Music Studies: A Select International Bibliography*, London: Mansell.

Shepherd, J., Virden, P., Vulliamy, G. and Wishart, T. (1977) *Whose Music?*, London: Latimer.

Shevory, T. (1995) 'Bleached Resistance: The Politics of Grunge', *Popular Music and Society*, 19, 2: 23–48.

Shore, M. (1985) *The Rolling Stone Book of Rock Video*, London: Sidgwick & Jackson.

Shuker, R. (1994) *Understanding Popular Music*, London and New York: Routledge.

—— (1998) *Key Concepts in Popular Music*, London and New York: Routledge.

Shuker, R. and Openshaw, R. with Soler, J. (1991) *Youth, Media and Moral Panic in New Zealand*, Delta Monograph, Palmerston North: Department of Education, Massey University.

Shuker, R. and Pickering, M. (1994) 'We Want the Airwaves: The NZ Music Quota Debate', in Hayward, P., Mitchell, T. and Shuker, R. (eds), *North Meets South: Popular Music in Aotearoa/New Zealand*, Sydney: Perfect Beat Publications.

Sinclair, D. (1992) *Rock on CD: The Essential Guide*, London: Kyle Cathie.

Sluka, J. (1991) 'Censorship and the Politics of Rock', unpublished paper, Department of Social Anthropology, Massey University, Palmerston North, New Zealand.

Small, C. (1987) 'Performance as Ritual', in White, A. (ed.), *Lost in Music: Culture, Style and the Musical Event*, London: Routledge.

—— (1994) *Music of the Common Tongue*, London: Calder (first published in 1987).

Smith, G. (1995) *Lost in Music*, London: Picador.

Spencer, J. (ed.) (1991) *The Emergence of Black and the Emergence of Rap*, a Special Issue of *Black Sacred Music: A Journal of Theomusicology*, 5, 1 (Spring).

Stambler, I. (1989) *The Encyclopedia of Pop, Rock and Soul*, rev. edn, London: Macmillan.

Stephens, M.A. (1998) 'Babylon's "Natural Mystic": The North American Music Industry, the Legend of Bob Marley, and the Incorporation of Transnationalism', *Cultural Studies*, 139–67.

Steward, S. and Garratt, S. (1984) *Signed, Sealed, and Delivered: True Life Stories of Women in Pop*, Boston, MA: South End Press.

Stockbridge, S. (1990) 'Rock Video: Pleasure and Resistance', in Brown, M.E. (ed.), *Television and Women's Culture*, London: Sage.

—— (1992) 'From Bandstand and Six O'clock Rock to MTV and Rage: Rock Music on Australian Television', in Hayward, P. (ed.), *From Pop to Punk to Postmodernism: Popular Music and Australian Culture from the 1960s to the 1990s*, Sydney: Allen & Unwin, pp.68–88.

Stokes, M. (ed.) (1994) *Ethnicity, Identity and Music: The Musical Construction of Place*, Oxford: Berg.

Stratton, J. (1982) 'Between Two Worlds: Art and Commercialism in the Record Industry', *Sociological Review*, 267–85.

—— (1983) 'What is Popular Music?', in *Sociological Review*, 31, 2: 293–309.

Straw, W. (1990) 'Characterizing Rock Music Culture: The Case of Heavy Metal', in Frith, S. and Goodwin, A., *On Record: Rock, Pop, and the Written Word*, New York: Pantheon Books, pp.97–110.

—— (1992) 'Systems of Articulation, Logics of Change: Communities and Scenes in Popular Music', in Nelson, C., Grossberg, L. and Treichler, P. (eds), *Cultural Studies*, London and New York: Routledge.

—— (1993) 'The English-Canadian Recording Industry since 1970', in Bennett, T. *et al.* (eds), *Rock and Popular Music: Politics, Policies, Institutions*, London: Routledge.

—— (1996) 'Sound Recording', in Dorland, M. (ed.), *The Cultural Industries in Canada: Problems, Policies and Prospects*, Toronto: Lorimer.

—— (1997) 'Sizing Up Record Collections: Gender and Connoisseurship in Rock Music Culture', in Whiteley, S. (ed.), *Sexing the Groove: Popular Music and Gender*, London: Routledge, pp.3–16.

—— (1999) 'Authorship', in Horner, B. and Swiss, T. (eds), *Key Terms in Popular Music and Culture*, Oxford: Blackwell, pp.199–208.

Straw, W., Johnson, S., Sullivan, R. and Friedlander, P. (eds) (1995) *Popular Music – Style and Identity*, Montreal: The Centre for Research on Canadian Cultural Industries and Institutions.

Street , J. (1986) *Rebel Rock: The Politics of Popular Music*, Oxford: Blackwell.

—— (1993) 'Local Differences?: Popular Music and the Local State', *Popular Music*, 12, 1: 42–56.

—— (1997) *Politics and Popular Culture*, Cambridge: Polity Press.

Swingewood, A. (1977) *The Myth of Mass Culture*, London: Macmillan.

Swiss, T., Herman, A. and Sloop, J.M. (1998) *Mapping the Beat: Popular Music and Contemporary Theory*, Malden, MA and Oxford: Blackwell Publishers.

Szatmary, D.P. (1991) *Rockin' in Time: A Social History of Rock and Roll*, 2nd edn, New Jersey: Prentice Hall.

Tagg, Philip (1982) 'Analysing Popular Music', *Popular Music*, 2: 37–67.

—— (1990) 'Music in Mass Media Studies: Reading Sounds for Example', in Roe, K. and Carlsson, V. (eds), *Popular Music Research*, an anthology from NORDICOM-Sweden, NORDICOM, University of Goteborg, pp.103–14.

—— (1994) 'From Refrain to Rave', *Popular Music*, 14, 3: 209–22.

Task Force (1996) *A Time for Action: Report of the Task Force on the Future of the Canadian Music Industry*, Ottawa: Department of Heritage, March.

Taylor, P. (1985) *Popular Music Since 1955: A Critical Guide to the Literature*, London: G.K. Hall.

Théberge, P. (1991) 'Musicians' Magazines in the 1980s: The Creation of a Community and a Consumer Market', in *Cultural Studies*, pp.270ff.

—— (1997) *Any Sound You Can Imagine: Making Music/Consuming Technology*, Hanover, NH: Wesleyan University Press.

—— (1999) 'Technology', in Horner, B. and Swiss, T. (eds), *Key Terms in Popular Music and Culture*, Oxford: Blackwell, pp.209–24.

Thomas, B. (1991) *The Big Wheel*, London: Penguin.

Thornton, Sarah (1995) *Club Cultures: Music, Media and Subcultural Capital*, London: Polity Press.

Toop, David (1991) *Rap Attack 2*, London: Serpent's Tail.

Tosches, N. (1984) *Unsung Heroes of Rock 'n' Roll*, New York: Scribners.

Treagus, M. (1999) 'Gazing at the Spice Girls: Audience, Power and Visual Representation', in Bloustien, G. (ed.), *Musical Visions*, Sydney: Wakefield Press.

274

Trondman, M. (1990) 'Rock Taste – on Rock as Symbolic Capital: A Study of Young People's Tastes and Music Making', in Roe, K. and Carlsson, V. (eds), *Popular Music Research*, an anthology from NORDICOM-Sweden, NORDICOM, University of Goteborg, pp.71–86.

Tsitsos, W. (1999) 'Rules of Rebellion: Slamdancing, Moshing, and the American Alternative Scene', in *Popular Music*, 18, 8: 397–414.

Tunstall, J. (1977) *The Media are American*, London: Constable.

Turner, G. (1992) 'Australian Popular Music and its Contexts', in Hayward, P. (ed.), *From Pop to Punk to Postmodernism: Popular Music and Australian Culture from the 1960s to the 1990s*, Sydney: Allen & Unwin, pp.11–24.

—— (1994) *British Cultural Studies: An Introduction*, rev. edn, Boston, MA: Unwin Hyman.

Turner, K. (1984) *Mass Media and Popular Culture*, Chicago, IL: Science Research Association.

Vermorel, F. and Vermorel, J. (1985) *Starlust. The Secret Fantasies of Fans*, London: W.H. Allen.

Vernallis, C. (1998) 'The Aesthetics of Music Video: An Analysis of Madonna's "Cherish"', *Popular Music*, 17, 2: 153–85.

The Virgin Encyclopedia of Rock (1993), London: Virgin Press.

Vogel, H.L. (1994) *Entertainment Industry Economics: A Guide to Financial Analysis*, 3rd edn, New York: Cambridge University Press.

Wakesman, S. (1998) 'Kick out the Jams!: The MC5 and the Politics of Noise', in Swiss, T., Sloop, J. and Herman, A. (eds), *Mapping the Beat: Popular Music and Contemporary Theory*, Oxford: Blackwell, pp.47–76.

Wallis, R. and Malm, K. (1984) *Big Sounds from Small Countries*, London: Constable.

—— (eds) (1992) *Media Policy and Music Activity*, London: Routledge.

Walser, R. (1993) *Running With the Devil, Power, Gender and Madness in Heavy Metal Music*, Middletown, CT: Wesleyan University Press.

Ward, E., Stokes, G. and Tucker, K. (1986) *Rock of Ages: The Rolling Stone History of Rock and Roll*, New York: Rolling Stone Press/Summit Books.

Weinstein, D. (1991a) *Heavy Metal: A Cultural Sociology*, New York: Lexington.

—— (1991b) 'The Sociology of Rock: An Undisciplined Discipline', *Theory, Culture and Society*, 8: 97–109.

Welsh, R. (1990) 'Rock 'n' Roll And Social Change', *History Today* (February): 32–9.

Wertham, F. (1955) *Seduction of the Innocent*, London: Museum Press.

Wesband, E. with Marks, C. (1995) *SPIN Alternative Record Guide*, New York: Vintage/Random House.

Whitburn, J., compiler (1988) *Billboard: Top 1000 Singles 1955–1987*, Hal Leonard Books: Milwaukee.

Whitcomb, I. (1972) *After the Ball*, Harmondsworth: Penguin.

White, A. (ed.) (1987) *Lost in Music: Culture Style and the Musical Event*, London: Routledge & Kegan Paul.

White, T. (1989) *Catch A Fire: The Life of Bob Marley*, rev. edn, New York: Holt, Rinehart & Winston.

Whiteley, S. (1992) *The Space Between the Notes: Rock and the Counter-Culture*, London: Routledge.

—— (ed.) (1997) *Sexing The Groove: Popular Music and Gender*, London and New York: Routledge.

—— (2000) *Women and Popular Music: Sexuality, Identity and Subjectivity*, London: Routledge.

Widgery, D. (1986) *Beating Time: Riot 'n' Race 'n' Rock 'n' Roll*, London: Chatto & Windus.

Wiener, J. (1984) *Come Together: John Lennon in his Time*, New York: Random House.

Williams, R. (1981) *Culture*, London: Fontana.

—— (1983) *Keywords*, London: Fontana.

Willis, E. (1981) *Beginning to See the Light: Pieces of a Decade*, New York: Knopf.

Willis, P. (1978) *Profane Culture*, London: Routledge.

Willis, P., Jones, S., Canaan, J. and Hurd, G. (1990) *Common Culture. Symbolic Work at Play in the Everyday Cultures of the Young*, Milton Keynes: Open University Press.

Winfield, B.H. and Davidson, S. (eds) (1999) *Bleep! Censoring Rock and Rap Music*, Westport, CT: Greenwood Press.

Wynette, T. with Drew, J. (1980) *Stand By Your Man: An Autobiography*, London: Hutchinson.

York, N. (ed.) (1991) *The Rock File: Making it in the Music Business*, Oxford: Oxford University Press.

Zappa, F. with Occhiogrosso, P. (1990) *The Real Frank Zappa Book*, London: Pan Books.

Zemke-White, K. (2000) 'Rap Music in Aotearoa: A Sociological and Musicological Analysis', Ph.D. University of Auckland, New Zealand.

Indexes

SUBJECT INDEX

A&R (artist & repertoire) 46, 72
aesthetics 7, 18, 24, 41–2, 117, 155
aficionados 213
alternative music 111, 200
Amnesty International 235–6
amplification 53–4
art/commerce dichotomy 34–5, 116, 117, 118
audiences 36, 37, 193ff
auteur, authorship 115–19; examples of 120–37
authenticity 8, 34, 36, 55, 107; and live performance 106–7; songwriting and 101, 103; and
 Springsteen 123, 149

baby boomers 36, 37
blues 144–5, 156
bodgies 221, 222–3
brass bands 52
Brill Building 102, 103

cassette audio tape 59; cassette culture 60
CD 56–7
CD-ROM 60–1
censorship 122, 223ff
class 14, 199
classical music 4, 5
clubs 106–7
commodification 32, 45
composition 101–4
concerts 109–9, 205–6
conscience rock 236–8

consumer sovereignty 12, 13,64
consumption 10, 16, 21, 23, 33, 45,193ff, 242; of
 MTV 190–1; see also cultural capital; taste,
 taste cultures
copyright 38–9
counterculture 106, 196
country music 132–3, 142
cover versions 103, 112–13, 158
cultural capital 13, 15, 96, 215, 216
cultural imperialism 20, 67, 69–72, 184
cultural policy, and State 67–8; in Canada 72–8; in
 New Zealand 78–81
cultural studies ix, 1, 11ff
culturalism 22–3
culture x, 5, 14, 68; see also high culture; popular
 culture
culture industries 28–9

dance 178ff; dance narratives 178–9; styles of
 203–4
dance music 100, 135, 149, 153–4, 199; magazines
 94
dance pop 164, 165, 231
demographics 35–7, 193–5
DJs 42, 100, 108, 136
documentaries 180
doo wop 19
Dunedin Sound 210

electric guitar 53

ethnicity 199

fans, fandom 212–15
fanzines 89
film 175–81, 220
formats 40, 45, 51, 55–7; and radio 62
Frankfurt School 18, 20, 235

gatekeepers 63, 83, 95–6
gender 119, 199, 231–3
Generation X 195
genre 6, 149–51
globalisation, glocalisation 72

heavy metal 151–3, 234; fanzines 89; magazines 90–1
hegemony 22–3
high culture 4, 11, 17, 68; high/low culture dichotomy 4, 18, 69, 219
home taping 60, 203
homology 208–9

indies/independents 27, 30, 41–2, 79; and music press 91–2
Internet 64–5

jazz 18, 19
journeymen 114

Live Aid 237–8
locality 211
lyrics, lyric analysis 139, 141–2, 146–7

majors 27, 29, 30, 79
making music 99ff; as Darwinian struggle 101, 110; see also musicians; producers; songwriting
Manchester sound/scene 211
market cycles 33, 43–5
marketing 4, 45–6, 72, 132; of dance pop 130, 166–7; of reggae 47–8
mass culture/society 17, 18
media literacy 2, 9–11
microphone 52–3
mods 159
moral panic 16, 153, 217, 218–19, 229
moshing 204–5
MP3 65–6
MTV 168, 171, 172, 188–91; and Spice Girls 130–1
music industry 20, 27–8; in Canada 73–7; consolidation/development of 31, 33, 35, 41; in New Zealand 78–81; study of 31–5
music journalism, music critics 84, 94–5, 95–7
music press 83, 85–7; examples of 89–94; study of 88–9

music video 24, 175, 185–8; analysis of 155, 167–74
musicals 176–8
musicians: career paths for 101, 110–12; definitions of 99–100; magazines 87
musicology 21–2, 139–41, 148

New Right 223–4
New Journalism 84–5, 87
New Pop 32, 214
Northern soul 209
nostalgia rock 194

performance, live performance 105ff
phonograph 57–8
political economy 20–1, 31–2, 33, 35, 235; see also music industry
politics 21, 125, 217–39; and Springsteen 145–6
pop, definition of 8
popular culture, study of 1–25, 68
popular music: definition of ix, 5–8; study of xi, 1–2, 16–25
postmodernism 23–5, 167–8
preferred readings 14
producers 42, 105
production of culture 37–8
punk rock 44, 89, 160, 161–2

radio 49, 40–1, 61–4, 202–3; and local content quotas 75–7, 79–81
rap 14, 163–4, 226–30
record collecting 200–2, 213; magazines 87
reggae 47–8
rehearsing 103
retail 52, 65
Riot Grrrl 233
rock, rock'n'roll: concerts 108–9; definitions of 6, 8; emergence of 36ff; moral panic and 220ff
royalties 39–40

sampling 54
scenes 210–11
school curriculum (and media studies) 11
semiotics 21
session musicians 114
sexuality 233–5
slam dancing 205, 206
song families 144
songwriting 101–3
sound: dissemination of 61ff; fidelity of 55; sound mixers 53; sound recording 52–4; sound systems 59; stereophonic sound 58
Soundies 187–8
soundtracks 181
stage diving 204
stars, stardom 115–37

structuralism 21–2
subcultures 23, 206–9

taste 14; taste cultures 197, 215
techno 153–4
technology 7, 51–66, 105
teenagers 195, 199; magazines for 90, 166, 199
television 175, 181–6
textual analysis 135; examples of 142–6, 156–76
Tin Pan Alley 19, 102
touring, tours 109–10
trade papers 86–7

tribute bands 113–14
trip-hop 154

ubiquitous musics 6

venues 106–7

world beat, world music 6, 8–9
World Wide Web 64

youth, youth culture 195–7

NAME INDEX

Abba 113
Abbs, P. 17
Abdul, Paula 165, 190
Abrams, Mark 195
Absolute 130
AC/DC 134
Adams, Bryan 73, 74, 134
Adorno, T. 19, 28
Aerosmith 152
Alexander, Arthur 113
Amos, Tori 103
Animals 22, 144
Anthrax 152
Ardolino, Emile 178
Armatrading, Joan 297
Arnett, J. 234
Arnold, Kokomo 156
Arnold, M. 164

Babes in Toyland 111
Baez, Joan 134, 135, 277
Bagdikian, B. 20
Baker, Ginger 145
Baillie, Russell 116
Ballard, Greg 102
Ballard, Hank 220
Band Aid 236–7
Bangs, L. 85, 152
Banks, J. 190
Baptiste, Jean 172
Bare Naked Ladies 74
Barlow, W. 156
Barnes, K. 62
Barry and Greenwich 102
Bats 210
Bayton, M. 232–3
Beach Boys 44, 54
Beadle, J. 54
Beastie Boys 164
Beatles 103, 116, 117, 118, 119, 177, 179, 194,
    205, 210, 231

Beats International 136
Beck, Jeff 114
Benitez, John 127
Bennett, A. 2, 49, 113, 211
Bennett, T. 104
Benwell Floyd 113
Berkenstadt, J. and Cross, C. 101
Berland, J. 73
Berliner 57
Berns, Bert 102
Berry, Chuck 37, 220
Bikini Kill 233
Bjorn Again 113
Black Sabbath 89, 151
Blackwell, Chris 46, 48
Bloom, B. 18
Blue Cheer 151
Bolan, Marc 214
Bon Jovi, John Bon Jovi 152, 214
Booker T and the MGs 114
Bordo, S. 174
Bourdieu, P. 13, 34, 215
Bowie, David 114, 214, 234, 237
Boy George 237; see also Culture Club
Boyzone 214
Brake, M. 207
Breen, M. 2, 150, 153, 204
Brooks, Garth 132–3
Brothers, Pastor Fletcher 224
Brown, James 118, 119
Brown, Willie 156
Browne, Jackson 103
Bruce, Jack 145
Burchill, Julie 85
Burdon, Eric 22
Burnett, R. 6, 182, 189

Cantin, P. 102
Captain Beefheart 122
Carey, Mariah 190
Carpenter, Mary Chapin 133

Carr, Leroy 156
Cawelti, J.117
Chambers, I. 1, 23, 149, 204
Chapman, Tracy 103, 146
Chapple, S. and Garofalo, R. 23, 32
Chapple, William 5
Charlebois, Robert 73
Charters, Samuel 157
Chater, Brian 77
Che Fu 79, 199
Cheap Trick 231
Chemical Brothers 92
Chess Brothers 42
Childs, Toni 103
Chills 210
Chimes 113
Chinn and Chapman 102
Christenson, P. and Roberts, D. 198
Christgau, R. 8, 85
Christianen, M. 33
Clapton, Eric 145, 190, 237
Clarke, D. 16, 123, 124, 127, 164
Clash 114, 162
Clinton, George 153
Coasters 102
Cobain, Kurt 101, 118; *see also* Nirvana
Cochran, Eddie 259, 263
Cohen, Sara 2, 100, 104, 110
Cohen, Stanley 218
Cohn, N. 85, 120, 219, 220
Collins, Phil 237
Communards 188
Considine, D. 126
Cook, Norman; *see* Fat Boy Slim
Cooper, Alice 44, 122, 230
Cooper, B. 142
Cope, N. 12
Cornershop 136
Costello, Elvis and the Attractions 97, 103, 108, 116
Cream 145, 151, 156
Crowded House 190
Cubbit, S. 172
Culture Club 214
Cunningham, M. 54
Cure 234
Curtis, J. 37
Cyrus, Billy Ray 133

Daltrey, Roger 159
Danielsen, S. 183
Davis, A. 130, 131
Dead Kennedys 218, 225–6
DeCurtis, A. 14; and Henke, J. 85, 123, 125
Deep Purple 151, 152
Def Leppard 134, 152
Demme, Jonathon 180

Denselow, R. 238
Devlin, Johnny 222
Diamond, Neil 103
Dickerson, J. 130, 131
Dion, Celine 73, 96, 194
Dire Straits 69
Dixon, Willie 144
Dobbis, Rick 194
Doctor Hook 92
Doggett, P. 84
Doors 107
Dr Dre 229
Drifters 102
Dunbar, Aynsley 122
Dunbar, Sly 114
Duran Duran 170–2, 190, 214, 237
Dylan, Bob 44, 103, 118, 119, 146, 194, 237

Eagles 62, 110, 194, 205
East 17 130
Edison, Thomas 219
Eisenberg, E. 55, 201
Eminem 229
Entwistle, John 160
Estefan, Gloria 165

Fabian 234
Fairport Convention 46
Falwell, Jerry 224
Fat Boy Slim 115, 135–6
Feelers 79
Fink, M. 38
Finn, Neil 79
Finnegan, R. 99
Fiske, J. 173–4, 212
Fleetwood Mac 62, 205
Flohel, R. 76
Flying Burrito Brothers 242
Ford, Mary 53
Freakpower 136
Free 46
Freed, Alan 42, 62
Frith, S. 1, 22, 24, 32, 39, 83, 91, 92, 94, 96, 110, 117, 140, 142, 147, 148, 149, 173, 185, 195; and Street 236
Fugs 97
Fuller, Simon 129, 130

Gallagher brothers 109, 131; *see also* Oasis
Garnham, N. 68
Garofalo, R. 2
Garon, P. 148
Gaar, G. 231
Geldof, Bob 238
Gendron, B. 137–8
Genesis 13
George, Lowell 122

George, Nelson 1
Gerry and the Pacemakers 177, 210
Giger, H.R. 225
Gilmore, M. 85
Gilroy, P. 59
Godley and Creme 170, 171
Goffin, Gerry 102, 164
Goldstein, Richard 147
Gomez 242
Goodman, Dave 173
Goodwin, A. 24–5, 54, 169, 189
Gordy, Berry 44
Gore, Tipper 225
Graham Bond Organisation 145
Gramsci, Antonio 85, 163
Grand Funk 151
Grandmaster Flash 163
Grant, B. 129–30
Grant, Brian 171
Grateful Dead 110, 210
Grenier, L. 78
Grossberg, L. ix, 1, 35, 36, 212, 215, 229, 235
Guns 'n' Roses 152

Hager, B. 134
Haley, Bill (and the Comets) 33, 177, 220
Hall, S. x, 22; and Whannel, P. 196
Hall, Vera 140
Hammond, John 123
Hanf, J. 58
Happy Mondays 211
Harder, Don 60
Harker, D. 34, 146–7
Hatch, D. and Millward, S. 112–13, 144
Hayward, P. 2
Haza, Offra 9
Hebdige, D. 93, 163, 206–7
Henderson, L. 173, 191
Hendrix, Jimi, Jimi Hendrix Experience114, 118, 151
Herbert, Bob and Chris 129, 131
Herbert, T. 52
Herman, G. 159, 160; and Hoare, I. 14–15
Hernandez, Patrick 126
Herschel, Sir John 18
Hill, D. 8, 24
Hole 199
Holland, Dozier, Holland 102
Hollows, J. and Milestone, K. 209
Holly, Buddy 37, 118, 233
Hornby, Nick 201, 202
Horner, B. and Swiss, T. 2
Housemartins 136
Hurt, Mississippi John 29
Hutchins, Stuart 136

Ice-T 13, 164, 199, 218, 227–8

Inspiral Carpets 211
Iron Maiden 152

Jackson, Janet 165
Jackson, Michael 119, 182, 189
Jactars 104
Jacobs, Dani 188
Jagger, Mick 116
James 211
James, Skip 156
Jameson, F. 23, 168
Jenkin, Barry 184
Johnson, Brian 133, 134
Johnson, Bruce 52–3
Johnson, Lonnie 152
Johnson, Robert 156–8
Jones, Howard 214
Jones, Simon 47–8
Jones, Steve 2, 7
Joplin, Janis 118, 179, 231
Joy Division 211
JPS 210

Kamins, Mark 126
Kaplan, A. 167, 168, 169, 172, 173, 190
Kaplan, Howard 122
Kassabian, A. 6
Kealy, E. 53
Keil, C. 147
Kellner, D. 126
Kelly, Christina 130
Kennedy, Eliot 130
Kennedy, R. and McNutt, R. 42
Kershaw, Nick 214
Keshishian, Alek 128
King, Ben E. 102, 120
King, Carole 103, 164
Kirschner, T, 101, 112
Kong, L. 210
Kraftwerk 153
Krall, Diana 74

L7 233
Laing, D. 1, 45, 71, 161, 162, 187
Landau, J. 8, 117, 134
lang, k.d. 234
Lange, David 69
Lange, Robert (Mutt) 133–4
Lanza, J. 6
Lauper, Cyndi 165
LeBon, Simon 171, 172
Led Zeppelin 56, 151
Leiber and Stoller 102–3
Lennon, John 102
Lennox, Randy 74
Leonard, M. and Strachan, R. 85, 87
Lester, Richard 177

Lewis, L. 191, 212, 215
Leyshon, A. 211
Lipsitz, G.1
Little Eva 164
Little Richard 37, 220
Little Steven 236
Lockward, Robert Jr. 157
Logan, Nick 93
Lopes, P. 33
Lucas, Reggie 127
Lydon, John 161

McCartney, Paul 102, 205, 237
McClary, S. 141
McEntire, Reba 133
McLachlan, Sarah 74
McLaren, Malcom 161
McRobbie, A. 1, 88, 160, 178, 204; and Garber, J. 90, 199
Madonna 115, 126–9, 164, 172–4, 189, 190, 234
Manilow, Barry 214
Mann and Weil 102
Manning, A. 223
Marcus, G. 85, 160, 162
Marilyn Manson 218, 229, 230
Marley, Bob: and the Wailers 28, 46–8, 107
Marsalis, W. 174
Marsh, D. 8, 85, 97, 160, 163, 194
Martin, George 105
Massive Attack 154
Masterman, L. 10
Matlock, Glen 161
MC Hammer 44, 164
MCA 41
Mellers, W. 140
Melly, G. 44
Mercury, Freddie 234
Metallica 152
Middleton, R. 1, 5, 22, 23, 208
Midnight Oil 235
Millard, A. 58
Miller, J. 53, 85
Milsap, Ronnie 142
Minogue, Kylie 102, 151, 164–5, 199
Mitchell, Joni 103
Mitchell, T. 2, 72
Moby Grape 210
Moon, Keith 160
Morissette, Alanis 27, 73, 74, 102
Moroder, Georgio 98
Morrissey 270
Morrison, Jim 231
Morrison, Van 242
Moss, Ian 113
Most, Mickie 276
Motley Crue 224

Mountain 151
Motown 44
Mud 102
Muesterberger, W. 201
Mulcahy, Russell 170, 171
Muldoon, Robert 69
Murdoch, G. (and Phelps, G.) 199
Murphy, Geoff 116
Murray, C. 85
My Bloody Valentine 119

Negus, K. 2, 34, 46, 105
New Kids on the Block 199, 214
New Order 211
New York Dolls 44
Newbern, Willie 156
Newman, Randy 119, 146
Nirvana 101, 200
NOFX 200
NWA 164, 227

Oasis 12, 13, 36, 53, 153, 236
Ochs, Phil 103
OMC 79
O'Neil-Joyce, T. 65
Orb, The 119
Orbit, William 129
Osbourne, Ozzy 224
O'Sullivan, T. 70
Our Lady Peace 74

Page, Jimmy 114
Palmer, Robert 157
Parker, Alan 179
Parker, M. 49
Parliament 153
Parsons, Gram 114
Paul Revere and the Raiders 97
Pearl Jam 200, 242
Peking Man 69
Penguins 220
Penn, Sean 127
Perry, J. 159
Peterson, R. and Berger, D. 28, 37, 38, 40, 43
Petty, Tom and the Heartbreakers 114
Phillips, Sam 54, 105
Pink Floyd 54, 184
Pitch Black 104
Poison 152
Police 48
Pomus and Sherman 102, 103
Ponty, Jean Luc 122
Portishead 154
Pratt, R. 126, 146
Presley, Elvis 37, 42, 54, 103, 118, 175, 176, 221, 234

Price, Alan 22
Prince, The Artist Formerly Known As Prince 103, 119, 181, 225
Pringle, Doug 76
Public Enemy 164, 199

Queen 213, 237
Queensryche 60
Quicksilver Messenger Service 97

Race, Steve 221
Radiohead 119
Rage Against the Machine 35, 153, 200
Raitt, Bonnie 194
Ray, Johnny 219
Read, O. and Welsh, W. 59
Red Rodeo 74
Redhead, S. 197
Reid, Jamie 161
REM 28, 119, 189, 235
Rex, I. 165
Reynolds, Simon 94, 95, 149
Richard, Cliff 176
Riesman, D. 196, 215
Righteous Brothers 113
Rijvin, S. 237, 238
Rimmer, D. 32, 85, 190
Robertson, Brian 74
Robinson, Dave 48
Robinson, D. et al. 72
Roe, K. and Lofgren, M. 187
Rogers, Jimmie 150
Rogers, Nick 127
Rolling Stones 28, 106, 110, 119, 144, 156, 194
Rosselson, L. 20
Rubey, D. 190
Runca, Bic 79
Russell, D. 166–7
Rutten, P. 78

S Club 7 111, 165–7, 199, 204
Savage, J. 85, 89, 160, 161
Schulze, L. 128
Searchers 97, 210
Seeger, Pete 134
Seigworth, G. 129
Sex Pistols 160–2, 179
Shakespeare, Robbie 114
Shamen 154
Shapiro, B. 126, 128
Shepherd, J. 1
Sherrill, Billy 142
Shihad 79
Shines, Johnny 156, 157
Shore, M. 170
Sinclair, D. 6, 123, 125, 128, 159

Sinclair, Pete 183
Slayer 152
Sluka, J. 223–4
Small, C. 205
Small Faces 97
Small, Millie 46
Smith, Trixie 220
Smiths 211
Soich, Karen 229
Son House 156
Spandau Ballet 214
Spears, Britney 199
Specials 96
Spector, Phil 102, 105, 115, 120–1
Spice Girls 111, 115, 129–132, 134, 165, 195, 214
Springsteen, Bruce 97, 103, 115, 119, 123–6, 145–6, 149, 184, 242
Stannard and Rowe 130
Steel, Tommy 176
Stephenson, Michelle 129
Steppenwolf 151
Steward, S. and Garratt, S. 231
Stock, Aitken, Waterman 102, 164
Stockbridge, S. 191
Stone Roses 211
Stravinsky 55
Straw, W. 2, 74, 119–20, 135, 136, 201, 202, 213, 237, 238
Street, J. 8
Strong, Andrew 181
Suede 234
Swaggart, Jimmy 224
Sweet 102
Swing Shift 113

Tagg, P. 7, 141
Take That 130, 214
Talking Heads 180, 188
Taylor, P. 84
Temple, Julian 171, 179
Théberge, P. 51, 87
Thomas, Bruce 108
Thomas, Chris 161
Thompson, Richard 116
Tikaram, Tanita 103
Tosh, Peter 255
Townshend, Pete 119, 158–60
Traffic 46
Tricky 154
Troggs 97, 113
Trondman, M. 216
Tsitsos, W. 204, 205
Tunstall, J. 70
Turner, G. 107
Turner, K. 3
Twain, Shania 73, 74, 108, 115, 132–5, 194
2 Live Crew 218, 227

USA for Africa 237
U2 111, 113, 118, 199, 235, 237

Van Morrison 242
Vega, Suzanne 103
Vengaboys 204
Vermorel, F. and J. 214
Vig, Butch 105
Village People 234
Vincent, Gene 233
Volman, Mark 122

Wailer, Bunny 47
Wainman, Phil 102
Waites, Tom 119
Walser, R. 152, 234
Ward, Billy 220
Ward, Tony 172
Weinstein, D. xi, 2, 86, 89, 104, 107–8, 110, 150,
    152, 204
Wenner, Jann 92
Wertham, F. 218
Westwood, Vivienne 161
Wet Wet Wet 113

Wexler, Jerry 258
Whalley, Chas 188
Wham 214
Wheatstraw, Peetie 156
White, Timothy 95
Whitely, S. 136
Who 107, 158–60, 182
Wildchild 136
Williams, Hank 73
Williams, Raymond 5
Williams, Robbie 116, 182
Willis, E. 85
Willis, P. et al. 198, 202, 203, 208
Wilson, Brian 54
Wolfman Jack 62
Wynette, Tammy 142–4

Yardbirds 144
Yoakum, Dwight 133
Young, Neil 103, 242

Zappa, Frank and the Mothers of Invention 115,
    119, 121–2, 226, 242

SONG AND ALBUM TITLE INDEX

Albums are in italics; music videos are indicated by (MV)

Absolutely Free 121
'Anarchy in the UK' 155, 160–2
Antichrist Superstar 230
'Anyway, Anyhow, Anywhere' 160
Apostrophe (') 122
As Nasty as they Want to Be 227

'Baby Let Me Bang Your Box' 220
Back To Mono 121
'Be My Baby' 120
'Beautiful People' 230
Bedtime for Democracy 226
Bedtime Stories 129
Better Living Through Chemistry 136
'Billie Jean' 182
'Black Eyes, Blue Tears' 135
Black Sabbath 151
Body Count 228, 229
'Born in the USA' 124, 139, 145–6
Born in the USA 124, 184–5
'Born To Be Wild' 151
'Born to Run' 97, 123, 124
Born to Run 123
Boss Drum 154
'Brimful of Asha' 136
'Bring it All Back' 155, 166–7
Bruce Springsteen and the E Street Band: Live 124

Buena Vista Social Club 180
Burnin' 47

'California Uber Alles' 226
'Caravan of Love' 136
Catch a Fire 47
Clumsy 74
Come On Over 134
'Cop Killer' 227–9

'Da Doo Ron Ron' 120
'Dancing in the Dark' 124
Dark Side of the Moon 54
Darkness On The Edge of Town 124
'D-I-V-O-R-C-E' 143
'Do they know it's Christmas?' 236–7
'Don't Be Stupid' 135
'Don't Eat the Yellow Snow' 122
'Don't Leave Me this Way' (MV) 188
'The Dope Show' 230
'Dreams' (MV) 188
'Dub Be Good to Me' 136
'Dust My Broom' 157

Efil4zaggin 227
'Everybody' 126

'Factory' 124
Fat of the Land 153
Frankenchrist 225
Freak Out 121
'Freedom 90' 189
Fresh Cream 145
'Fuck the Police' 227

'Gangsta trippin' ' 136
The Ghost of Tom Joad 125
'Girls On Film' (MV) 170, 171
'Glad to be Gay' 235
'Good Vibrations' 54
Greetings From Asbury Park, NJ 123

'Hell Hound On My Trail' 157–8
'He's A Rebel' 120
'Holiday' 127
'Holiday in Cambodia' 226
Home Invasion 228
'Honey I'm Home' 135
'How Bizzare' 79
'How High is the Moon' 53
'Hungry Like the Wolf' (MV) 155, 167, 170–2

'I Can't Explain' 160
'I Still Haven't Found What I'm Looking For' 113
'If U Can't Dance' 130
'(I'm A) Stand By My Woman Man' 142
'I'm A Steady Rollin' Man' 157
'I'm Crying' 22
'Im Nin Alu' 9
'Imagine' 120
'Into the Groove' 127
'It Ain't Me Babe' 147

Jagged Little Pill 27, 95
Jazz From Hell 122
'Jungleland' 123
'Justify My Love' (MV) 127, 172–4, 191

'Last Time Lover' 130
'Lawdy Miss Clawdy' 222
Legend 48
Let It Bleed 158
Licensed To Ill 164
Like a Virgin 127
'Listen to Your Heart' 56
Live at the BBC 194
'Locomotion' 155, 164–5
'Lola' 235
'Love In Vain Blues' 155, 158
'Love Is All Around' 113
Love Scenes 74
'Love Thing' 130

Madonna 83 126
The Marshall Mathers LP 229
Mechanical Animals 230
'The Message' 155, 163–4
Music 129
'My Boy Lollipop' 46
'My Daddy Rocks Me' 220
'My Generation' 155, 159–6
'My Sweet Lord' 120

'Naked' 130
Natty Dread 47
Natural Mystic 48
Nebraska 124
Nevermind 105
No Fences 133
Northern Star 132

Off the Wall 182
'One Week' 74
'Open Your Heart' (MV) 127, 155, 167, 174

'Part of the Union' 14
Perfect Stranger and Other Works, The 122
Please Hammer Don't Hurt 'Em 44
'Praise You' 136
Purple Rain 225

'Ramblin' On My Mind' 157
Ray of Light 129
'Reach' 166
'Relax' 235
'Renegade Master' 136
Rio 171
The River 124, 184
'River Deep, Mountain High' 120
'Rock Around the Clock' 177, 220
'The Rockafeller Skank' 136
Ropin' the Wind 133

'S Club Party' 166
Sergeant Pepper's Lonely Hearts Club Band 121
Shaday 9
'She Loves You' 147
'Should I Stay or Should I Go?' 186
'Sixty Minute Man' 220
'Something Kinda Funny' 130
Songs of Freedom (boxed set) 48
'Spanish Harlem' 120
Spice 130, 131
Spice World 132
'Spinning Around' 165
'Spoonful' 139, 144–5
'Stand By Your Man' 139, 142–4
'Start Me Up' 28
Stop Making Sense 180

Strictly Commercial 122
Stripped 61
Stunt 74
'Summertime Blues' 151

Tapestry 103
'The Tennessee Waltz' 177
'Terraplane Blues' 157
'That's All Right Mama' 37, 54
'Then He Kissed Me' 120
Thriller 29, 182
'Thunder Road' 123
'To Know Him Is To Love Him' 120
'Too Drunk To Fuck' 226
Tracks 125, 146
'Traveling Riverside Blues' 157
'Trouble so hard' 140
Trout Mask Replica 122
True Blue 127
Tunnel of Love 124
'Turn On Tune In Drop Out' 136
'Tutti Frutti' 235
'2 Become 1' 130
200 Motels 122

'Viva Forever' 132

'Walk on the Wild Side' 235
'Wannabe' 130, 131–2
'We are the world' 237
We're Only In It For The Money 121
'What Made You Say That' (MV) 133
Wheels of Fire 145
When I Look in Your Eyes 74
'Who Do You Think You Are' 130
The Wild, the Innocent and the E Street Shuffle 123
The Woman in Me 134
'Work With Me Annie' 220

'You Take My Breath Away' 186

'You'll Never Walk Alone' 14
'You're My Number 1' 166
'You're Still the One' 134
You've Come a Long Way Baby 136
'You've Lost that Lovin' Feelin'' 113, 120